The New Institutional Politics

The New Institutional Politics is a comparative study of the impact of political institutions upon outcomes, covering several of the major themes in the new institutionalism. It starts from a theoretical examination of the concept of an institution, contrasting the rational choice and sociological approaches to institutional analysis.

The book presents a framework for the analysis of institutions, based on the fundamental distinction between rules and interests. Since institutions constitute the rules of the game, constraining interest maximization behaviour, we ask: how much of the macro political outcomes can be accounted for by political institutions?

The evaluation of the performance of political institutions covers the executive, the legislature and the judicial system in a broad sense. The book examines the existence of institutional effects in democracies as well as dictatorships, providing at the same time analyses of some of the most important models in political science.

It looks at the impact of various democratic institutions in order to assess how political institutions connected with parliamentarianism or presidentialism perform as well as how the institutions of Konkordanzdemocratie and corporatism display better outcomes than Westminster institutions. The book also looks at economic outcomes such as affluence and GDP growth as well as social aspects like income distribution, gender issues and quality of life.

This book explores how political institutions matter for political, economic and social outcomes and estimates their impact in relation to other major factors such as culture and social structure. It is written for political scientists, scholars and students studying comparative politics.

Jan-Erik Lane is Professor of Political Science at the University of Geneva; he has published widely in public management and political theory. **Svante Ersson** is a lecturer at Umea University. They are joint authors of a number of comparative books, including *Politics and Society in Western Europe, 4th edition.*

The New Institutional Politics

Performance and outcomes

Jan-Erik Lane and Svante Ersson

London and New York

First published 2000
by Routledge
11 New Fetter Lane, London EC4P 4EE

Simultaneously published in the USA and Canada
by Routledge
29 West 35th Street, New York, NY 10001

Routledge is an imprint of the Taylor & Francis Group

Typeset in Times by
Exe Valley Dataset Ltd, Exeter, Devon, England
Printed and bound in Great Britain by
Biddles Ltd, Guildford and King's Lynn

British Library Cataloguing in Publication Data
A catalogue record for this book is available
from the British Library

Library of Congress Cataloguing in Publication Data
Lane, Jan-Erik.
    The new institutional politics: Performance and outcomes / Jan
-Erik Lane & Svante Ersson.
        p.   cm.
    Includes bibliographical references and index.
    (pbk.: alk. paper)
    1. Comparative government.   2. Quality of life.   I. Ersson,
Svante O.   II. Title.
JF51.L356   1999
320.3—dc21   99–32334
                                                              CIP

ISBN 0-415-18320-0 (hbk)
ISBN 0-415-18321-9 (pbk)

We dedicate this book to the memory of the Swedish political scientist Pär-Erik Back (1920–88). He was not only our common teacher, mentor and friend, but he also gave us both, though independently, a vision of what the conduct of enquiry could and should be like.

Contents

List of figures and tables   ix
Preface   xiii

Introduction: Rousseau's problem   1

Theoretical Section

1 What is an institution?   23

2 Institutions and interests   38

3 Outputs, outcomes and institutions   58

Substantive Analyses Section

PART I
Basic state institutions   75

4 Federalism: Althusius   77

5 The institutionalization of human rights: Locke   102

PART II
The Montesquieu system   115

6 Presidential or parliamentary executives: Linz   117

7 Impact of legislative institutions   143

8 Judicial institutions   166

PART III
The Lijphart system 179

9 The Duverger theory: impact of election rules 181

10 Westminster versus Consensus democracy – a tenable
distinction? 207

11 Konkordanzdemokratie and corporatism 225

PART IV
The Friedman system 245

12 The economic outcomes of market institutions: theory 247

13 The economic outcomes of market institutions:
empirical tests 260

14 Economic institutions and political freedom: Friedman 274

15 Conclusion: constitutionalism matters 286

Bibliography 304
Index 322

Figures and tables

Figures

0.1	Interpretations of institutions	6
2.1	Motivation and rules	42
5.1	Democracy versus aristocracy	108
5.2	Real equality and positive liberties	109
7.1	The cube root law of national assemblies	161
9.1	Regimes and party-systems	187
12.1	Economic growth 1960–73 and 1985–94	259
14.1	Economic freedom and democracy: 1990s	280
14.2	Economic freedom and social expenditures: 1990s	282

Tables

2.1	Key political institutions	52
3.1	Variation in policy outputs in the 1990s	67
3.2	Variation in socio-economic outcomes in the 1990s	68
3.3	Variation in political outcomes in the 1990s	69
3.4	Stability over time among policy output and policy outcome variables from the 1970s to the 1990s: measured through explained variance of the first factor in a factor analysis	71
4.1	Federal states – classifications	82
4.2	States with federative arrangements	83
4.3	Federal states	88
4.4	Federalism and public sector size: comparing means	91
4.5	Federalism and decentralization/centralization: comparing means	92
4.6	Federalism and affluence: real GDP/capita: comparing means	93
4.7	Federalism and human development: HDI: comparing means	94
4.8	Federalism and economic growth: comparing means	95

4.9	Federalism and income distribution: comparing means	96
4.10	Federalism and democracy scores: comparing means	97
4.11	Federalism and constitutional longevity: no. of years: comparing means	98
4.12	Regressions: federalism, affluence and decentralization: 1990s	100
5.1	Democracy, outputs and outcomes: correlations	110
5.2	Regression analysis: democracy and level of human development, welfare state, equality and corruption: the 1990s	111
6.1	Classification of regimes: around 1989 and 1995	124
6.2	Presidentialism 1970, 1984 and 1995	125
6.3	Parliamentary regimes around 1990 and 1995 including mixed executives	127
6.4	Correlations: presidentialism versus non-presidentialism: political outcomes	136
6.5	Correlations: presidentialism and non-presidentialism: socio-economic outcomes	136
6.6	Correlations: presidentialism versus parliamentarism: political outcomes	137
6.7	Correlations: presidentialism versus parliamentarism: social and economic outcomes	137
6.8	Regressions: presidentialism and democracy in the 1990s	140
A6.1	Stable presidential countries 1970–1995	142
A6.2	Stable non-presidential countries 1970–1995	142
7.1	Types of referenda	150
7.2	Number of referenda (Ln)	151
7.3	Number of national referenda in the OECD countries 1970–97: ranking order	151
7.4	Chamber system	156
7.5	Asymmetrical and symmetrical bicameralism	159
7.6	Absolute and relative size of national assemblies in the 1990s (lower house)	160
7.7	Status of central banks	162
7.8	Autonomy of the central bank 1970–1990 in OECD countries	163
7.9	Impact of legislative institutions: regression analysis	164
7.10	Inflation: regression analysis	165
8.1	Legal families in the world	168
8.2	Occurrence of judicial review around the world	172
8.3	Occurrence of the ombudsman institution around the world	175
8.4	Impact from judicial institutions on democracy and corruption: regression analysis	177
9.1	Democratically stable countries (n=45)	184

9.2	Electoral systems in the 1990s	185
9.3	Electoral systems: stability over time: 1970s to the 1990s	185
9.4	Disproportionality and district magnitude (natural logarithm) by election systems: means	194
9.5	Party system properties by election systems in the 1990s	197
9.6	Government instability properties by election systems in the 1990s: all and parliamentarian countries	199
9.7	Party system and election system: correlations	202
9.8	Government instability and party systems: correlations	204
9.9	Government instability and election system: correlations	204
10.1	Factor analysis of institutions in democracies: 1990s	222
11.1	Scales of macro-corporatism	228
11.2	Trade union density and Drittelparität	230
11.3	Indices of Konkordanzdemokratie	232
11.4	Types of governments after World War II: 1945–1994	234
11.5	Correlations between corporatism and Konkordanzdemokratie	235
11.6	Power-sharing institutions and Konkordanzdemokratie	237
11.7	Sources of corporatism and Konkordanzdemokratie	238
11.8	Corporatism, Konkordanz and policy outputs	240
11.9	Konkordanz, corporatism and policy outcomes: correlations	241
12.1	Research on the connection between economic freedom and economic growth	247
13.1	Economic systems around 1985 (Gastil)	263
13.2	Economic freedom index 1975–95	264
13.3	Economic systems in South East Asia	265
13.4	Correlations: economic systems and economic growth	267
13.5	Number of patents (per capita ×1000) registered in the USA by inventor country	269
13.6	Correlations: innovations (Ln of patents per capita) and economic growth	269
13.7	Regression analysis: economic growth 1960–94 and economic institutions	271
14.1	Economic regime and democracy: correlations	279
14.2	Economic freedom and public sector size: correlations	281
14.3	Economic freedom and social expenditures: correlations	281
14.4	Regression equations: the effect of economic freedom and wealth on democracy and human rights	283
14.5	Economic freedom and human development: correlations	284
14.6	Economic freedom and female parliamentary representation and income inequalities: correlations	284
15.1	Constitutional longevity in years by major world regions: means	295
15.2	Constitutional longevity in various regions in 1996	296

15.3 Constitutionalism in 1900 and 1950 by world regions: means — 298

15.4 Constitutionalism and constitutional longevity: correlations — 299

15.5 Constitutionalism and human development: correlations — 301

15.6 Constitutionalism and perceptions of corruption: correlations — 301

Preface

The origins of this book are to be found in a few separate papers that were published some years ago. First, there is a short article that one of the authors published in 1993 in a Festschrift to Gunnar Sjöblom, long-time Swedish professor in political science at the University of Copenhagen: 'Opportunistic behaviour and institutions' (in Bryder, T. (ed.) *Party Systems, Party Behaviour and Democracy: scripta in honorem professoris Gunnar Sjöblom sexagesimum annum complements*, University of Copenhagen; Institute of Political Science, pp. 51–71). It is reprinted here in a revised version in Chapter 2.

This paper posed the question whether political institutions could restrain the negative impact of opportunistic behaviour, but it did not answer it, as that would require a vast empirical investigation. We went on to investigate whether federalist institutions matter in the paper 'Is federalism superior?' (in Steunenberg, B. and van Vught, F. (eds) (1997) *Political Institutions and Public Policy: perspectives on European decision making*, Dordrecht: Kluwer, pp. 85–113). There we saw the relevance of comparative institutional analysis, both for the new institutionalism and for the analysis of macro level politics; these findings constitute Chapter 4.

The analysis of the relationship between institutions and outcomes proved interesting, so that one of the authors suggested that we examine the institutions of Konkordanz as well as those of corporatism. The outcome was the paper 'The institutions of Konkordanz and Corporatism: how closely are they connected?' *Swiss Political Science Review* 3, 1997, 5–29. We have drawn upon this paper in Chapter 11.

At the end of the day, we decided to engage in a major empirical effort to map institutional performance and establish the occurrence of institutional effects. It seemed to us that for the purposes of empirical analysis we could arrange institutional theory at the macro level around three major theoretical approaches: Montesquieu, Lijphart and Friedman.

Before we arrived at that conclusion we had to clarify where we stood on some difficult questions in neo-institutionalism, especially the meaning and reference of 'institution'. We decided to link up our investigations about the outcomes of institutions with the rational choice understanding of an institution as a rule or a norm that is backed by sanctions of some sort.

The enquiry into institutional effects is done solely on the basis of a comparative approach focusing upon institutional performance and institutional outcomes at the macro level, i.e. that of society. It would be interesting to examine whether institutional effects occur by means of a case study or by focusing upon micro data. However, we have restricted ourselves to the macro level exclusively in the hope that the book will be suitable for teaching in comparative politics.

All but three of the chapters have thus been written specifically for this volume. The three papers included here but published elsewhere have been revised for the purpose of the coherence of this volume, searching for institutional effects using a comparative institutional approach. This book has been produced as part of the project 'Institutional Arrangements and Conflict Resolution: Theoretical and Comparative Perspectives' (Grant no. 5004-0487882/1) by the Swiss Science Foundation.

Geneva and Umeå, September 1999
Jan-Erik Lane and Svante Ersson

Introduction

Rousseau's problem

Jean-Jacques Rousseau testified more than once about how he came to understand the distinction between the nature of man and woman and the institutions that society harbours (Rousseau [1782] 1972). Rousseau took the extreme position that men and women were good but that the prevailing institutions were bad. What we want to research in this book is whether, and to what extent, the operation of political institutions has specific results that one may wish to label 'good' or 'bad'. Examining the major political institutions of today's societies, we ask: Are there institutional effects?

In general, the new institutionalism in political science or neo-institutionalism in the social sciences claim that institutions or rules are extremely important for the outcomes of human interaction. Yet there are, in addition to rules, other factors that may explain results, such as the preferences of actors, macro social conditions, cultural patterns and belief-systems. How can one be sure that institutions are so important for outcomes?

Do institutions govern the behaviour of men and women, giving rise to determinate results, i.e. policy outputs or social outcomes? Or do men and women take institutions into account when they act, suggesting that behaviour is orientated in terms of institutions? But it is hardly the case that institutions constitute a powerful determinant of outcomes, because other factors impact too. Perhaps there is so much institutional variation that the existence of one institution or another does not matter much, because they constitute institutional equivalents in the sense that the operation of different institutions has the same outcomes. Key questions about institutional variation and performance will be addressed in this book. In addition, we raise the question of the existence of institutional effects in a comprehensive manner.

Thus, the overall problem analysed in this volume is whether institutions matter for macro political and social outcomes and if so, in what ways. We ask whether it is possible to corroborate the theories that adduce a major role for institutions in determining outcomes, as well as whether the evidence supports one or the other hypotheses about institutional effects when institutional theories contradict each other.

A comparative approach

A broad set of outcomes, including democracy and constitutional stability, affluence and economic growth, social and gender equality and democracy as well as policy outputs like welfare state spending, may be examined in terms of an evaluation of a few well-known institutional models on the basis of a data set covering some 150 states. The analysis will cover all countries with a population larger than one million inhabitants and use a data set covering the post-Second World War period.

In the search for institutional effects, working with two sets of countries is desirable. Here we consider: (1) all political systems whether democracies and non-democracies; and (2) only constitutional democracies. This separation allows for a systematic test of a variety of institutional models, some covering all states but others referring only to constitutional democracies. The organization of the materials is focused upon the examination of several well-known institutional models in political science. Actually, some of the most discussed institutional models today are not entirely 'modern', but may be traced back to early institutionalists in political thought.

As we set out to make a comparative study of the impact of political institutions on outputs and outcomes, we intend to cover some of the major themes in the new institutionalism, which has become such a dominant area of study in the social sciences in the 1990s. The institutional revolution in political science can be carried further only if it can be shown that different political institutions really have different consequences for important outputs (policies) or outcomes (results). The book explores how political institutions matter for political, economic and social outcomes and estimates their partial impact in relation to other major factors such as culture and social structure.

Institutionalism

A fundamental feeling of caution lies at the basis of this book. The new institutionalism is still a loose set of different models which may not have that much in common. The idea that institutions matter is such a general one that it may harbour almost any general hypothesis. One may wish to know both what specific entities institutions are and what it is that they have an impact upon.

The strong recent attention paid to institutions in society by social scientists with backgrounds as different as political science, economics and sociology, has been hailed as evidence of convergence and growing interdisciplinarity. If the social sciences concentrate on understanding the role of institutions in human behaviour, then it is to be hoped that the excessive fragmentation of the social sciences as expressed in the extreme proliferation of approaches and frameworks may come to a halt. Let us pursue this line of thought and use the new institutionalism within the field of comparative study.

Political institutions can be structured in a variety of ways. There is hardly any limit to how much variation in institutional details that one may wish to cover when institutions are considered interesting. Yet, we deal with a limited set of macro political institutions that lend themselves to comparative institutional analysis. A few major institutions give a format to the state: unitarism–federalism, as well as the institutionalization of human rights in constitutional democracies, are examples of macro institutions. In the history of political thought we already find institutional theories about the state format when the modern concept of a state emerges in the sixteenth century. We discuss Althusius' theory about federalism and Locke's human rights approach to government. The classic Montesquieu separation of state power – executive, legislative and judicial competencies – must be covered, especially the structuring of the executive institutions including the Linz argument about presidentialism. This old institutional system may be contrasted with the recent Lijphart system for institutional analysis, which brings together in a macro fashion a number of diverse institutional themes, including the early Duverger focus upon the importance of election rules for political life. Finally, one may wish to take up the macro distinction between state and market and examine whether alternative ways of structuring economic institutions by means of state interference play a role for either economic outcomes, as with Williamson and North, or for political liberty as with Hayek and Friedman.

Institutionalists – old and new – claim that institutions bring about or enhance outcomes. Following this approach, it is important to specify the key institutional models in an accurate manner, theoretically speaking. Upon theoretical reasons a number of competing institutional models are conceivable, between which only empirical tests can decide when it comes to how well they perform on criteria of truth or evidence.

Concept of institution

A rule that has been institutionalized identifies an institution. Institutionalis-ation is the process through which rules or norms are implemented in the sense that they meet with acceptance and that violations towards them are met with sanctions, in one form or another, that are considered legitimate by the group concerned.

When employing the institution concept, one may ask how one draws the boundary between what belongs to an institution and what lies outside of the same institution. It is also relevant to ask how one institution becomes part of a system of institutions, or how simple institutions form part of complex institutions. The boundary problem and the composition problem have been given different answers in the literature, reflecting the basic difference between holistic approaches, on the one hand, and atomistic approaches on the other (Powell and DiMaggio 1991; Ostrom 1990).

The boundary is a source of contention, because it raises critical ques-tions about how institutions are related conceptually to other entities such as behaviour, interests and information. The composition problem relates to difficult questions of how single items of institutions form macro institutions.

The boundary problem

According to what one may call the thin interpretation, an institution is a norm that has been institutionalized, meaning that it actually governs behaviour by means of sanctions. Such a thin conception of institutions entails that the concept has a very broad range of applications, covering all norms that somehow govern human activity.

The thin conception of an institution entails that a group can be governed by alternative institutions. When it is argued that institutions matter, then the assumption is that if one institution is replaced by another, then group behaviour will change. Logically, the thin conception implies that institutions are analytically distinct from other factors that shape behaviour, such as interests or preferences and information. If the institutions are changed, then behaviour may change, even though the interests of the people participating in the group remain the same. A thin conception of an institution is to be found in the social choice literature examining the set of voting rules for groups. Given the same preferences in a legislative body, alternative decision rules result in different choice outcomes as the aggregation rule used matters (Kelly 1986; Nurmi 1987).

In contrast, a thick conception of an institution consists of more than merely a rule or a norm. Thus, for example, the Dutch or English monarchy is often said to be an institution, which would comprise (besides quasi-constitutional provisions) life-long practices, memories and personalities. Actually, people may become an institution in the thick conception, such as Winston Churchill or Alexander Solzhenitsyn. According to the thick conception of an institution, it is more generally considered as a practice, and practices are behaviour patterns that people form expectations about and that tend to involve interests and belief-systems (March and Olsen 1989).

In the neo-institutionalist literature, one must link up the thin conception of an institution as a rule with the rational choice orientation, whereas the thick conception of an institution as a practice is to be found within the sociological approach to institutions. In the latter one may find the perspective that institutions comprise 'routines, procedures, conventions, roles, strategies, organizational forms, technologies, beliefs, paradigms, codes, cultures and knowledge . . .' (March and Olsen 1989: 22). From the rational choice perspective, institutions are rules in the strict form of norms which are seen as choice options, between which actors may decide deliberatively as when Italy changed its election rules from proportional to a mixed system.

The composition problem

The composition problem concerns how simple institutions may be added together to form 'wholes'. Simple institutions enter into structures or a web of institutions such as universities or parliaments. What is critical here is how the aggregation from the micro level to the macro level is conceived. Thus, one speaks of, for example, the university as constituting a more or less coherent institutional body of simple rules governing the behaviour of scholars, students and administrative staff in the conduct of research and education. These institutional bodies constitute a whole system of practices or beliefs which are more or less tightly knitted together, forming the university institution as it were.

Institutions as 'wholes' consist of simple institutions that may be coupled together into a system. Thus, there arises the problem of how institutional pieces are to be combined together to form an entire institution. The atomistic viewpoint sees institutions as separate entities that are connected more or less accidentally into a whole. Additional institutions may be added now and old ones may be deleted as institutions change or develop. Thus, institutions adapt in relation to exigencies by transforming some but not all of its institutions. What is referred to as a parliament may consist of simple institutions that have become coupled due to accidental circumstances and which need not always co-exist.

The organic viewpoint looks upon the coupling question in a totally different way. It is true that institutions consist of parts, but the connections between the overall structure and the parts are conceived of as being much tighter, meaning that the parts are moulded by their place in the whole. The practices of a national parliament like the British one or the Norwegian Stortinget are based upon a cohesiveness without which each single institutional item would be meaningless. The organic approach looks at institutions as organized wholes of simple institutions that somehow fit together in a pattern that defines the parts. The organic starting point emphasizes the system as determining the pieces, whereas the atomistic starting point proceeds from the institutional pieces to the structure.

Thus, for instance, simple majority voting and the various institutions of parliamentarism – investiture, vote of no-confidence, dissolution – may be seen as a collection of institutional items with a variety of alternative framings. In each country they have been connected together in a certain form due to mere accidental reasons. Or, one could argue, that the country institution may be seen as having an internal logic from which derives the sense of each of the subinstitutions.

In Figure 0.1, we combine the two distinctions introduced above: the thin–thick interpretations and the atomistic–organic perspectives on institutional linkages.

	Atomistic	Organic
Thin	I	II
Thick	III	IV

Figure 0.1 Interpretations of institutions.

The rational choice approach to institutions tends towards the combination I whereas the sociological approach tends towards type IV in Figure 0.1.

The difference between the two conceptions of an institution – type I and type IV – is that between saying that chess is a game governed by institutions in the form of rules and that chess is an institution in itself. In the former sense an institution is a clearly written down norm about how to make valid moves, whereas in the latter sense it is an entire practice. In the latter interpretation, the chess institution would not simply be an unambiguous set of valid rules enacted by an international body, but would also be made up of the available information about strategies like various chess openings as well as the interests of players that are connected with the game.

Atomistic versus holistic conception

One could speak of two radically different interpretations of institutions, one holistic and one atomistic. On the one hand, there is the Montesquieu belief in country-specific institutions – the spirit of institutions as it were, or the idea that each country has a special set of institutions which may be compared with regard to similarities and differences, at least to some extent. Thus, one may see references being made to British or the German political institutions. Actually, the sociological version of neo-institutionalism tends towards such an assumption about country-specific institutions that have developed over time. Specific institutional origins and a special developmental trend have given a unique aura to the institutions of a country, as if each and every country has its own distinct institutions, reflecting its institutional legacy, determining present behaviour as well as shaping the future of the country.

The rational choice version of neo-institutionalism rejects such an interpretation of institutions as having some kind of national identity. Instead it looks upon institutional aggregation, meaning that it takes the atomistic point of view. Thus, a parliament is a collection of a large number of rules, which may be changed at will one by one, e.g. agenda setting and voting rules, rules about legislation of various kinds as well as rules about the expression of non-confidence in cabinets or rules that divide the work between the committees and the plenum assembly.

Neo-institutionalism based upon rational choice claims that there is a set of general institutions that tend to be present in one form or another in country after country. Actually, each country's institutional set may be seen as a way to combine general institutions into a country-specific pattern, as for instance in the institutions that structure government – business relationships. In some countries such interaction involves three players – government, firms and trade unions – whereas in others only government and business are really important. In addition, one may focus upon the institutions that identify what functions governments have in relation to business, e.g. where the relevant rules in the main economies in South East Asia are very different from the ones that Western economies institutionalize (Whitley 1994).

One may identify such general institutions by positing an ideal-type institution such as the Walrasian market with fully specified property rights. Perhaps the most well-known example of such a construct of an institution is the Weberian bureau model, combining a number of subinstitutions under the restriction of efficiency (Weber [1922] 1978). Another instance is the Coase model of the firm as a general institution (Coase 1988) or the Schmitter model of corporatism (Schmitter 1983). The ideal-type approach to institutions tends to be highly abstract, constructing an artificial institution with extreme properties which real-life institutions more or less resemble.

Political institutions and institutional approaches

If we follow the two main approaches in neo-institutionalist literature, institutions can be said to be either rules or organizations, rational choice institutionalism, on the one hand, and sociological institutionalism on the other. While rational choice institutionalism insists upon the equality between rules and institutions, sociological institutionalism does not deny that institutions include rules but it claims that institutions consists of more than rules, for instance interests, culture and behaviour.

This basic difference in the concept of an institution between atomistic and holistic neo-institutionalism is not just a matter of choosing a definition for the word 'institution'. The controversy reflects two alternative theories of collective behaviour.

Political institutions like parliament, the government with its ministries, and the judiciary all involve the behaviour of lots of persons, but such behaviour is not random or accidental. It consists of people interacting in a more or less predictable fashion, based upon expectations of the individuals in relation to each other. Such collective behaviour tends to be institutionalized, i.e. the expectations of the participants focus upon rules that prescribe how interaction is to take place. And behaviour tends to obey the directives contained in the rule, whereas failure to follow directives meets with disapproval and sanctions.

To a rational choice institutionalist, institutions play a key role in structuring collective behaviour, but they constitutute only one part of collective behaviour, namely the rules directing interaction. To a sociological institutionalist, the collective behaviour in its entirety is the institution. Whereas a rational choice institutionalist looks upon collective behaviour as framed by institutions as rules, the sociological institutionalist regards institutions as collective behaviour including all its aspects, not only institutions as rules.

Thus arises a fundamental divergence in outlook upon political institutions within the neo-institutionalist literature, which is so large that adherents of the two approaches hardly speak to each other. The difference between rational choice institutionalism and sociological institutionalism becomes most critical in their entirely different opinions about the nature of interests or preferences in collective behaviour.

The outcomes of collective behaviour such as voting in a parliament, decisions by a government and the rulings of a supreme court reflect the interests or the preferences of the choice participants – both rational choice and sociological institutionalism agree on this, but thereafter the disagreement becomes large enough to create another gulf between the two approaches.

To the rational choice institutionalist, collective behaviour is the outcome of the interaction of individual choice participants' preferences, framed by means of the rules of the game. To the sociological institutionalist, collective behaviour establishes institutions as organizations which have interests of their own, such as the promotion of the institution or its survival.

In rational choice institutionalism, it becomes a major question to clarify whether outcomes of collective behaviour depend more upon preferences (interests) or institutions as rules. Yet, what a parliament, cabinet or supreme court or constitutional court decides is nothing but the aggregation of individual choice participants' preferences into a group of collective decisions in accordance with rules.

In sociological institutionalism, the interests of institutions as organizations reflect historical legacies, national interests and community needs. Parliaments, governments and courts promote interests that reflect their images of themselves and what they can contribute to society. Thus, institutions become actors, which is impossible in rational choice institutionalism.

The main objective of this volume is not to look into all the aspects of the controversy between rational choice and sociological institutionalism, which concerns basic philosophical issues about the nature of human agency and the relationship between parts and wholes (Nagel 1961). In Chapters 1 and 2, we will state our preference for rational choice institutionalism and why we believe it is to be preferred. Yet, the problem that we will pursue arises within both these two approaches, namely: Do political institutions have a major impact upon political outputs and outcomes in a comparative perspective?

Political institutions are – to us – the rules that structure the interaction between individuals when they focus upon power and the public sector. It is always persons who act, but the setting varies depending upon the political institutions, or the rules of the game. Thus, the parliamentary arena follows certain kinds of rules and the judicial arena other kinds of rules. Political institutions frame the setting in which individual actors participate and act in accordance with their interests or preferences. One may, if one so wishes, regard these choice-setting 'institutions' as being organizations.

Now, what is the contribution that political institutions make to major outcomes, whether social, economic or political? In order to respond to this challenging question, we will employ a comparative methodology, looking at whether outcomes vary when political institutions change.

Importance of institutions: for what?

We should underline already from the outset that neo-institutionalism includes very different frameworks (March and Olsen 1989; North 1990). But all the various approaches adhere to the institutionalist tenet (IT) claiming:

(IT) Institutions are important.

However, we do not really have a set of established models on the basis of the format (IT) above. As a matter of fact, there is a huge distance between the general idea that institutions are important (for what?) and a set of precisely specified and empirically tested models that combine specific institutions with determinate outcomes. March and Olson state:

Politial democracy depends not only on economic and social conditions but also on the design of political institutions.

(March and Olsen 1989: 17)

This is almost like a research programme, because one would need to have a set of distinctive models about institutional effects, having empirical support based upon comparative research. Thus, one may wish to know more about which specific institutions are critical for what identifiable outcomes as well as what the relative contribution of rules is in relation to, for example, structural or cultural forces.

There is a real danger that neo-institutionalism will become just another fad, if we cannot replace the vague statement (IT) with more specific ones modelling for which outcomes institutions are important. This is the reason why we test a number of specific institutional models. The purpose of the chapters below is to examine the basic commitment (IT) of the new institutionalism in relation to a couple of outcomes that have been given much attention in recent research. If institutions are of such a fundamental importance in social life, then perhaps they help us understand why countries differ in terms of such macro outputs and outcomes as civil and political rights, affluence and economic growth, welfare state ambition and social or gender equality?

As neo-institutionalism sweeps the social sciences on the basis of the claim that institutions are important in social life or are the most important determinants of human interaction, then one may wish to stop and pause to reflect. Important for what? And how important are they?

Intrinsic and extrinsic importance

Generally speaking, the new institutionalists claim that (IT) is true or that:

(IT) Institutions are important.

(IT) can be interpreted in two different ways: either institutions are intrinsically important, or their importance derives from extrinsic aspects, i.e. their influence upon social outcomes, broadly speaking.

As long as one takes the intrinsic approach, one can always study institutions for their own sake. Thus, the public institutions in a country are interesting objects of analysis by merely being such institutions or having been so for many decades or even centuries. However, if one takes the extrinsic approach, then one needs to specify, at least tentatively, the policy outputs or outcomes that one connects with an institution.

The intrinsic approach to institutions needs hardly to be argued. One could always pose the relevant question: Which are the major political institutions in a country? The intrinsic approach is suitable for under-standing the internal logic and dynamics of institutions as well as for pinning down the overall similarities or differences between the political institutions of various countries. Perhaps one could claim that institutions are important simply because of the fact that they have been in existence for a long time.

Yet, the extrinsic approach to institutions asks more specific questions about the consequences of the operation of institutions, i.e. the results or so-called outcomes. The strength of a few much discussed institutional models in the literature is that they are explicit about both the institution and the outcome(s). Let us pin down a few such macro models which connect institutions with policy outputs or political, social and economic outcomes, in particular democratic stability as well as socio-economic performance.

Institutional importance and institutional counter-factuals

The separation between performance and causality in relation to the operation over time of institutions may be further elucidated by a discussion of the concept of institutional importance. In the causal sense, institutional importance implies a counter-factual proposition. When one affirms the proposition '(IT) Institutions are important', then the word 'important' can be used in different senses. One may distinguish between three different connotations: (1) the orientation of behaviour in terms of the institution in question; (2) the moral value attached to the institution; (3) the causal impact of the institution upon social results.

In recent literature on political institutions such as presidentialism and parliamentarism there has been a strong focus on the outcomes of various institutions under the classical heading of policy efficiency and electoral representativeness. Actually, one find this theme also with an early institutionalist such as Duverger. One needs to research how policy efficacy and voter representativeness is to be measured in terms of outcomes.

First, institutions may be considered important simply because they have been in existence for some time. Obviously, they have had an impact upon behaviour since they exist. It may matter a great deal for ongoing practice whether a country has a one-chamber national assembly or a two-chamber national assembly. Even in countries where the senate is much less powerful than the lower chamber, the use of a two-chamber system channels political activity and is thus of importance. 'Importance', meaning existence over time, may be claimed by several political institutions, as institutions often change slowly. Since people orientate their behaviour in terms of the prevailing institutions, then this implies that the institutions in question have impact.

Second, institutions that have existed for a long time may be important in still another sense, namely because they are considered distinguished, or carry moral and social values. Perhaps many people would consider the US Congress or the Norwegian Stortinget as important institutions in both these two meanings of 'important'. 'Importance', meaning here valuable, may be a contested aspect of institutions though, as various groups may have different opinions about how valuable existing institutions are.

Third, institutions may be important because they bring about other results than simply their own existence. Thus, institutions may enhance political stability or political performance, such as a vibrant democracy, or socio-economic performance such as economic growth and social equality. 'Importance' in the third sense means causality or the impact that the operation of an institution has upon political and social conditions. We focus upon this third meaning of 'importance' when we examine whether institutions matter.

It is one thing to say that an institution like the German constitutional court is important since it often acts and is a highly regarded institution. It is quite another thing to claim that the constitutional court in Karlsruhe has been of critical importance for stabilizing democracy in Germany. No one would deny the importance of the Karlsruhe court in the sense that it has played a major role in post-war political developments in Germany. But no one has shown conclusively that a stable democracy with much vitality needs the specific institution of an activist court that intervenes in public life often by means of legal review.

When one claims that an institution such as the French presidency under the Fifth Republic has not only contributed to the stabilization of the French political system but also enhanced affluence and economic modernization of the country (Suleiman 1995), then one must be able to answer the counter-factual question: if France had remained within the institutions of the Fourth Republic, would it then not have experienced the same outcomes? Perhaps the crisis in 1958 was merely transient, meaning that French parliamentarism could be made operative? What we wish to emphasize here is that every statement about an institutional effect that goes beyond saying merely that the institution existed, involves a counter-factual claim: had the institution not been present, then the outcome would have been different.

When an institution such as presidentialism is claimed to be the cause of Latin America's major political and economic problems, then there is, again implicit, an institutional counter-factual. We need to know whether the absence of presidentialism would have made a difference in Latin America, i.e. with regard to outcomes such as authoritarianism and poverty. Only empirical research can give clues as to whether the institutional counter-factual is correct: had this institution not been present, then the outcome would have been another one. In order to test counter-factuals in the social sciences as well as in the natural sciences, one must research generalizations (Goodman 1965). Institutional counter-factuals entail models that probabilistically connect determinate outputs and outcomes with specific institutions. Institutional analysis then becomes causal analysis of general relationships between institutions and outcomes.

'Getting the institutions right'

The argument that institutions matter, what we translate in the notion of an institutional effect, surfaces in the discussion about countries getting their institutions correct. Many countries have in the 1990s engaged in a far-reaching reform of their political institutions, placing the country in a great transitional stage. Two major transitions have aroused much interest, namely the transition from authoritarian political regimes and the transition to a market economy. Several countries have made one of these institutional reforms, whereas a few others have made both transitions, on the basis of the hope that outcomes will change.

The transition from an authoritarian regime to democracy has been guided by institutional arguments about the importance of putting the correct rules in place, i.e. not only enacting a constitution that promises the Rule of Law but also practising a Rechtsstaat. 'Getting the institutions right' is nothing but a theory about institutional effects. Here, we have some major hypotheses about which rules promote the full respect of civil and political rights: (a) a Western legal system; (b) legal review; (c) an Ombudsman; (d) a two-chamber parliament; (e) parliamentarism, etc. – many of which are analysed in Chapters 7 and 8.

The reform of the economy has in many countries focused upon the transition from state interventionist institutions towards the acceptance of the rules of a market economy. Thus, the command economies have been dismantled almost everywhere, and the countries which practised economic nationalism have cut back the role of the state in the economy, moving more towards so-called laissez-faire. Why? Because 'getting the institutions right' for the economy would – it is believed – increase wealth, i.e. certain types of politico-economic rules enhance economic growth. Again, we have some ideas concerning these institutional effects.

Since the basic institutions of the economy tend to be regulated by the state, either by law or in the constitution, we will in this volume include a few economic institutions in our search for the occurrence of institutional effects, especially those that define the borderline between the public and the private sectors.

However, fundamental economic rules may not only be of importance for economic outcomes. They may also have an impact upon political outcomes. In Chapters 13 and 14, we test a couple of models which claim institutional effects from the institutions of the market economy, the first set of models dealing with the explanation of differential growth rates in the economy itself, and the second set of models using the institutionalization of economic freedom to explain civil and political rights.

At the same time, political institutions have been mentioned as a major condition for economic and social outcomes. Thus, the debate about the socio-economic consequences of Consensus institutions and Corporatist institutions for rich countries is at heart a discussion about alternative models concerning institutional effects. Chapter 11 evaluates the theory that the institutions of Konkondanz democracy and Corporatist democracy are closely linked by focusing upon their institutional effects, for the economy as well as for social and gender equality.

The most well-known institutional model in modern political science, Duverger's law about the impact of electoral institutions, is an argument about the occurrence of a very strong institutional effect. Duverger, in reality, claimed not only that the party system was shaped by the electoral laws but also that electoral systems played a major role for the type of government via their impact upon the party system. Chapter 9 examines the evidence for and against these two institutional effects. All the arguments about institutional effects are hypotheses about probabilities. They boil down to statements about contributory conditions, where institutions figure prominently as one of the explanatory factors and outputs and outcomes constitute the phenomena to be explained. From a comparative institutional perspective, the use of statistics, especially the use of regression analysis, provides a suitable methodology for testing alternative theories about institutional effects.

Performance and causality

When countries adhere to different legal traditions such as Western traditions – the Common Law and Civil Law legacies – or Oriental legacies such as Sharia Law, one may ask whether different legal institutions are reflected in institutional performance. When looking at the typical policies and outcomes connected with an institution, then it is vital to underline a distinction between performance and causality, especially when engaging in comparative institutional analysis. Examining how institutions perform involves mapping what policy outputs and what social outcomes tend to accompany the operation of various regimes.

Evaluating institutional performance on policy outputs and outcomes is very common in so-called regime analysis. A regime is a distinct set of institutions combined into a whole according to an institutional logic that makes sense (March and Olsen 1989). One might mention federalism, corporatism or Westminster democracy and Consensus democracy as examples of political regimes. Various combinations of state and market result in alternative politico-economic regimes (Gastil 1987; Gwartney *et al.* 1996).

The performance configuration of regimes tells us what the characteristic policies of such composite institutions tend to be as well as what the overall profile of the outcomes attending such policies looks like. Here, we have fascinating questions about how different regimes tend to engage in different policy mixes concerning welfare state expenditures as well as alternative sizes of the public and the private sectors. In terms of outcomes, various political or politico-economic regimes tend to display differences in terms of such macro aspects as political development and human development, but also on such matters as inflation, social equality and economic growth. To map these patterns of institutional performances is a very important task in comparative institutional analysis.

However, performance is not causality. The new institutionalism, in its search for institutional effects, must remain aware of the problem of spurious correlations as well as the difficulty in separating cause from effect. All that we can arrive at are probability connections between institutions, on the one hand, and outputs and outcomes, on the other, where one cannot jump to any conclusions about causality. First, factors other than institutions may be at work. Policy outputs and outcomes tend to depend upon party preferences, peoples' cultures and social forces. Comparative institutional analysis must employ regression analysis to try to separate the impact of institutions in relation to the effect of other factors. Second, outcomes may cause institutions, meaning that we face the difficult problem of causal interpretation, when two entities go together in constant conjunction, which one is the cause and which one is the effect.

We do both an analysis of regime performance and an analysis of institutional causality. In the various analyses of macro institutions, we first set out to map the policy outputs and outcomes that go together with regimes. The next step is to identify institutional effects, attempting to show that an institution really matters for outcomes when other relevant factors have been taken into account.

The statement that '(IT) Institutions are important', runs the risk of rapidly becoming a dogma. Whether an institution is simply a rule or a mechanism for decision-making or the practice of an entire country, whether it is a general governance mechanism or some country-specific arrangement, what is referred to as an 'institution' is said to be very important. How are we to know? Such claims can in the last resort only be validated by means of empirical research about, first, performance and, second, causality.

Evaluating institutional models

By evaluating models that claim that specific institutions have determinate outcomes, the chapters in this volume basically proceed in a two-step fashion. First, we examine the findings from an analysis of the performance record of various macro institutions. Second, we proceed to causal analysis and employ the regression technique.

One may get a first glimpse as to whether the occurrence of an institution is accompanied by a specific outcome by resorting to dichotomies. In an analysis of variance one may look at whether a set of countries that exhibits the institution in question tends to be different on the outcomes as compared with a set of countries which lacks the institution. Such an approach, based on simple dichotomies, evaluating the performance record of entire sets of countries, is only helpful in directing research into directions where a regression analysis may reveal more about the interaction between the variables, given the *ceteris paribus* clause.

Once we move to an examination of correlations between, on the one hand institutional variables and, on the other, outcome variables, we broaden the analysis by considering other factors known to be of causal relevance for the explanation of the performance record of a country. We argue that social structures contain a host of factors that are of importance for country performance and that these should be included when one finally arrives at regression analysis. Looking at developmental outcomes – economic, social and political – we test a set of well-known institutional models. The general and vague claims of the new institutionalism may thus be replaced by a set of models backed by a number of relevant and interesting empirical associations between identifiable institutions, on the one hand, and specific developmental outcomes, on the other, arrived at by means of the tools of comparative research.

Thus, there is a set of institutional hypotheses that has been much debated in the 1980s and 1990s, although clear-cut evidence has not been provided for these hypotheses or their counter-hypotheses. Thus, many scholars argue to the effect that parliamentarism has a better performance record than presidentialism; judicial institutions may be highly conducive to a stable democratic regime; majoritarian election techniques may promote governmental stability, but reduce the influence of minorities; equality is enhanced in corporatist institutions; and that set of institutions that promotes economic freedom is likely to result in higher levels of affluence and democracy. We wish to enquire into these institutional effects by using a comparative institutional approach, focusing upon macro outputs and outcomes.

Unpacking an institutional model may be an effective strategy to gauge the impact of institutions upon policy outputs and outcomes. Comparative politics offers the tools for such an approach to the problem of institutional effects. If an institution makes a difference to a country, then perhaps it will have the same impact in other countries. One should not expect to find deterministic relationships between institutions and outcomes, as one can be sure that other factors play a role. Yet, probabilistic support in the form of correlations or regression analysis findings are clearly relevant when one examines the impact of institutions in comparative politics.

Democratic institutionalism

The attention given to Lijphart's *Democracies* (1984), outlining two ideal-type patterns of political institutions, Westminster democracy and Consensus democracy, reflects the power of institutional analysis in interpreting concrete country institutions, resulting from the combination of a few general institutional features. In Lijphart we clearly face the composition problem, as the two concepts of Westminster democracy and Consensus democracy consist of seven or eight institutions which need not logically co-vary. Basically, the distinction between these two types of democratic regime is focused upon governmental institutions, in particular the difference between a minimum winning and minimum-sized cabinet, on the one hand, and a grand coalition or oversized cabinet, on the other. One may view the idea of Konkordanzdemokratie as a smaller version of the Consensus model of democracy.

It is possible to test not only whether real-life institutions cluster the way Lijphart predicts but also enquire empirically into how each of the seven or eight abstract institutional features listed by Lijphart relate one by one to a set of outcomes. Perhaps when one pins down which one of them matters and how much, one discovers that they are not of the same importance for different conceivable outcomes. One of the institutions in the Lijphart cluster is the form of the electoral system, already identified by M. Duverger in 1950 as of critical importance for a few political outcomes, despite the fact that Lijphart and Duverger hold completely opposite views about the institutional effects of various election systems.

Lijphart particularly focused on the difference between British democracy and European Continental democracy, but never scrutinized closely the general executive institution of presidentialism in order to find out how it works in reality, i.e. what the main outcomes of presidentialism tend to be. Linz's argument is that presidentialism is not conducive to democratic stability, which has been criticized (Linz and Valenzuela 1994; Horowitz 1992). Presidentialism involves a number of subinstitutions that may differ somewhat from one country to another, such as the possibility of a presidential veto in relation to the legislature and the existence of different executive prerogatives. One also has to take into account the possibility of an eventual combination of a strong presidential head of state and a premier as the head of cabinet, as in the case of European presidentialism, and enquire into the effects of such an institutional mixture of parliamentarism and presidentialism.

Thus, it is relevant to conduct inductive research to find out which countries have strong, medium or weak presidentialism, the institutions of which admit an interesting variation across countries around the world (Shugart and Carey 1992). One soon discovers that the subinstitutions of presidentialism admit of a large institutional variation (Tsebelis 1990), i.e. the composition problem referred to above. Yet, however important it is to understand the variety of presidentialism on the globe on its own terms, the research emphasis has tended to focus on the outcomes of presidentialism in terms of democratic stability and economic performance. Shugart and Carey argue that presidentialism may constitute both an effective and representative institution. We will test in a systematic manner whether political institutions such as presidentialism or parliamentarism can be connected with key political or socio-economic outcomes.

One can look at the institutions of the national assembly in a similar manner. Thus, Taagepera and Shugart examine at great length how parliaments are assembled in various countries (Taagepera and Shugart 1989). They argue that the rules governing the composition of parliaments in the countries around the world express a basic law, namely the inverse square law according to which the number of parliamentarians will vary from one country to another as a function of the size of the country population. What one would want to know is whether alternative institutional arrangements such as a one-chamber parliament or a two-chamber parliament affect outcomes. Is it true that the mere size of a parliament in terms of members has an impact upon the size of the public sector, smaller parliaments being conducive to a smaller public sector for instance? Tsebelis and Money thus presented an argument in 1997 about the strong institutional effects from the existence of bicameral national assemblies.

In relation to the judicial system, the institutionalists underline the importance of strong legal review, meaning that judges or a court may test legislation for constitutionality. Naturally we ask: Important for what? Is it possible to establish any links between judicial review and political and economic outcomes at the macro level? In relation to the existence of legal review one encounters the problem present in all institutionalist writings, namely the separation between formal institutions in written constitutional documents and real-life institutions that actually work. Several countries claim they have judicial review but without really accepting its real-life functioning. Instead of legal review several countries employ the ombuds-man institution. Whether countries operate legal review or an ombudsman, does it matter for outcomes such as democratic stability or the longevity of democracy? In terms of the variation in legal institutions, what does the evidence from each country reveal?

One could examine the state format by asking, in a similar fashion, whether federalism or unitarism matters. This links up with a strong claim in federalist literature that federal institutions have specific effects. Federalism in a modern interpretation by Elazar and Ostrom is the theory that not only presents an analysis of a federal state framework but also claims that it results in better outcomes than a unitary state (Villiers 1994). We test this claim by looking at how federal states perform in terms of democracy, affluence and economic growth. The research on the outcomes of federal institutions is, however, hampered by the lack of a concise definition of the concept of a federal state. Are federal institutions the institutions that occur in states that designate themselves 'federal', or is federalism a theory about the positive implications of decentralization in a general sense so that decentralized unitary states can also be called 'federal' if they are character-ized by extensive regionalization such as, for instance, Spain and Italy. The difficulty is again the composition problem, as one may wish to know the parts and pieces of a federal state in more detail in order to find out what their respective consequences are.

Williamson's *The Economic Institutions of Capitalism* from 1985 is an example of how institutional research may combine a few subinstitutions – the existence of private property rights, joint stock companies and bourses or stock exchanges – into a model of one key economic institution, namely that of competitive capitalism, or as we will call it, the 'market economy'. As a matter of fact, the question as to the meaning of the word 'capitalism' has been much debated in economic research. The concept of capitalism has been interpreted in different ways, Sombart listing a variety of types of capitalism as they have occurred throughout history (Sombart 1916–1927). Yet the model where one type of capitalism – the market economy – enhances affluence and economic growth can be tested by focusing upon the amount of economic freedom in the economic life of a country. What is at stake is the place and force of market institutions, which may be limited not only in command economies but also in countries which adhere to economic nationalism or, as it is also called, state capitalism. We look at the interaction between indicators of economic freedom and key macro outcomes, including also democracy.

The emphasis in this volume is upon political institutions and their institutional effects. But we will examine also macro economic institutions, especially those that refer to the separation between state and market. Here we find the classical argument by Friedman that economic institutions are critical for enhancing political liberty, expressed in his *Capitalism and Freedom* in 1962. What are the chief types of economic regime and what are their institutional effects?

Institutional effects in comparative analysis

Political outputs and outcomes are often analysed at the macro level, i.e. at the most general level, meaning that of society or a country. Thus, policy analysts have examined why total public expenditures vary between countries, i.e. outputs; and comparativists have enquired into the sources of the variation in political stability and democracy between countries, i.e. outcomes. Chapter 3 contains a concise summary of such outputs and outcomes that figure prominently in studies at the macro level. What explains this variation in policy outputs and social, economic and political outcomes?

The rational choice approach would underline one factor: preferences or interests. Sociologists would suggest another explanation: social forces. Anthropologists would argue that it is culture that explains such phenomena. Historians point to the relevance of time, or the impact of traditions such as historical legacies. And instititutionalists point out still another factor, namely institutions. There is no other way to find out which factor explains the most – interests, social structure, culture or institutions – than to employ regression analysis and run measures of these factors through a computer in order to arrive at estimates of causal influence.

In the rational choice approach, the key explanatory factor is preferences. Macro outcomes could be related to preferences in two ways. Either preferences are aggregated from the micro level to the macro level, or the preferences of persons with macro status is focused on. In rational choice theory, preferences tend to be more or less selfish interests, although rational choice is not the same as public choice, which exclusively focuses upon egoism and its consequences in politics. Sociologists tend to reject the rational choice approach, denying that human beings act in accordance with the *homo economicus* model. Human behaviour is heavily influenced by the social environment in which it takes places. Social behaviour involves not only taking altruism into account, but also the social structure which impacts upon human beings to such an extent that the notion of a utility-maximizing individual becomes almost impossible.

The rational choice approach is also rejected by the anthropologists, using the concept of culture to interpret human behaviour. The variety of cultures can only be understood if one moves away from the assumption of human nature being one and the same, focusing upon self-interests. Cultural analyses of society could encompass religious belief, ethnic identities and universal values.

For instance, one could look for the conditions of democratic stability amongst several factors in a country: (a) the preferences of elites; (b) the culture of the population; (c) the structure of society or the economy and (d) historical legacies. A number of well-known hypotheses have been formulated, adhering to one of these explanatory factors. What institutionalists add to this debate concerning the conditions for democracy is the emphasis upon the role of institutions, especially political institutions but also to some extent economic institutions.

Conclusion

The new institutionalism or neo-institutionalism can only succeed if more specific models about the impact of institutions upon clearly identified outcomes are developed. Such models, of course, need empirical corroboration by means of comparative research covering preferably as many countries of the world as possible. The crucial question in relation to the new institutionalism is: important – yes, but for what?

What follows in the various chapters in this volume is an enquiry into the links between political institutions of various kinds and policy outputs and outcomes searching ultimately for institutional effects. Each chapter starts from a key model or theoretical framework within neo-institutionalism and then proceeds to an empirical test by means of comparative data. Much emphasis is placed upon getting the model right, i.e. discussing the theoretical underpinnings of hypotheses which claim that the operation of certain institutions results in determinate outcomes. The institutionalist tenet (IT) must be qualified, as one must specify very clearly the kinds of institutions that one is talking about and the kinds of outputs and outcomes that one has in mind when one talks about institutional importance, especially extrinsically.

Right from the outset of this enquiry, one must recognize that institutions are not the only important factors for outcomes. We will also deal here not only with the impact of culture upon macro outcomes but also discuss the causal relevance of structural factors such as affluence and the level of socio-economic modernization. Thus a number of specific institutionalist models will be discussed theoretically and then the empirical evidence for these models will be probed, using the most recently available information about the countries of the world. Sometimes we will consider the entire set of states with more than one million in population as the test set, whereas at other times we will only examine a set of states that fulfil the criteria on democracy. Before we embark upon the analysis of several themes in the neo-institutionalist research, we will theorize the place of institutions in human interaction.

Theoretical Section

1 What is an institution?

Introduction

The advent of the new institutionalism as a framework for social science analysis has been hailed as the kind of scientific revolution that one has had in mind when analysing theoretical developments in the natural sciences (Kuhn 1962). Since it is stated that the new institutionalism or neo-institutionalism is radically different from the old institutionalism, it is regarded by many as a radical innovation in the way in which social science concepts are to be framed as well as in the manner in which social science modelling is to be made. What is different in institutionalism compared with other major approaches such as behaviouralism, rational choice and structuralism is the focus on the concept of an institution (Keman 1997). What, then, is meant by this key term 'institution'?

The institutionalist trend in the social sciences is broad enough to encompass a number of different approaches (Steinmo 1992; Koelble 1995; Hall and Taylor 1996; Rothstein 1996; Immergut 1998). One basic division is that between individualist, economic or rational choice neo-institutionalism, on the one hand, and sociological neo-institutionalism, on the other. The first adheres to the doctrine of methodological individualism while the second is to be regarded as holistic in its approach. Yet, this is not the place to discuss the pros and cons of various institutionalist approaches, but to link the contention between rational choice institutionalism and sociological institutionalism to the double-natured core of the concept of an institution.

Thus, the purpose of this chapter is to examine the concept of an institution in order to make a distinction between two senses of institution, namely rule and organization. We will argue that there is one fundamental difficulty connected with the word 'institution' in that the word is ambiguous between these two senses. It may stand for either a norm or for an organization. An institution may be a rule that directs behaviour by means of sanctions, i.e. it is a norm that has been institutionalized. Or an institution may be a system of behaviour that is directed by means of a set of rules, i.e. it is organized activity. In Max Weber's taxonomy of fundamental concepts in the social sciences, we find the very point where the rule conception turns into the organization conception.

Ambiguity of 'institution'

One promising approach to the discussion about the concept of an institution is to ask how this concept is related to other key terms in the social sciences such as 'rule', 'behaviour', 'practice', 'organization' and 'order'. The more one probes into the variety of meanings given to the word 'institution', the more difficult it becomes to arrive at one common conceptual core. We will employ the well-known Weber taxonomy over basic social science terms to show that it is far from evident what the connotation (meaning) and denotation (reference) of 'institution' is or should be. Asking for the connotation of a word focuses upon properties whereas asking for the denotation of a term pinpoints what the word stands for.

From surveying the literature within neo-institutionalism, it is apparent that the word 'institution' may be either defined as a norm or it may be defined as an organization or a system of organs or offices. Interestingly, the *Oxford English Dictionary* contains these two definitions of 'institution':

> An established law, custom, usage, practice, organization, or other element in the political or social life of a people.

Whereas 'institution' as a law points towards the norm interpretation, 'institution' as an organization or organ is a behavioural interpretation. Thus, the *Oxford English Dictionary* speaks of an institution as:

> a regulative principle or convention subservient to the needs of an organized community or the general ends of civilization.

This is very much the norm interpretation. It should be separated from the following definition in the *Oxford English Dictionary* of an 'institution' as:

> An establishment, organization, or association, instituted for the promotion of some object, esp. one of public or general utility . . .

This then is the organizational interpretation of institution, or 'institution' defined as an establishment or association or organ. Associations tend to have institutions in the sense of 'institution' as rules, but 'institution' as organization covers much more than merely norms, and includes behaviour, interests and belief-systems. Not only is the connotation different in these two definitions, but also the denotation is not the same. Let us therefore give a few more examples from the many definitions of 'institution'.

Walton H. Hamilton also identifies institutions as rules or norms or conventions. He wrote in 1932:

> Institution is a verbal symbol which for want of a better describes a cluster of social usages. It connotes a way of thought or action of some prevalence and permanence, which is embedded in the habits of a group or the customs of a people.
>
> (Hamilton 1932: 84)

'Institution' may stand for practices that are more or less codified into a set of rules. One author identifies the institutions of democracy in the following manner:

> There were (1) a written constitution; (2) with a declaration of rights implying a limitation of the sphere of government; (3) majority rule, usually control of a government by an elected legislature; (4) the separation of powers of government so that each power might check and balance the other; (5) public education to produce the knowledge and spirit appropriate to democratic government.
>
> (Finer 1962: 78)

Democratic institutions according to this quotation would consist of constitutional norms in so far as they correspond to actual practices. Democratic norms and realities need not be the same phenomena, if the rules have been unsuccessfully institutionalized.

It is always stated that the use of sanctions is typical of an institution. This entails that an institution includes norms, as the sanction must be directed against behaviour which violates rules:

> Institutions derive from particular, established codes of conduct, which shape the behavior of particular groups of men who implicitly or otherwise have a loyalty to that code and are subject to certain controls (anxiety, guilt, shame, expulsion, etc.) if they violate the norms.
>
> (Bell 1988: 51)

Doing institutional research may involve focusing upon certain important rules. Or such research may look at a web of institutions that cover an entire practice:

> Since institutions provide society with the framework that enables it to operate as an organized whole, in which individuals and social groups, their symbols and ideas can act and interact, institutional history offers many ways of looking at society without losing sight of its unity. Intellectuals, officials, economic leaders and workers, priests, and professional figures function within the institutional structure and contend for place there.
>
> (Anderson and Anderson 1967: vii–viii)

One may interpret 'institution' in this quotation as comprising a web of rules that give the framework for major practices in social life. When institutions are considered as frameworks for practices, then one is not far away from considering institutions as macro practices:

> The concept of 'institution' refers to a pattern of supraorganizational relations stable enough to be described – polity, family, economy, religion, culture.
>
> (Alford and Friedland 1985: 16)

The danger of confusing institutions as rules with institutions as practices appears clearly when institutions are identified with certain types of practices, namely the activities of corporations or organizations:

> Since the Roman law, two main forms of the juridical personality have been distinguished: (1) Corporations (universitas personarum or the medieval collegia personalia) where the union of the members as persons is stressed – such as most of various corporations, incorporated societies, firms etc. (2) Institutions (universitas bonorum or the medieval collegia realia) as a complex of property with a specific purpose, endowed by the law to act as a single person, such as various universities, asylums, etc.
>
> (Sorokin 1966: 38)

In all debates about institutions, we tend to find two basic definitions of 'institutions', either as rules, i.e. the sense (2) above, or as organizations, i.e. the sense (1) above. 'Corporations' and 'institutions' are different words, both on the level of connotation and the level of denotation. The ambiguity of 'institution' referring either to norms or to organizations reappears in all discussions about institutions, e.g. in theories about the design of institutions or constitutional engineering (Sartori 1994).

Organizations act, but rules are never said to be actors or to have preferences. Political organs or bodies such as a parliament, a government or a supreme court are often spoken of as 'political institutions', as behaviour in such bodies tends to be heavily institutionalized. At the same time one may distinguish the institutions of such bodies, i.e. their rules, as an aspect that is separate from other characteristics of such bodies, such as their resources or capacity to take action.

It would hardly serve any purpose to legislate here for or against one of these two definitions. What is crucial, however, is to make the separation between the two definitions, because it goes a long way to explain the contrast between rational choice institutionalism (rule interpretation) and sociological institutionalism (organization interpretation). A political institution may be simply a rule that is upheld with sanctions or it may be a complex organ in the state.

Thus, it is perfectly legitimate to speak of national assemblies or legislatures as institutions or, even more strongly, as the most important national institutions of a country. This use of the word 'institution' is, however, different from when one is speaking of the voting rules of parliaments as examples of their institutions. A parliament like the British one is an organization that follows certain rules. When 'institution' stands for an organization, then the meaning of the word is much wider than when 'institution' stands for a norm or rule. This distinction is vital if one wishes to understand why the new institutionalism in the social sciences harbours so many divergent approaches, because, to a large extent, they are speaking about different phenomena.

The cause of the confusion about what 'institution' stands for is the link between rules and organization, i.e. institutionalization. Note that not just any norm is an institution. Far from being the case, an institution is a norm that is upheld in behaviour by means of sanctions. Organizations, obviously, do have rules that are combined with sanctions. Institutions are essential to organizations, as they could not operate without them. But that is not saying that an organization is the same as an institution. The command 'Drive on the right side of the road' is an institution in several countries, but it does not constitute an organization. Let us develop this argument more below.

Epistemology and ontology of institutions

Reflecting on the meaning (connotation) and reference of 'institution' (denotation) brings us into both ontological issues (what institutions exist?) and epistemological issues (how do we come to know about institutions?). Theorizing institutions entails that one not only identifies what 'institution' stands for, but also states how we can gather knowledge about these phenomena in accordance with the canons for the conduct of scientific enquiry (Kaplan 1964).

Taking a broad look at the neo-institutionalist literature, one is confronted with not only very different views about what an institution is – ontologically speaking – but also with different positions as to how one goes about acquiring knowledge about institutions – the epistemological aspect. Whereas many scholars take the view that institutions may be investigated by the ordinary canons of scientific enquiry, others claim that institutions require a special approach, the so-called 'logic of appropriateness' (March and Olsen 1989). Institutions call for approaches that are more hermeneutic in spirit, it is argued.

Neo-institutionalism, state March and Olsen, is a reaction against various reductionist perspectives that attempt to explain how political institutions work by means of non-political factors. Institutions have a logic of their own, the understanding of which requires approaches that are not reductionist, explaining politics with only preferences (economic man) or with simply social structure (sociological man).

In order to understand the place of institutions in social and political life one can use the analogy of a chess game as a model of human interaction. In chess, people interact under a clearly given and transparent set of institutions about how to move the pieces. These are the rules of the game. The behaviour of each actor is orientated in terms of these rules, acknowledging them in every move. Yet, the actual moves are determined by the strategies of each player, which aim at maximizing their advantages. What the rules do is to restrain the choice of alternative strategies so that they comply with the idea of chess. Thus, chess is both institutionalized practice and rules. It is also organization, as chess may be played at clubs on a competitive basis which involves arranging tournaments all over the world.

New institutionalism and institutional design

One finds in the institutional literature simple definitions as well as complex definitions of 'institution'. One philospher writes: 'a social institution is nothing more than a stable, valued, recurring pattern of behavior' (Goodin 1996: 21), which implies that institutions are behaviour patterns. And 'institutionalization' he defines as 'the stable, recurring, repetitive, patterned nature of the behavior that occurs within institutions, and because of them' (Goodin 1996: 21), which implies, we take it, that institutions are different from behaviour. This difficulty with introducing a clear definition of the concepts of institution or institutionalization is endemic.

What is an institution? If it is a rule or a code, then it is not behaviour. One must make a very clear distinction between, on the one hand, the rules of the game, which are crystal clear, informing us about how one makes moves and when the game is over with a determinate outcome, and, on the other hand, the actual play of the game. Social life, modelled on the analogy of the chess game, would include both the rules and the behaviour, although these are separate entities.

Suppose that an institution is a system of action. To those who argue that the rational choice perspective is the most promising framework for institutional analysis, one could argue that there is a basic difficulty involved in the application of economic decision models to institutions. Self-interests are not the sole consideration within institutions as systems of action, which could involve social or altruistic interests to a considerable extent.

Suppose that institutions are rules or norms. Then one may certainly examine the morality of institutional design, meaning the questions surrounding whether an institution promotes purposes that are indeed morally acceptable. Internal and external morality relating the individual and the institution may be distinguished on the basis of the idea that 'the moral theory of institutions and of the behavior of institutional office holders must be derived from the nature of the institutions' (Hardin 1996: 152). Yet, since it is difficult to establish the contribution of each individual to institutional performance – the crux of the matter is individual responsibility – the conclusion is that institutions could be outside of the realm of moral discourse. Yet, institutions as norms are certainly critical in resolving problems of how persons as members relate to groups, both the instrumental rules of the group and those that identify its ultimate purposes.

If institutions are first and foremost moral norms, then perhaps they should be examined by means of the publicness requirement, as in Kantian ethics. However, a legal scholar has shown that the requirement that institutions as maxims or norms satisfy publicness is far from being as self-evident as one might think (Lubin 1996). The acceptance of institutional publicness could depend upon shifting empirical circumstances, namely whether one can enhance justice secretly.

What is the import of the publicity principle for the evaluation of institutions? Kant thinks about publicness as a sufficient criterion of justice: an action is wrong if their maxim is incompatible with publicity. It means that publicness is only a necessary condition. It does not hold that an action that satisfies publicness *ex ante* is thereby just. Even if Hitler had made public the decision to eliminate the Jewish population in Germany and if it had met with little resistance among Germans at that time, it would still have been wrong, for both Germany and the Germans. All German governments after the war have admitted this, satisfying publicness *ex post*.

If institutions are organized behaviour or organizations, then one may wish to consult the sociological analysis of institutions, i.e. codes. Interestingly, one sociologist says that institutions are codes, but he writes about them as if they are actors: 'Institutions generate vested interests in their own preservation' (Offe 1996: 208), he writes, but only men/women can have interests and take action, not codes themselves. Similarly, 'institutions are designed to redesign themselves' (Offe 1996: 209), but it is men/women who change the codes, not the codes themselves This is a macro perspective of institutions conceived of as organizations having purposes and responsibilities to individual members.

Suppose that institutions are codes. Then one would focus on how codes function in social life by governing behaviour, and especially how they develop over time. Questions of institutional design loom large, quite naturally, and cover here not only intentional rule-making but also the evolution of rules. In a micro approach to institutions one would wish to separate codes from actors and rules from behaviour. Yet, if one goes back to a macro perspective on institutions, then institutional design loses its intentional aspects and one enters the evolutionary perspective, where institutional selection is a slow process, only partly the result of the actions of actors. It is a commonplace observation that institutions constrain behaviour, but perhaps they also select actors. Proper selection procedures identifying the correct people are as important as rules that restrict the activities of the incorrect people (Brennan 1996).

Institutions as rules, moral norms, codes, behaviour regularities, organizations – this is a substantial set of connotations taken from the institutional literature (DiMaggio and Powell 1991).

Holistic institutionalism

When we turn to holistic, or sociological, institutionalism, then the meaning of institution becomes complex (Brinton and Nee 1998). Let us quote the places where 'institution' is mentioned in an already classical text – *Rediscovering Institutions* (1989):

> traditional political institutions, such as the legislature, the legal system, and the state.
>
> (March and Olsen 1989: 1)

institutions, such as law and bureaucracy.

(March and Olsen 1989: 1)

the ways in which political behavior was embedded in an institutional structure of rules, norms, expectations, and traditions.

(March and Olsen 1989: 5)

It seems from these quotations that March and Olsen are inclined to link up the definition of an 'institution' with the concept of an organization. Since organizations can be considered as actors, institutions would not be the rules or norms that govern the activities of actors, but would constitute actors themselves. Yet, March and Olsen often refer to institutions as rules: 'Thus, political institutions define the framework within which politics takes place' (March and Olsen 1989: 18).

The danger involved in such a wide definition of 'institutions' as both rules and organizations are twofold. First, we have reification or the fallacy of misplaced concreteness when institutions are looked upon as actors. If institutions regulate the behaviour of actors, then how could institutions be actors themselves? Second, when institutions are included in the set of organizations, then institutions take on a number of the properties of organizations. Thus, we read:

> Political democracy depends . . . also on the design of political institutions. Bureaucratic agencies, legislative committees, and appellate courts are arenas for contending social forces, but they are also collections of standard operating procedures and structures that define and defend values, norms, interests, identities and beliefs.
>
> (March and Olsen 1989: 17)

But if agencies, committees and courts are institutions, if institutions are activity, values and beliefs, then maybe institutions are everything and by entailment nothing?

Sociological neo-institutionalism suggests that one should look at: (1) the physical structure; (2) the demographic structure; (3) the historical development; (4) personal networks; (5) the temporal structure (decision points in time) (Olsen 1988: 35). Institutions may be analysed as: (a) normative orders; (b) cognitive orders; or (c) symbolic orders; but how about the action aspect? Are institutions primarily norms, belief-systems or symbols, and do they comprise action phenomena meaning that collective activity takes place and leads to social outcomes? If all state organizations are looked upon as institutions, then the concept becomes a wide one indeed.

Institutions come before interests; institutions shape the wishes and desires of individual persons, their preferences. Already this position is risky, but March and Olsen move to the doctrine of holism (Nagel 1961), i.e. public institutions constitute a social reality that involves more than simply the acting persons. March and Olsen argue that the emergent properties of institutions as organized social systems give public institutions a life of their own, a destiny that even the social researcher finds it difficult to unravel. Institutions are not only an important part of the common sense equation of rules plus interests, they also determine individual preferences or interests.

The sociological version of the new institutionalism looks upon institutions as something more than constraints on choices. The identities and conceptions of the actors, perhaps even the notion of an actor itself, are formed by the institutional structures. The distinction between interests and institutions gets blurred. In sociological neo-institutionalism, institutions seem to assume the role of actors, i.e. resulting in reification or the fallacy of misplaced concreteness. In this perspective, interests are endogenous, as the individuals or the actors are formed in the institutional context which they live. Common sense, though, teaches us that interests and institutions are separate entities in social reality. Preferences are determined exogeneously with regard to institutions – this is a basic tenet of rational choice institutionalism which, however, raises the question of where and how the interests of actors originate (Wildavsky 1987).

Old institutionalism: Weber

The institutionalist paradigm has become fashionable in the social sciences since the 1980s. A long-known framework for social analysis dating back to Montesquieu's emphasis on the importance of rules, i.e. laws and customs (1748) has been revitalized. The new institutionalism may be seen as an attempt to revitalize the old institutionalism in political science that, we were once told, had mutilated political research for such a long time (Eulau 1963). By confining the conduct of political enquiry to history and case studies, institutionalism was accused of provincialism by emphasizing country-specific formal rules to the neglect of real-life behaviour and its law-like regularities.

How do we single out the political institutions in the general set of institutions? Acknowledging the existence of political, economic, social and cultural institutions, the distinctive features of the public institutions are, it is assumed, that they constitute a political order orientated towards conflict resolution. More specifically, the new institutionalism answers that the concept of the state is crucial in designating those institutions that are political and it regards the revival of state theory as an institutionalist trend (Skocpol 1979; Evans *et al.* 1985; Dunleavy and O'Leary 1987).

It cannot be emphasized enough that not all of old institutionalism was deficient (Eisenstadt 1968; Apter 1991; Selznick 1996; Stichcombe 1997). Among the old institutionalists we have Weber, who launched a sociological kind of institutionalism which was not, however, holistic. Here, we have an analysis of institutions that pinpoints the connection between institutions as rules and institutions as organization.

In 1913 Weber published an article where he attempted to systematize several concepts about various forms of social life. It was included in *Economy and Society*, published shortly after his death in 1920. The ultimate unit in human interaction is, argued Weber in 'Basic Sociological Terms', behaviour that is orientated or intended in terms of expectations about people – social action (Weber [1922] 1978). All aggregate units such as organizations and states consist of such units, i.e. actions. Weber moved from the most simple unit to the most complex entities by doing two things: aggregating actions and adding what he called 'maxims'.

These maxims enter social life when one looks at the occurrence of orders in social life. An order, writes Weber, is more than a mere uniformity of social action, as it involves behaviour that is determined by orientation to a norm or rule which is held to be valid or 'legitimate'.

Actions and norms are the building-blocks in the Weber system. By distinguishing between various kinds of actions as well as between various types of norms, Weber was able to compile a long list of definitions of key terms used in political science. We will look at some of these distinctions below, but the key one for our purposes now is the separation between action and norm. By moving from simple to more complex social science concepts Weber managed to pin down a concept of an institution which is suitable for present-day research endeavours.

Using 'social action' we may introduce more complex concepts. Thus, we proceed to 'social relation', which stands for an interaction between two or more people. A social relation is a more complex term, as it requires more than merely the aggregation of social actions. The emphasis in Weber's taxonomy lies upon social relations and their ever more complex properties resulting from the combination of properties into successively more complex constructs. Some types of relations consist by definition of several actions (e.g. friendship), while other types may contain only a few actions (e.g. buying or selling). A one-sided relation would be a social relation where the orientations of the persons are neither of the same type nor complementary. A two-sided relation would occur when the orientations are either of the same type or complementary.

More complex concepts can be introduced as various kinds of social relations. A communal relation would be a relation based upon approval between persons. A relation of interest occurs when there is mutual neutrality between persons interacting. 'Communal relation' stands for relations of deference and erotic relations, whereas 'relation of interest' refers to market relations, for instance. Obviously, these types of social relations involves different forms of co-operation, one based on mutual feelings and the other based on shared interests or a compromise of interests.

Anyone may enter into open social relations, whereas in a closed relation participation is restricted. As types of examples of closed relations where participation is confined to certain persons, Weber mentions the family, the religious association and the monopoly in economic life. Market interaction under conditions of complete competition is an example of an open relation, where entry is without restrictions. Over time, social relations may hover between these two extreme types.

More types of social relations may be identified: a relation of solidarity is a social relation, where both are responsible for what goes on. A relation of representation is different, as one party is responsible to another for what he/she does, but not the other way around. The property solidarity is most usual among communal and closed relations like the family and the tribe. Representation occurs in rationally established corporations and almost always in some form or another in formal organizations.

Weber links up the state with a relation of representation, but before we arrive at such a highly abstract construct we must pay attention to the specific qualities which are, in general, connected with a political action. Thus, Weber links politics with power, of which authority is the form of power that he underlines. Authority is a social relation in which there is obedience between two or more persons. This type of social relation is of central importance for Weber as he employs it in his theory of domination. Weber's word 'Herrschaft' is synonymous with the other word he also employs in this connection, namely 'Autorität' (authority) (Weber 1964: 157).

Let us turn to the definition of power or 'macht' in Weber before we move to the concept of an institution. A relation of selection is, according to Weber, the most basic general predicament in societies of whatever conceivable kind they may be. Note that it is not a social relation, as it is not necessary that persons orientate towards each other in order for selection to occur. When we add that the relation of selection should also be a social relation, then we arrive at conflict as a relation among actors. Thus, we have a relation of conflict which involves a relation of selection where two or more parties confront each other about the advantages in social life.

Weber distinguishes between biological and social selection, but conflict is the most general construct for selection when it takes place within social interaction. Relations of conflict may involve the use of force or they may be peaceful as in competition. Violent conflict is the opposite to co-operation as it involves a clash between different orientations in a relation of selection. Weber distinguishes between various types of conflict relations such as competition and regulated conflict. Power occurs in a social relation when one of the actors exerts his will against that of another actor. Thus, a power relation is a social relation in which one party carries through his/her will against the will of the other party, even if it meets with resistance.

This brings us to the introduction of a few definitions containing one term that is essential for the concept of an institution. The word 'legitimacy', meaning 'considered binding', allows Weber to introduce an 'order' as a legitimate system of rules. A valid order occurs when the behaviour in a social relation is orientated in terms of a system of norms.

Weber speaks about these rules of behaviour as the so-called maxims of social life, indicating that the norms that persons orientate towards tend to be generalized. What makes these maxims into institutions is the additional property that they tend to be guaranteed, not only by belief in their legitimacy but also by activity. Thus, an institution is a system of norms towards the rules of which there is obedience. We arrive now at two types of institutions, depending on how the maxims are guaranteed.

A legal order is an institution which is guaranteed by means of the employment of physical violence against non-compliance. A convention is an institution which is guaranteed by other means. Institutions may thus be of two types: legal orders and conventions. They both have three distinctive properties: (a) a regularity of behaviour; (b) a set of maxims in terms of which the behaviour regularity is orientated; (c) the occurrence of a mechanism of some kind through which the maxim is upheld in the sense that behaviour tends to occur that complies with the maxim. Weber shows in the further development of his taxonomy that such a concept is useful in order to introduce other concepts which elaborate somewhat upon the properties of institutions and that are very relevant for the purposes of social science analysis.

It is readily seen that the concept of an institution is different from that of an organization, as the latter concept requires more than the former: a corporation is an institution that is guaranteed by the activity of leaders. A corporation is the combination of three properties: social relation, norms and activity by leader(s) in order to implement the norms. As examples of corporations, Weber mentions the family, the formal organization, the State and the Churches.

The concept of corporation has a central place in Weber's taxonomy. It is a necessary component in his definition of the state. Weber introduces terms for properties of corporations but also terms for types of corporations. A territorial corporation is a corporation whose system of norms is valid for a specific territory. An organization is a corporation which involves interest relations between the members of the corporation. To Weber, formal organizations need not have a territorial property but they are always based upon the interests of participants, not their affections.

Weber ends up with his definition of the state as a special territorial corporation, and in order to arrive at the definition of the state he separates voluntary and compulsory corporations: a compulsory corporation is a corporation whose system of norms is valid for each and every member of the corporation whether he/she wishes it or not. A voluntary organization is a corporation whose system of norms is valid for the members of the organization in so far as they accept them. States belong to the general set of compulsory organizations. Their distinctive properties are introduced as follows: a state is an authority corporation whose system of norms is guaranteed within a territory by physical violence or the threat of physical violence by its leaders.

Following Weber's list of concepts with their increasingly more complex constructs has allowed us to identify a concept of institution that is more distinct than that employed in sociological neo-institutionalism.

Rational choice institutionalism

The holistic or sociological approach is challenged by the rational choice approach, which has two sources within neo-institutionalism, one in political science and the other in economics (Weingast 1996). The sociological view of institutions originates in organization theory (DiMaggio and Powell 1991), while the rational choice perspective is based upon the neo-classical decision model within economics (Eggertson 1990). Between these two approaches stands the new institutional economics, which is atomistic but models behaviour in terms of bounded rationality also originating within economics (Williamson 1986).

The rational choice perspective on institutions has been heavily influenced by the many new developments within so-called social choice, i.e. the analysis of how decision rules affect outcomes when groups come together and aggregate individual preferences (Arrow 1963). The many results concerning the paradoxes of voting, path dependencies and the chaos theorem all indicate the same, namely that the rules of the game play a profound role, alongside preferences, in shaping outcomes (Moulin 1983; Kelly 1986; Nurmi 1987). Institutions are regarded as stability conducive mechanisms, reducing the turbulence that stems from the lack of so-called core solutions in collective choice, i.e. solutions that cannot be defeated by some strategy or coalition. Institutions help derive stable outcomes, so-called equilibria (Shepsle 1989).

The rational choice perspective on institutions has also been much influenced by developments in economics, especially the emergence of new institutional economics (Coase 1988; North 1990). In the economic insitutionalist models there is a focus upon those institutions that are basic to economy (Eggertson 1990) such as the market, property rules and the firm whilst not taking the existence of institutions for granted, these new models emphasize the crucial importance of social rules for social interaction, modelling how men/women make rational choices about which institutions they wish to live with in order to maximize economic output and minimize the dissipation of rents. Somehow society tends to find the institutions that are transaction-cost minimizing.

As in economic institutionalism, the word 'institution' is, without exception, defined as rules. Institutions as rules are looked upon as constraints within which actors may maximize their self-interests. Or they are considered as transaction-cost saving devices regulating the interaction between men/women. In the public choice literature, institutions tend to be regarded as rent-seeking mechanisms that reduce economic efficiency or total output (Stigler 1988; Mueller 1989). Yet, in law and economics, rational choice institutionalism has been developed in a theory about the consequences of various legal institutions for economic life, such as property rights, the limited liability company as well as alternative arrangements within contract law, tort law and public regulation – all rules enhancing economic efficiency (Posner 1992).

Thus, among the rational choice institutionalists, those social phenomena which are to be called 'institutions' range from simple to complex rules, which are implemented by means of some form of sanctions. Matthews (1986) distinguishes between four kinds of institutions: property rights, conventions, types of contracts and specifically contracts about authority or governance structures like the firm or the limited liability company. Williamson (1985: 15), concentrating on governance mechanisms in a world of bounded rationality, states: 'Firms, markets and relational contracting are important economic institutions'. North stresses the importance of distinguishing conceptually between the rules of the game (institutions) and the strategies (organization) which the players in the social game find it advantageous to adopt (1990: 5).

Conclusion

The new institutionalism has been hailed as a most promising approach in the social sciences in the 1990s. There is interesting work on institutions going on in the disciplines of political science, sociology and economics. Our focus in this analysis of public institutions is to establish to what extent do institutions have an impact upon outcomes. Thus, we are less interested in discussing the variety of nuances in various concepts of an institution, which is after all basically a matter of choosing a definition, than in finding out whether the claim that '(IT) Institutions are important' is a valid statement about the world.

The sociological institutionalism of March and Olsen, rejecting each and every reductionist interpretation of the public sector, has a basic holist twist which upsets the balance between the motivational aspects – interests – and the rule aspects – institutions – in public sector behaviour. In contrast, there is a tendency in the neo-institutionalist approach developing from the economic man decision model, to expect that institutions can be derived from interests in a manner that could satisfy criteria on optimality and rationality. We remain sceptical about both the sociological and the economic versions of neo-institutionalism.

Following Weber, a clear separation between interests and institutions may be upheld, while at the same time remaining within the confines of methodological individualism. When a set of maxims are obeyed in a society through the orientation of the actions of the members of that society, there is in Weber's theory an order. An order can be guaranteed in two ways, says Weber: first, by subjective reason: affectual, value-rational or the belief in legitimacy; and second, by expectations of specific external effects, i.e.

through the employment of sanctions in the form of group approval or disapproval – convention – or in the form of physical or psychological coercion – law (Weber 1978: 33–4). Maxims or norms that are connected with sanctions are called 'institutions'. Maxims that are not institutions lack enforceability.

In the rational choice approach to neo-institutionalism, institutions are looked upon as (or comply to) simple rules or norms. They constrain the actors, who take the existence of institutions into account when they orientate their behaviour. Institutions are thus webs of rules that constitute phenomena that are of a different order to individuals or organized collectivities such as organizations. In rational choice institutionalism, institutions are sharply distinguished from interests or preferences and complex institutions may be decomposed atomistically into simple institutions.

From a political science standpoint, public institutions structure governance relations involving the electorate, the leaders or politicians and agencies or bureaucracies. Public institutions may be looked upon as responses to the search for structuring principal-agent relationships in politics. What could this mean? The next chapter suggests an answer.

2 Institutions and interests

Introduction

In Chapter 1, we chose the definition of 'institution' according to which institutions are the rules or norms that govern behaviour, whether individual or organizational. To 'govern' actions means to restrain activity by narrowing down possible means and ends. Thus, institutions constitute governance mechanisms. Why do governance mechanisms of various types exist? What would life be like if there were no governance mechanisms? This question logically precedes the question about the consequences of an alternation in governance mechanisms, which is the topic discussed in the empirical chapters that follow below.

Suggesting an answer to the problem of the reason for institutions in human interaction brings us into the theoretical debate about the micro foundations of institutionalist theory. Insisting upon a clear distinction between interests and rules, we must present an argument to the effect that the institutionalization of rules is necessary in human interaction as governance mechanisms, directing action in society based upon the interests or preferences of actors.

In this chapter, we wish to elaborate upon another idea of Weber's, namely that political institutions restrain authority relations. We will focus especially upon the modern state, which Weber connected with the employment of legal authority, which he claimed is the rational type of domination. Legal authority means a relation between rulers and the rules that is highly institutionalized in terms of an explicit and rationally instituted set of rules. Why is this superior to the two other classical forms of domination: traditional authority and charismatic authority?

We argue that their role derives from the ever present dangers of outright opportunistic behaviour. Opportunism is self-intererest seeking with guile. If one starts from an assumption which claims that not only human beings behave in accordance with the assumptions of rational choice, but that they also consider opportunism if not restrained by rules, then what follows? This basic assumption about human motivation will be combined with a principal-agent framework for the analysis of the rules governing the interaction between political leaders and their people.

Rationale of institutions

Now, the key question is the following: why are institutions forthcoming? Whether one emphasizes the importance of spontaneous institutional evolution or underlines the possibility and desirability of institutional design, one has to ponder about why institutions are needed in society at all. Each and every society consists simply of persons, whatever role they may occupy in organizations. Individual behaviour is determined by the interests of persons, one may assume. Why could not people interact without institutions, solely on the basis of their preferences?

Samuel P. Huntington has suggested an answer that we wish to elaborate upon:

> In the total absence of social conflict, political institutions are unnecessary; in the total absence of social harmony, they are impossible.
>
> (Huntington 1968: 9)

Thus, institutions are connected with conflict, peaceful or violent, among men and women. Huntington explains:

> The level of political community a society achieves reflects the relationship between its political institutions and the social forces which comprise it. . . . A political organization or procedure, on the other hand, is an arrangement for maintaining order, resolving disputes, selecting authoritative leaders, and thus promoting community among two or more social forces.
>
> (Huntington 1968: 8–9)

Institutions are, therefore, needed for the organization of society – this is the argument. How can it be proved?

The typical feature of traditional authority, which is, historically speaking, the most frequent institution for regulation of political domination, is that it offers weak restraints upon the use and abuse of power. As political leadership has developed into a formidable source of domination due to technological developments in the twentieth century, we must pose the question: how is such a capacity to affect millions of people to be channelled into socially acceptable activities? What political institutions restrain political leaders so that they do not use the people or the country for their own self-interests? In the Weberian analysis of forms of authority, charismatic leadership has been one such institution for defining the principal-agent relationship, but it is a very weak one (Weber 1978).

Perhaps the concept of charisma comes readily to one's mind when there is a discussion about the personal element in the politics of the twentieth century. Charismatic leaders direct their states with *personalismo*, if they reach leadership positions, or undermine existing state structures if they carry revolutionary momentum. In spite of the fact that politics involves millions of people, single individuals like Nelson Mandela, Lech Walesa and Corazon Aquino can bring down an entire system of rule like apartheid, Communist Poland and Marcos's Philippines, whereas Ruholla Khomeini identified a whole new concept of the state under modern Muslim rule (Goldstone, Gurr and Moshiri 1991). State persistence may be promoted by the employment of shrewd tactics and strategies on the part of traditional rulers like King Hassan II of Morocco or the late King Hussein of Jordan. Established systems of rule were undermined by embarking on proper action at a suitable time and in the right circumstances by key actors like Kemal Ataturk, Fidel Castro and Mahatma Ghandi.

The tragedy of politics is that charisma could be employed for engaging in activities that spell catastrophy, such as with Hitler and Stalin. Single actors could have a fatal impact upon state performance, bringing about catastrophy for millions of people, if disastrous opportunities are presented to persons with ruthless determination and fervent zeal. The impact of single individuals such as Pol Pot in Cambodia, Ceausescu in Communist Romania and Idi Amin in Uganda, indicates that charismatic leadership may deteriorate, meaning that the self-interests of rulers take precedence over the accomplishment of the broad interests of various citizens. In charismatic leadership it is impossible to remove opportunistic behaviour on the part of political leaders. During certain events, or under certain time periods, pure charisma will not restrain political leaders. Another more relevant restraining mechanism is the basic rules of the political game, the constitution, which is characteristic of the modern state with its drive towards legal or rational authority.

Institutions and their enforcement

When one looks at the view of men and women in the history of political philosophy one finds two alternative philosophies, the egoistic perspective versus the altruistic one. They are in agreement that men and women are inclined to look after their own interests such as protecting their lives, their offspring and their property. They disagree about whether men and women are inclined also to care for others.

The Epicurean line of thought places the emphasis upon the self-interests of men and women. Epicureanism argues that human motivation is profoundly shaped by the love of oneself. The question then becomes: if egoism is correct, then what prevents men and women from doing harm to each other? In one way or another, the Epicurean philosophers answer: rules of proper conduct. But how do rules come about, where do they come from, if one accepts the naturalist starting point that man only looks after his own interests?

The rules of proper conduct limit egoism, channelling it along certain paths of behaviour which make social life possible. Thus, in all societies there are maxims that prohibit certain behaviour, restricting the harmful consequences of naked egoism. One may conceive of these maxims as divinely inspired as in religious thought or as imposed by means of the domination of rulers, but also as pacted from within society, by mutual consent. Such maxims instruct men and women to limit their egoistic drives, respecting other people, their lives, liberty and property.

In Epicureanism, the need for rules is obvious, as without them men and women would act like wolves: homo homine lupus. Although one may argue that rules would be forthcoming in one way or another, the question of enforcement of these maxims then becomes the second basic difficulty. Why comply with maxims that restrict the basic drives of men? Are certain rules self-enforceable or is there a need to set up an enforcement mechanism for each and every rule? When one argues not only that maxims are necessary in simple as well as complex human interactions but also that these rules tend not to be self-enforceable, then one arrives at the conclusion: institutions must exist in every society.

In the competing philosophy of man and woman, Stoicism, the basic tendency in man is towards virtue. Men and women form humanity, which is a union of human beings respecting each other and naturally taking care of each other – altruism. Egoism is a threat to justice, which demands that each and every one respects all. The Stoicist line of thought claims that man/woman knows by his/her reason that certain maxims are valid for man. Natural rules of equity make social life possible, but there is still somehow a need for institutions restricting the negative consequences of egoism, as reason does not always control egoistic drives. What becomes critical in the Stoicist line of thought is first to clarify how much human beings have in common, the scope of sociability as it were, and second to devise an implementation mechanism, as egoist tendencies remain a threat towards sociability, feelings threatening the rule of reason.

Whether one pursues the Epicurean line of thought or the Stoicist line of thought, one arrives at two conclusions: (a) the importance of maxims for human interaction and (b) the lack of self-enforceability of rules concerning human interaction. In egoist philosophies one needs to explain how such norms of proper conduct emerge and are implemented. In Stoicist philosophies one needs to account for how far sociability reaches out and how it is protected against the vices of man. Paradoxically, one arrives at the same conclusion: the necessity of institutions in social life. It is not enough to identify by fiat or evolution the maxims that regulate human interaction. These maxims must also be institutionalized, i.e. they must be enforced by some mechanism.

In the history of political philosophy, one has debated not only whether men and women are basically egoistic or altruistic – the first problem of institutions – but also the second problem – what is the enforcement mechanism in institutions? One may argue for the necessity of rules in order to arrive at social stability. Without rules, behaviour would become unpredictable, if not violent. But can one have a society which has rules but which relies upon self-enforceability in the sense that the members of the society implement the rules by their own initiatives and policing? How is the observation of rules forthcoming?

A person may obey the maxims either because he/she believes them to be valid or because he/she is afraid of the consequences of not respecting the norms of society. In the first case, self-enforceability is forthcoming, whereas in the second case this is not so, and a mechanism must be devised that achieves the enforcement of the rules. Institutions arise when a society possesses rules which are enforced by means of a mechanism. The enforcement of rules may be accomplished by means of either group pressure – conventions – or by means of the employment of physical violence – law.

Egoism versus altruism, self-enforceability versus mechanisms for enforcement – making these distinctions allows us to make four combinations (Figure 2.1).

	Basic Motives	
	Egoism	*Altruism*
Rules		
Self-enforcement	I	II
Mechanism for enforcement	III	IV

Figure 2.1 Motivation and rules.

In political philosophy there may be wide disagreement about the issue of altruism versus egoism, but there seems to be agreement about the need for explicit mechanisms for the enforcement of rules, i.e. institutions in general and law in particular. Let us here adduce the argument launched by David Hume, which claims that viable societies tend towards category III, meaning that institutions are really needed for social order.

In his *A Treatise of Human Nature I–II* (1739–41) Hume states a plausible argument for the need of not only institutions in general but political institutions in particular. Hume starts from the epicurean position:

> Nothing is more certain than that men are in a great measure governed by interest, and that, even when they extend their concern beyond themselves, it is not any great distance; nor is it usual for them, in common life, to look further than their nearest friends and acquaintance.
>
> (Hume [1741] 1966: 235)

After having established egoism as a powerful motivation, being conducive to the state of nature – 'wretched and savage condition' – if unchecked, Hume, however, admits the Stoicist starting point as well, stating that man has a natural interest in society and justice:

And as this interest which all men have in the upholding of society, and the observation of the rules of justice, is great, so it is palpable and evident, even to the most rude and uncultivated of the human race.

(Hume [1741] 1966: 235)

Hume rightly states that if the Stoicist assumption is correct – that the interest of men/women 'is so much concerned in the observance of justice' – then one may ask: 'how any disorder can ever arise in society' (Hume [1741] 1966: 235).

Yet, Hume resolves the contradiction between egoism and altruism by adding a third assumption – myopia. He states:

This is the reason why men so often act in contradiction to their known interest; and, in particular, why they prefer any trivial advantage that is present, to the maintenance of order in society, which so much depends on the observance of justice.

(Hume [1741] 1966: 236)

Combining the assumption of myopia – 'the consequences of every breach of equity seem to lie very remote, and are not liable to counterbalance any immediate advantage that may be reaped from it' – with egoism and altruism tips the balance in favour of the first force in human motivation. The implication is clearly that 'the violations of equity must become very frequent in society, and the commerce of men, by that means, be rendered very dangerous and uncertain'. (Hume [1741] 1966: 236). How, then, is social order possible and peaceful human interaction feasible?

Interestingly, Hume anticipates the manner in which the dilemma of reconciling social order with human motivation is modelled in the Prisoner's Dilemma game in modern social science (Rapoport *et al.* 1976). He writes, in a marvellous passage, that it is rational for one person to break the social order if another person does so:

You have the same propension that I have in favour of what is contiguous above what is remote. You are, therefore, naturally carried to commit acts of injustice as well as me. Your example both pushes me forward in this way by imitation, and also affords me a new reason for any breach of equity, by showing me that I could be the cully of my integrity, if I alone should impose on myself a severe restraint amidst the licentiousness of others.

(Hume [1741] 1966: 236)

Thus, if the natural inclination towards altruism and the wish to respect the precepts of justice are not strong enough to hold back the negative consequences of egoism and myopia in human motivation, then what explains social order according to Hume? Hume's answer is: the state.

There is no other way out of the Prisoner's Dilemma situation than to change the logic of the situation, as 'the utmost we can do is to change our circumstances and situation, and render the observation of the laws of justice our nearest interest, and their violation our most remote' (Hume [1756] 1966: 237–8). The change in the situation, not in the motivation, is brought about by the introduction of persons 'whom we thus immediately interest in the execution of justice' (Hume [1741] 1966: 238). Hume writes:

> These are the persons whom we call civil magistrates, kings and their ministers, our governors and rulers, who, being indifferent persons to the greatest part of the state, have no interest, or but a remote one, in any act of injustice; and, being satisfied with their present condition, and their part in society, have an immediate interest in every execution of justice, which is so necessary to the upholding of society.
>
> (Hume [1741] 1966: 238)

One may argue that institutions or the precepts of justice play a profound role in social life, making social order or stable and peaceful human interaction possible given basic facts about human motivation, i.e. the tendency for egoism to prevail over altruism. This is an argument one often encounters in the literature on the Prisoner's Dilemma (Elster 1989). However, Hume adds that the rules of civilized behaviour must be enforced by means of one special apparatus, the state.

Thus, in the Humean analysis of human motivation versus the rules of society, the state is assigned a key role. Actually, here we find at the same time 'the origin of civil government and society' (Hume [1756] 1966: 238):

> By means of these two advantages in the execution and decision of justice, men acquire a security against each other's weakness and passion, as well as against their own, and, under the shelter of their governors, begin to taste at ease the sweets of society and mutual assistance.
>
> (Hume [1741] 1966: 238)

Suppose we accept Hume's solution to the Prisoner's Dilemma game, which in reality amounts to changing it into another kind of game – an Assurance game, where it is individually rational to co-operate and not defect. Hume manages, by introducing government, to explain why men in their ordinary conduct respect the simple rules of society, restricting the consequences of egoism and myopia. These natural precepts of justice make social life stable by offering rules about proper conduct, the respect of others and the protection of life and property. Without the state, however, they will not be enforced safely and predictably.

Yet, the problem of social order has only been moved somewhere else, as we may now ask how one can be sure that government and its officials and judges will really be as beneficial for ordinary citizens as Hume claims.

Perhaps institutions of a higher order are necessary in order to structure the public sphere? Hume actually makes an *ad hoc* assumption about the people in the state, stating that they have no motive to be selfish and all kinds of motives to care for the public interest. Rejecting such an *ad hoc* assumption, we insist that one speaks of the people in the state in the same manner as ordinary people, i.e. we assume the same constellation of forces: myopic egoism being stronger than altruism. Let us assume that political elites are also driven by rational egoism. Then what follows? One could argue that Hume solves the Prisoner's Dilemma game – the conflict between individual rationality and collective rationality – by a very simple and *ad hoc* assumption about the so-called principal-agent relationship between the population and the elites in the state.

One may find a similar confrontation to the one between Epicureanism and Stoicism in the debate between rational choice on the one side and communitarianism (Mulhall and Swift 1996) or the socio-economics school on the other (Etzioni 1988). It seems impossible to construct social life only on the basis of individual motives, especially if these are conceived of as mainly egoistic or self-interested ones. Without rules that people obey not even the most simple forms of human co-operation such as agreements and contracting appears to be stable (Bromley 1989). The difficulty in deriving co-operative solutions to games that model human interaction has received much attention in modern game theory, focusing upon the well-known Prisoner's Dilemma situation (Heap 1989).

Within the rational choice school, building upon the assumption about the maximization of self-interests, one admits the difficulty of founding social life only upon self-interests. What is needed is a choice of rules before individuals can begin to maximize their self-interests, as people could choose institutions rationally. People could either first come to an agreement on the rules of the game and, after that, play the game. Or they could simultaneously come to an agreement about both the contract as well as a mechanism for the implemenatation of the contract.

Within the communitarian school, people are benevolently social in orientation and they act in institutions that are naturally given. In a soft version, institutions influence the preferences of the actors in the sense that people wish to respect the rules as a matter of adherence to social principles about truthfulness, fairness and honesty, i.e. the Prisoner's Dilemma situation does not often arise. In a radical version, a person's self is constituted by the norms that are valid in a society, meaning that people are defined by the collective ideals that are also expressed in institutions. This position would be equivalent to category IV in Table 2.1.

Yet, whether we start from a rational choice approach or a sociological perspective, we still arrive at categories III or IV in Table 2.1, which entails that institutions exist in stable societies where social order prevails. This is only a first step, as we also need to present an argument as to why political institutions such as a state are necessary in a society. Let us pursue the argument by Hume and focus upon so-called principal-agent relationships. What, more specifically, is involved in such interaction and where does politics enter?

Principal-agent theory

Human interaction is based upon agreements. One set of institutions regulates exchange between individuals as one form of contracting – private sector contracting. The market institutions of the private sector offer one framework for contracting based upon property rights. Another set of institutions regulates contracts in the public sector, based upon the authority of the state over the population in its territory. The rules about democracy and bureaucracy offer institutions through which so-called principal-agent contracting may take place.

Public policy or the making and implementation of policies in the public sector may be interpreted as responses to fundamental governance problems in society. At heart of the policy process and the implementation stages is the attempt of the principal to monitor the efforts of different agents to live up to the terms of agreement made between them. The governance relationships stretch from the election arena to the parliamentary theatre and to the bureaucratic setting. And the operation of public institutions structure the interaction between the rulers and those ruled. The design of political institutions is fundamentally different in a democracy from an authoritarian regime in precisely the principal-agent relationship: the institutions really restrain the rulers in their exercise of political power, meaning that they handle the problems in principal-agent interaction.

The principal-agent relationship was identified firstly within the private sector, where certain types of human interaction had a longer duration than was typical of market behaviour (Ross 1973). Thus, one was able to see that long-term contracting took place where one party instructed another party to work to his/her benefit and received compensation. Examples of principal-agent interaction may easily be found in the insurance sector and within the legal setting. Modelling such contracting involves certain specific problems, related to the occurrence of asymmetric knowledge, giving rise to incomplete contracts as well as strategic behaviour on the part of the agent in order to gain advantages in relation to the principal, who faces monitoring difficulties (Campbell 1995).

Once the existence of principal-agent interaction had been verified in market situations, it was soon realized that relational contracting and incomplete contracting occurred in many other settings as well (Molho 1997). A classical case is the use of sharecropping in agriculture as an alternative to other institutional regimes such as the labour contract or the rental/franchise regime. Other examples of principal-agent interaction include the employment relationship in firms or organizations, including not only the salaried employees but also the managing directors or CEO's (Ricketts 1987).

The theory of principal-agent interaction in the private sector has developed quickly since the first analyses appeared around 1970, as it has benefited from game theoretical modelling of so-called mechanism design (Hiller 1997). Taking the model of principal-agent interaction into the public sector, one may mention the economic theory of bureaucracy (Niskanen 1971), or the logic of public regulation (Stigler 1975) and so-called rent-seeking behaviour (Tollison 1982). In principal-agent interaction the governance problems are non-trivial except under exceptional circumstances. They include both problems *ex ante*, i.e. the arrival at an agreement between the principal and the agent about what is to be done, and problems *ex post*, i.e. the implementation of the agreement in accordance with the terms arrived at *ex ante*.

First, there is bound to arise a conflict of interest between the principal and the agent, as they are supposed to co-operate but at the same time the agent asks for a remuneration for his/her efforts to enhance the objectives of the principal. If the agent happens to want to do what the principal wants him/her to do, there would be no reason to set up a monitoring device to check whether the agent's level of effort corresponds to his/her payment. Second, the agent tends to possess information that is relevant to the principal, which the principal cannot obtain without incurring considerable search costs. If the principal had the same information as that on which the agent acts, and if he could monitor the effort of the agent easily, then the principal could design an efficient contract. Asymmetric information in combination with the conflict of interest concerning effort level versus remuneration are conducive to governance problems both *ex ante* and *ex post*, which are identified as moral hazard, or hidden action, and adverse selection, or hidden information.

In principal-agent interaction, there is bound to arise uncertainty about what the principal can reasonably expect from the agent *ex ante* and *ex post* as well as incompleteness in the agreement between the two, as not all circumstances that are relevant to the execution of the contract can be foreseen. Contractual incompleteness tends to become exaggerated by two factors: hidden actions and hidden information. In principal-agent interaction agents may maximize their own utility to the detriment of the utility of the principal in situations where agents do not bear the full consequences of their actions (Eatwell *et al.* 1989).

Moral hazard (hidden actions) results even though the principal has the same information as the agent at the time when they come to an agreement over the contract. The problem is that the principal is often unable to observe the actions taken by the agent, and consequently has to base his evaluation of the agent's contract performance on the results of those actions. If the result depends on unobservable random variables beyond the agent's control, the principal cannot make reliable inferences from the results of the activities of the agent to the level of effort made by the agent, simply by monitoring the results of those activities alone. It allows the agent not to follow the terms of the contract *ex post*.

Adverse selection (hidden information) occurs *ex ante*, i.e. at the time when the contract is established, when the agent possesses information about the services that he will not render to the principal and which is inaccessible to the principal. The agent may misrepresent the fundamentals of contract negotiation to obtain better terms of agreement than he would otherwise have been able to secure. When the principal comes to realize this, he/she may design terms according to the expected performance of the would-be agents discouraging better-than-average candidates and encouraging worse-than-average candidates. The degradation of the quality of the agents may continue resulting in an outcome similar to the description of the market for lemons (Akerlof 1970).

We suggest, therefore, that one looks upon political institutions as structuring principal-agent interactions in the state, focusing upon political elites. Thus, we arrive at our main question: Assume that political elites, in whatever manner they have come to power, are looked upon as the agents of the population, paid for by them as well as instructed by them to act in the interests of the population. Which institutions exist that regulate this interaction between the leaders and the population and what are their macro consequences?

Democracy and principal-agent theory

Without political institutions governing principal-agent contracting between political elites and the people, there would be strategic behaviour on the part of the agents, the political elite, as a result of moral hazard and adverse selection. Institutions contribute to handling the principal-agent difficulties in political interaction, some political institutions more than others though, as they restrain the scope of activity of the agents more. We are referring, of course, to the institutions of democratic regimes.

The principal-agent model starts from a contractual perspective. Agreements establish a reciprocal relationship between the contractual parties where one party in return for compensation agrees to follow the directions of the other. One party, the principal, is given the right to instruct the other, the agent, whereas the agent promises to work for the promotion of the interests of the principal. Such relationships are established when it is impossible to specify all the details in a contract and, at the same time, it is risky to leave room for discretion. Such agreements are expressed in the public contract between the electorate, politicians and bureaucrats (Moe 1988).

The principal-agent model is more easily applicable in a democratic context than in an authoritarian one. In democracies, the population possesses a number of institutions by which it may instruct the political elite and make agreements, these include elections of various kinds, referendums and opinion polls. One may speak of election contracts where political parties offer various policies from which the electorate may choose. The period up to the next election would then be a long monitoring process, during which the electorate seeks information about the achievements of the governments in order to hold it accountable for its promises. The constitution of a democratic country offers several institutions with which political elites may be checked, one of which is the set of competition rules between alternative agents.

In the case of authoritarian settings, the principal-agent model seems more remote, as the population is mastered by its political elite. Yet, even in such systems political elites regard themselves as somehow the servants of the basic interests of the population, despite the fact that the people do not always fully or correctly understand the fundamental interests of the nation, the true religion or the state. Thus, kings and emperors, the Caudillo or der Führer and Il Duce, the secretary of the Party, the Junta – all attempt to legitimate their rule by considering themselves as agents of the population promoting the interests of the principal, whatever that may be. Thus, there also arises a principal-agent interaction in dictatorships. However, one realizes immediately that the problems within principal-agent interaction – moral hazard, adverse selection – are endemic to such public contracts, both *ex ante* and *ex post*.

In all political systems there is thus a principal-agent relationship, political leaders acting on behalf of the population. There is a line of thought in political theory where this relationship is modelled as involving very few restrictions. Machiavellism or the so-called neo-Machiavellians in classical elite theory proceed from the assumption that leaders can do what is rational in order to stay in power, viewing their people as simply an instrument or hindrance in their own power aspirations. Yet, even Machiavelli acknowledges that princes have to pay attention to the best of their people, not only from a moral point of view but also out of strict self-interest. In democratic political systems, the modelling of principal-agent relationships between leaders and the population must take institutions into account, which restricts what one may refer to as opportunism on the part of political leaders.

What are the degrees of freedom for action by the political elites in democratic and non-democratic regimes? Assuming that all act upon the basis of self-interest, i.e. not only ordinary people, as with Hume, but also leaders, we would arrive at the frightening conclusion that leaders will handle their people in whatever manner suits their interests. Political leadership could involve not only brutal warfare against other states or people but also the entire elimination of people within a country such as happened in the major examples of genocide in the twentieth century – the cases of the Armenians, the Jews, the Cambodians and the Tutsis come to mind. What prevents leaders from not only defeating their opponents among the political elites, but also eliminating them, either by putting them out of action or simply killing them? We argue: institutions. Institutions structure the interaction between the principal – the population – and their agents – the political leaders.

The leadership problem become acute within a principal-agent framework as soon as one considers opportunism, or self-interest-seeking with guile. What is it that restrains political leaders from resorting to vicious actions in order to prevail over their opponents? Atruism? Perhaps. But few political leaders are of the same calibre as Gandhi. And even Lincoln fought a bloody civil war in order to implement his ideas of political justice and the nature of the American state. What are the restraining mechanisms when political leaders do not have an altruistic bent? We suggest: institutions.

Even if one travels along the route of Machiavellianism and assumes the omnipresence of opportunistic behaviour, one would still ask: what institutions tend to emerge in order to control and limit the occurrence of opportunism? Assuming that opportunistic behaviour plays a major role in politics, then what institutional mechanisms tend to emerge in order to counteract the negative consequences that opportunism implies? Let us briefly go to the Williamson theory of hierarchy in order to examine what is involved in the occurrence of opportunism in contracting, whether private sector or public sector.

Williamson (1986) considers whether a hierarchical system as an institutional arrangement is the most transaction cost efficient way of handling exchanges or interaction between people. The answer is that hierarchies offer governance structures as the most cost efficient framework with the aim of reducing the cost of transacting when it involves relatively higher costs of writing and enforcing contracts in the market when compared to internal organization. In the private sector, hierarchies take the form of the firm institution whereas in the public sector we find the institutions governing the executive, the representative assembly and the judiciary as well as the bureau institution.

Williamson rejuvenated Simon's concept of bounded rationality (Simon 1957) as an alternative to the rational choice approach (Williamson 1975). Referring to the limited capacity of man to be informed about all the alternatives and consequences of action, the new institutionalism of Williamson addresses the same basic questions that institutional economists work with in terms of the neo-classical model. Williamson points at two human factors and two environmental factors which when combined help explain why hierarchies exist alongside markets. The human factors are bounded rationality and opportunism whereas the environmental factors include uncertainty and the small numbers problems.

Bounded rationality refers to the limited ability of man to receive/process information as well as to communicate it. Individuals are not typically capable of handling large amounts of information, making it difficult to foresee all contingencies in a complex and changing environnment. Opportunism refers to self-interested behaviour through deliberate manipulation of information about attributes of the object of exchange, as well as own preferences and intentions. Uncertainty should perhaps rather be termed 'complexity'. The environment of an organization is complex and changing, offering risks but also opportunities. The small numbers problem means that only a few actors participate in the exchange, which enhances opportunism.

The combination of bounded rationality with uncertainty means that writing contracts that cover all contingencies that may occur over a long period of time is impossible. Any attempt to approach the goal of rational decision-making will tend to be very costly. The market solution to this co-ordination problem would be an incomplete long-term contract or recurrent short-term contracts. However, both these alternatives are subject to the problems that appear when opportunism is paired with the small numbers condition. This condition assures that competitive pressures do not eliminate the potential gain of opportunistic action. Incomplete contracts may leave room for behaviour contrary to the intention of the contract when unforeseen contingencies arise. Even though a small numbers condition does not obtain at the outset, this condition tends to evolve as the contractual partners invest in transaction-specific capital and acquire transaction-specific skills. This process makes maintenance of the contractual relation all the more important for the parties to the contract, as the consequences of termination become severe. Market contracting becomes risky as the pay-off resulting from hold-up strategies increases.

The relative advantages of relying on internal or vertical organization instead of market-contracting consist of the attenuation of incentives by subgroups in an organization to behave opportunistically, as their behaviour can be monitored more closely and an incentive system be designed to further the interests of the organization. In addition, disputes may be more easily settled within an organization than across markets. As for bounded rationality, the advantages include the possibility of a step-by-step approach to problem-solving in the exchange process, as well as a process of convergent expectations serving to reduce uncertainty.

Institutions may be interpreted as governance systems that regulate contracts. The governance system that minimizes the costs involved in establishing and enforcing contracts will be chosen by the contractual partners. As a matter of fact, this basic hypothesis is highly relevant for the interpretation of political institutions, because the political and administrative organization of the public sector stems from the handling of social problems with high transaction costs involved – issues which could not be resolved by contracting in terms of a simple voluntary exchange approach.

Let us now join together the two ideas about opportunistic behaviour and principal-agent interaction to see what the implications are for the occurrence of institutions. Admitting not only the relevance of but also the frequent occurrence of altruism in human interaction, we still place the main weight upon institutions in preventing or counteracting the negative consequences of leadership opportunism in political principal-agent relationships. Political institutions, we argue, are critical for restraining leadership and holding political elites accountable, as well as for identifying proper selection procedures for choosing people in various positions in political leadership. In a principal-agent perspective on politics, selection procedures are as important as rules that restrict and control the activities of elites.

Public institutions: rules restraining opportunism

Public contracts, pervading the state and local government, involve the principals' task of designing a governance system which gives the agent incentives to act in accordance with the principals' interests, that is to act as the principal would have done had he/she had the capacity and competence to do it him/herself. The contractual perspective highlights the possibility for contractual failure and implies a search for mechanisms to be established in order to control whether the agent lives up to the terms of the contract, and sanctions to be employed to enforce the contract. Is it possible to design public institutions in such a way that they reduce the possibility for opportunistic behaviour?

Public contracting in the state and local government results in double governance relationships in a democracy. On the one hand, there is the relationship between the population as the principal and its agents in their capacity as rulers of the population. On the other hand, the rulers may wish to employ a staff to be active in the implementation of the policies of the rulers, which implies that the latter become the principal of the former. Here, we have the gist of the relevance of neo-institutionalism to political science as public institutions structure governance relationships. Table 2.1 presents an overview of public institutions that structure the interaction between leaders and their population, when examined from a principal-agent perspective.

This list in Table 2.1 is not meant to be in any way exhaustive. There is no limit to how many institutions one may wish to cover in comparative institutional analysis, as one may go very deep into institutional details. However, we wish to argue that these institutions are of key relevance for interpreting the structuring of principal-agent relationships in politics. Let us comment shortly upon some of the institutions listed in Table 2.1.

Table 2.1 Key political institutions

Human rights: implemented or not
Constitution: codified or not
State format: unitary or federal
Executive: presidential or parliamentary
Legislature: uni- or bicameral
Judiciary: legal review or not, ombudsman
Election system: proportional or not
Democracy: Consensus or Westminster
Legal system: Common law, Civil law or other
Civil society: free market economy or corporatism

Civil society institutions

If political institutions do not themselves suffice as constraints upon opportunistic behaviour in principal-agent interaction, then there are civil society institutions available. The private sector, if vibrant, would be a major force containing opportunism in the public sector. Non-political organizations may set limits to what is acceptable conduct. One such set of institutions are the rules that protect the set of all voluntary organizations, denoted by the expression 'civil society'. The classical argument in favour of civil society as the guarantee for democracy and the public interest is to be found in Tocqueville's remarkably fresh analysis of the United States, published in 1835–40: *Democracy in America*. Here, Tocqueville linked the emergence of free associations with the coming of the industrial society and the market economy.

Where the private sector is vibrant, there are considerable constraints stemming from civil society, which may be of crucial importance for limiting the occurrence of opportunistic behaviour among politicians. The firm institutionalization of the distinction between political and economic power is highly conducive to constraining political opportunism. Such restraints on the power of the state depends upon the extent to which economic power is decentralized.

A decentralized market economy is a condition for achieving a real constraint on political oppotunism, but how large should the private sector be in relation to the public sector. Hayek stated a clear case for so-called decentralized capitalism (1944), where he argued that any kind of state planning would threaten freedom in a democracy. The opposite argument to libertarianism has been stated by Lindblom (1977), claiming that state interference in the economy in the form of planning and welfare spending may increase democracy. Questions about the public–private distinction are thus highly political.

One important element of civil society is trade union activity, although Tocqueville focused much upon religious organizations. Freedom to form and belong to associations in civil society is one thing, and the actual strength of trade unions is another matter. Left-wing authoritarian states have tried to boost trade union membership in order to employ the unions as vehicles for regime goals, while freedom of collective action tends to be accepted only in democratic states. In several states the trade unions are almost non-existent, in particular in right-wing authoritarian regimes.

In several democracies, the interest organizations have established a mode of interaction with the state that is institutionalized to a high extent: corporatism (Schmitter 1983). In other democracies, the freedom of association guaranteed in the human rights protection in the constitution involves that interest organizations can interact with the government and the political parties in a free manner, but the interaction is less institutionalized: lobbyism.

We will examine below a few theories which attribute socio-economic development as well as political freedom to the institutions of civil society, especially the institutionalization of the market economy. We will concentrate upon the basic economic institutions of society but also enquire into the outputs and outcomes of corporatism.

Constitutions and constitutionalism

Constitutional documents single out the normative framework for the operation of the state. As the actually employed rules of governing the state may not be identical with the rules in the documents, it remains a fact that constitutions can only constrain political leaders if it is long-lasting. Merely having a written constitution is not enough to restrain political elites in relation to their principal, the people.

But when a constitution really restrains in a state that respects human rights and the division of powers, then the doctrine of constitutionalism applies in that very country.

Rules for competition between political elites

What is crucially important for principal-agent relationships is the occurrence of institutions allowing for contestability among political leaders, or agents of the population as principal. If leaders may be challenged and removed from office according to established rules, then opportunististic behaviour could be checked. Modern democracy offers mechanisms for competition between elites (Schumpeter 1944).

The institutions of party systems differentiate between open and closed party systems, the separation of which is intimately connected with the position of human rights in a country. The right to vote and join free associations tend to exist only in countries with a clear human rights record. Furthermore, the party system is shaped by the electoral institutions employed, both the rules governing how elections take place and the rules for the allocation of mandates to the national assembly. It has been much debated whether the employment of majoritarian or proportional election techniques makes a difference, i.e. is conducive to different policy outputs and outcomes.

It has also been much debated as to which form of executive is the most sensitive to the wishes of the principal. In a democratic setting one may choose between either presidential and parliamentary executives or the special European mixture of the two. In parliamentary regimes one finds three kinds of cabinets: grand coalitions, minimum winning coalitions and minority governments. Some democratic countries foster adversarial relations between political elites, whereas other democracies promote a consociational atmosphere. Legislatures may be formed as uni- or bicameral, and their competencies may be symmetrical or asymmetrical.

Another important feature is the amount of centralization in the modern state. It has been argued that federalism is the 'mother of democracy' (Elazar 1995). In the federal state format, bureaucracy is dispersed onto several levels of government, including a more or less clear-cut division of competencies between the central government and the governments of the member states. Federalism entails the idea that political decentralization will restrain political opportunism, either the states keeping the federal government in check or the federal government controlling state practices.

Judicial or quasi-judicial controls

It would be a serious omission not to mention the extremely important contribution of the legal system to constrain opportunism in political life. What is law but institutions? And public law when fully institutionalized constrains political life through a plethora of devices. Independent judges constitute a bulwark against excessive use of executive or legislative powers. Countries that provide for legal review go even further and provide judges or a separate constitutional court with a role in legislation, testing law and sometimes also executive actions with the criterion of constitutionality.

The role of the judiciary becomes most conspicuous when countries allow for legal review, but the impact of the legal system is much more extensive. Administrative law regulates the competencies of public officials, from top politicians to street-level bureaucrats, guarded by a system of public courts of one kind or another, and sometimes upheld in the last resort by the supreme court. In addition, more and more countries have put in place so-called ombudsmen, who check that public administration is conducted in terms of the Rule of Law.

The most distinctive feature of a Rechtsstaat is the independence of the judiciary. When political opportunism becomes excessive, then it is the Rule of Law nature of the state that is hurt or destroyed. Constitutionalism can only be protected vigorously by an independent judiciary, which explains why in countries with unlimited presidentialism or military junta the executive arm of government wishes to control the judicial arm, appointing the judges who will not speak against political opportunism.

Institutional degeneration

Theoretically, one may suggest a conceptual opposition between institutions as rules and opportunistic behaviour, where institutions would constrain self-interest-seeking with guile. The distinction between institutions, on the one hand, and interests or preferences, on the other, works itself out within a basic principal-agent interaction, where political leaders act as agents of their principal, the population, institutions regulating this interaction.

At the most general level of analysis, one may launch a theory to the effect that institutions constrain political leadership by, for instance, limiting the scope of the public sector, by instituting contestation among political parties, or by enhancing constitutionalism (human rights and *trias politica*) and by structuring the bureaucracy in terms of administrative law.

However, political institutions vary as there are alternative institutional set-ups for the executive, the legislature and the judiciary as well as for the state format itself. In the chapters to come we proceed to analyse the outcomes of alternative sets of institutions, searching for the existence of institutional effects.

Finally, we wish to remind of the ever-present risk of institutional degradation, when institutions begin to malfunction as the result of the pressure from opportunistic behaviour. One may, in relation to many institutions, make a distinction between an ideal-type version and a real-life-based version of the institution. Thus, sometimes presidentialism works well, sometimes parliamentarism operates in accordance with model requirements; but, at times, institutions degenerate, presidentialism resulting in authoritarianism and parliamentarism in government instability. One must all the time in institutional analysis be aware of the danger of institutional malfunctioning.

Looking at policy outputs and outcomes, testing whether institutional variation makes a difference, one must make clear the specific model that one is examining. Institutional models may take the form of ideal-types, but in reality one often encounters degenerated versions of such ideal-type models. Institutions may actually exist only on paper as constitutional articles, such as federalism in Nigeria. In institutional evaluation, it is necessary to focus upon the real-life copies of the ideal-types, which may be far apart. Stating that institutions matter is not enough. One must clarify which institution has what effect.

Conclusion

In a neo-institutionalist approach one may look upon institutions as responses to interaction and transaction problems in human behaviour. Assuming, like James Madison in *The Federalist Papers* (Hamilton *et al.* [1787–8] 1961), that men organize in factions in order to protect their vested interests, political institutions may be interpreted as devices for constraining opportunistic behaviour among political elites. Political groups pursue their broadly defined self-interests within the framework of interaction set by political institutions. Madison's position is close to a few key notions of economic organization theory (Williamson 1975) or the new institutionalism (Williamson 1986), which offer a framework for the analysis of institutions on the basis of the assumption of opportunistic behaviour. Institutions restrain individual behaviour – this is the basic idea.

Selecting the institutions that we will focus upon in this macro study we follow Montesquieu's *The Spirit of the Laws* with its famous doctrine of '*trias politica*', or the three branches of government. Thus, we will enquire into the consequences of executive, legislative and judicial institutions. The classical Montesquieu model may be compared with the Lijphart model that has received much attention recently. We examine electoral institutions before finally launching our argument that constitutionalist institutions matter most. Constitutionalism is with the man from Bordeaux, but in 1748 he conceived of a limited or restricted version of constitutionalism, not advocating universal human rights in the form of male and female suffrage for example. We will state a case for a full version of constitutionalism, combining Montesquieu's separation of powers with the institutionalization of human rights. It seems appropriate to examine briefly the consequences of the legal system a country adheres to. One may distinguish between two major Western systems of law, Common law and the Romano-Germanic family, as well as other systems such as Sharia law (David and Brierley 1993; Schacht 1993). However, to start our empirical enquiry we first need to look at what institutions may have an impact on outputs and outcomes. This is the task of the next chapter.

3   Outputs, outcomes and institutions

Introduction

Our book is about macro political institutions in general and the institutional effects of these institutions in particular. It basically aims to scrutinize theoretically and evaluate empirically statements occurring in all brands of neo-institutionalism – sociological as well as rational choice institutionalism – claiming that: (IT) Institutions are important.

Now, institutions as rules or norms may matter in a number of ways. But here we are primarily interested in enquiring into the impact which macro political institutions may have on macro policy outputs and macro outcomes, be these of political, social or economic nature.

Since (IT) is basically an opaque sentence, we need to specify it more in order to be able to test (IT). Thus, we need to know what political institutions are important for as well as which political institutions matter for what outputs or outcomes. (IT) should be replaced by a set of scientific hypotheses about institutional effects.

In this chapter, we attempt first to clarify what is meant by 'outputs' and 'outcomes' in comparative institutional analysis. Second, we map a variation in time and space of the occurrence of outputs and outcomes which we will relate to the operation of specific political institutions. Macro comparative institutional analysis of outputs and outcomes would lack its *raison d'être* if there did not exist a substantial variation between countries in outputs and outcomes.

The two key questions about macro outputs and outcomes that we attempt to answer here is the extent of variation as well as the stability of that variation. First, we enquire into how large the output and outcome variation between countries tends to be. Second, we test whether this variation tends to be stable over time. Since institutions tend to be in existence for decades, the argument about their impact upon outputs and outcomes (IT) can be properly tested, especially if the variation in outputs and outcomes also tends to be stable. The neo-institutionalist tenet that institutions are important for the variation in outputs and outcomes entails, we argue, that when different political institutions have been in operation for a long period of time, then it is probable that average policy outputs and average social, economic and political outcomes also differ. The meaning of 'probability' here is frequency of occurrence, according to a Humean theory of causality.

Institutional effects as probabilities

Institutional analysis would take a huge step forward towards a set of testable models if it could show that institutions matter for outcomes. In this book we attempt to advance neo-institutionalism by showing to what extent macro institutions are important for political, social and economic outputs and outcomes. We will use a Humean methodology concerning causality, enquiring into whether there is constant conjunction in a large set of countries between an institutional variation and a variation in outputs and outcomes. Thus, we will use a cross-sectional approach to the understanding of policy outputs and social, economic and political outcomes.

Two questions are central in a Humean approach to institutional importance: (1) What is average institutional performance? (2) Does institutional performance involve institutional causality in addition? We approach these two problems in a macro analysis, meaning that we examine data about whole societies, using countries as cases, focusing upon their macro political institutions and the outputs and outcomes that attend institutions.

We can hardly emphasize enough that neo-institutionalist theory needs empirical social science research in order to substantiate the claim about the existence of institutional effects. Much analysis in neo-institutionalism has been directed towards conceptual matters, distinguishing between various meanings of terms like 'institution' or 'institutionalization', or towards methodological questions such as the choice of an adequate approach in institutional analysis (March and Olsen 1984). In neo-institutionalism, a great deal of attention has also been devoted towards theoretical paradoxes such as whether institutions may solve the collective action problem of how to unite individual rationality with group rationality – the Prisoner's Dilemma question (Ostrom 1990).

It is now time to engage in empirical research, directed towards the main argument in neo-institutionalism, namely: (IT) Institutions are important. In empirical research, we are no longer talking about concepts or theoretical constructs but real-life institutions and their impact upon politics and society. Talking about the world as it exists is a different enterprise from discussing the meanings of words or the choice of a proper approach (Armstrong 1973, 1978, 1980; Danto 1968). Describing the world of political institutions and their effects involves laying claims to truth, which can only be tested by observations, or the presentation of data. Yet, theoretical and empirical steps in the conduct of enquiry go hand in hand (Kaplan 1964). Without concepts and theories, empirical research is blind. Without empirical research, conceptual constructions are empty.

Social science is just like natural science, a web of beliefs, consisting of hypotheses, adopted or entertained, because these, when true, explain the world (Quine and Ullian 1970). Hypotheses about institutions are no different from any hypotheses about the world:

> What we try to do in framing hypotheses is to explain some otherwise unexplained happenings by inventing a plausible story, a plausible description or history of relevant portions of the world.
>
> (Quine and Ullian 1970: 43)

Scientific hypotheses have certain distinctive features, explored in the philosophy of science (Popper 1959, 1972; Nagel 1961; Hempel 1965; Glymour 1980). Here, we emphasize that hypotheses tend to be: (a) conservative, i.e. the less rejection of already established beliefs required, the more plausible the hypothesis; (b) general, i.e. the more of observations that it covers, the more plausible it is; (c) simple, i.e. the fewer entities it assumes, the more plausible it is; and (d) refutability, i.e. some imaginable event could falsify the hypothesis (Quine and Ullian 1970: 42–53).

In the social sciences, the generalizations tend to take the form of probability statements. Thus, we seldom find the true law-like statements or universal generalizations that Hume had in mind, which, as a matter of fact is also becoming more and more characteristic of the natural sciences (Cartwright 1994). However, probabilities may be good enough as the basis for causal explanation (Suppes 1970).

In neo-institutional research, the proposition (IT) should be replaced by a set of hypotheses about institutional effects, having the properties (a) to (d) outlined above. In comparative institutional research, the hypotheses link institutions with macro outputs and outcomes. Now, what do we mean by 'outputs' and 'outcomes' in comparative institutional analysis? Outputs tend to be approached as independent variables, whereas outcomes are looked upon as dependent variables, but this distinction often breaks down, as outcomes may be employed as independent variables.

Semantics of 'outputs' and 'outcomes'

The words 'outputs' and 'outcomes' have different meanings in various scientific contexts. In economics, one talks about industrial output during a certain time period, while at the same time one may speak of the outcomes of running various strategies in game theory. Our usage of these two concepts goes back to the discourse formulated by scholars focusing upon political development, on the one hand, and the political system, on the other, during the 1950s and 1960s.

Thus, 'outputs' refers to measures decided by and implemented within a political system, while 'outcomes' stands for the consequences of these outputs within as well as outside the political system. Sometimes we may also talk about close outcomes (outputs) and distant outcomes (outcomes).

When a government seeks to fulfil certain elementary needs (MacIver 1965: 318), such as the achievement of external security, internal order, justice, general welfare and freedom (Merriam 1966: 31), then one may examine these measures by means of the output–outcome approach. Outputs would then be the measures taken by government – decisions and actions, or to use the language of the policy framework: public policies – and outcomes would cover the consequences of the outputs in a very wide sense, comprising not only political results but also social and economic consequences. The outputs–outcome framework is thus a way to evaluate whether the means of governments have been effectuated and whether or to what extent their ends have been attained (Dahl 1967; Barry and Rae 1975).

Perhaps the most well-known example of the employment of the output–outcome approach is Easton's so-called systems analysis of political life, launched in the 1960s. According to Easton (1965: 351), 'outputs produced by the authorities include the binding decisions, their implementing actions and . . . certain associated kinds of behaviors'. The output–outcome approach was also used in so-called functionalism, where Almond and Powell (1966: 27) identified four different types of outputs: extractions, regulations of behaviour, allocations or distribution of goods, and symbolic outputs. In a later work, Almond *et al.* (1993: 156) slightly rephrase this, stating that outputs are 'the kinds of actions government take in order to accomplish their purposes' including the following: extraction of resources, distributive activity, regulation of human behaviour, and symbolic per-formance.

Both Easton and Almond state that outcomes are something different from outputs. Easton (1965: 351) stated: 'We must distinguish the outputs from their consequences or what we may call, their outcomes'. Using a metaphor he says (1965: 352): 'In short, an output is the stone tossed into the pond and its first splash; the outcomes are the ever widening and vanishing pattern of of concentric ripples.' The same distinction is made by Almond *et al.* (1993: 20) who write: 'We have to distinguish between the efforts, the things a government does, and the actual outcome of these efforts.'

Yet, one can ask whether there is such a neat separation between outputs and outcomes. Suppose that we are faced with certain social outcomes but we cannot attribute them to any outputs. Are they still to be called 'out-comes'? Outcomes of what? Moreover, are outcomes the more or less intended effects of outputs, or can we also include completely unintended outcomes? The importance of the distinction between intended and unintended outcomes is crucial in not only policy analysis (Stokey and Zeckhauser 1978), but also in general social analysis (Levy 1952).

Yet, if the set of outcomes includes all kinds of consequences that attend policies however distant they may be, then there is no limit to how far the output–outcome scheme could be extended in its application. Everything would be a potential outcome. If 'outcomes' are defined in such a broad manner, then outcomes cannot be seen as mainly dependent variables of outputs as independent variables. Outcomes will become crucial independent variables in policy research, determining policies in their turn. It is difficult to specify once and for all which factors or variables are to be considered exegenous and which are to be seen as endogeneous – this distinction really depends upon the problem posed.

The breakthrough for the output–outcome framework came with the arrival of policy analysis as a central concern of political science in the 1960s and 1970s (Levy *et al.* 1974). Discussing whether 'Politics Matter', a number of scholars identified so-called determinants of public policies (Sharpe and Newton 1984). A major branch in this literature was the attempt to explain the growth of government in industrial democracies during the twentieth century, especially after the Second World War (Borcherding 1985), focusing upon social, economic and political factors that increase or decrease public expenditures (Castles 1998).

The analysis of the state as a set of public programmes for reforming society called for new concepts, replacing traditional public administration. 'Policy' became the new key term, and this concept was approached in terms of the distinction between policy-making and policy implementation. Policy analysis without impact analysis was considered incomplete. Thus, a number of new approaches to the analysis of policy consequences were launched, focusing basically upon the outcomes of policies and their measurement (Wildavsky 1979).

Although the link between policy-making and implementation was conceived of in different ways, some placing the emphasis upon policy while others underlined implementation, the basic understanding was that the running of programmes and budgets was one thing and the achievement of real-life consequences quite another matter (Pressman and Wildavsky 1984). In order to come to grips with the extent to which public policies really achieved their objectives, a host of evaluation techniques were developed dealing with the measurement of a number of different aspects of outcomes. Thus, outcome analysis in evaluation research came to include all kinds of results that were relevant to the understanding of policies, including outcomes that had no link whatsoever with a policy but affected the evalaution of whether a policy had succeeded or not.

Real policies and real outcomes

In order to substantiate the above argument, let us finally refer to the standard definitions of 'output' and 'outcome' in the policy literature. In a standard text from the 1990s we read about the concept of an output:

> Here policy is seen as what government actually delivers as opposed to what it has promised or has authorized through legislation.
>
> (Hogwood and Gunn 1992: 16)

This first distinction concerning the concepts of policy outputs and outcomes is that between intention and action, as stated in the quotation above. An output is government action, never merely statements of objectives or ambitions. Hogwood and Gunn continue saying that outputs as actions:

> can take many forms – the payment of cash benefits, the delivery of goods and services, the enforcement of rules, the invocation of symbols or the collection of taxes. The form of output varies between policy areas.
>
> (Hogwood and Gunn 1992: 16)

Underlining the real nature of policy outputs, one would focus primarily upon the provision of public services – government consumption – as well as the transfer of pay cheques to individuals – income maintenance programmes. The provision of goods and services such as police, defence, infrastructure, education and health care must be paid somehow, which is as true about income maintenance policies. Thus, one would wish to cover also the income side of the public sector, i.e. taxes and charges, and state to what extent the real programmes are totally financed or not, in which case there is deficit spending. In comparative institutional analysis, the information on policy outputs in the form of public finance statistics from international organizations comes in handy.

The second distinction that is vital in order to employ the framework of policy outputs and outcomes concerns the separation between real outputs and real outcomes. Hogwood and Gunn state:

> Another way of looking at policy is in terms of its outcome, that is, in terms of what is actually achieved. This distinction between outputs (the activities of government at the point of delivery) and outcomes (the impact of these activities) is often blurred over, and is sometimes difficult to make in practice, but it is an important one.
>
> (Hogwood and Gunn 1992: 17)

Thus, outcomes are the things that have actually been achieved, whatever the objectives of policies may have been. Outcomes are real results, whether intended or unintended, at the same time as outcomes are not government actions.

Finally, there is a third distinction that is helpful when employing the policy approach, for instance in comparative institutional analysis. Outcomes need not be the main effect of a policy output, because the occurrence of outcomes as results depend upon other factors than the operation of a policy. Hogwood and Gunn explain that outcomes may the product of the actions of several government organizations. Thus:

> The overall outcome will be the product of the outputs of these organizations and their effect on the environment and on one another. This

product of the impact need not necessarily reflect the sum of the purposes of the organizations concerned or of the original decision-makers.

(Hogwood and Gunn 1992: 17)

One would want to add that outcomes may be more the product of other factors than the actions of government. They may be the product of the activities of organizations other than governmental ones, or they may be conditioned by vast forces such as culture, religion and social structure.

Measures of outputs and outcomes

Outputs and outcomes may be operationalized in numerous ways. If we stick to the distinction between what government does – policy – and what government achieves – outcomes, then there is a set of standard measures that one encounters in the literature that employs the output–outcome framework. On the one hand, one may turn to the literature analysing public policies and their consequences in a comparative fashion. Most of the time, policy outputs refer to public expenditures of different kinds. Thus, these measures include total public expenditures or total tax receipts. Furthermore, public expenditures can cover various public finance items such as allocative expenditures, i.e. the amount of money spent on allocating services: health care, education or military spending. Other public finance items include transfer payments or redistributive expenditures such as pensions and other forms of income compensation. One often employed item combining allocative and redistributive expenditures is social expenditures, employed in welfare state research (Dye 1972; Danziger 1978; Dye and Gray 1980; Castles 1982; Hicks and Swank 1992; Schmidt 1997; Castles 1998). In these studies public spending as a percentage of the GDP is used as the main dependent variable of the making of public policies, although more recent literature has tried to widen the set of indicators to cover also non-monetary aspects.

On the other hand, one may consult the literature dealing with national policy outcomes. There we find a set of more or less standard indicators upon factors that may enter as variables when modelling what political institutions effect. Looking at studies of various comparative forms of outcomes, one observes that there is a number of standard variables used in this literature. Yeung and Matheison (1998) identify six different outcome areas: economic performance, competitiveness, education, health, environment, and democracy and freedom. Economic performance often refers to outcomes including unemployment, inflation and economic growth as well as the distribution of income or measures on income inequalities (North 1989; Alvarez *et al.* 1991; Golden 1993; Crepaz 1996). Other aspects of political system outcomes may refer to social performance such as income distribution and political performance including democracy scores, political stability, representation measures and female participation (Lijphart 1994a).

These variables have also been chosen as dependent variables. Thus, we find in the literature on policy-making a large number of variables that attempt to measure various aspects of policy outputs and political system outcomes by means of variables and indicators that may be used in comparative research.

Variables and indicators

It remains to clarify the variables and indicators as measures of outputs and outcomes that we will employ in our study. Which measures are relevant for an enquiry into the truth of the statement:

(IT') Political institutions are important for outcomes,

when it refers to macro institutions and macro outcomes?

The output indicators mainly refer to variables measuring the size of the public sector, like public spending or taxation, while the outcome indicators take into account various aspects of economic, social and political development in society. To be more precise, the following list has the main output indicators, and the sources they are based on:

- central government revenue (CGRE) (World Bank)
- general government consumption (GGCO) (World Bank)
- central government deficits (DEFI) (World Bank)
- social security benefit expenditures (SOCB) (ILO)
- military spending (MILE) (SIPRI)

For the chief outcome indicators we rely on the following data concerning political, social and economic results:

- economic growth per capita (ECGR) (World Bank)
- inflation rates (INFL)(World Bank)
- human development index (HDIN) (UNDP)
- income distribution (GINI) (World Bank; ILO)
- real GDP per capita in US dollars (RGDP) (Summers and Heston)
- level of democracy (DEMO) (Freedom House)
- number of years of present constitution (COYR) (Encyclopaedia Britannica)
- female participation in politics (FEMR) (IPU)
- party system fractionalization (PART) (Banks)
- number of effective executive changes (EXEC) (Banks)
- indicators of political protests (PROT) and violence (VIOL) (Banks)
- the level of corruption in a country (CORR) (Transparency International).

It is obvious that once we go from the OECD area, now covering twenty-nine rich countries with democracy and a market economy, and attempt to cover more states, then we also face increasing problems as to the validity and reliability of both output and outcome data (cf. Taylor 1983; Jackman 1993). Yet we also know that data reported by the World Bank and other similar international organizations are the best data available so far.

What we can do is to map the variation in data in various ways in order to be able to draw conclusions about whether data is more or less reliable. We will also, in several instances, report the distributions for both the 'total set' and 'subtotal sets'. This mapping is done primarily for descriptive reasons, consisting of, in addition to an 'OECD set', various subsets, one for the 'rest of America', 'Africa', 'Asia', and one for 'post-communist states' in Europe. The first step of mapping the variation consists of identifying the states with high and low values on the variables measuring outputs and outcomes.

An important aspect in the design of the present study is to enquire about how stable outputs, outcomes and institutions tend to be over time. This means that a second step when mapping the variation in outputs and outcomes is to measure the stability over time for both data sets. This stability measure is arrived at through the employment of a factor analysis of the same variable measured at three different time periods. A first factor explaining 85 per cent or more of the variance may indicate stability over time.

Policy outputs

The output variables that we include cover measures of various aspects of public expenditure. One has to keep in mind that once we attempt to cover states outside the set of OECD countries, then the data availability is more limited. Here we employ data on both general and central government expenditures/receipts and consumption, although in many countries the distinction between central and general government tends to be blurred. In addition to overall spending, we also focus on social spending and military costs.

The pattern of variation in policy outputs for the 1990s is displayed in Table 3.1. Public spending and receipts is highest among the OECD countries. In terms of percentage of GDP, central government receipts tend to be higher in industrial democracies than in Third World countries.

Another measure of public spending is General Government Consumption as it is presented by the World Bank in publications like World Development Report and World Development Indicators. From these data we may see that public consumption in general increases over time, but this pattern varies within the different subsets. In Latin America there is a rise between the 1970s and the 1980s while we may note a decrease in the 1990s. A similar trend holds true for Africa, while the OECD set and the Asian set display an increase over time.

So far we have mapped more general output variables. The two remaining variables capture more specific forms of public spending, namely social

Table 3.1 Variation in policy outputs in the 1990s

Country-set	CGRE	GGCO	DEFI	SOCB	MILE
OECD	33.3	17.5	−5.4	21.1	2.1
Latin America	19.4	10.5	−1.8	4.8	1.4
Africa	25.7	15.1	−3.5	0.9	2.9
Asia	20.4	15.6	−3.6	2.2	5.5
Post-communist	32.1	17.9	−3.2	15.3	3.2
Total	26.0	15.4	−3.7	8.8	3.0

Sources: CGRE=World Bank 1992, 1997; GGCO=World Bank 1983, 1997; DEFI=World Bank 1992, 1997; SOCB=ILO 1992, 1998; MILE=SIPRI 1980, 1988, 1997.

Note: CGRE=central government receipts as a % of GDP; GGCO=general government consumption as a % of GDP; DEFI =central government deficits as a % of GDP; SOCB=social security benefit expenditures as a % of GDP; MILE =military expenditures as a % of GDP.

spending and military spending. The pattern of social spending is very stable over time, and it is also obvious that social spending is something we find mainly in the industrialized countries of the the so-called First and former Second World, while it is more or less non-existent in many countries in the Third World. Military spending also follows a stable pattern over time, although we may note a slight decrease from the 1980s to the 1990s. Military spending is highest among the Asian set of countries, where the impact from the countries in the Middle East is highly salient.

To what extent are these output variables really related to each other? It is obvious that public spending is not one-dimensional, since it makes a difference when looking at public expenditures which include social spending and public consumption which excludes social spending. The data indicates that it may be fruitful to maintain the distinction between total public expenditures and government consumption. The former item is much larger than the latter item and includes the transfer payments. The latter item consists of expenditures on so-called public goods, which occur in all societies, whether they are welfare states or not. In addition, general government consumption also covers education and health care to the extent that they are publicly provided.

Outcomes

To map the outcomes of political systems, we have identified a number of variables measuring results. These include economic outcomes (economic growth, inflation and affluence), social outcomes (human development, income distribution), political outcomes (democracy, female representation, party system stability) and also some event outcomes (protest and violence events). How stable are these outcomes over time?

Economic outcomes

Speaking generally, it holds true that economic outcomes, in particular, vary over time. Countries displaying high economic growth at one period of time may come out otherwise at another period, and this holds true both for the narrow OECD set of countries and the total set. The period 1960–73 was indeed a period of economic growth in most parts of the world, whereas there is more variation in the other two periods. Latin-American countries had, on average, negative figures for the 1973–85 period while the same was true for the African countries during the 1985–94 period. The picture is slightly different when it comes to the development of inflation. Here we find very high rates of inflation at certain periods among countries from the post-communist, Latin-American and African countries. Table 3.2 contains information about the variation in socio-economic outcomes in the 1990s.

The two social outcome variables – human development index and GINI index – follow another pattern over time. The spatial distribution for the Human Development Index (HDI) was roughly the same in the 1970s as it is in the 1990s, and this is valid both for the OECD set and the total set. The HDI increases over time and this applies to all five subsets of countries, although there is a distinctive difference between the levels of HDI for OECD countries and African countries.

Perhaps the major difference in the variation in human development is first and foremost that between Africa and the rest of the world and then between the rich industrial democracies and Latin America, Asia and the post-communist countries, where the scores for the last mentioned is probably somewhat too high. The country variation in income inequality is entirely different. GINI-indices measuring inequalities of income distributions seem to have decreased from the 1970s to the 1980s but are on the increase again in the 1990s. The distribution of affluence as measured by Real GDP per capita follows a similar pattern. The OECD countries are the rich countries whereas we find the poor countries in Africa.

Table 3.2 Variation in socio-economic outcomes in the 1990s

Country-set	ECGR	INFL	HDIN	GINI	RGDP
OECD	1.6	6.8	0.90	33.2	13326
Latin America	0.5	76.3	0.70	48.0	3385
Africa	−0.2	116.7	0.37	46.8	1475
Asia	2.2	10.6	0.60	36.4	4691
Post-communist	−0.2	367.4	0.86	28.1	4560
Total	−0.2	96.4	0.61	39.3	5589

Sources: ECGR=World Bank 1975, 1987, 1996; INFL=World Bank 1982, 1997; HDIN= UNDP 1994; GINI=Deininger and Squire 1997, Tabatabai 1996; RGDP=Summers and Heston 1994.

Note: ECGR=growth in real GNP/capita 1985–94; INFL=average inflation rate 1990–95; HDIN=human development index 1992; GINI=gini index measuring income distribution; RGDP=real GDP per capita in US $ 1992.

Political Outcomes

The next set of outcome variables refers to various kinds of political out-comes more or less related to attempts to measure democracy. Data on developments over time seem to confirm that democracy has been on the rise over the last decades, and this is particularly true for data on the level of democracy, which shows a rise from an average score of 4.3 in the 1970s to 5.2 in the 1990s. Table 3.3 displays data for the political outcome variables.

The changes were most dramatic in the late 1980s and the early 1990s. On the other hand we find no straightforward development over time when it comes to female representation in parliaments. The slight decline of female representation in the 1990s is mainly explained by the drastic decline in the post-communist states from the highest rates in the 1970s and the 1980s to very low rates of representation in the 1990s. We may also add that it is noteworthy that there is still no country-set where the average female rate of representation even comes close to 50 per cent.

Democracy has the strongest standing in the OECD countries, but it is clearly on the rise both in Latin America and among the post-communist countries, while African and Asian countries, on average, display lower scores. Looking at the stability over time for these political outcomes, the picture is somewhat scattered. Globally, the spatial variation over time for democracy scores is stable, but among the OECD countries we may note the impact of the transition to democracy in Mediterranean Europe in the 1970s. On the other hand, female representation and voter turnout is very stable over time among the OECD countries, but displays less of stability if we take a look at it worldwide. Corruption seems to follow a similar pattern as democracy: less (=higher scores) in Western countries and more (=lower scores) in non-Western countries.

Table 3.3 Variation in political outcomes in the 1990s

Country-set	DEMO	COYR	FEMR	PART	EXEC	PROT	VIOL	CORR
OECD	9.5	64.9	17.6	0.681	0.24	0.96	0.42	7.7
Latin America	6.4	20.2	9.9	0.608	0.24	1.92	1.76	3.4
Africa	3.5	10.4	7.6	0.245	0.14	1.08	0.93	3.6
Asia	3.4	22.0	6.8	0.365	0.18	1.56	0.91	4.5
Post-communist	5.3	6.6	7.3	0.608	0.24	1.28	0.57	3.7
Total	5.2	22.2	9.4	0.463	0.20	1.33	0.90	4.9

Sources: DEMO=Freedom House 1990–97; COYR=Banks 1978, Encyclopaedia Britannica 1986, 1996; FEMR=IPU 1995; PART=Banks 1996; EXEC=Banks 1996; PROT=Banks 1996; VIOL=Banks 1996; CORR=Transparency International 1995, 1998, Mauro 1995.

Note: DEMO=average democracy index for 1991–96; COYR=number of years of present constitution; FEMR=female parliamentary representation in %; PART=party system fractionalization index; EXEC=average number of effective executive change; PROT=average number of protest events 1990–95; VIOL=average number of violence events 1990–95; CORR=corruption perception index for 1998.

Party system fractionalization is highest in the OECD countries and lowest in Third World countries of Africa and Asia reflecting the variation in democracy worldwide. This also holds true for the distribution of effective executive changes worldwide; democracies display more of regular executive changes while non-democracies have less of such regular changes.

Let us finally take a look at two political event outcome variables, namely frequency of protest and violent events. It is obvious that we have here the kind of event that varies over time, and the pattern of variation in space over time is also marked. We may note that the late 1980s was a period of revolutionary upheaval not only in the post-communist countries but also in parts of Asia and Latin America, while the early 1990s display less protest and violent events; again the OECD countries deviate, displaying less violence and protests during the 1990s.

We do not expect that these outcome variables will constitute only one dimension. Rather there are reasons to believe that there will be one political, one social and one economic subdimension.

Stability of variation

Let us finally take a look at the variation over time among these variables measuring policy outputs and policy outcomes. This analysis is based on data covering three different periods of time, i.e. roughly the 1970s, the 1980s and the 1990s. We employ factor analysis in a strict descriptive way in order to arrive at a suitable measure of stability over time. The amount of variance explained by the first factor estimated in the factor analysis using these three variables indicates whether there is stability over time or not. We may somewhat arbitrarily say that measures around or above 0.85 indicate stability, while lower figures indicate a less stable pattern of variation over time. These stability measures are displayed in Table 3.4 below.

There are different patterns of variation over time if comparing the total set with the OECD set as well as comparing different output and outcome variables. In general, the policy output variables display a high degree of stability over time. Countries having a relatively high level of social or military spending at one period of time also tend to have a similarly high level at a later period of time. It is only for deficit spending that we may identify a pattern of instability over time.

Looking at the outcome variables there is less stability over time and more time-varying patterns. It is only for the variables measuring human development (HDIN), affluence (RGDP) and perceived corruption (CORR) where we can find stability. Economic growth and inflation display, as might be expected, a great deal of fluctuation over time, meaning that a country experiencing high levels of growth in the 1970s cannot necessarily expect a similar growth in the 1980s or in the 1990s. Most of the political outcome variables also display instability over time. The pattern of variation in the levels of democracy is quite stable over time if we look at the total sample,

Table 3.4 Stability over time among policy output and policy outcome variables from the 1970s to the 1990s: measured through explained variance of the first factor in a factor analysis

		Total set	*OECD set*
Policy outputs:	CGRE	88.0	95.0
	GGCO	69.4	88.1
	DEFI	51.5	61.0
	SOCB	96.7	89.3
	MILE	87.1	90.5
Socio-economic outcomes:	ECGR	56.0	54.4
	INFL	51.4	83.7
	HDIN	98.1	98.5
	GINI	91.4	81.2
	RGDP	97.5	97.6
Political outcomes:	DEMO	88.1	69.4
	COYR	78.9	82.2
	FEMR	76.2	95.5
	PAST	80.1	80.1
	EXEC	56.3	68.0
	PROT	71.5	66.2
	VIOL	63.2	75.6
	CORR	93.4	90.1

Note: The figures reported in the table refer to the explained variance of the first factor in a factor analysis which includes three variables measuring the same indicator at three different time periods, i.e. roughly the 1970s, the 1980s and the 1990s. This measure may be interpreted as a stability measure where figures around 85 or higher indicate stability over time.

while within the OECD sample there is more fluctuation over time, and this is a reflection of the process of democratization in Mediterranean Europe in the 1970s.

To sum up, we may establish that in addition to a substantial variation in space among the different output and outcome variables, there is also a distinct pattern of variation over time. In a few cases – social spendings, human development and affluence – the pattern of variation over time is stable, but in most other cases we have fluctuations over time in the spatial patterns of variation. This means that it is meaningful to enquire into the sources of variation of policy outputs and policy outcomes worldwide.

The problem of induction

We have surveyed a number of variables, drawn from outputs and outcomes, stating a measure of their variation as well as a measure of how stable this variation tends to be over time. It is time to return to our key question, namely testing the validity of the claim:

(IT') Political institutions are important for outcomes.

Is neo-institutionalism relevant for explaining the variation in outputs and outcomes described above on a country basis, meaning that we must speak about macro phenomena? How would we go about examining whether institutions are relevant?

Methodologically speaking, whatever the connection may be between institutions, on the one hand, and outcomes, on the other hand, that relationship must be *synthetical a posteriori*, to use the words of the Kantian philosophy of science (Pap 1958). First, the relationship between an institution and an outcome is synthetical, meaning that these two entities are logically independent of each other. Thus, the relationship is not an analytical one, but an empirical regularity. Second, the nature of that regularity can only be discovered by means of empirical research, testing hypotheses against a body of data. Thus, there is no *a priori* valid knowledge about the relationships between institutions and outcomes, as any hypothesis about such a link can be refuted by empirical evidence. Theories about institutions and outcomes are in principle falsifiable.

Enquiring into the connections between institutions and outcomes, the only possible research strategy is to make qualified guesses and then proceed to put them up for the most severe test possible – following a falsification methodology (Popper 1963; Lakatos and Musgrave 1970). In all the research on the connection between institutions and outcomes there is an openness which can only be limited by means of empirical research, attempting to find out what the regularity that connects the two entities is like.

Basically, this is the problem of induction in a Humean approach towards researching causality in the social world. Since the link between institution and outcome is empirical and not logical, we must observe how the two entities go together in the real world. But what is the inductive power of one set of evidence or one set of tests? If we can observe a strong correlation in one set of data, then it is far from certain that the same correlation will be observed in other data.

Our research strategy attempts to cover as many states as possible in the present post-World War Two period. However, we will from time to time make a distinction between a 'total set', covering a larger number of states, and an 'OECD set', basically covering the 'old' twenty-four states which over a number of years constituted the set of OECD countries. For each of the variables we attempt to collect data for three different time periods, mostly referring to the 1970s, the 1980s and the 1990s; there will, however, be some deviations from this framework.

In institutional analysis, we face the riddle of induction: what justifies the conclusion from one observation today about institutional effects in future observations (Goodman 1972)? Only if one assumes that regularities stay the same for ever is such an induction a valid inference. And this assumption cannot be proved by means of itself, as the link between two entities in any regularity is not a necessary one but an accidental one. Empirical regularities being constant conjunctions, how can one be sure that what has been observed to look like an empirical regularity is not merely an historical fact, which will not reoccur in the future? There is no other way of knowing than examining empirical evidence, testing alternative hypotheses, guessing the true nature of a regularity, i.e. the probability that two entities go together (Salmon 1984, 1998).

Conclusion

We have here attempted to map the variation in time and space of a number of output and outcome variables at the macro level. One may always question the inclusion or exclusion of specific variables among the set of output and outcome variables. It is our belief, however, that the variables chosen cover reasonably well various aspects of macro policy outputs and policy outcomes worldwide. It is obvious that neither outputs nor outcomes are uni-dimensional phenomena. Rather they identify various macro aspects like public consumption, public expenditure, level of welfare, democracy, political change and economic growth.

When mapping this variation we have been primarily interested in variation in time and space. There is a huge country variation in many of the variables that calls for explanation. However, even more interesting is the stability over time in these output and outcome measures, which we have computed using factor analysis. Is the spatial variation in different output and outcome variables roughly the same for the 1970s, the 1980s and the 1990s? We face stability over time if the spatial variation over time is limited.

From the preceding analysis, we may conclude that outputs in general are quite stable over time. One exception may be general government consumption as measured by the World Bank and the deficit spending measure. The picture is somewhat different when we look at the outcome variables. Economic growth and inflation is – almost by definition – not stable over time, and this is also the case with protest and violent events. We find more stability when we look at human development, income distribution, and levels of democracy.

The remaining chapters of the book address the key research questions about institutional performance and effects, or how institutions may explain the variation in space and time in outputs and outcomes. Could institutions – given that institutions tend to be stable over time – explain a variation in outputs and outcomes that also tend to be rather stable over time ? Let us begin with the most basic state institutions and search for their impact upon macro outputs and outcomes.

Substantive analyses section

Part I

Basic state institutions

Political life tends to be highly institutionalized, in constitutional democracies more so than in authoritarian states. In many countries, there is huge set of rules that govern political life. For instance, voting on bills in a legislature is regulated through numerous institutions about agenda-setting, committee preparation, the making of amendments and the final resolution of the matter. In a macro approach to comparative institutional analysis, one cannot go too deep into institutional details, as one would like to focus upon the main characteristics of the overall institutional framework.

There are two institutional distinctions that separate the states of the world, which now number almost two hundred. First, each and every state declares whether is has a unitary or federal state format. One can always debate whether a country is *truly* a federal state, i.e. really implements the institutions of the doctrine of federalism, however it may have been interpreted since Althusius introduced the idea of a federation (*consociatio*) as the foundation of a state in his *Systematic Analysis of Politics* of 1610. Second, one may classify any state in terms of whether it has institutionalized human rights or not. These two macro institutions will be the first institutions that we examine from the perspective of occurrence of institutional effects.

4 Federalism

Althusius

Introduction

Concerning the phenomenon of federalist institutions, several modern interpretations claim that the federal state format performs better than unitarism. This chapter challenges this position by examining developmental outcomes for a large number of states, divided into federal and unitary ones.

Neo-institutionalism in the social sciences harbours claims about the consequences of institutions. 'Institutions matter', it is stated. We ask: for what? The basic distinction here is the one between institutions as systems of rules, on the one hand, and social, economic and political outcomes, on the other. We need models to test whether a variation in institutions is accompanied by or occurs together with a variation in outcomes. A chief difficulty in institutionalist theory is that the model linking the institution with the outcome is often not stated explicitly.

We know that real social life events depend upon things other than institutions, i.e. rules or mechanisms for interaction. There is a whole body of literature that underlines the modernization of social structure as well as culture. Why isolate institutions as of special relevance? Well, presumably because they matter, i.e. matter for various outcomes. This is a question about causality. In neo-institutionalism one faces both an identification problem – Which is the institution? – as well as a problem concerning causality: what is the probability that an institution is attended by certain outomes?

Let us in this chapter examine these two questions in relation to a very well-known theme in neo-institutionalist theory, namely federalism. Federalism amounts to a theory that federal states have an advantage over unitary states – all other things being equal (Ostrom 1991; Burgess and Gagnon 1993; Elazar 1987, 1995, 1997; Watts 1998). But it is difficult to understand why federal states would be superior to unitary ones if it were not for better performance, meaning better outcomes – social, economic or political ones under a *ceteris paribus* clause. Is this a valid claim?

Once one starts examining the thesis about federalist superiority, a number of difficult questions arise. Why would federalism promote better outcomes? What is the mechanism involved in connecting state format with outcomes? First, however, we must discuss what a federal state is, because it may be shown that it is far from easy to identify the federal state format itself or a unique set of federal states.

Institutional evaluation

It would enhance institutionalist theory if the models about institutional performance could be specified clearly and stated explicitly. This general remark applies to the federalist argument about the assumed superiority of federal political institutions. We need to identify the federal states and test models of institutional performance, comparing them with unitary states as looking at only federal states is not enough. It is the idea that federal states do better than unitary states that should be examined in relation to data about the countries of the world today (Hesse and Wright 1996).

Federalism is as relevant today as it was in the nineteenth century, when Walter Bagehot rejected the model in favour of a unitary state with the argument that its outcomes were inferior (Bagehot [1867] 1993), focusing upon the risk of secession of member states. It is now argued that the federal state format is the best conceivable one, given the strong demand for democracy today, as well as the existence of many multicultural societies.

Thus, Elazar states that 'Federalism must be considered a "mother" form of democracy like parliamentary democracy or direct democracy' (Elazar 1995: 475). Can we, then, make the deduction that federal states are democracies? Certainly not, because federalism does not automatically produce the virtues of democracy such as the implementation of human righs. Why would federalism be more conducive to the establishment of civil and political rights than unitarism? Elazar also claims that 'Federalism can be understood as constitutionalized power sharing through systems that combine self-rule and shared rule' (Elazar 1995: 474–5). Is this a true generalization of how real world federal states tend to perform? Or is it ideology, explicating the legal doctrine of what federal states ideally ought to be?

Ostrom starts out from a neutral definition of federalism as 'constitutional choice reiterated to apply to many different units of government where each is bound by enforceable rules of constitutional law' (Ostrom 1987: 25), but moves in *The Meaning of American Federalism* (1991) to the much stronger claim that a federal state is the most appropriate form for a 'self-governing society'. Is this a statement about real-life institutions or is it state ideology?

Evaluating Federal Systems (1994), edited by B. de Villiers, takes a close look at the actual and recent performance of federalism in a number of countries. Thus, Ronald L. Watts states:

> an attempt to assess the respective effectiveness of confederations and federations and of different variants of federations in meeting the long-

run needs for both unity and diversity might be helpful to those considering the establishment of new federal systems or the reform of older ones.

(Watts 1994: 23)

Perhaps one should not only contrast alternative federal institutions against one another but move to a full-scale evaluation of the relative benefits of federalism compared with its chief competitor, the unitary state format. In such an assessment of real world state performance, one has to cover a broad range of outcomes, not only the rather vague requirement of a need to strike a balance between unity and diversity.

One could argue that part of the secret of the successes of the Swiss and US polities and the German developments after the Second World War lies in their federal constitutions (Sturm 1994; Gress 1994; Schmitt 1994); moreover, one might think that a move towards more federalism in South Africa would bring about more stability (Welsh 1994; Wamala 1994). But these claims must be corroborated by performance evidence. And, we underline, one highly relevant approach is to examine the comparative performance records of federal states in relation to unitary states.

Before we enquire into the performance profile, we need to look at the nature of federal institutions in themselves. What, more specifically, is a federal state? And how many are there in the world of today? We look at the identification problem through the combined angles of the denotation and the connotation of a 'federal' state, meaning that we search for both a set of federal states and the characteristics that make them federal (Sartori 1984).

Identification: which states are federal?

Although it is fairly easy to tell what states there are in the world, it is quite difficult to identify a set of federal states. There are cases, moreover, where one can reasonably have different opinions about the actual existence of a state, and not only about the nature of the state in question. Is there a state in Bosnia, Somalia or Liberia today? Are some of the small states like the Vatican, Androrra or San Marino really states themselves or merely enclaves within a larger state? How is one to handle Taiwan now that it is not recognized by the UN as a state? These problems all concern the question of how to decide when a state has begun to exist as well as ceased to exist, and they require criteria for the identification of states, which international law provides. In most cases, then, this is not problematic.

Can law also solve the other problem of identifying the set of federal states, which strictly speaking is a proper subset of the set of all states? There is nothing in public international law that gives guidance about the criteria that distinguish unitary states from federal states. One may also wish to include confederal states, but their number is so small that we can disregard them; in fact, there are so few, that one can identify them by simple enumeration, e.g. the Commonwealth of States in the former USSR territory. Also, one counted certain international organizations such as the EU, for instance, as a confederal state, then things immediately becomes confused. But this question is related more to the problem of identifying a state than establishing the criteria for separating federal and unitary state frameworks.

One can identify things in two ways. Either one points them out, listing them by name – the denotation approach. Or one employs abstract properties which describe the things in questions – the connotation approach. Enumeration versus characterization involves a methodological choice which may be resolved in various ways. In relation to the question of federalism one would preferably use both approaches, the denotation and the connotation perspectives as it were, using the language of the philosophy of science.

A number of criteria can be suggested that would somehow shed light on the set of federal states. One may derive such a list of properties either from constitutional and administrative law or from a behavioural perspective, that is from either formal rules or actual action patterns. Thus we have:

1   Language: symbols and constitutional self-identification
2   Origin: act of federation – real or fictive
3   Composition: states within a state, separate state constitutions
4   Double governments: double executives, legislatures and judicial bodies
5   Real power structure: fiscal decentralization or the decentralization of competences to lower levels of government
6   Judicial review and constitutional court

Should one employ all six criteria or focus upon one of them to the exclusion of the others? From a legal point of view, one may emphasize constitutional formalities, but from a political science point of view, one may underline institutional realities. Is federalism merely talk about a federation or is it a real-life institutional autonomy, or perhaps both? Starting from the constitutional criteria one can list a set of countries that call themselves 'federal states', or one can start from one or two criteria like the ones above and tentatively list the federal states. One can regard federalism as a nominal variable or as an ordinal one.

Riker argues that federations would be useless without a military threat. Moreover, he claims that all federal states originate from external threats or war with neighbours (Riker 1996). If this is an historical fact, then we still need to understand why federal states remain intact after a temporary military threat has been removed or gone away. Riker's thesis can be contrasted with another argument about the condition or rationale for federations, namely social heterogeneity. Just like the military threat argument, this argument about social fragmentation in terms of ethnicity or religion seems plausible, but one can find counter instances. Many of the tiny islands federations are homogeneous (Anckar 1998).

By simply using the occurrence of federalist terminology one may arrive at a list of formal 'federal states' as of 1995, by resorting to sources such as Blaustein and Flanz, *Constitutions of the Countries of the World* (1972–), *The Statesman's Yearbook* 1990–1995, *Fischer Weltalmanack* (1996) or *L'états du monde* (1995). However, one may certainly ask: are these the states that uniquely make up the federal set? One may question such a classification by invoking the often used distinction between appearance and reality. By employing the behavioural criteria one would wish to include more states as 'federal' than those that employ the term. Perhaps one would then also wish to include some states that are unitary in language but operate with much institutional autonomy, the so-called semi-federal states as it were.

Adding to the problem of identifying federal states, one may also point out that federal states differ a great deal in terms of how they are constituted. In a federation it is crucial to specify the competences and the level of government. Typically, the constitution contains a list of exclusive competences and shared competences, stating also where the remaining, but not specified, competences are located. The specification of competencies can be done in very different ways, placing the residual powers either with the federal level or with the state level. There may be much shared competencies or few such shared powers.

Now, which list of federal states is the 'correct' one? Actually, one may ask what 'correct' means in this case, because establishing the set of federal states boils down to a question which does not have a clear-cut answer, nor is there available a straightforward method by which the problem can be resolved. A number of considerations will have to be taken into account. Let us look at how experts on federalism have approached the identification problem.

In Table 4.1 we have displayed how scholars like Watts, Elazar, Riker and Duchacek, as well as the *Encyclopaedia Britannica*, have identified states as being federal states in recent decades. These classifications are simply nominal, as a country either has or has not a federal state framework. In this table, twenty-seven countries are listed and fifteen among them are classified as a federal state in all of the classifications.

In the most recent classification, Watts (1996), considers Ethiopia and South Africa as federal states; he also identifes Spain as a federal state, as does Elazar (1995). Looking at the classifications made by the *Encyclopaedia Britannica* in 1995 and 1986, we may note that there have been a few changes, but they reflect the changing reality and do not result from a change of definition. Thus, Belgium has been added as well as Micronesia at the same time as Czechoslovakia has been omitted the set of federal states. Three countries have changed their federal framework to such an extent that one must talk about a new state: USSR – Russia, FRG – Germany, and former Yugoslavia – FR Yugoslavia (Serbia and Montenegro). Do the changes reflect any instability in the federal framework, or do they testify to the flexibility of such institutions? The Elazar listing of federations agrees

Table 4.1 Federal states – classifications

Country	Watts 1996	EB 1995	Elazar 1995	Elazar 1991	EB 1986	Riker 1975	Duchacek 1970
Argentina	x	x	x	x	x	x	x
Australia	x	x	x	x	x	x	x
Austria	x	x	x	x	x	x	x
Belgium	x	x	x	–	–	–	–
Brazil	x	x	x	x	x	x	x
Burma	–	–	–	–	–	–	x
Cameroon	–	–	–	–	–	x	x
Canada	x	x	x	x	x	x	x
Comoros	x	x	x	x	x	–	–
Czechoslovakia	–	–	–	x	x	x	x
Ethiopia	x	–	–	–	–	–	–
Germany/FRG	x	x	x	x	x	x	x
India	x	x	x	x	x	x	x
Malaysia	x	x	x	x	x	x	x
Mexico	x	x	x	x	x	x	x
Micronesia	–	x	–	–	–	–	–
Nigeria	x	x	x	x	x	x	x
Pakistan	x	x	x	x	x	x	x
Russia/USSR	x	x	x	x	x	x	x
St Kitts and Nevis	x	–	–	–	x	–	–
South Africa	x	–	–	–	–	–	–
Spain	x	–	x	–	–	–	–
Switzerland	x	x	x	x	x	x	x
United Arab Emirates	x	x	x	x	x	–	-
USA	x	x	x	x	x	x	x
Venezuela	x	x	–	x	x	x	x
Yugoslavia	x	x	x	x	x	x	x

almost completely with the classification in the *Encyclopaedia Britannica* with the sole exception of Venezuela and Spain.

The classification of federal states reflects not only conceptual matters but also changing empirical facts. Consequently, it would be interesting to see if a few classifications made in the 1960s or 1970s are very much different from the classifications presented above. Here we consult two well-known experts on federalism, I.D. Duchacek (1970) and W. Riker (1975).

There are few differences between these two classifications. Actually, Libya and Myanmar are the only countries listed as federal by Duchacek which Riker does not include. Both listings do not not include some of the tiny states that are often included as federations, as mentioned above. Both listings, however, may be criticized with the same argument, namely that they include countries that are obviously authoritarian states and thus hardly in accordance with federal state principles. If one bypasses formal federalism, or federalism as it occurs in constitutional articles, then what is real federalism and which states are true federal states?

Combining the above listings of federalism, we may arrive at a list of federal states that no one would question. Such a certain set would include: Argentina, Australia, Austria, Brazil, Canada, Germany, India, Malaysia, Mexico, Nigeria, Pakistan, Switzerland and the USA. One could start including other countries or one could identify a second set, the quasi-federal set. Indeed, one could order all countries in the world along one dimension – say the amount of fiscal decentralization – in order to have a classfication that runs from centralized states to decentralized states, but this is not the same as the federal/unitary distinction. All procedures are possible and one has to make a choice as to which one to work with.

The distinction between denotation/connotation cuts across another important separation, viz. that between formalia and realia. When one classifies federal states, is one looking at constitutional articles or real-life institutions?

The problem of indentifying federal states raises difficult questions in institutional research about their legal and political characteristics. In *Federal Systems of the World: A handbook of federal, confederal and autonomy arrangements* Elazar offered a listing of all countries that have either a federal state or have federative elements, that is having 'federacies/associated states or home rule arrangements'.

One may wish to know what state properties qualify as so-called federative arrangements. Is it decentralization, home rule or institutional autonomy on a regional basis? If a unitary state moves towards the acceptance of regional competencies for a regional body elected from below, then has it taken steps towards federalism? Elazar would probably say 'Yes', but we argue that it is not necessarily so. In Table 4.2 we have identified a number of states which are said to have some kind of federative arrangements.

As a matter of fact, Elazar widens the concept of federalism even further by speaking in addition of 'associated states, federacies and condominions'. Here, Elazar includes, for instance, Denmark, Finland and the United Kingdom, which all have a unitary state format from a constitutional point of view. The reason is that each of them includes a territory which is connected

Table 4.2 States with federative arrangements

Afghanistan	Georgia	Papua New Guinea
Antigua and Barbuda	Ghana	Portugal
Bhutan	Indonesia	Solomon Islands
China	Italy	Sri Lanka
Colombia	Japan	Sudan
Cyprus	Lebanon	Tanzania
Denmark	Namibia	Ukraine
Fiji	Netherlands	United Kingdom
Finland	New Zealand	Vanatau

Sources: Elazar 1991; Elazar 1995; Watts 1996.

to the state in question by means of a federacy. Elazar also mentions Greenland, the Faroe Islands, Aland and the Channel Islands, as well as the Isle of Man. But these territories are not linked up with a state through the mechanism of a federacy. It is true that these territories enjoy home rule, but is that the distinctive characteristic of a federacy? Why could not a unitary state offer home rule without using the specific format of a federacy?

Perhaps Elazar conceives of degrees of federalism with the federal states as close to one polar type of state framework and the unitary states as close to the other polar type, with a number of states somewhere in-between. Can one create a scale of degrees of federalism? In any case, it seems truly awkward to include unitary states like the United Kingdom and New Zealand among the federal or quasi-federal states. Can Finland and Japan really be classified as quasi-federal, even if one accepts such a designation for Spain and Italy?

The classification of federal states faces both problems of theory and questions of fact. On the one hand, what is the distinctive characteristic of these federal states – the connotation? What criteria can one employ for their identification? And on the other hand, which countries satisfy these criteria? And at what time in history – the denotation?

The list in Table 4.2 is, in our view, too comprehensive. All forms of decentralization, and even special home rule, are designated as 'federal' arrangements.

Federalist characteristics

Instead of looking at lists of federal states – the denotation approach – one may try the connotation approach, identifying the institutions that states need to have in order to qualify for federalism. As such state properties may indeed be abstract or complex ones, it would help if one could also have a list of criteria that more easily identifies a state as 'federal'. Having such a list of institutions, one may ask whether a state truly implements them, or merely claims to accept them.

One can find a number of criteria of federalism in I.D. Duchacek's *Comparative Federalism: The territorial dimension of politics* (1970), where the first three criteria consider the federation from the standpoint of the central government whereas the others take the perspective of the member states of the union. We have:

1 exclusive central government control over diplomacy and defence
2 constitutional immunity against secession
3 central government authority over citizens directly
4 member state protection against their elimination
5 collective sharing in federal rule-making by, for example, a bicameral representation
6 two independent sets of courts, one dealing with federal laws

7   legal review
8   significant and staying powers of the member states

(Duchacek 1970: 207–8).

Actually, Duchacek includes two other so-called yardsticks of federalism, but it is not quite clear how they are to be interpreted. On the one hand, he asks who has ultimate control over amendments to the federal constitution. And on the other hand, he requires that the territorial division of authority be clear and unambiguous. However, though both items may be important, one cannot tell from which perspective they are vital: that of the union or those of the member states. Let us concentrate upon the yardsticks 1– 8.

What is fundamentally unclear with these criteria on federalism is whether they concern the written constitution or the real-life regime. Duchacek's list of federal states includes several authoritarian regimes, but do they really fulfil yardsticks 4, 5, 7 and 8? In a country ruled by means of martial law, where the constitution has been suspended formally or a military junta has been provided with emergency powers, could there be federalism in the sense of these yardsticks?

Take the example of Nigeria, which has changed its territorial division of member states each time the constitution has been rewritten – is yardstick 4 fulfilled? The same argument actually applies also to yardsticks 1–3: formal articles or real-life institutions? When Biafra declared itself independent, then it may have broken federal articles about secession, but that did not prevent the civil war lasting for several years. Or take the example of Tanzania, where power has certainly rested with the CCM in Dar-es-Salam and not with Zanzibar.

How about the USSR or any communist regime that has a federal constitution? Real federalism or merely a constitutional facade? It seems awkward to use the Stalin 1936 constitution as a foundation for classifying the USSR as 'federal', given all the evidence about extreme power central-ization to the party secretary, displayed at times in arbitrary behaviour lacking institutional recognition. Did the supreme court of the USSR really engage in independent legal review of federal legislation and administration?

Given Duchacek's many yardsticks, one would opt for a more restrictive listing of federal states. A restriction of the number of states that could be federal to the set of constitutional states would also have rather drastic consequences for the analysis of the performance record of federalism. Typical of Duchacek's approach is the use of many yardsticks which is in contrast to Riker's approach to federalism.

Riker uses a different way of identifying the characteristics of federalism, trying in one definition to lay down a necessary and sufficient condition for a state to be federal. Let us quote from two formulations of this critical condition:

> a government of federation and a set of of governments of the member units in which both kinds of governments rule over the same territory

and people and each kind has the authority to make decisions independently of each other.

(Riker 1964: 5)

the activities of government are divided between regional governments and a central government in such a way that each kind of government has some activities on which it makes final decision.

(Riker 1975: 101)

The wordings from the 1964 book – *Federalism: origin, operation, significance* – and the 1975 article – 'Federalism' in *Handbook of Political Science* – are, apparently, close to each other. Whereas the 1964 definition speaks of 'independent' decision-making, the 1975 definition talks of 'final' decision-making, which both must be exercised by the central government and the regional governments or 'governments of the member units', as stated in 1964.

It seems as if Riker's definition is far weaker than Duchacek's set of yardstick criteria. Why could not a unitary state like the Nordic countries satisfy the 1975 definition, given their extensive local government autonomy? The 1964 definition would rule out such an application, since no one would suggest that in these countries the local governments constitute what is called 'governments of member states' – member states do not exist in unitary states. However, the 1964 definition is indeed a circular one, as it hinges critically upon the distinction between the government of federation and the governments of the member units, where, of course, the term 'federation' is the one that should be defined and which, therefore, cannot be used in order to define 'federalism'.

We cannot accept the 1975 defintion of 'federalism' as equal to 'decentralization'. Federalism involves more than political or administrative or fiscal decentralization. The 1964 definition points in the right direction as federal states are different to the extent that they involve the tension between two states, not governments as in many unitary states, as well as the institutional mechanisms for resolving that tension. Thus, we will limit our use of the concept of a federal state to states that consist of member states, i.e. they are federations whether the act of federating is a real historical event or not. But we require, in addition, that the federal states are constitutional states; otherwise they are merely federal in name.

To summarize: we have the following two conditions for a federation to constitute a true federal state:

1   It cannot be at the same time an authoritarian state. However, this does not imply that federalism is the same as democracy. There have been federal states that were not democratic and there exist today federal states that are clearly not democratic states, such as Mexico and Venezuela. But since federalism implies power-sharing between the central government and the governments of the states as well as power-

sharing between executives, legislatures and the judiciaries, then a strong authoritarian state where power is held by a military junta, for instance, cannot be recognized as a federal state. There is more to federalism than a set of constitutional paragraphs that speak of 'federalism'. For example, Nigeria, or Pakistan, could qualify as a federal state during the periods when it has not been ruled by an omnipotent military junta. Also it does not seem adequate to treat the former communist states as federal ones. Russia today would, however, qualify.

2 There is more to federalism than merely power-sharing between various levels of government. One cannot simply equate federalism with a decentralized state structure, because unitary states could also harbour considerable decentralization. One might wish to include the states with extensive regionalization like Spain and Italy in the set of federal states, but then one must remember that there is no clear demarcation line between these quasi-federal states and the decentralized or regionalized unitary states. The concept of regionalism is as difficult to handle as that of federalism. What is a regionalized state format, more specifically? Is the occurrence of regional assemblies elected from below enough? Or should the regional assemblies also possess considerable finanancial autonomy, including taxation? Instead of having a set of quasi-federal countries where it is difficult to include and exclude countries, one could develop a scale of centralization–decentralization that would cover all countries, whether formally federal or unitary. Such a scale could be based upon the extent of taxation autonomy at lower levels of government in relation to the central government.

Federalism is not only difficult to pin down, one may also wish to distinguish between different types of federalism. In Europe, Swiss federalism appears to be the pure type whereas all other forms – German, Austrian and Belgian – seem to include elements that are different from the classical Swiss type of federalism, i.e. dual federalism with a clear demarcation between the states and the federal government. One may wish to identify German federalism as implementation federalism, because typically the federal bodies, including the Bundesrat (the federal chamber), are in a strong position when it comes to finances and legislation, whereas the Länder enjoy considerable autonomy in the application of federal rules (Scharpf *et al.* 1976; Hesse 1978; Abromeit 1992). In any case, Austrian federalism seems very centralized whereas Belgian federalism is not strictly territorial.

Perhaps it is easier to tell what federalism entails if one sticks to the constitutional democracies in the OECD set of countries (Hesse and Wright 1996). Hesse and Goetz speak of 'the Austrian and German Länder, the Swiss Cantons, the Belgian regions, and the Spanish autonomous communities' in relation to the theme 'Federalizing Europe?' (Hesse and Goetz 1992: 9). One may wish to discuss whether Spain is federal or semi-federal, but the interesting point is that Hesse and Goetz also identify the European

Union as a 'political institution with unmistakeably federal features'. The Union is, as things now stand, more a confederation than a federation, but the borderline between these two kinds of units is anything but crystal-clear. Yet, it seems warranted not to include supra-international organizations in the set of potential federal states, even when admitting that there is little left of the concept of state sovereignty in today's realities. To be sure, Hesse and Goetz qualify their classification by speaking of the 'traditional Western European federations (Austria, Switzerland and Germany) and Belgium and Spain, whose constitutional make-up contains distinctive federal elements' (Hesse and Goetz 1992: 2) – a distinction that we noted above.

Now, when examining the outcomes of federalism, should one include states that score low on the standard democracy indices? Should one include the small tiny states with few inhabitants? Can one really include all states with autonomous institutions? We offer no solution to these questions about the identification of federalism, in theory or in practice. We suggest, though, that different sets of federal states should be employed when one tests the theory that federalism is conducive to better outcomes than unitarism: a full set, a medium set and a true set of federal states (see Table 4.3).

If it is true that federal instutions perform better than unitary ones, then we must be able to find evidence to that effect in at least one of these sets.

Does federalism matter?

If there is so much debate about what federalism can do for a country, if one can seriously contemplate moving to a federal format, if it is indeed claimed that more federalism will help solve a country's problems, then federalism must be attended by attractive outcomes. If a federal state displays a performance record that is only as good as that of the unitary format, then how can all these claims on behalf of the federal state be upheld?

If federalism is better than unitarism, then federal states should have better outcomes than unitary ones (Ostrom 1974; Buchanan 1995). Do they? Which outcomes are the relevant ones to focus upon? One can make a distinction between a configuration of outcomes and outcomes in the causality sense. First, we may see whether federal states are accompanied by a specific set of outcomes. Second, we investigate whether these configur-

Table 4.3 Federal states

	1970	1980	1990
Full	19	18	17 (total = 151)
Medium	10	10	11 (total = 37)
True	6	6	7 (total = 24)

Sources: Blondel 1969; Banks 1978; Encyclopaedia Britannica 1996.

Note: Full set = all states; medium set = constitutional democracies; small set = OECD countries.

ations were in any sense also caused by the federal framework. If federalism matters, then it matters for long-term performance, because a federal framework is not a policy instrument that can be put into practice or withdrawn from one day to another. Thus, one should focus upon outcome measures that evaluate permanent phenomena.

One may make a distinction between close and distant outcomes, or simply outputs and outcomes, from the perspective of federalism. Sometimes this distinction is expressed by separating outputs and outcomes, as typified in the policy approach. Close outcomes or policy outputs we measure by examining public expenditures. If, indeed, federal states can control their policy outputs, then such states may wish to operate a different system of public expenditure from the unitary states, allowing for the fact that there are always so-called outliers.

Roland Vaubel has suggested that federal states operate a different budget structure from the unitary states (Vaubel 1995). He claims that federal states have a decentralized public sector whereas the unitary states tend towards a centralized budget structure. This is an essential argument about the consequences of federalism that may be tested by an examination of available public finance data. Yet, one may question whether it is, in a sense, too close an outcome, meaning that it is inherent in the very concept of a federal state that the lower levels of government, especially the member states of the federation, have larger budgets than the federal government.

Vaubel's argument actually raises a number of questions about the close outcomes of federalism. If a federal state is a state in which the member states are the basic stakeholders and, according to the constitutional myth, have set up the federation entrusting powers or competencies to the federal government, then surely one would expect that the member states retain financial powers themselves. If, on the other hand, a state adheres to a unitary framework, then since all powers belong to the national assembly of the central government, except those delegated to the government at lower levels, such states must have a public sector where the latter play a minor role to that of central government. Although this is constitutional myth and not an institutional reality, there is a core insight here, namely that fiscal decentralization must be larger in federal states than in unitary states, all other things being equal.

One should generalize the Vaubel argument to include more aspects of the public sector than simply the division of expenditures between central government and the member states or lower levels of government. First, one needs to look at the total size of the public expenditures. A country like unitary Japan can have a much smaller public sector than federal Germany even though fiscal centralization is much higher in the former than in the latter. Second, one would like to examine whether fiscal decentralization also involves taxation, i.e. do the lower levels of government not only spend more money than the central government but also raise more money by their own decisions.

Here, we have a couple of critical output questions concerning federalism: (1) Does federalism result in a smaller public sector? (2) Does federalism build upon fiscal decentralization in the sense of real taxation powers? It would indeed be a strong case of institutional effect if federalism resulted in a smaller public sector than that of a unitary state, and not simply a smaller share of the public expenditure for central government, which, after all, is what one would expect as long as it was a matter of outlays and not revenues.

In relation to the close outcomes of political institutions such as policy outputs, one can always raise the question: so what? Does it really mean anything for the population or society if certain institutions result in certain policies? What are the real-life outcomes? Is life better or worse under one institutional regime than under another? The distant outcomes pertain to the living conditions of the average citizen, often measured by means of indicators concerning purchasing power, employment and income distribution. In order to examine the links between political institutions and distant outcomes one could select a few measurements of outcomes based upon average scores over a few decades, such as political stability, affluence and economic growth, unemployment and inflation.

Thus, the key questions include: do federal states tend to perform differently than unitary ones on policy outputs and outcomes? And is it federalist institutions that make the difference in such countries? These questions require rather strict methodological deliberations. It is crucial to make a distinction between country configurations and causality, because one set of countries may differ from another in terms of outcome measures, but this does not allow for the conclusion that institutional differences play a key role.

One finds in political theory the whole range of positions concerning the outcomes of federalism, from strongly positive claims with Elazar and Ostrom to the surprisingly negative analysis by Riker, who argued that federalism, when confronted with political realities, amounted to nothing more than simply a myth (Smith 1995: 1–28). We may add here that there is also a literature discussing the failures and break-downs of federal regimes. Federalism is not always a success (Franck 1968; Hicks 1978; Young 1994). Let us proceed to empirical data about federal and unitary states – which perform the best? Speaking of state evaluation it is necessary to distinguish between configurations of outcomes, whether close or distant, and causality. The fact that the federal set displays, for example, a higher level of affluence per capita need not be due to federalism, as other properties may also distinguish this set, for instance the institutions of the market economy.

Configurations of policies and outcomes

In the following sections we will attempt to map the variation in different policy outputs and outcomes with relation to a federal or a unitary state format. The design we will apply takes as a starting point the distinction between three data sets (see Table 4.3): first, we identify a full set containing all states; second, a medium set consisting of constitutional democracies; and finally, a small set defined as the set of old OECD countries. Before we use regression analysis to establish whether the performance profile of the federal set also results from the operation of federalism, we employ the analysis of variance to observe how the federal sets compare with the unitary sets. This means that we will compare the different means for federal states and unitary states in all three data sets. If there is an institutional impact this will be indicated by the size of the eta-squared scores and their corresponding significance levels.

Decentralization

One would indeed expect federal states to emphasize fiscal decentralization more than unitary states. However, whether federal states or unitary states have a larger public sector is a more open question, although one would predict that the private sector would be stronger in a federal state, given its overall commitment to power diffusion. Let us look how things stand when we compare the federal format with the unitary format for the three sets of states. Public sector size is measured here as public expenditure in relation to GDP (GGEXP92, GGC) or as taxation as a percentage of GDP (TAX).

It is difficult not to maintain on the basis of the results in Table 4.4 that

Table 4.4 Federalism and public sector size: comparing means

	GGEXP92	GGC70	GGC80	GGC95	TAX75	TAX85	TAX94
Full set	(n=87)	(n=106)	(n=109)	(n=126)	—	—	—
All	32.5	13.9	14.8	15.4			
Unitary	31.9	14.1	14.9	15.5			
Federal	35.5	12.9	14.2	14.4			
Eta-sq	0.01	0.01	0.00	0.00			
Sig.	0.38	0.35	0.68	0.57			
Medium set	(n=36)	(n=36)	(n=37)	(n=35)	—	—	—
All	40.4	14.0	16.7	16.1			
Unitary	40.3	14.3	17.4	16.8			
Federal	40.7	13.2	14.8	14.8			
Eta-sq	0.00	0.01	0.04	0.02			
Sig.	0.94	0.58	0.24	0.40			
Small set	(n=24)	(n=24)	(n=24)	(n=22)	(n=24)	(n=24)	(n=24)
All	47.3	14.3	17.5	17.5	32.5	36.6	38.5
Unitary	47.6	14.0	17.3	17.7	32.7	37.5	39.3
Federal	46.5	15.3	17.8	17.1	31.9	33.7	36.6
Eta-sq	0.00	0.03	0.00	0.00	0.00	0.04	0.03
Sig.	0.81	0.43	0.82	0.76	0.83	0.37	0.44

Sources: GGEXP92=IMF 1994; GGC=see Table 3.1; TAX=OECD 1996.

Note: GGEXP92=general government expenditures as a percentage of GDP in 1992; GGC= general government consumption; TAX=total taxation as a percentage of GDP.

federalism does not matter for the overall size of the public sector. The eta-squared scores are simply too low and none of them show any significance. The general public sector hypothesis is not confirmed. Actually, the public sector is somewhat larger in federal states than in unitary states, on average. How about the amount of fiscal decentralization? Fiscal decentralization is measured in two ways. First, we look at the proportion of public expenditure which stems from non-central government (DEC92) and the proportion of public taxation which stems from non-central government (DEC75, DEC85, DEC94). Second, we use central government expenditures as a proportion of GDP as a measure of centralization, i.e. the opposite of decentralization. This is displayed in Table 4.5.

Federal states are more fiscally decentralized than unitary states. This applies to all the three sets of states. We thus see that the fiscal decentralization hypothesis is confirmed, the eta statistic in most cases showing significance, as federal states give less financial resources to the central government than unitary states. How about more distinctly economic outcomes?

Affluence and economic growth

Neo-classical economic growth theory teaches us that GDP and its yearly rate of change depend first and foremost upon economic factors. But the

Table 4.5 Federalism and decentralization/centralization: comparing means

	DEC92	CGE72	CGE80	CGE95	DEC75	DEC85	DEC94
Full set	(n=86)	(n=80)	(n=90)	(n=84)	—	—	—
All	8.5	22.3	27.5	29.6			
Unitary	5.2	23.0	28.6	30.2			
Federal	24.3	19.1	21.3	26.5			
Eta-sq	0.31	0.02	0.05	0.01			
Sig.	0.00	0.18	0.04	0.29			
Medium set	(n=36)	(n=32)	(n=35)	(n=32)	—	—	—
All	16.3	24.4	30.7	33.9			
Unitary	11.1	26.6	34.1	36.1			
Federal	28.1	19.4	22.2	29.1			
Eta-sq	0.27	0.13	0.18	0.07			
Sig.	0.00	0.04	0.01	0.14			
Small set	(n=24)	(n=21)	(n=22)	(n=21)	(n=23)	(n=24)	(n=24)
All	20.4	26.8	33.5	38.8	17.3	16.9	17.0
Unitary	15.3	29.3	36.5	40.8	12.0	11.9	12.7
Federal	32.9	20.8	25.5	33.7	32.4	31.8	27.5
Eta-sq	0.33	0.25	0.25	0.13	0.45	0.46	0.29
Sig.	0.00	0.02	0.02	0.10	0.00	0.00	0.01

Sources: DEC92=IMF 1994; CGE=World Bank 1992, 1997; DEC=OECD 1996.

Note: DEC92=non-central public expenditures as a proportion of general government expenditure; CGE =central government expenditures as a percentage of GDP; DEC75–DEC94=non-central taxation as a proportion of total public taxation.

new institutionalism in the social sciences underlines the contribution of legal factors to a rich and dynamic economy. Is the state format a factor to be reckoned with here? State institutions could be relevant for economic growth theory, if it were the case that the state framework had an impact upon the economic factors that enhance affluence and GDP growth. In this section we will look at the impact on affluence, human development and economic growth. Table 4.6 contains data about affluence or the level of economic output as measured by real GDP per capita for all three sets of states for three separate periods of time.

There is, in fact, no straightforward evidence to the effect that federalism increases country affluence. Among the full state set we may find an impact of federalism. This also seems to be the case for the set of OECD countries. However, controlling for constitutional states we find no such impact, as the low eta-squared scores reveal. How about the impact on the level of human development? Look at Table 4.7.

The information in Table 4.7 indicates strongly our basic point, namely that it matters very much how one goes about examining the performance of federal states, both with regard to how federalism is identified and in relation to how the set of states is specified. What looks like the superior economic performance of federal states in relation to unitary states (the full set) goes away when one looks at countries with a similar socio-economic background and where it is crystal clear which states are truly federal ones (the medium and small sets). The eta-squared values indicate the same, as they are never strong, even though the averages differ substantially. Most of the variation in

Table 4.6 Federalism and affluence: real GDP/capita: comparing means

	RGDP70	*RGDP80*	*RGDP92*
Full set	(n=115)	(n=120)	(n=84)
All	3294	4643	5588
Unitary	2885	3918	4814
Federal	5499	8753	9461
Eta-sq	0.09	0.12	0.10
Sig.	0.00	0.00	0.00
Medium set	(n=37)	(n=37)	(n=32)
All	6448	8363	10555
Unitary	5922	7856	10165
Federal	7869	9731	11299
Eta-sq	0.06	0.04	0.01
Sig.	0.13	0.23	0.55
Small set	(n=24)	(n=24)	(n=22)
All	8208	10498	13325
Unitary	7404	9627	12491
Federal	10620	13113	15114
Eta-sq	0.28	0.27	0.18
Sig.	0.01	0.01	0.05

Source: See Table 3.2.

Table 4.7 Federalism and human development: HDI: comparing means

	HDI70	*HDI80*	*HDI92*
Full set	(n=108)	(n=108)	(n=108)
All	0.48	0.54	0.61
Unitary	0.45	0.51	0.58
Federal	0.62	0.71	0.77
Eta-sq	0.05	0.07	0.07
Sig.	0.02	0.01	0.00
Medium set	(n=37)	(n=37)	(n=37)
All	0.74	0.79	0.84
Unitary	0.74	0.78	0.85
Federal	0.73	0.79	0.84
Eta-sq	0.00	0.00	0.00
Sig.	0.95	0.96	0.87
Small set	(n=24)	(n=24)	(n=24)
All	0.83	0.86	0.90
Unitary	0.81	0.85	0.90
Federal	0.87	0.89	0.92
Eta-sq	0.06	0.06	0.10
Sig.	0.26	0.26	0.14

Source: See Table 3.2.

affluence and quality of life occurs within the categories of states and not between them. When the socio-economic background is held constant, then all differences practically disappear.

Let us look at the impact on economic growth. Economic growth is measured for three consecutive periods, namely 1960–73, 1973–85 and 1985–94. Table 4.8 has the corresponding data.

Given the eta-squared statistic in Table 4.8 it is hardly possible to claim that federal states do better on economic growth than unitary. The extremely low eta-squared values show that almost all country variation takes place within the sets and not between them. In any case, the differences between the averages are very small. In the small set, unitary states even tend to do better than federal states.

Thus, one may observe a certain difference in affluence between federal and unitary states. Is this a sign of some more fundamental connection? Before we discuss causality, let us first look at some social outcomes (social equality) and then some political outcomes (democracy and stability).

Social equality

One kind of social outcome could be evaluated by looking at the distribution of incomes within countries. Reliable income distribution data is mainly

Table 4.8 Federalism and economic growth: comparing means

	Growth 1960–73	Growth 1973–85	Growth 1985–94
Full set	(n=113)	(n=109)	(n=130)
All	2.9	1.1	−0.2
Unitary	2.9	1.1	−0.5
Federal	3.2	1.1	1.2
Eta-sq	0.00	0.00	0.02
Sig.	0.57	0.94	0.12
Medium set	(n=35)	(n=37)	(n=37)
All	3.7	1.2	1.8
Unitary	4.0	1.2	2.0
Federal	3.1	1.2	1.2
Eta-sq	0.06	0.00	0.04
Sig.	0.15	0.93	0.23
Small set	(n=24)	(n=24)	(n=24)
All	4.3	1.5	1.6
Unitary	4.6	1.5	1.7
Federal	3.5	1.6	1.4
Eta-sq	0.08	0.00	0.01
Sig.	0.19	0.85	0.60

Source: See Table 3.2.

available for what is called the small set of countries here, i.e. the OECD set. However, data have increasingly become available from other sets of states as they are reported by international organizations like the World Bank and the ILO. Can we find an impact of federalism on income distribution? Table 4.9 offers an answer.

It is obvious from Table 4.9 that federalism has no impact on this matter. There is no set of states for which we may find any significant eta-squared scores.

Democracy scores

If the modern version of federalism is correct, then federal states should tend towards democracy. We wish to know, in addition, whether federal states tend to be more democractic than unitary states. Making use of the estimates presented by Freedom House we may arrive at democracy scores covering three different periods, namely averages for 1972–83, 1982–93 and 1991–6. Table 4.10 contains information about the impact of federalism on democracy for three different sets of states.

As expected, in the OECD (small) set and the constitutional (medium) set there are no differences, as virtually all OECD countries are stable democracies. In the full set there are clear differences between the average

Table 4.9 Federalism and income distribution: comparing means

	GINI 1970	GINI 1980	GINI 1990
Full set	(n=61)	(n=73)	(n=63)
All	39.4	37.8	39.3
Unitary	39.9	38.0	40.2
Federal	37.9	37.2	34.9
Eta-sq	0.01	0.00	0.04
Sig.	0.49	0.78	0.13
Medium set	(n=31)	(n=32)	(n=37)
All	37.6	37.1	37.3
Unitary	37.3	35.9	37.8
Federal	38.6	40.1	36.0
Eta-sq	0.01	0.05	0.01
Sig.	0.68	0.21	0.65
Small set	(n=21)	(n=22)	(n=14)
All	34.2	33.0	33.2
Unitary	34.6	32.4	33.1
Federal	32.9	35.2	33.5
Eta-sq	0.02	0.07	0.00
Sig.	0.60	0.22	0.88

Sources: See Table 3.2.

scores, but the eta-squared statistic indicates that the 'within category' variation is much larger than the 'between category' variation. Perhaps the low average scores for unitary states simply reflects that there are more of them than of the federal kind?

Political stability

One may wish to complement the regime indicator on democracy versus dictatorship with a political stability indicator. Whether stability is a positive or a negative in the performance asssessments of regimes may be disputed. Suffice it to say here that a democracy may be stable or unstable just as a dictatorship. How about the political stability of federal states compared with unitary states? One indicator of political stability which we will use here is constitutional longevity, i.e. the length of time that the present constitution has been in operation for three different time periods (Table 4.11)

It is only in one set of states (the full set) where we may judge from the eta-squared scores that there is a difference between federal and unitary states in relation to constitutional longevity. Federal states tend to have constitutions that last longer. The average scores are considerably different for unitary and federal states, indicating that state stability could be higher in the federal format. However, again, when we hold the level of development

Table 4.10 Federalism and democracy scores: comparing means

	1972–83	*1982–93*	*1991–96*
Full set	(n=122)	(n=126)	(n=146)
All	4.3	4.8	5.2
Unitary	4.0	4.4	5.0
Federal	6.3	6.9	6.8
Eta-sq	0.06	0.06	0.03
Sig.	0.00	0.00	0.02
Medium set	(n=37)	(n=32)	(n=37)
All	8.6	9.0	8.8
Unitary	8.6	9.1	9.0
Federal	8.7	8.8	8.5
Eta-sq	0 .00	0.02	0.02
Sig.	0.91	0.44	0.39
Small set	(n=24)	(n=24)	(n=24)
All	9.3	9.6	9.5
Unitary	9.0	9.5	9.4
Federal	9.9	9.9	9.9
Eta-sq	0.10	0.04	0.05
Sig.	0.14	0.36	0.31

Sources: See Table 3.3.

constant in the medium and small set of states, there is no difference between unitarism and federalism as regards constitutional stability.

Comparing means for different outputs and outcomes for federal and unitary states differentiated in three different sets, we only find a few instances of an impact of federalism. Basically, there is only in one case where we find a consistent impact and this is with regard to fiscal decentralization (Table 4.5); there may possibly also be an effect on the level of affluence (Table 4.6).

Causality

We have been able to isolate only two distinctive traits of federal states when their performance is compared with that of unitary states. On the one hand, they display a higher degree of fiscal decentralization, meaning that lower levels of government spend more of the public sector outlays, relatively speaking. On the other hand, federal states tend to have high levels of affluence. Can we speak of institutional effects here?

We argue that the first feature here is an example of an institutional impact. Federalism is conducive to fiscal decentralization. The second feature is hardly an institutional effect, as federalism scarcely has an independent impact upon affluence. Other factors are at work, which

Table 4.11 Federalism and constitutional longevity: no. of years: comparing means

	1978	*1985*	*1996*
Full set	(n=123)	(n=123)	(n=143)
All	26.6	30.7	22.1
Unitary	22.7	27.4	18.5
Federal	49.1	51.1	47.0
Eta-sq	0.06	0.04	0.09
Sig.	0.01	0.02	0.00
Medium set	(n=36)	(n=36)	(n=36)
All	53.8	55.5	52.6
Unitary	48.1	52.2	46.4
Federal	66.6	64.1	66.6
Eta-sq	0.03	0.01	0.04
Sig.	0.30	0.56	0.26
Small set	(n=23)	(n=23)	(n=23)
All	69.0	68.2	64.9
Unitary	59.8	63.1	57.9
Federal	94.8	82.7	80.7
Eta-sq	0.07	0.02	0.04
Sig.	0.21	0.52	0.39

Sources: See Table 3.4.

account for the fact that federal states tend to have a higher level of affluence than unitary states. What might these be?

One may employ regression analysis in order to establish an institutional effect. By holding other relevant factors constant one may observe whether the institution makes any difference to explaining an outcome, whatever that may be. Any argument about an institutional effect is merely tentative, as one cannot be sure that one has indeed specified the correct model, including the factors that are causally related to the outcome to be explained or predicted.

Starting with federalism and affluence, one may point out that affluence summarizes many years of economic development. Federal states do not perform better than unitary states when one looks at economic growth during most of the post-war period. The implication is that federal states were already rather rich around 1950. If federalism promotes economic performance more than unitary states, why is there no short-term effect to be discovered in the various growth data for 1960–94?

A similar interpretation may be reached if one considers that the number of unitary states is much larger than the number of federal states. Averages are sensitive to the number of cases included in the computation. It is telling that there is hardly any difference between federal and unitary states when one looks at the OECD countries, where other things are more equal. What is at stake in the analysis of institutional effects is the *ceteris paribus* clause.

Now, affluence as measured by some economic indicators on total output reflects a long period of economic development as it takes decades of even high economic growth to reach a substantial level of affluence. First, one may expect affluence to be related to the starting point in time of economic modernization, the longer the time span the higher the level of affluence. For each country there is typically a starting point for economic modernization, when, for instance, the industrialization period got under way – what W. Rustow called the 'take-off stage'. Black has given a rough estimation of when economic modernization started, which data may be employed in a regression analysis of the impact of federalism on affluence, holding economic modernization constant (Black 1966).

Second, it would be surprising if federalism was the only institution that had an impact upon affluence, because any institutionalist theory of economic development would underline the role of economic institutions, not political institutions. In economic neo-institutionalism, scholars like, for instance, O. Williamson and D. North have emphasized the contribution of the market economy to a high level of affluence. Let us therefore also look at the connection between federalism and affluence when one enters the degree of economic freedom into the regression equation. One may use an index measuring the strength of market institutions in a country, as suggested by Wright (1982) or Gwartney *et al.* (1996).

Third, take, in addition, political modernization or the level of democracy. If decentralization does not reflect the federal–unitary distinction, then maybe it depends upon state longevity. States with a longer time span of uninterrupted institutionalization would, all other things equal, be more decentralized than states which have been recently founded. State maturity would promote trust, which is fundamental to the delegation of powers to lower levels of government from the central or national government. Thus the institutional sclerosis factor or the year of the introduction of modern state institutions (Black 1966) is also introduced in the regression analysis.

Finally, another reasonable explanation of the variation in the levels of fiscal decentralization is whether a state is democratic or not, as authoritarian regimes would, one may assume, be less willing to grant fiscal decentralization. Since many federal states are democracies, the connection between federalism and fiscal decentralization could be spurious, simply reflecting the association of both variables with democracy. Since several unitary states are authoritarian regimes, the same explanation would apply. Table 4.12 displays the outcome of the regression analysis where these variables are included in order to explain the variation in fiscal decentralization on both federalism–unitarism and the degree of democratization.

The finding is that the pattern of variation in affluence today is to a considerable extent explained by the process of industrialization or, more specifically, to the time when this major process was initiated. Federalism or unitarism matters little for country affluence when one controls for the start-up year of economic modernization. The analysis also shows that the struc-

Table 4.12 Regressions: federalism, affluence and decentralization: 1990s

		Affluence	Decentralization
Federalism	coeff	−0.03	15.91
	t-stat	−0.21	5.37
Econ free	coeff	0.14	0.24
	t-stat	2.57	0.26
Econ modern	coeff	0.01	—
	t-stat	5.21	
Inst scler	coeff	—	0.06
	t-stat		2.31
Dem 1990s	coeff	—	0.91
	t-stat		1.57
Constant	coeff	6.89	−6.94
	t-stat	25.41	−1.76
adj rsq		0.57	0.50
n		52	76

Sources: Affluence=see Table 3.2; decentralization=see Table 4.5; economic freedom=
Gwartney *et al.* 1996; economic modernization and institutional sclerosis=Black 1966;
democracy 1991–96=see Table 3.3.

Note: Affluence=Ln RGDP 1990; decentralization=DEC92 (see Table 4.5); federalism
=see Table 4.3; econ free=economic freedom index for 1993; econ modern=economic
modernization; inst scler=institutional sclerosis or political modernization; dem 1990s=
democracy score 1991–96.

ture of economic institutions like the mechanisms of exchange and allocation are more important than the federal–unitary distinction.

The key finding in Table 4.12 is not that state longevity has a stronger
impact than federalism upon fiscal decentralization, state longevity being
measured by the year of introduction of modern state institutions. What it
clearly shows is that federalism also matters. Again, the institutional effect is
there, federalism promoting fiscal decentralization in addition to the positive
impact of democracy upon fiscal decentralization.

Things are different when one interprets the second institutional
configuration, viz. the tendency of federal states to display lower levels of
fiscal centralization. Here, we argue, there is an institutional effect. It is not
possible to explain away this finding by regressing the extent of decentralization onto other factors. From Table 4.12 we can find the outcome of
regressing economic freedom and federalism on fiscal decentralization. Now,
it would appear that political institutions are more important than economic
institutions, the extent of fiscal decentralization reflecting more the federal–
unitary separation than the structure of the economy.

The key finding in Table 4.12 is not that state longevity has a stronger
impact than federalism upon fiscal decentralization, state longevity being
measured by the year of introduction of modern state institutions. What it
clearly shows is that federalism also matters. Again, the institutional effect is
there, federalism promoting fiscal decentralization in addition to the positive
impact of democracy upon fiscal decentralization.

Conclusion

It has been argued that federal states tend to perform better than unitary
states. We cannot confirm such a sweeping generalization. Actually, there is
no evidence whatsoever for the strong claims launched by the adherents of

federalism (Ostrom 1991; Elazar 1995). What federalism means is first and foremost what it should mean according to constitutional theory, namely less central government spending and more sub-national government spending (King 1982; Bakvis and Chandler 1987; Watts 1996). Federalism has one institutional effect that makes itself apparent, however one identifies the set of federal states, and that is fiscal decentralization. After all, how could a true federal framework be viable if the provincial governments had few budgetary competences? This clear finding does not mean, however, that federalism is simply decentralization, because unitary states may also exhibit substantial fiscal decentralization, especially when the communes have been granted taxation powers.

We found one certifiable institutional effect evaluating the claims put forward in recent federalist literature, namely fiscal decentralization. And this is no surprise, because if a federal state is at all radically different from a unitary state, then it must relate to the capacity of lower levels of government to balance the central or national government. The capacity for provincial autonomy would be larger if the national government did less – all other things being equal. This entails that in federal states the amount of fiscal decentralization should be greater – again, all other things being equal.

Already in 1968 Elazar stated that federalism may work very well, if supported by certain conditions. He argued:

> The successful operation of federal systems requires a particular kind of political environment, one which is conducive to popular government and has the strong traditions of political cooperation and self-restraint that are needed to maintain a system which minimizes the use of coercion.
>
> (Elazar 1968: 365)

Of the countries that Elazar classified as federal or semi-federal in 1995, only just over half would qualify according to his 1968 criteria for the 'successful operation of federal systems'. But even when we include only the successful federal states, we cannot detect any other institutional effect other than that federal states tend to have more vibrant provincial governments, or so-called 'states', 'länder' or 'cantons'.

5 The institutionalization of human rights
Locke

Introduction

The institutional distinction between federalist and unitary states seems in reality to have little to do with another institutional separation, which distinguishes between states that have successfully institutionalized human rights and states that have not. Adherents of federalist theory connect federalist institutions with democracy, but in the real world several federalist countries do not respect civil and political rights, which, by the way, is also true of many unitary states. One must not forget that Althusius advocated federal rights, not human rights. The case for civil and political rights was presented almost a century after *Systematic Politics* (1610) in Locke's *Two Treatises of Civil Government* (1690).

A macro analysis of human rights, or democracy, on the basis of a neo-institutionalist approach would have to satisfy three requirements: (1) that the extent to which civil and political rights have been institutionalized can be clearly identified at the macro level and preferably measured in terms of an index; (2) that the performance profile of human rights countries can be described; and (3) that it is, in principle, possible to distinguish cause and effect in relation to human rights.

Human rights, all seem to agree, are important, constituting a major element in constitutional law. But, we ask in this chapter, with regard to the institutionalization of civil and political rights in relation to a set of outputs and outcomes, important for what? The difficult problem in a comparative institutional analysis of human rights is to show that human rights is the cause of policy outputs and outcomes and not the effect. As a matter of fact, it may be almost impossible to make this distinction even when countries institutionalizing human rights have a certain distinct profile of outputs and outcomes. When human rights are focused upon, then one is speaking about constitutional democracy.

Human rights and democracy

Human rights constitute institutions that are often mentioned in relation to the concept of a democratic regime. In an institutionalist approach to the concept of democracy, one would focus upon the institutions that secure government of the people or by the people or for the people, as Lincoln expressed it in his Gettysburg address. The key question in democracy theory is to lay down these institutions that secure participation and representation as well as freedom and equality.

Democracy is one kind of group decision-making where votes are allocated to choice participants and the group decision is the aggregation of the preferences of the participants. What democracy excludes is the imposition of the will of an external person or the declaration of the preference of one participant as being the group choice against all the preferences of the other participants. Democratic decisions are non-dictatorial from within the group and are not imposed from outside of the group either. However, simple majority institutions may not suffice to accomplish these requirements, as one may need a stronger institutional set-up, including immunity as one form of human rights protection.

In political democracy, there is an institution that safeguards equality, as implied by the one man, one vote rule. All citizens – men and women – are equal and count for the same. In political democracy, there is, in addition, a preference for one group decision-making rule, simple majority. Although political democracy may employ qualified majority decision-making, real-life democratic countries tend to use simple majority in most of their institutions. Thus, we arrive at a minimalist definition of democracy: equal citizen voting rights and simple majority decision-making. Equal voting rights and simple majority implies a thin definition of democratic institutions, called populist democracy or Rousseau democracy.

One may arrive at a thick definition of democracy by increasing the number and types of citizen rights, including negative or positive freedoms, group rights, and immunities such as, for instance, property. One thick definition of democracy is based upon using group decision-making rules that are more complex, including a variety of qualified decision-making or the allocation of veto possibilities to various players – so called Madisonian democracy.

Human rights are clearly connected with democracy, but the relationship is a complex one. Some human rights such as the right to vote, to form associations and the one man, one vote principle are at the core of democracy. Several so-called negative freedoms are human rights that democratic regimes very much respect, including habeas corpus rights and the right to freedom of conscience, religion and the press. Whether and how far a democratic regime can restrict these negative human rights is a debated topic, involving a potential conflict between popular sovereignty and individual freedom. In relation to positive freedoms, or human rights that call for state programmes, the debate about democracy is more open-ended, some regarding these rights as essential to democracy, whereas others deny that.

In order to map the occurrence of civil and political rights, we employ a human rights index, of which there are various versions (Humana 1983,

1987, 1992; Jaggers and Gurr 1995; Freedom House 1990–7). There is a variety of indices measuring the institutionalization of human rights, ranking countries from 0 to 10 in terms of their extent of democraticness. These indices may be seen as basically an institutional definition of the concept of democracy in relation to a macro unit such as the country. The various indices on democracy not only correlate highly with each other, they also involve a considerable distance between democracies and dictatorships. Thus, they are not only reliable but they also demarcate between countries that respect human rights and countries that do not (Bollen 1980, 1986, 1990, 1993; Jabine and Claude 1992; Beetham 1994; Schmidt 1995).

Although the institutionalization of human rights is an extremely reliable indicator of macro democracy, one could define democracy in a less institutional way and more in a behavioural one, focusing less upon law and more upon real popular participation in politics. Let us spell out the difference between the behavioural approach to democracy and the neo-institutionalist approach.

Dahl's concept of polyarchy

The behavioural research on democracy looked for the conditions that are necessary or sufficient for the stability a democratic regime. Thus, R. A. Dahl identified a number of conditions that are conducive to democratic viability. In the neo-institutionalist research on democracy, the focus is decisively upon the outputs and outcomes of the operation of democratic institutions. Let us develop this distinction between the conditions for democracy, on the one hand, and democratic performance, on the other hand.

'Polyarchy' was the term employed by Dahl in his book of the same name from 1971, which presented a theory of modern democracy. Dahl argued that democracy in the original sense of the word, that is the rule of the people, could not be fully accomplished in a country with a large population, meaning roughly more than one million. Only polyarchy was feasible. Polyarchies were thought of as relatively (but incompletely) democratized regimes. Most recent research on democracy has hardly taken up and followed the Dahl distinction between polyarchy and ideal democracy. Why? Because it is more a behavioural than institutional distinction, running counter to the emergence of neo-institutionalism.

Dahl identified two behavioural dimensions of political systems and elaborated a typology by means of these two variables: (1) closed hegemonies or a low degree of public contestation and a low degree of participation; (2) inclusive hegemonies or a low degree of public contestation and a high degree of participation; (3) competitive oligarchies or a high degree of public contestation and a low degree of participation; (4) democracies or a high degree of public contestation and a high degree of participation. The difficulty with the Dahl typology is that as long as one does not know what is a high degree of contestation or participation, then how can one identify the set of democracies around the world. Stating that real-life democratic regimes – polyarchies – underperform, because ideal democracy – with a high degree of contestation and participation – is not feasible, only makes it even more problematic to tell which country is democratic and which is non-democratic. A behavioural definition will probably not do when one wants to separate between democracies and dictatorships.

Dahl argued that the way a democracy is created does affect the possibility of its persistence and survival, underlining the peaceful evolution of democratic institutions that transfer legitimacy from the old regime to the new one, which becomes accepted by large segments of the citizens. Dahl also emphasizes the importance for democracy of a decentralized economy. Ownership of economic assets is not the crucial issue, but a centrally directed economy is not likely to coexist with democratic institutions. Democracy may exist in agrarian societies; again, the degree of hierarchy is the crucial issue, because a society with a system of free farmers is conducive to democracy. Generally, the relationship between socio-economic conditions and democracy depends on how resources are controlled. Most favourable conditions for democracy exist when the control over resources for repression (police and military) and socio-economic sanctions (economic resources, means of communications, education opportunities) are dispersed between groups that have some degree of autonomy versus each other and which may oppose attempts at a monolithic concentration of various kinds of power, political, economic and social.

The level of socio-economic development affects democracy; the richer a country is, the more likely is the existence and survival of democratic institutions. In addition, Dahl finds a significant connection between equality and democratic institutions. Extreme inequalities in the distribution of key values are unfavourable to competitive politics and to polyarchy because this state of affairs is equivalent to extreme inequality in the distribution of key political resources which most probably generates resentments and frustrations, weakening allegiance to the regime (Dahl 1971: 103). Democracies, though, may survive inequalities as long as they do not become a focus for contention among large segments of the population.

Dahl's analysis also covered the relationship between heterogeneity and democracy with the implication that democracy functions better in homogeneous societies than in fragmented ones, although there are deviant cases. Heterogeneity may be accommodated to democracy by means of a few mechanisms: collaboration between the subcultures, devices which guarantee the various subcultures some influence (veto, proportional representation, federalism).

Moreover, belief systems are important for the possibility of creating a democratic regime; Dahl emphasizes the crucial significance of what various elite groups believe. Democracy needs legitimacy: a belief among political activists that democratic institutions are valid in their own right. Adhering to an idea proposed by Eckstein that beliefs about one kind of authority (political authority in democratic institutions) must be consonant with beliefs about authority structures in other kinds of institutions like the family, the church and voluntary associations (Eckstein 1966), Dahl underlines the belief in the effectiveness of democratic government to solve problems as well as trust in the sincere objectives of contending political activists.

Finally, Dahl argues that democratic political systems are not only dependent on the structure of society but are also vulnerable to the operations of other nations in their environment. Democracy may be threatened by overt foreign intervention. But, drawing on the experiences of the West European countries during the Second World War, he proposes that foreign intervention may not be fatal to an existing democracy but may strengthen it (Dahl 1971: 197). These various conditions that all somehow enhance the probability of democratic longevity are relevant today in the debate about the many democracies that have come forth in the 1990s.

Yet, in the eyes of an institutionalist, the question of effects is just as important as that of conditions. Institutionalism implies a belief in the crucial role of institutions. Thus, while not denying all the conditions for democratic stability that Dahl identifies, an institutionalist would still insist upon the crucial importance of getting the democratic institutions right in the first place and then have them effectively implemented, even when the surrounding conditions may be negative towards democratic longevity. And here is where we enter human rights as being critical to the establishment of a constitutional democracy.

Thus, following neo-institutionalism, we will search for the effects of the institutionalization of human rights. Do human rights countries have a different performance profile than non-democratic countries? The distinction between institutional performance and institutional effects is highly relevant when enquiring into the outputs and outcomes in countries where human rights are respected. These countries may display a distinct performance profile on outputs and outcomes, but to conclude that human rights is the key factor explaining such a distinct performance profile would require much effort in causal analysis, including other relevant factors besides institutions.

Tocqueville and human rights

Democracy as a decision-making process implies freedom. Without the right to associate and the right to religion, opinion and press, democracy cannot operate. Democracy as a decision process entails citizen participation in some form or other. Without free and fair elections where political parties contest, democracy cannot operate. Thus, intrinsically, democracy is linked up with freedom and participation, meaning one man, one vote. In a constitutional democracy one goes to great lengths in defining and protecting institutions that harbour these human rights about liberty and equality.

Here, we are concerned with the question of the extrinsic value of constitutional democracy: will the protection of human rights in countries be attended by policy outputs and social and economic outcomes that are better than the outputs and outcomes of other kinds of macro political institutions? What is at stake is not the intrinsic value of the institutions of human rights, but whether they are linked up with political, social or economic policies or outcomes. This is a question about empirical probabilities, referring to the evaluation of the performance record of countries with human rights institutions.

One side of democracy is about rights, and another side refers to citizen participation under these institutions. The evaluation of the performance profile of the institutions of constitutional democracy may be based upon the Tocqueville theory about the coming democratic period, replacing the aristocratic society in which men and women had lived since the beginning of civilization. What would be distinctive of government policies and socio-economic development in the democratic era that Tocqueville predicted with such accuracy in the 1830s?

In his two-volume *Democracy in America*, the first volume published in 1835 and the second volume in 1840, Tocqueville started out from the institutional foundation of a democratic society and state, making a sharp distinction between it and the institutions of an aristocratic society. Whereas in an aristocratic society human beings face formal inequality as well as having few or no liberties, the democratic society is founded upon formal equality and safeguards many liberties. The institutional difference between aristocracy and democracy as the ordering principle for both society and state refers to how equality and freedom is defined and mixed in the laws and customs of a country (see *L'ancien régime et la révolution* [1856] 1988).

The combination of formal equality and negative liberties that for Tocqueville were distinctive of a democratic society and state, meant not just an entirely different social structure when compared with aristocratic society. Such institutions as equality and liberty also mattered for government outputs and socio-economic outcomes, or – it is better stated – will in the future matter, as outlined in the famous Tocqueville predictions about the twentieth century.

When looking backwards, comparing the new society that he saw emerging for the first time in the United States with all past societies in history, Tocqueville made the distinction between the aristocratic and the democratic society. Thus, Tocqueville relied heavily upon how the rights of individuals are defined and upheld, either by explicitly made government decisions – statute laws – or through the customs and habits of people. What is decisive is how rights and duties are institutionalized by the moral codes operating in the minds of people. Aristocracy is based upon formal inequalities, and such a society leans towards despotic government. Aristocratic societies are based upon status distinctions, enshrined in law in the form of political, social and economic privileges: e.g. the three estates in France or the caste society in India. In an aristocracy there may be some degree of liberty, although restricted to the upper classes, as in a feudal society or under l'ancien regime.

	Formal Equality	
	Low	High
Liberty		
Low	Monarchy	
Medium	Aristocracy	
High		Democracy

Figure 5.1 Democracy versus aristocracy.

On the contrary, democracy is founded upon formal equality or equality under the law, and it favours a government that respects the liberties of men and women (Figure 5.1).

When looking forward to the coming of the democratic era, when all societies would be democratic, Tocqueville pinned down two developmental paths that he predicted.

In a democratic society, men and women will fully enjoy its institutions: freedom and equality. Thus, a democratic society is conducive to individualism, each person acting on the basis of his/her self-interests. With social distinctions loosing their discriminatory force, men and women are left to themselves to relentlessly pursue their individual happiness. The democratic society is a highly mobile society, both geographically and in relation to different income groups, and may move upwards as well as downwards. Moreover, it is linked to the industrial society, whereas the aristocratic society has a greater agrarian basis.

Excessive individualism is the major risk with a democratic society, because it could lead to atomism, where solitary men and women find simple solutions to complex social and economic problems by giving support to strong leaders who appeal directly to the people. Only if the economy with its market institutions creates wealth, will the negative consequences of atomism then be counteracted through men and women joining free associations, which were the schools of democracy to Tocqueville. Thus, the institutions of democracy, human rights, will only thrive if society becomes affluent – this is the first major prediction by Tocqueville.

In an affluent society, men and women will not rest content with formal equality. Tocqueville sees another force besides affluence that may destabilize the democratic society, namely the quest for real equality. Formal equality not being enough, men and women will lend their support to political forces that wish to use government to intervene in the economy and the private sector in order to enhance equality of results (Figure 5.2).

Real equality, and not merely equality of opportunities such as the one man, one vote principle or the quality of entering the market economy as a consumer, can only be enhanced by state action, i.e. public sector expansion. Whereas negative liberties restrict the state, positive liberties result from the public policies that government can conduct in order to present people with opportunities: education, health and social care.

	Formal Equality	Real Equality
Negative Liberty	Tocqueville's preference	
Positive Liberty		Tocqueville's fear

Figure 5.2 Real equality and positive liberties.

Human rights today is a composite of both positive and negative liberties with tensions built into any mixture of the two types of freedoms. One human rights tradition places the emphasis upon the negative liberties, since they tend to be strictly enforceable in courts, whereas another human rights tradition argues that positive freedoms are as important as the negative liberties, at least as policy principles. Tocqueville favoured the negative liberties and he argued that too many positive liberties could hurt the freedom of the individual as against the state, although he predicted that the love for real equality would lead men and women to increase the public sector in the century to come.

To sum up: Tocqueville argued that countries that institutionalized human rights would experience both affluence or wealth and real income equality. Have these predictions come true ?

The performance profile of human rights countries

One may start the performance evaluation of human rights institutions by pointing out that richness and income equality are not logically linked up with each other. Affluence is a measure of total or aggregate economic output in a country and equality deals with how aggregate wealth is distributed. Distributional matters are affected by factors such as the culture of a country as well as the political forces operating in that country. When mapping the performance profile of countries on aggregate wealth as well as distribution, one may wish to include a number of measures that somehow tap how rich a country is and how equal groups tend to be, i.e. income groups or gender groups.

Table 5.1 indicates that countries that institutionalize human rights in a successful manner tend to have a distinct performance profile in terms of policy outputs and socio-economic outcomes. The democracy index employed here is based upon the ratings of political rights and civil rights made by Freedom House (Gastil 1987, 1988; Freedom House 1990–97). These scores have been added and normalized so that democracies scoring high comes close to 10 and non-democracies scoring low comes close to 0.

It is hardly an exaggeration to state that all of the Tocqueville predictions are confirmed in the data about outputs and outcomes among democratic and non-democratic countries around the world. The many findings in Table 5.1

Table 5.1 Democracy, outputs and outcomes: correlations

		LnRGDP	HDIN	SOCB	CGRE	GINI	FEMR	CORR
DEM 1970s	r	0.71	0.81	0.58	0.36	−0.17	−0.19	0.65
	p	0.000	0.000	0.000	0.000	0.097	0.025	0.000
DEM 1980s	r	0.68	0.80	0.64	0.34	−0.09	0.04	0.62
	p	0.000	0.000	0.000	0.000	0.239	0.330	0.000
DEM 1990s	r	0.72	0.70	0.68	0.51	−0.23	0.37	0.68
	p	0.000	0.000	0.000	0.000	0.037	0.000	0.000

Sources: LnRGDP=see Table 3.2; HDIN=see Table 3.2; SOCB=see Table 3.1; CGRE= see Table 3.2; GINI=see Table 3.2; FEMR=see Table 3.3; CORR=see Table 3.3; DEM=see Table 3.3.

Note: LnRGDP=Natural logarithm of real GDP per capita; HDIN=Human development index; SOCB=social benefit payment expenditures in % of GDP; GINI=gini index; FEMR=female representation in parliament; CORR=index of perceived corruption; DEM=democracy scores.

validate Tocqueville's images of democracy as conducive to richness and a high level of human development, as well as towards equality by reducing income differences and promoting the equal status of women by means of female parliamentary representation. Democracy also gives the state a major role in providing for equality by means of state intervention in the form of welfare benefits. At the same time, the level of corruption also seems to be low in the democracies. What Tocqueville warned against was centralization, which is also corroborated in the data about the size of central government.

This is all to do with performance, and the data indicate a very good record for countries which have successfully institutionalized human rights. Human rights countries tend consistently to do better on affluence, on equality and on welfare state programmes than countries which do not respect human rights.

But how about causality? Are there any institutional effects? Do human rights institutions really contribute to the outputs and outcomes listed in Table 5.1? Here we have a very clear case of interaction between entities, but it is difficult to tell which is cause and which is effect. One could very well argue the other way around, namely that human rights is the effect and affluence the cause.

Institutional effects

What we need to do in order to vindicate the basic belief in neo-institution-alism that '(IT) Institutions matter', is to prove causality, i.e. to establish the existence of institutional effects from the implementation in a country of human rights to affluence and equality, as conceived in the Tocqueville theory about the effects of the democratic society.

Let us turn to some regression analyses concerning the level of human development, the size of the welfare state and income equality. Holding constant the factors usually considered relevant for the explanation of these outcomes, can we detect an institution effect from the operation of human rights? This effort to really establish the institutional effects of human rights takes us somewhat into unknown territory, where the task is to explain why countries vary so much in terms of socio-economic development, welfare state effort and equality. Estimates from a regression analysis estimating the impact of democracy on different outputs and outcomes are summarized in Table 5.2.

Let us comment upon the findings in Table 5.2 systematically.

Human rights and socio-economic development

To test for an institutional effect on socio-economic development we regress the level of human development (HD) upon human rights and a few other relevant factors. The standard index on human development (HDI) allows us to rank most of the countries of the world. It is basically a composite index taking into account first and foremost total economic output or the GDP, but it adds measures of other dimensions of affluence such as literacy, life expectancy and child mortality. In the 1990s the variation in the HDI is most substantial ranging from 200 for the poorest countries and close to 1,000 for the most affluent countries. Is the institutionalization of human rights an explanatory factor for the variation in the HDI in the 1980s and 1990s ?

Table 5.2 Regression analysis: democracy and level of human development, welfare state, equality and corruption: the 1990s

Independent variables		HDIN92	SOCB94	GINI90	FEMR90	CORR90
Democracy	coeff	0.059	0.252	0.469	0.029	0.050
	t-stat	11.06	0.54	0.74	0.09	0.60
Ln RGDPCH	coeff	—	5.630	−4.250	0.413	1.690
	t-stat		4.03	−1.92	0.39	6.47
Econ free	coeff	0.026	—	—	—	—
	t-stat	2.44				
Trade union density	coeff	—	0.215	—	—	—
	t-stat		4.23			
Protestants	coeff	0.000	—	0.009	0.197	0.032
	t-stat	0.10		0.19	7.11	5.42
Family system	coeff	—	—	0.541	−0.799	0.049
	t-stat			0.59	−1.81	0.46
Constant	coeff	0.187	−43.179	68.898	7.960	−10.075
	t-stat	4.08	−4.76	3.45	0.84	−4.38
rsq adj		0.67	0.68	0.20	0.46	0.75
n		92	60	56	100	75

Sources: For the dependent variables, see Table 5.1; democracy=see Table 3.3; Ln RGDPCH= see Table 3.2; econ free=Gwartney *et al.* 1996; trade union density=ILO 1997; protestants= Barrett 1982; family system=based upon information in Todd 1983.

Note: For the dependent variables, see Table 5.1; democracy=democracy score 1991–96; Ln RGDPCH=natural logarithm for real GDP per capita 1990; econ free=economic freedom index 1995; protestants=percentage protestants c. 1970; family system=classification of different types of family systems.

Since the HDI includes GDP, we would expect to find among its determinants factors that promote affluence, for instance economic institutions that allow for economic freedom. Since the HDI includes other things in addition to the GDP, such as quality of life, we expect that cultural factors play a role, for instance a religion that underlines well-being and individualism such as Protestantism.

Table 5.2 reports on a regression model predicting the variation in HDI in the 1990s by means of economic freedom, Protestantism and democracy. The major finding here is that civil and political rights remain strongly associated with human development, even when one holds constant the nature of the economic system (economic freedom) and the nature of the religion (work ethics). However, one cannot conclude that human rights is the cause and level of human development the effect, as it could still be the other way around.

Tocqueville argued that in a democratic period people will be almost exclusively occupied with promoting their material interests. Thus, liberty and formal equality would promote economic growth. This is actually one of the Tocqueville predictions about democratic outcomes that receives substantial empirical support when one moves from surface correlations to deep structure causality.

Does one dare to suggest on the basis of this finding that if only more countries in the world institutionalized human rights completely, then the world would also reach a higher level of socio-economic development ? It is often argued in relation to Third World countries that poverty can only be counteracted successfully on a long-term basis if human rights are respected by their government. Although rights cannot produce economic output in the short-run, it can certainly do so in the long-run.

Human rights and the welfare state

There is a huge literature discussing the determinants of welfare state effort, which varies considerably today among the countries of the world. Some countries are full-scale welfare states with massive social expenditures – allocative and redistributive expenditures – whereas several countries provide little state-guaranteed welfare, trusting markets or simply refraining from doing much in the social sphere. Why this variation in terms of welfare effort, which is measured by means of public expenditures as a percentage of GDP (Castles 1998)?

Theory claims that there are two main determinants, economic resources and the strength of the left in politics and society. An affluent society would make a welfare state possible (Wagner's Law), but the strength of the left in government or society makes the welfare state a reality, whereas the strength of the right makes welfare less likely. Let us test a model predicting social expenditures from the GDP (Wilenksy's factor), the length of time of the right in government (Castles' factor) or the strength of the position of the left in society (Schmidt's factor) and finally democracy. The major finding in Table 5.2 with respect to the impact on social expenditures is that both the Wagner–Wilensky hypothesis and the Schmidt hypothesis receive support. However, the Tocqueville factor – human rights – becomes insignificant when one includes both resources (affluence) and political will (trade union density) in the regression equation. The implication is that the welfare state is less dependent upon institutions and more a reflection of economic resources, especially when these can be commanded by the left, either through government power or through the influence of the trade unions.

Human rights and equality

In a democratic society, formal equality or equality under the laws requires government based upon one man(woman) one vote. Thus, civil and political rights open up the possibility of electing governments that aim to correct the inequalities in society by enhancing real equality. For Tocqueville, the search for equality would be one of the most dominant tendencies in the democratic era.

We approach real equality from two angles: income equality measured as income distributions and gender equality measured as female representation in parliament. Both dimensions of equality vary considerably among countries, but they are not the same phenomenon. Does democracy reduce both kinds of inequalities? If so, then it would have to be added to other factors, mainly economic ones such as affluence or cultural ones such as a Protestant religion or an individualist family system.

Table 5.2 also contains estimates of a model predicting income inequalities and female representation in parliament from affluence (GDP per capita), democracy, Protestantism and the family system. It is often argued that there exists a Kuznets' curve, meaning that income inequalities even out as countries grow richer. Besides, there is the cultural theory which links inegalitarian outcomes with collectivist attitudes or cultures. The findings in Table 5.2 indicate that human rights, or democracy, have little impact upon equality. Income inequalities seem to depend more upon richness, whilst gender equality is definitively associated with Protestantism, the religion that most underlines individualism for both men and women.

Human rights and corruption

Corruption is also a societal malaise which is assumed to be associated with non-democracies, or at least non-Western societies. Table 5.2, also displays estimates from a regression estimating the impact of democracy on corruption. In this case we may note that there is no effect of democracy on the level of corruption when we are controlling for affluence (Ln RGDPCH) and the effect of Western influences in the form of Protestantism.

Conclusion

When considering democracy in general and its impact on outputs and outcomes, we find that democratic countries display a performance profile that is much more attractive than the performance profile of non-democracies. Where there is democracy, there also tends to be a decent level of human development, a welfare ambition in terms of public expenditures and, finally, only modest inequalities. However, it is more difficult to argue that the performance profile of democracy reflects the occurrence of institutional effects. Comparing findings with the Dahl analysis of the conditions for democratic stability, we note a striking parallelism. What we have considered as outputs and outcomes of democracy are looked upon as conditions for democratic longevity in his analysis.

However, in the literature on empirical democratic theory one encounters a much stronger claim, namely that different kinds of democratic regimes have different performance profiles in terms of outputs and outcomes. Moreover, it is stated that special democratic institutions bring about special outcomes. We will examine these claims in the next chapter in relation to a variety of particular democratic institutions.

Theorizing the impact of democratic institutions may be done in two ways. Either one focuses upon the *genus proximum* of democracy, or the institutions that are always present in any democratic regime. Or one brings up the question of the *differentia specifica*, or the different types of democratic regimes around the world. Perhaps the most discussed model of democratic effects is Lijphart's which considers the differential consequences of the operation of Westminster democracy and Consensus democracy. Before we evaluate this *differentia specifica* model, having discussed the *genus proximum* one, we must consider whether any type of democratic regime brings about a difference for outputs or outcomes (it does not matter whether it is one kind or another)? The *genus proximum* model of institutional effects is concerned with the distinction between democracy and non-democracy and what this institutional separation may bring about for outputs and outcomes. The *differentia specifica* models claim that alternative democratic institutions matter. We will analyse such models through the perspectives of Montesquieu ([1748] 1989) and Lijphart (1999).

Part II

The Montesquieu system

We wish to state that the analysis of political institutions that Montesquieu set forth in 1748 remains the best framework for comparative institutional analysis. But it has to be complemented by the search for institutional effects. Montesquieu's *trias politica* distinctions framed constitutions in all countries adhering to the Rule of Law. Thus, Montesquieu is one the sources of the presidential regimes but he is also very much present in the parliamentary regimes, especially in those countries where constitutional monarchies preceded democracy.

Montesquieu inspired presidentialism in the American constitution of 1787 but he also framed the first constitutional institutions in France, viz. the 1791 Constitution. These model institutions were copied in one country after another, where presidentialism spread from the United States to Latin America and the rest of the world outside of Europe. In Europe, constitutionalism became linked up with the constitutional monarchy, which later developed into a parliamentary regime. Presidentialism, parliamentarism and the constitutional monarchy cannot be understood without knowledge about the institutionalist from Bordeaux.

We will base our search for institutional effects on the *trias politica* system. Thus, we devote one chapter each to the three competences of the state. However, we will not repeat Montesquieu's message, but take a comparative institutional approach. If it is the case that the executive, the legislative and the judicial powers can be structured differently, does it matter for policy outputs and outcomes? This is our key question, as we set out to map how the Montesquieu powers vary institutionally. Let us start with the alternative institutions of the executive where parliamentarism entails a rejection of the Montesquieu theory of the virtues of the separation of powers.

6 Presidential or parliamentary executives

Linz

Introduction

Presidentialism is a theory about the executive, focusing in particular on the relationship between the executive and the legislature. Basically, in presidential systems the head of state – the president – wields real power, and does not only possess a symbolic function. Presidents may exercise various powers or prerogatives, by themselves or together with other offices and organizations. It is necessary to pay attention to the variation in presidential executives, as, for instance, European presidentialism is very different from the American brand which tends to be the type of presidentialism found outside of Europe (Lijphart 1992; Mainwaring 1993; Stepan and Skatch 1993; Moe and Caldwell 1994; Döring 1997; Riggs 1997).

Drawing mainly upon the experiences of Latin America in the twentieth century, J. Linz argues that the only case of successful presidentialism is the USA. In Latin America, as well as in Africa and Asia, presidentialism has not worked well. What is the evidence for such a general rejection of this set of institutions for the executive? If there is a bad performance record among the presidential systems, can one then also be sure that it is the executive and not something else, such as poverty, that makes the difference? In other words: we ask whether an institutional effect can be detected in the operation of presidential regimes. Where and how is presidentialism practised?

Below we discuss the nature of presidentialism and after that we test the model that parliamentarism does better than presidentialism in terms of promoting desirable outcomes. Along this route we also find space to make a few distinctions between various kinds of parliamentarism. To clarify both presidentialism and parliamentarism we must talk about premiers and their role in both presidential and non-presidential systems. Finally, one must state explicitly which outcomes one is referring to, state stability or aspects of performance.

The executive: heads of state and premiers

Linz takes a very firm institutionalist position concerning presidentialism versus parliamentarism, claiming that: 'the institutional characteristics to which we have referred directly or indirectly shape the whole political process and the way of ruling' (Linz 1994: 18). This is in one sense obviously true, if one looks at the way government operates – a presidential regime is not a parliamentary regime. But the key question is whether it also matters for outcomes, i.e. whether the way government operates impacts upon state stability and state performance.

The basic logic of structuring the executive is the following: presidents are always heads of state when the office of the president exists in a country. Premiers are always the head of government when the office of the prime minister exists. In addition, presidents may be the head of government, in which case there is strong presidentialism. When presidents are not heads of government, then there exists a prime minister. If there is no president when there is a prime minister, then there is usually a king or queen, i.e. we have a monarchy. If there is both a president and a premier, then we face either weak presidentialism or cohabitation in the form of power-sharing or a power struggle between the two offices.

Typically, the present kingdoms of the world are more ceremonial than real. In only a few countries are there heads of state that are true monarchs, i.e. a king, queen or an emir, recruited hereditarily or by election. Ceremonial monarchies employ the office of the premier, meaning that they practise parliamentarism. True monarchies may also use the premier, but then parliamentarism is not strongly institutionalized. Besides monarchies and presidential heads of state, there seem to exist few alternative arrangements concerning the head of state. Political systems where much of the real executive power is vested elsewhere employ either monarchs or presidents, such as the few still existing communist systems and the religious regime in Iran. Even military juntas may put up a president as the head of state, although the military actually rules.

When the premier is the head of government, he/she may face a powerful president meaning that executive competences are shared (Duverger 1980; see also Elgie 1997, 1998; Bahro *et al.* 1998). In European presidentialism this is always the case (including Russia), whereas outside of Europe pure presidentialism is the usual procedure where the president exercises all the prerogatives of the executive, although we also find premiers in some such countries. Thus, one may classify the presidential regimes into three types: (1) pure presidentialism; (2) semi-presidentialism; and (3) weak presidentialism. Since the set of semi-presidential and weak presidential regimes is the same as the set of parliamentary regimes, we may say that only real monarchies and military juntas fall outside of the set of presidential regimes.

One may wish to mention a few strikingly odd cases when it comes to structuring the executive. First, there is collective presidentialism or the directorate model used during the French Revolution (1795–99) and the collegiado in Uruguay (1918–33, 1952–67), where the presidential office circulates every year among the members of government. Today, only Switzerland employs collective presidentialism. Second, there is the new South African constitution which provides for strong presidentialism even though the president is elected by parliament and is accountable to parliament on a political basis. This president is thus the head of state and the head of government, some executive decisions being taken as presidential prerogatives whilst others belong to the cabinet. The president of the Republic of South Africa is both a US head of state and an English premier. Third, one may point out the special features of the Israeli prime minister, who is elected in direct election but is politically accountable to parliament at the same time as parliament elects the president of the country.

The general pattern is that premiers are appointed by parliament whereas presidents are elected in direct popular elections and are able to exercise real executive powers (Blais *et al.* 1997). Weak presidents may be elected by parliament. However, there are deviations from this general pattern, as a strong president may be elected by parliament and a weak president directly by the people. Perhaps one is witnessing a break-up of the general pattern, as premiers could in the future be elected directly. Besides parliamentary and presidential executives, one may wish to identify executives that deviate from parliamentarism or presidentialism, viz. the real kingdoms, the military junta and the communist executive.

On the surface, according to the written constitution, a communist executive may have the appearance of some blend between parliamentarism and presidentialism in the form of a dual executive. But in reality there is the principle of parallelism, according to which actual power is vested in the shadow structure of decision-making bodies of the communist party and its officers.

Executive institutions

To understand the variety of ways in which an executive may be structured institutionally, one may survey the formal side of the executive by looking at constitutional articles. As things now stand, we have a number of pure presidential constitutions, i.e. constitutions where the president does not share power with any premier, meaning that he/she has complete executive responsibility. Here, we have the American constitution from 1787 as well as numerous present-day constitutions in Latin America, Africa and Asia.

Comparing the oldest presidential constitution of the world – the constitution of the United States of America – with the more recent presidential constitutions in Third World countries, one notes one striking difference. We are referring to the vast scope of the prerogatives of the president in Third World presidential constitutions.

Let us take the example of the Brazilian constitution of 1988. The president is vested with all the executive powers, which constitute a list that is truly extensive and which touches in a not insignificant manner upon legislative and judicial competencies. Thus, the president may: (a) appoint and dismiss ministers; (b) initiate and approve legislation; (c) veto bills wholly or partially; (d) decree a state of defence or a state of siege; (e) decree and enforce federal intervention; (f) grant pardons and commute sentences; (g) exercise supreme command over the armed forces; and (h) appoint, after approval of the federal senate, the ministers of the supreme federal tribunal. The checks and balances in the US constitution are missing here.

One may contrast these constitutional articles with those of weak presidentialism. In countries which harbour weak presidentialism one certainly finds the president mentioned in the articles of the constitution, but the office of the premier takes precedence over the office of the president, confining the latter to matters strictly in relation to the head of state, i.e. ceremonial tasks.

The constitution of Estonia from 1992 may serve as an example of the clear-cut institutionalization of a 'premier' system of executive powers. The president of Estonia is only the head of state and does not enter the government. His first duty is representing the republic. The competences of the president include either doing things on the proposal of other bodies, or himself/herself proposing things to other bodies. Who makes decisions in the executive branch of government is crystal clear:

> Art 86: Executive power shall rest with the Government of the Republic.
>
> Art 93: The Prime Minister shall represent the Government of the Republic and shall direct its work.

Now is the time to also consider the parliamentary constitutions which have monarchical heads of state. Here we find mainly countries in Western Europe. In so far as the constitution explicitly introduces parliamentarism, which is not always the case, it identifies the office of the prime minister as the head of government and the leader of the cabinet.

The rules for investiture, censure and dissolution of parliament focus upon head of government, i.e. the premier, and not the head of state, i.e. the monarch.

Yet, surprisingly, one may find many royal competences in the written constitutions of West European countries with a king or queen as head of state. Evidently, there is a hiatus between formal wording and real practice. Take, for instance, the case of the Dutch constitution in its 1983 wording, where we read the following:

> Art 42: (1) The Government shall comprise the King and the Ministers. The Ministers, and not the King, shall be responsible for acts of government.

This is the old legal construction, employed when constitutional monarchies were introduced in the nineteenth century before the advent of the democratic regime. What is at stake is juridical responsibility, not political responsibility in the form of parliamentarism. Royal decrees can only become valid if they are signed by the monarch and by one or more ministers or state secretaries – the counter signature that is meant to place the juridical responsibility with the minister and not the monarch, because the former can be removed from office but not the latter, if a decree is legally incorrect.

The Dutch constitution states expressly:

> Art 43:   The Prime Minister and the other Ministers shall be appointed and dismissed by Royal Decree.

There is no article which states that the ministers must have the political confidence of the Dutch parliament, the States General. According to constitutional practice, the monarch cannot exercise this power in confrontation with the will of the States General.

What creates difficulties when analysing the structure of the executive is that the division of competences between the premier and the president is not always clear-cut, which means that the distinction between weak presidentialism and strong presidentialism with a premier is also far from clear. Let us exemplify from the semi-presidentialism of the Portuguese constitution according to its wording from 1992.

The executive competences in Portugal are shared between the president and the government, led by a premier in a most complicated manner. The president appoints and dismisses the ministers, including the premier. He/she may dissolve the National Assembly, call a referendum, declare a state of emergency, give pardons, act as supreme commander of the armed forces, exercise leadership over the administration at both national and regional levels, including appointing diplomats. However, the president has to share almost all of these competencies with the government, or, when it comes to legislation, with the National Assembly. Thus, the president has only suspensive veto against bills, and several of his/her decisions must be countersigned by the ministers or ratified by the National Assembly. The president is not part of the government, whose leader, the premier, must be acceptable to the National Assembly.

The muddy waters on the borderline between parliamentarism and presidentialism become even more difficult to penetrate when one takes constitutional practice into account. In several countries the constitution states in a transparent manner that the prime minister is the head of government or the cabinet, and that the president as head of state exercises presidential prerogatives. In reality, executive powers will float between the president and the premier depending upon personalities, parties and the overall situation of the country.

Thus, examining the constitutional articles is only a very rough way to describe how executives work in relation to legislatures and judiciaries. What matters most is constitutional practice, which may deviate from constitutional theory in not only Third World countries but also in constitutional democracies. In, for example, Romania, Bulgaria and Hungary the constitutions indicate clearly a parliamentary executive, but constitutional practice has thus far been much more turbulent, as the presidents in these countries claim more than the ceremonial powers of a weak president (Baylis 1996; Frye 1997; Taras 1997). Which executive powers belong to the president and which ones to the prime minister? European presidentialism is seldom clear-cut, dividing executive functions neatly between the head of state and the leader of the cabinet, as one can observe in Finland, Portugal, Poland and Lithuania.

Here we will not deal much with real monarchical regimes, even if they have modern constitutions containing an office of premier. The question is whether presidentialism or parliamentarism has better outcomes, and this does not require us to discuss quasi-parliamentary systems where the head of state is a monarch, such as in Morocco, Jordan or Thailand. In these real monarchies the amount of constitutionalism laid down in the written constitution tends to be considerably circumscribed by monarchical prerogatives.

Thus, in the constitution of the Hashemite Kingdom of Jordan from 1984 it is stated in an Occidental manner that:

> Art 24: (i) The nation is the source of all powers.
> (ii) The nation shall exercise its powers in the manner prescribed by this Constitution.

However, it is then stated that the king or the 'throne of the Hashemite Kingdom', 'limited by inheritance to the dynasty of king Abdullah ibn Al-Hussein' is to be involved in the exercise of all three branches of state powers:

> Art 25: The Legislative Power shall be vested in the National Assembly and the King.
> Art 26: The Executive Power shall be vested in the King who shall exercise His powers through his Ministers. . .
> Art 27: The Judicial Power shall be exercised by the different courts of law, and all judgements shall be given in accordance with the law and pronounced in the name of the King.

When these provisions are made more concrete in the constitutional articles that follow, then the royal power position is even more underlined. The king appoints his ministers himself, he may dissolve both chambers of parliament and he may declare war, conclude peace and confirm treaties single-handedly. As if these competences were not enough, the king appoints the judges of the civil and sharia courts (Art 98) and he also appoints members of the senate.

In Europe, strong presidentialism always takes the form of cohabitation between a president and a prime minister. Outside of Europe, presidentialism tends towards the pure presidentialism, or the institution where almost all executive powers are vested in one office, viz. that of the president. But outside of Europe there are also countries which practice cohabitation, such as Turkey and Pakistan, as well as countries which adhere to weak presidentialism or symbolic presidentialism, for instance India.

One has discussed at great length whether semi-presidentialism is a new kind of regime, or if it is merely presidentialism and parliamentarism, each practised half of the time, as it were. The decisive thing is whether there is cohabitation or not. When the president and the premier belongs to the same party, then we have presidentialism, but when there is cohabitation we would have parliamentarism. Linz argues that his critique of presidentialism applies equally to the semi-presidential regimes, meaning that they are also conducive to political instability. Is this really true?

M.S. Shugart and J.M. Carey employ a detailed classification of executive functions as well as decision-making capacities in order to map how presidents may exercise executive powers. In *Presidents and Assemblies* (1992), they focus upon how presidential prerogatives are listed and defined in relation to mainly the legislature, including the power of the president to appoint and dismiss a premier, if indeed there is such an office. Presidential prerogatives also include legislative and budgetary/financial functions, where presidents may possess certain rights to act on his/her own or have been entrusted with various forms of veto power in relation to the national assembly. One special kind of presidential prerogative is the capacity to declare a state of emergency under certain conditions.

Shugart and Carey examine presidentialism in some thirty-five countries where the president is elected in direct popular election, which is a condition for strong presidentialism, ranking countries in accordance with the extent of presidential powers (1992: 155). The overall finding is that European presidentialism scores much lower than non-European presidentialism, especially since countries with weak presidentialism are included. However, whereas the average score for presidential power is around 12 in Latin America, France is only given 4 and Portugal 6, while, somewhat astonishingly, Finland and Iceland are ranked at 8.

Let us now try to map the occurrence of presidentialism around the world after the Second World War. One needs to separate the presidential executives from the parliamentary systems, on the one hand, and to draw the distinction between presidential regimes and some types of executives that are not parliamentary, on the other hand.

Mapping presidentialism

In order to map the occurrence of presidentialism around the world, we will resort to an attempt to classify countries in terms of various kinds of executives in Derbyshire and Derbyshire (1989, 1991, 1996). They employ a few distinctions that come close to the discussion above: first, a separation between limited and unlimited presidentialism; second, a separation between mixed executives and a strictly parliamentary executive; third, a separation between communist, military and absolutist executives.

Table 6.1 has the occurrence of the three types of presidentialism in various parts of the world in the 19980s and the 1990s.

Table 6.1 Classification of regimes: around 1989 and 1995

	OECD		Latin Am		Africa		Asia		Post-com		Total	
	1989	1995	1989	1995	1989	1995	1989	1995	1989	1995	1989	1995
Parliamentary	18	19	2	2	1	2	7	9	—	4	28	36
Mixed	3	3	—	1	—	1	—	3	—	4	3	12
Limited presid	3	2	18	18	11	25	7	5	6	13	45	63
Unlimited presid	—	—	—	—	19	10	4	5	2	—	23	21
Communist	—	—	1	1	—	—	5	4	2	—	8	5
Military	—	—	1	—	11	5	1	1	—	—	13	6
Absolutist	—	—	—	—	1	—	7	6	—	—	8	6

Sources: Derbyshire and Derbyshire 1989, 1991, 1996.

As Table 6.1 shows, the sheer number of presidential regimes is no doubt very large. Out of the 149 classified countries included in the overview for the 1990s, no less than 96 countries have some type of real presidential executive. During the 1980s, 71 out of a total of 128 countries included in this overview had a presidential executive. According to this classification, most presidential executives are of either the limited or constitutional type or the unlimited or non-constitutional type.

We note, though, that the number of mixed executives has risen from the 1980s to the 1990s; mixed meaning dual or that there is a president as head of state and a premier as the leader of the government, where the two share executive competencies. Here we find the increasing attraction of European presidentialism, which is always of the dual type, as exemplified in the adoption of the mixed executive in countries such as Portugal, Russia, Lithuania and Romania. It should be pointed out that the dual executive may result less from explicit constitution-making than from the unintended outcome of a power struggle between the president, on the one side, and the premier/parliament on the other side, as in Poland, Hungary and Bulgaria, for example.

Thus, the form of presidentialism which one tends to place in-between presidentialism and parliamentarism, called semi-presidentialism or quasi-parliamentarism, has received increasing attention in constitution-making in the last decade. Linz calls it 'bipolar system', because it involves a double executive, dividing real executive powers between the president and a premier. Such systems are seem to attract increasing attention in countries switching from authoritarian rule to democracy, mainly in Eastern Europe. One could say Finland is the country which first practised this mixed type of executive, which was introduced in its 1919 constitution, modelled partly on the Swedish 1772 Royal constitution. But France has definitely served as a model with its 1958 Gaullist constitution, to which Portugal also come close.

Taking into account that the number of countries included in the survey for the 1990s is larger than those covered in the survey for the 1980s, we may still assert that the number of presidential regimes has increased during the last decade, reflecting the decrease in other kinds of executives, chiefly the communist, the military and the absolutist types. At the same time, the number of parliamentary regimes has increased, meaning that one faces a clear choice between parliamentarism and presidentialism, when structuring the executive.

In the 1990s, limited presidentialism occurs in sixty-three countries, whereas unlimited presidentialism is to be found in twenty-one countries. The occurrence of limited and unlimited presidentialism shows a very clear geographical pattern, as it is a Third World phenomenon to a considerable extent. Presidentialism dominates in Latin America, Africa and in the post-communist countries and is frequently found in Asia. The practice of parliamentarism dominates among the OECD countries, especially if one also takes the mixed or dual executive into account. Outside of the OECD area there are few countries with parliamentarism or a mixed executive.

This distribution of presidentialism in the world today reflects how the diffusion of the model occurred in history. Presidentialism in Latin America was introduced in the nineteenth century whereas in Africa and Asia it followed upon the events of the late 1950s and 1960s when several colonial regimes were dismantled. Many countries in Africa and Asia started out as constitutional regimes, parliamentary or presidential, but degenerated rapidly into unconstitutional presidential regimes. Presidentialism in Latin America has hovered between the limited and unlimited version (Jones 1994).

Following Table 6.1, classifying countries as presidential depends upon the time period selected. Due to constitutional changes, a country may move quickly from one type of executive to another. Table 6.2 also displays classifications of the occurrence of presidentialism where one observes rather extensive changes in the executive institutions.

Table 6.2 Presidentialism 1970, 1984 and 1995

	Presidentialism				*Non-presidentialism*				*n*	*First factor*
	1970	1984	1995		1970	1984	1995			
OECD	3	2	2	(2)	21	22	22	(21)	24	96.1
Latin America	18	20	19	(17)	4	2	3	(2)		
Africa	29	29	20	(10)	11	13	22	(4)		
Asia	4	3	7	(1)	26	31	27	(21)		
Post-com	0	2	2	(0)	8	6	25	(5)		
Total	54	56	50	(30)	70	76	99	(53)	119	66.1

Sources: Blondel 1969; Europa Yearbook 1985; Encyclopaedia Britannica 1996.

Notes: Within parentheses we have identified the countries which have one and the same executive during all three decades; see also Appendix 6.1 and 6.2. First factor stands for the amount of explained variation in a factor analysis based on data for three time periods; the greater the explained variation, the greater the stability over time.

Interestingly, this alternative classification of the structure of the executive agrees with the Derbyshire and Derbyshire classification in the distribution of presidential regimes over space, but it counts far less countries as presidential. Why is this so, one may ask. The divergences between Table 6.1 and Table 6.2 stem from three circumstances.

First, the mixed executives in Table 6.1 have been classified as non-presidential regimes in Table 6.2 because it only counts those regimes as presidential where one and the same person is the head of state and at the same time the leader of the government or cabinet. Thus, there is no need for the dual executive category. Second, some of the countries that are listed as limited presidentialism in Table 6.1 have been listed as non-presidential regimes in Table 6.2 because these regimes have both a president and a premier. Finally, there is also real disagreement about how to classify certain countries. Just as the borderline between limited presidentialism and parliamentarism may be a fine one, so the distinction between unlimited presidentialism and other types of executives such as the communist type, the military junta type and the absolutist type is far from clear. Thus, how does one classify countries which are placed in-between presidentialism and military rule?

Due to the fact that the number of countries with dual executives has increased from 1989 to 1996, Table 6.2 will contain in its non-presidential category numerous quasi-presidential regimes. Dual executive countries tend to belong to the set of constitutional presidential regimes, as the sharing of executive powers between the president and a premier would be difficult without institutional restrictions which limit opportunistic behaviour. When one asks the critical question whether presidentialism is conducive to bad outcomes, then one must take care to spell out what is included in the set of presidential regimes. Now, what is a parliamentary regime?

Mapping parliamentarism

The classical model of parliamentarism stems from British practice as it evolved during the eighteenth and nineteenth centuries, carried by the great premiers and only formalized in conventions. However, the constitutional recognition of parliamentarism in many European countries deviates considerably from British practice, which provides the prime minister with all the prerogatives of parliamentarism, including the formation of the cabinet, the dissolution of the cabinet and the posing of the question of confidence in government. The right to censure the cabinet belongs to parliament as its right to express non-confidence at any time, either against individual ministers or the entire cabinet.

In British unwritten parliamentarism there rests with parliament only the power to express a vote of non-confidence towards the government. In Continental European parliamentarism the rules guiding investiture, the decision to dissolve and the posing of the question of confidence vary considerably, as the president or the parliament may also be involved in these decisions (de Winter 1995). Yet, one also speaks of strong premier parliamentarism in Continental Europe in the form of Kanzlersdemokratie. The basic alternative is committee parliamentarism, where the main power resides in the committees of parliament – *regime d'assemble.*

Actually, British parliamentarism is not only special due to the strong prerogatives of the premier. Equally important is that the parliament is weak in relation to the premier when there is a single party government with majority support, as there is no formal separation between the cabinet and the parliament, cabinet members always sitting in parliament and serving on its committees. In English constitutional practice the cabinet is just the first executive committee of parliament whereas in Continental European parliamentarism the government is formally separated from parliament, cabinet members not serving at the same time as members of parliament (Döring 1995).

In parliamentary practice in Europe one seldom sees the power concentration on the premier that is typical of English parliamentarism – 'minister caesarism'. Perhaps 'Kanzlersdemokratie' comes close to the British version. But what needs to be emphasized is that one often finds an altogether different kind of parliamentarism in Continental Europe, where the power of parliament is much larger. In countries where cabinets do not have majority support, the country tends to be ruled from the different committees of parliament – committee parliamentarism. One may refer here to the experiences of the French Fourth Republic, Italian parliamentarism and Scandinavian practice.

What is the occurrence of parliamentarism around the world? Table 6.3 maps the existence of the institutions of parliamentarism around 1990. One should note that many African states started out as parliamentary regimes when becoming independent, but soon turned towards presidentialism. There are parliamentary regimes outside of Europe, but only in Europe do they prevail over presidentialism.

Table 6.3 Parliamentary regimes around 1990 and 1995 including mixed executives

	1989	1995
Western Europe	17	17
Eastern Europe	0	9
North America	1	1
Central America	2	3
Southern America	0	0
Northern Africa	1	3
Sub-Saharan Africa	1	2
Middle East	4	6
Extreme Orient	2	4
Oceania	3	3

Source: Derbyshire and Derbyshire 1989, 1991, 1996.

Parliamentarism is widely used in Europe and outside Europe in countries with a legacy of British colonial rule, i.e. India, Australia, New Zealand and Canada. However, there is also parliamentarism in Japan. Actually, one could find elements of parliamentarism in countries such as Sri Lanka, Iran (1906 constitution), Thailand and Morocco, but it is an open question as to whether parliamentarism in these regimes was really practised for any length of time.

Virtues of parliamentarism

Now, what are the theoretical reasons for claiming that parliamentarism, when fully implemented, is superior to presidentialism? What performance or outcomes are involved in this argument in favour of parliamentarism?

One of the advantages of parliamentarism is that it implements the Montesquieu separation of powers, although only halfway (Linz 1990b). Parliamentarism separates the judiciary from both the executive and the legislature, but it makes the executive dependent upon the legislature by a very special mechanism of trust between parliament and the government. Another advantage of parliamentarism is that it emphasizes the role of the legislature along the lines of the doctrine of legislative supremacy. As long as parliament is elected in democractic elections, parliamentarism offers a good protection for democracy by underlining the sovereignty of the popular assembly. A final advantage of parliamentarism is that parliament tends to accept limits on its sovereignty, which derives from either a constitution that it has created or from principles of right reason or from conventions that parliament would not wish to dissociate itself from. It seems to be the case that human rights and parliamentarism go smoothly together.

Thus, parliaments seek to maintain their legislative competence in a separation of powers perspective and they claim that they have a mandate to rule from the people by being the chief representative body of the population. Parliaments tend to respect human rights, because why would Parliaments want to be unreasonable ?

Parliamentarism is the prevailing regime type in Europe, meaning that parliaments must accept the executive or at least tolerate them. The only non-parliamentary government is the Swiss cabinet, which always sits for a fixed period of four years. However, in some European countries a president holds a people's mandate to exercise certain powers in relation to the government and its leader the premier – European presidentialism.

The prerogatives of the president may relate to cabinet formation, cabinet dismissal and dissolution of assembly. In France, Finland, Portugal and Poland the president may play a very active role in both composing the government and in dissolving parliament for new elections. It may be pointed out that none of the semi-presidential systems in Europe, among which one may also count Lithuania, Romania and Croatia, goes as far as the Russian constitution in providing a major role for the president in shaping the government. Presidential prerogatives in mixed parliamentarism may also include the competence to enact regulations replacing parliamentary law and to declare a state of emergency.

In pure parliamentary systems, the representative assemblies face the premier, who may have certain competencies in relation to parliament. Actually, these prerogatives of the premier are rather similar to those of the president in countries which adhere to European presidentialism. Thus, the premier competencies focus upon his/her rights in forming the cabinet, in hindering censure of cabinet members by parliament, in dismissing cabinet members and in dissolving the assembly. The institutions of European parliamentarism include various rules for expressing a vote of non-confidence in the cabinet by parliament, for how a premier may force a vote of non-confidence and how a premier may call for new elections to parliament.

The French government possesses a large number of prerogatives in relation to parliament: (1) the block vote; (2) the mechanism of confidence declaration; (3) limited censure. The critical question under the Fifth Republic is whether it is the president or the premier who takes the lead in exercising these rights as the leader of the government. In some countries, the censure is restricted by the requirement of a positive vote of confidence in the sense that parliament may only bring down a cabinet if it can appoint a new premier, as in Germany. In other countries, the prerogatives of the premier may be limited by allowing the head of state a role in forming and dismissing governments as well as dissolving Parliament. In Norway, parliament cannot be dissolved.

Presidentialism presents a challenge to the claim of parliaments to monopolize the mandates of the people. When the president is directly elected, then he/she may receive a people's mandate to rule. There is no example of pure presidentialism in Europe, although some heads of state are directly elected. Pure presidentialism is a non-European phenomenon, but it goes back to Montesquieu's separation of powers doctrine, which presidentialism actually implements better than parliamentarism, i.e. when there is limited presidentialism. Yet, pure presidentialism, it is argued, tends towards unlimited presidentialism. Thus, the virtues of parliamentarism basically are the perils of presidentialism.

Why is presidentialism inferior?

The most convincing argument against strong presidentialism is outlined by Linz in the book chapter 'Presidential or Parliamentary Democracy: Does it make a difference?' (Linz and Valenzuela 1994; see also Linz 1990b). Strong presidentialism has two basic features, states Linz: (1) 'dual democratic legitimacy'; (2) 'rigidty' (Linz 1994: 6). The first feature refers to the fact that the people directly elects a president and a legislature, and the second feature covers the relationship between the two in so far as the legislature cannot remove a president which it does not like, as long as the president commits no constitutional wrong or legal error. Now, what could be the consequences of these two institutional features – dual popular legitimation and immobilism between the legislature and the executive? The consequence of the joint operation of the two conditions is a high risk of deadlock in the political regime.

Linz is evidently thinking about political stability. When there are two independent powers that are entrusted with democratic legitimacy, then the stability of the state is in danger, Linz seems to argue. To arrive at this conclusion Linz needs to argue two things: (1) the probability of conflict between the executive and the legislature is great all the time; (2) when both the executive and the legislature possess independent legitimation, then the conflict between the two branches of government will endanger democratic stability. Linz states:

> Since both derive their power from the vote of the people in a free competition among well-defined alternatives, a conflict is always latent and sometimes likely to erupt dramatically; there is no democratic principle to resolve it, and the mechanisms that might exist in the constitution are generally complex, highly technical, legalistic, and therefore, of doubtful democratic legitimacy for the electorate.
>
> (Linz 1994: 7)

Thus, we derive the implication that presidential systems tend towards deadlock between two of the branches of government, i.e. towards state instability. This is a test implication which can be researched empirically. Another implication of the same argument is that this deadlock tends to be resolved by extra constitutional means, meaning that presidential systems tend to deviate from the democratic constitutional state. Again, this can be tested by examining whether presidential democracies tend towards dictatorship or plebiscitary systems. Even if one can establish an empirical connection between presidential regimes and instability/authoritarianism, it is still not possible to conclude that presidentialism causes instability/authoritarianism. One must recall that many presidential regimes operate in Third World polities, where instability and lack of democracy occur frequently whatever the regime looks like.

Linz is well aware that his thesis about the negative consequences of the presidential regime has a 'ceteris paribus' clause attached to it. Thus, he acknowledges that the state with the longest record of constitutional democracy happens to be a presidential regime – the United States of America. What is extraordinary in American exceptionalism? Linz hardly presents a serious answer to this key question of why one presidential system seems to be performing so exceptionally well, when, at the same time, there is a general tendency for most presidential systems to face difficulties. This objection against Linz seems plausible as one may require that there must be a stable institutional environment for presidentialism to operate. In many Third World countries such an environment is lacking, as not even mass political parties always support democratic constitutionalism, without which presidentialism cannot work.

Linz underlines the importance of fragmentation or polarization, stating that presidentialism can work when there is homogeneity in the electorate and the flank parties are not large or extremist. This would be Linz's explanation of the success of American presidentialism. But do we not have to take into account other institutions that restrict presidential power as well, such as the judiciary and federalism? However, Linz also argues that presidentialism is conducive to a weak party system, which in turn reinforces the bad tendencies of presidentialism. But cannot political parties also be irresponsible under parliamentary regimes?

The kernel of Linz's critique of the attractiveness and relevance of presidentialism, however, is not focused upon the conditions for the application of the presidential model. It is an attack upon the core of the model, which is that the head of state is also the leader of the team having executive powers. Thus, Linz could not be more at odds with the *trias politica* model of Montesquieu. Linz states:

> The presidential office is by nature two-dimensional and in a sense ambiguous because a president is the representative of a clear political option, a partisan option, and of his constituency, sometimes in addition representing his party within the coalition that brought him to power. But the president is also the head of state.
>
> (Linz 1994: 24)

We believe this is the essence of the Linz rejection of presidentialism, which would also apply if there was no social heterogeneity or polarization. Presidentialism is bad, because its institutions mix two different roles: neutral umpire versus partial government leader.

Does presidentialism have to result in deadlock? Linz actually argues that many more of the characteristics typical of a presidential regime – high stakes, little chance of re-election, term limits – are also conducive to the very same effect, namely uncertain relations between the president and the legislature. This uncertainty may call for extra constitutional activity, for example the creation of special links between the president and the bureaucracy or the military. It is astonishing that Linz says nothing about the potential contribution of judiciaries to compensate for this uncertainty between the executive and the legislature.

In relation to Linz's general critique of presidentialism as inherently bad, one remembers the classical Montesquieu model stating a clear positive preference for the kind of regime that presidentialism expresses. Who is right: Montesquieu or Linz? Here is the place to remember the distinction between institutions that operate according to the ideal and institutions that degenerate. Linz is not only saying that presidentialism may degenerate due to the bad use of its institutions but also that the institutions of presidentialism, even when operating according to the Montesquieu model, enhance instability in government.

Could not parliamentarism result in deadlocks of the kind that Linz speaks of? Perhaps parliamentarism can also degenerate and cause political instability? One must always remember the distinction between institutional ideals and institutional realities. Institutional blueprints may look attractive in theory, but when confronted with realities, in particular the omnipresence of opportunistic behaviour, then institutions may not operate as envisaged in the ideal-type conceptions.

It is true that parliamentarism avoids dual popular legitimation as well as rigidities between the executive and the legislature, but parliamentarism also involves dangers such as governmental inefficiency or political instability. It can degenerate under the form of *regime d'assemble* into permanent governmental crisis such as under the Fourth French Republic. At times it may even be impossible to form a government on the basis of an election result, whereas presidential elections tend to score winners. Yet, the critical question is not whether strong presidentialism makes a difference, but to what outcomes it makes a difference.

To sum up: Linz has launched a forceful argument against the use of presidential institutions. He claims that they result in political instability threatening democracy, because presidentialism involves a confusion of two executive functions: head of state versus leader of the government – a distinction that Montesquieu never made. Presidentialism feeds a conflict between the executive and the legislature, when political parties dominate the latter but refuse to fully endorse the former. These two arguments are very different, the first referring to presidentialism in general whereas the latter assumes a certain kind of developed party system, where disciplined mass parties dominate the legislature. One may accept the latter argument, which favours parliamentarism, although one may reject the former, which is directed against any form of presidentialism. Linz states:

> The incompatibility between the president with considerable powers and a parliament in which a party or parties not acceptable to him are in the majority can lead to a serious impasse generating a crisis of the political system.
>
> (Linz 1994: 54)

This argument is not the same as the argument about the confusion of umpire–government leader. Suppose the president is acceptable to the major party in the legislature. He would still sit upon two chairs.

Linz states that the form of the party system is very important for how institutions operate, including the executive ones:

In my view, the development of modern political parties, in contrast to the American type of parties, particularly in socially or ideologically polarized societies, is likely to make those conflicts especially complex and threatening.

(Linz 1994: 7)

What Linz is referring to here is the emergence of mass political parties with a high degree of party discipline in parliament. Where such parties dominate politics there would arise the risk for double popular legitimacy in a presidential system.

Now, the first argument against presidentialism, concerning the fundamental role confusion, goes to the heart of the presidential regime, whereas the second argument about the conflict between the president and a major party in the legislature is *ad hoc*, depending upon the accidental results in various elections. The second argument against presidentialism involves actually a *petitio principii*, as one may question why a major party in the legislature would tend to challenge a popularly elected president within a system of power-sharing to such an extent that democracy is threatened. American presidentialism offers evidence that this confrontation between the major party in the Congress and the president may not be such a serious threat to political stability.

When we evaluate Linz systematically, we wish to separate between the general effects of presidentialism, on the one hand, and its effects when combined with a certain party system, on the other. These two ideas are really distinct, one arguing that presidentialism is bad no matter what and the other arguing that presidentialism could be bad, but it depends upon the party system.

The strength and weakness of presidentialism reflects both the ideal-type properties of this model and its tendency to degenerate when its institutions cannot be maintained properly. Much of the Linz argument against presidentialism is phrased as an attack upon the ideal-type model, but in reality it deals more with its tendency to degenerate, not least because of the ever present tendency towards opportunistic behaviour.

When one lists the pros and cons of presidentialism, then one notices that both are real, meaning that how presidentialism operates involves trade-offs. When this is the case, then it is certainly vital to examine empirical evidence in order to check which among the pros and cons tend to prevail. Linz never offers any systematic evidence for his theses that both presidentialism and semi-presidentialism are conducive to political instability. It is true that Linz examines at length the specific country experiences in Latin America with great insight into specific events and special circumstances, but one should employ a different kind of evidence, i.e. data collected systematically covering presidentialism as it occurs on all continents (Mainwaring and Shugart 1997). Perhaps one may also wish to enlarge the set of outcomes against which presidentialism is to be evaluated, including also developmental results such as socio-economic outcomes.

The performance of presidentialism

When one argues that presidentialism performs badly, or that parliament-arism has done better than presidentialism, or predicts that a parliamentary regime will be better for a country searching for new political institutions, then which are the relevant outcomes in the performance assessment? Linz focuses mainly upon political stability in a democratic context. There is no inherent reason why one could not include other outcomes as well, for instance socio-economic outcomes. Thus, it has often been argued that a strong state, for instance strong presidentialism, is needed in order to promote economic development, which a democratic regime would not necessarily enhance, especially in a Third World context.

How to measure the concept of democratic stability? This becomes a key problem in relation to the Linz argument for, when speaking of the prob-ability of a deadlock in a presidential regime, he refers to a drift towards dictatorship or maintains that democracy is not stable. However, the concept of stability is not easily handled in relation to politics, including democracy. A number of different indicators has been suggested in the literature, but they do not identify one and the same dimension. Testing the Linz argument is not a straightforward task of simply applying one standard indicator with a high degree of validity and reliability.

One may relate the concept of instability to various political aspects. First, there is the continuity of the regime, where political instability would be a predicament of regime fluctuations where the constitution is not fixed for a very long time. One may tap this aspect by measuring the length of time that has lapsed since the constitution was enacted, provided that it has been implemented fully. Second, one may look at governmental stability, which in a parliamentary regime has a straightforward measurement in the form of the average length of cabinet duration in relation to the possible score, i.e. the full election period. It is not as easy to measure executive stability in a presidential regime, but one may look at the length of time that the same president has held power in relation to what the constitution allows. Third, one may examine the occurrence of political unrest or violence in the form of political strikes, death from domestic violence etc. We suggest that one takes a broad look at the indicators that are relevant for the evaluation of presidentialism.

Dividing the set of relevant outcomes into political, social and economic ones, then which would be the critical ones in a test of the theory that presidentialism performs badly, or that parliamentarism does better than presidentialism? It seems fair to say that political outcomes are given a major role in Linz's argument. What counts is, no doubt, political stability or democratic viability, as this theory definitely claims that countries with presidential regimes tend to be different from countries with a parliamentary regime in terms of democratic longevity. How the Linz argument is to be tested is controversial, as he has been criticized for using evidence from only one subset of countries – the Latin-American countries. Such a narrow focus upon one subset could be one-sided, because these countries could be unstable politically for reasons other than their employment of presidential institutions (Horowiz 1992).

Among the political outcomes of alternative institutional arrangements one would first want to emphasize the character of the regime, i.e. whether it tends towards democracy or not. The regime may hover between dictatorship and democracy – this is one aspect of political instability. Or it may be stable but undemocratic. Thus, it is essential to test for democracy. The socio-economic performance of presidential regimes may be evaluated by examining their records on affluence, economic growth, level of human development, income inequality and gender equality.

What is the overall evaluation assessment of the presidential regimes? We first compare them with non-presidential regimes of whatever kind they may be and then with only parliamentary regimes, excluding completely traditional regimes as well as military juntas and communist regimes.

Presidential–non-presidential regimes

If presidentialism matters in a negative way for outcomes, then is a presidential regime a necessary or sufficient condition for a bad performance record? If the thesis is that presidentialism is a necessary condition for bad outcomes, then we would expect to find only bad outcomes among what we have identified as the stable set of presidential regimes. The countries in this set are listed in Appendix 6.1.

This set is extremely heterogeneous, containing not only a number of countries with profound problems politically and economically but also a few extremely successful countries, if standard evaluation criteria are employed. Since the United States, Switzerland, Costa Rica and Botswana are in the set, we may conclude that presidentialism is not a sufficient condition for a bad performance record, but it could still be a necessary condition. This would require that all or most of the stable non-presidential countries do well on the evaluation criteria. Appendix 6.2 contains these countries.

Also, this set is very heterogeneous, covering not only parliamentary and mixed executives but also communist, military and absolutist executives, as in Vietnam, Libya and Saudi Arabia. One would not expect to find that the performance record of these countries is uniformly superior to that of the countries in Appendix 6.1. Table 6.4 has the comparison.

Here, we have hardly any corroboration of the theory that presidentialism performs much worse than non-presidentialism. As the set of non-presidential regimes includes not only parliamentary regimes and mixed

executives but also regimes with a military, communist or absolutist executive, we see that presidential regimes only do very slightly worse on the
evaluation criteria than non-presidential regimes.

Examining socio-economic outcomes in Table 6.5, we find, though,
stronger evidence for the argument that presidentialism tends to display
more negative outcomes than non-presidentialism.

The finding in Table 6.5 is that affluence and human development tend to
be lower in the presidential set, despite the inclusion of the United States
and Switzerland in that set, than in the non-presidential set. Also, the
inequality of the income distribution is worse in the presidential set, as is the
low rate of female representation in parliaments.

On the whole, there is not enough empirical support for the hypothesis
that presidentialism constitutes a necessary condition for a bad performance
profile, at least when only political performance is taken into account.
However, the proper comparison may be to restrict the comparative institutional analysis to only stable presidential systems and stable parliamentary

Table 6.4 Correlations: presidentialism versus non-presidentialism: political
outcomes

		DEMO	*VIOL*	*PROT*	*EXEC*	*DISP*	*VOTE*	*PART*	*COYR*
Pres70	r	−0.18	0.07	−0.04	−0.10	−0.09	0.02	−0.12	−0.01
	p	0.054	0.273	0.366	0.198	0.326	0.464	0.193	0.450
Pres84	r	−0.13	0.14	−0.08	0.11	−0.18	−0.28	−0.02	−0.01
	p	0.124	0.102	0.233	0.156	0.141	0.045	0.445	0.472
Pres95	r	−0.14	0.30	0.11	−0.07	−0.23	−0.13	0.01	−0.07
	p	0.098	0.003	0.156	0.277	0.075	0.212	0.468	0.281

Sources: Presidentialism=see Table 6.2 (presidentialism=1, non-presidentialism=0); DEMO,
VIOL, PROT, EXEC, PART COYR: see Table 3.3; VOTE=see Table 9.5; DISP=see Table 9.2.

Note: DEMO=democracy scores; VIOL=violence scores; PROT=protest scores; EXEC=
executive change; DISP=party system disproportionality; VOTE=effective number of parties;
PART=party system fractionalization; COYR=number of years of present constitution. Only
stable regimes have been included; see Table 6.2.

Table 6.5 Correlations: presidentialism and non-presidentialism: socio-economic
outcomes

		ECGR	*RGDPCH*	*HDI*	*GINI*	*FEMR*
Pres70	r	−0.30	−0.37	−0.39	0.57	−0.19
	p	0.005	0.001	0.000	0.000	0.050
Pres84	r	−0.40	−0.44	−0.38	0.63	−0.30
	p	0.000	0.000	0.001	0.000	0.006
Pres95	r	−0.05	−0.49	−0.37	0.71	−0.18
	p	0.345	0.000	0.001	0.000	0.059

Note: ECGR=economic growth; RGDPCH=real GDP per capita; HDI=human development
index; GINI=gini index; FEMR=female parliamentary representation. Only stable regimes
have been included; see Table 6.2.

systems, omitting entirely all other kinds of executives such as real monarchies, military dictatorships and communist executives.

Presidential–parliamentary regimes

Let us proceed to examine Table 6.6 where we use the Derbyshire and Derbyshire classification of executive institutions, deleting the countries that have executives other than presidential, mixed or parliamentary. One would expect a stronger confirmation in Table 6.6.

The Linz argument receives support from Table 6.6, as the correlation between presidentialism and democracy is negative and fairly strong. We also note that presidential regimes tend to be slightly more unstable than parliamentary regimes. Finally, presidential regimes operate within party systems that are less fractionalized than the party systems of parliamentary regimes. Presidential elections are basically majoritarian, but this fact does not imply that the party system must tend towards a two-party system, as parliamentary elections could produce a party system with a higher effective number of parties than two.

How about performance based upon social and economic criteria of evaluation? Table 6.7 indicates clearly a more negative performance profile for presidential regimes.

Perhaps one would even wish to say, given the findings in Table 6.6, that presidentialism has an even worse performance profile in terms of socio-economic criteria than in terms of political ones. Poverty and a low level of human development tend to characterize presidential regimes and the inequalities are more pronounced, on average.

Table 6.6 Correlations: presidentialism versus parliamentarism: political outcomes

		DEMO	VIOL	PROT	EXEC	DISP	VOTE	PART	COYR
Presid 1990s	r	−0.54	0.13	0.02	−0.26	−0.19	−0.10	−0.31	−0.30
	p	0.000	0.065	0.416	0.001	0.109	0.258	0.000	0.000

Sources: See Table 6.4.

Note: See Table 6.4; presidentialism here according to Derbyshire and Derbyshire 1996. Three groups: (1) Parliamentary; (2) Mixed; (3) Presidential.

Table 6.7 Correlations: presidentialism versus parliamentarism: social and economic outcomes

		ECGR	RGDPCH	HDI	GINI	FEMR
Presid 1990s	r	−0.29	−0.59	−0.50	0.50	−0.31
	p	0.001	0.000	0.000	0.000	0.000

Sources: See Table 6.5.

Note: see Table 6.5; presidentialism according to Derbyshire and Derbyshire 1996. Three groups: (1) Parliamentary; (2) Mixed; (3) Presidential.

Thus, one may establish that presidential regimes face worse outcomes than the other two kinds of regimes, the strictly parliamentary ones and the dual executives. But one cannot draw the conclusion that the institutions of the executive are decisive here, because there could be other factors at work in countries which practice the presidential executive. One needs to use regression analysis in order to make causal inductions.

Suppose one encounters a country 'A' which is not democratically stable and which adheres to a strict presidential type of executive and not a parliamentary one. Can one then make the counterfactual statements on the basis of the evidence shown above, namely if A were not a presidential regime, then A would be a stable democracy? Such a statement is hardly supported by the evidence concerning presidentialism versus non-presidentialism, because A could be a communist, military or absolutist regime, with the consequence it would still not be a stable democracy. However, the evidence about presidentialism versus parliamentarism lends support to this counterfactual statement. But is it really presidentialism that makes country A an unstable democracy? Could it not be some other factor present in country A? In order to establish an institutional effect from presidentialism, we must employ regression analysis.

Presidentialism and institutional effects

Presidentialism tends to display political, social and economic outcomes that are worse than those of parliamentary regimes. Above we mentioned one interpretation of these differences in regime performance, namely that the deficit in the performance profile of the presidential regimes compared with that of the parliamentary regimes indicates bad institutional effects from presidentialism. However, one may wish to suggest a second and perhaps more plausible interpretation, namely that the often weak socio-economic conditions that happen to be associated with presidential regimes have a sharply negative impact upon the capacity of presidential regimes to support democracy.

We need to test the hypothesis that presidentialism reduces the probability of a democratic regime while at the same time controlling for the impact of affluence, or more correctly poverty. Thus, we ask: is it the case that presidential regimes which often are situated in poor countries reduce democratic viability in addition to the negative impact of poverty upon democracy?

Contrary to what Linz argues, there is not much of an association between presidentialism and the short-term indicators on political instability. Depending upon how presidentialism is measured, we find a negative relation between presidentialism and long-term political stability, measured by means of state longevity (Table 6.6). Presidential regimes were most often introduced in states that have fought for their independence against the European colonial powers. The attraction of a European model of governance may have been less than the appeal of the American preference for presidentialism as the executive institution of the New World. In any case, presidentialism offered to the new elites in the Third World an executive with much power.

Here, we may be reminded of the position taken by several scholars that a firm and strong executive – a presidential executive for instance – could be strategic in succeeding to amass enough state capacity to steer economic development towards the promotion of the rapid achievement of objectives (Myrdal 1968; Leftwich 1995). Such an executive would be critical in the main model of economic strategies in the Third World, namely economic nationalism, besides, of course, the communist model of a command economy.

One may wish to include not only aggregate indicators on socio-economic development, total output or affluence, but also pay attention to the distribution of income. Equality is often considered as a highly valuable outcome, fostering solidarity and thereby political stability. Although data on income inequality are not available for all countries studied here, Table 6.6 indicates that income equality and gender equality is much lower in presidential regimes than in parliamentary ones. Perhaps the inegalitarian nature of societies with presidential executives contribute to their instability and undemocraticness?

With presidentialism occurring in newly created states or recently independent states, would it make a difference if the state in question had been older? State longevity may perhaps have an impact on democratic viability in addition to any negative effect of presidentialism. Thus, we wish to hold constant what is called institutional sclerosis, or the length of time of uninterrupted statehood. The indicator on institutional sclerosis in the literature targets the occurrence in time of political modernization in a country, whether it occurred early or late. Modernization or, as it is also called, modernized leadership is based upon a Weberian notion of the modern state as involving stable formal institutions, resulting in rational or legal authority.

In order to really say that parliamentarism contains a superior executive to presidentialism one must establish some causal links between the shape of the executive and political, economic and social outcomes. The only other factor that Linz takes into account when claiming that presidentialism matters is the party system. But why not hold constant other factors such as affluence, inequalities and institutional sclerosis? Linz not only places a great emphasis upon the party system in maintaining good presidentialism, but he also claims that bad presidentialism contributes to a party system that operates less well. He claims that the regime interacts with the party system, the two shaping each other. At the same time he claims that a presidential system in reality needs a two-party system in order to function well.

It is now time to examine the empirical evidence about the institutional effect of presidentialism. Table 6.8 estimates a number of regression models concerning presidentialism and democracy at the same time as a few other

Table 6.8 Regressions: presidentialism and democracy in the 1990s

| | | Democracy in the 1990s | | | |
		(1)	(2)	(3)	(4)
President	coeff	−0.63	−0.51	−0.60	−0.39
	t-stat	−2.41	−2.04	−2.40	−1.48
Affluence	coeff	1.01	1.20	0.74	1.31
	t-stat	3.02	4.91	2.27	3.36
Inst scler	coeff	0.01	—	0.01	0.01
	t-stat	2.51		2.10	1.52
Party syst	coeff	—	3.55	3.28	2.31
	t-stat		3.83	3.57	1.26
Constant	coeff	−1.61	−4.11	−1.03	−5.44
	t-stat	−0.59	−1.89	−0.40	−1.55
adj rsq		0.54	0.58	0.60	0.50
n		95	95	95	69

Sources: Democracy=see Table 3.3; presidentialism=see Table 6.1 and 6.6; affluence (Ln RGDPCH)=see Table 3.2; institutional sclerosis=see Black 1966; party system=see Table 3.3.

Note: Models (1) – (3): total set excluding communist, military and absolutist regimes; model (4): excluding one-party systems.

relevant conditions are controlled for; the time period covered here is the 1990s.

There are two major findings in Table 6.8. One finding is that the institutions of a presidential executive matter, but the other finding is that affluence as well as state longevity (institutional sclerosis) have a stronger impact than presidentialism.

It is a fact that many countries that have had presidential regimes have witnessed a change in their democraticness in the 1990s, especially in Latin America. Perhaps the negative impact of presidentialism upon democratic stability as revealed in Table 6.8 is a temporary phenomenon? Repeating an analysis on the basis of data for the 1980s (not reported here), we still find that poverty is a more powerful predictor of a lack of democracy than presidential executives. However, the negative impact of presidentialism seems clearly more pronounced during the 1980s, when many more countries in Latin America failed in terms of democracy than in the 1990s.

Can one argue that the negative impact of presidentialism upon democracy will further diminish? We would be inclined to reply: NO. There is ample evidence for the Linz effect, but all the evidence indicates that it is not as strong as is believed, because social and economic factors must be considered when accounting for the variation in democracy and authoritarianism.

It remains to comment upon the special version of the Linz argument which claims that it is not presidentialism in general that fosters a tendency towards authoritarianism, but that it is presidentailism combined with a multi-party system that is conducive to democratic instability. Table 6.8 indicates that the party system matters, but it is not the Linz effect that is confirmed. On the contrary, a multi-party system enhances the probability of democratic stability. It is in countries where few parties operate that democracy is not stable. Party systems dominated by one party present a particular threat to democracy.

In order to exclude the effect of a one-party system upon democracy, we could test the second and special Linz argument about presidentialism threatening democracy when combined with a multi-party system, in a slightly different way. When the one-party system countries have been excluded, then we find that the number of parties does not matter for the variation in democracy. We must conclude that the special version of the Linz argument is probably wrong – see model 4 in Table 6.8. We may, however, conclude that Linz's main hypothesis about the relation between presidentialism and democracy is confirmed, but the impact of presidentialism is not as strong as that of poverty.

Conclusion

The purpose of this chapter has been to examine the evidence for Linz's preference for parliamentarism. Is it true that presidentialism is conducive to bad outcomes? All countries that are not in a state of anarchy have some executive institutions. Since there are many countries which have either presidential or parliamentary regimes, there is no difficulty in principle in testing the Linz argument on a much larger set of countries than he developed the argument in relation to. What are the main features of executive performance around the world?

Linz is both more right and less right than he can claim to be. On the one hand, he is more correct than he pretends when stating that presidentialism is attended by a worse performance profile than parliamentarism. Had he also taken socio-economic performance into account, his case against presidentialism would have been even stronger. On the other hand, we must remind ourselves that association is not strictly causality, because it is not easy to show, in addition, that presidentialism is the cause of authoritarianism. We have ample evidence that economic factors play an even greater role when accounting for democratic instability.

One needs to separate between two versions of the Linz argument. First, there is the general theory that presidential executives lower the probability of democratic stability. We have found that there is considerable support for this hypothesis. Second, there is the special theory that presidentialism when it occurs in a multi-party system is more conducive to democratic instability or authoritarianism. We think there is no evidence at all for this hypothesis. Instead, multipartism tends in general to increase democratic viability.

Whether or not the institutions of presidentialism work well has been debated since Walter Bagehot raised the issue in his *The English Constitution* of 1867, no doubt drawing heavily upon the severe experiences of the Americans during their civil war. To Bagehot it was beyond any doubt that parliamentarism would operate better than presidentialism, as he, in a theoretical argument, listed a number of reasons why presidentialism leads to immobilism whereas parliamentarism supports flexibility. Since we have many examples of both parliamentarism and presidentailism in the twentieth century we may ask which one set of institutions work best today according to empirical evidence. The evidence shows that parliamentarism does better than presidentialism, but the institutional effect is not as strong as Linz has claimed, because poverty explains some of the bad performance record of presidential systems.

It is now time to move to the analysis of the legislature. One may wish to broaden the analysis of institutions to include in more detail the judicial branch of government. In Chapter 7 we focus upon the outcomes of a number of alternative institutions for making law, whereas in Chapter 8 we examine the judiciary, including the power of judges in legislation, viz. the capacity to test laws and actions for their constitutionality, i.e. the occurrence of legal review.

Appendix 6.1.　Stable presidential countries 1970–1995.

ANG, ARG, BOL, BOT, BRA, BURUN, CHIL, COL, COSRI, CUB, DOM, ECU, ELSA, GHA, GUA, GUI, HON, INDO, IRAQ, KEN, LIBER, MALAW, MAUIA, MEX, MOZ, NIC, NIGRIA, PAN, PAR, PER, SIEL, SWI, USA, URU, VEN, ZAMB.

Appendix 6.2.　Stable non-presidential countries 1970–1995.

AFG, ALB, AUSL, AUT, BEL, BHU, BUL, CAN, CHIN, CZE, DEN, EGY, FIN, FRA, GAB, GER, GRE, HUN, INDIA, IRE, ISR, ITA, JAM, JAP, JOR, KAMP, KORN, KORS, KUW, LAO, LEB, LES, LIBYA, MAD, MALAY, MAUUS, MON, MOR, NEP, NET, NEWZ, NOR, OMA, PAK, PAPNG, POL, POR, SAU, SING, SPA, SWE, TAIW, THA, TRI, TUR, UNIAR, UNIK, VIE, YEM, ICE, LUX, HONG (crown colony).

7 Impact of legislative institutions

Introduction

Institutional theories deal with all the Montesquieu branches of government, not only the effects of alternative structures of the executive. In the neo-institutionalist literature one often meets theories which point out that legislatures are critically important for politics. We wish to know for what aspects of politics, more specifically.

Legislative institutions may be described either in a general fashion by means of a few categories or in great detail by paying attention to a subtle variation in the rules at work in legislatures. Whether one should focus upon the overall structure of institutions for legislature or upon the many special rules that may be employed in structuring legislative work depends upon how one conceives of its importance in relation to institutions.

Institutional importance, it has been pointed out several times, is a concept that stands for two very different things. Institutions may matter either intrinsically or extrinsically.

(a) Intrinsic importance. One could argue that the institutions of parliaments are extremely important, because they provide the rules in terms of which political behaviour is orientated. How could the modern state or the constitutional democracy work without them? Understanding how a national assembly works involves analysing its institutions in great detail, because they are important in and of themselves, legislative behaviour tending to follow them to a very large extent.

(b) Extrinsic importance. Rules may be important for politics due to the contribution of various institutional arrangements to policy outputs as well as social, economic and political outcomes. Whether a parliament has a one-chamber or two-chamber structure may not only have a profound impact upon how legislation is done, but it may also favour certain outcomes. Thus, a two-chamber system could reduce welfare state spending and reduce state deficits, because majorities are much more difficult to arrive at.

The purpose of this chapter is to try to distil a limited number of institutional models about the legislative branch of government, which could help us understand the macro variation in policy outputs and political or socio-economic outcomes. Does it matter if legislation is forthcoming inside or outside a parliament, when a country applies the referendum frequently? Does the chamber system have an impact, meaning that two-chamber systems have outcomes other than one-chamber systems? Finally, what is the impact of institutions that present a major legislative role for independent bodies, such as an independent central bank? But before we move to examine these empirical questions, we have to enquire into the theoretical reasons for expecting extrinsic importance, even when the case for intrinsic importance is so obvious.

Legislative institutions: The macro variation

Legislation can be done in several ways. Here, we will make use of a couple of distinctions that have been researched in the literature on legislatures. Our list is not exhaustive, but pinpoints a macro level variation that is relevant to the explanation of policy outputs and outcomes.

One may distinguish between rule-making inside a formally designed legislature and rule-making outside the legislature. Thus, not only military juntas engage in legislation by means of the use of emergency powers, but also democratically appointed executives promulgate administrative laws, either on delegation or by means of regulatory powers. In the modern state, the legislature tends to dominate legislative work, especially if the country has a constitutional democracy. Authoritarian governments also employ legislatures extensively, if only in their legitimizing capacity.

Legislation outside of parliament may take the form of the referendum. Or decisions with legislative import may be handed over to an independent body, such as the central bank, exercising discretion on monetary policy. The relevance of the referendum and central bank autonomy has increased much in the 1980s and 1990s, but for different reasons. The referendum is seen as a method for having the electorate participate in legislation, bringing legislation very much into the centre of political attention. Central bank independence on monetary matters is a legislative institution with the very opposite intention, namely to withdraw decision-making on monetary policy from the political process and hand it over to autonomous regulators.

When legislation is done by a legal rational mechanism such as a national assembly, then one may conceive of various structures: unicameralism, asymmetrical bicameralism and symmetrical bicameralism. There is a clear connection between the state format – unitary versus federal states – and the chamber system in parliament. Federal states tend towards symmetrical bicameralism, whereas unitary states tend towards unicameralism or asymmetrical bicameralism. However, the match is not perfect.

As a matter of fact, there is considerable institutional variation in the legislative branch of government. If one takes a detailed look – the micro perspective – at how legislation is done, then one finds a plethora of institutions structuring how parliament or the national assembly should work. Yet, at the macro level, legislative institutions may vary in terms of the use of the referendum, independant bodies and the two-chamber system.

Returning to the distinction between intrinsic and extrinsic importance, it seems to us almost self-evident that legislative institutions would be 'important' due to their intrinsic aspects. Whether they are also extrinsically important is an open question that requires both theoretical and empirical research. However, we will look for indications that suggest that legislative institutions have an impact upon public policies or political, social and economic outcomes. The case for intrinsic importance is crystal clear, as constitutional countries cannot live without legislation and legislation is at the heart of politics in the modern state. But what about the extrinsic importance?

When legislation is done in terms of alternative institutions, then which are the macro outputs and outcomes? The theoretical problems involved in answering this question are painstaking, because it is far from an easy task to specify an outcome or output model that could be tested in relation to the variation in legislative structures.

All countries need legislation – this is trivially true, whether one adheres to a minimalist theory of the role of government or a maximalist theory advocating massive state intervention. It is true that in some authoritarian states legislation is basically done by the executive in the form of martial law, based upon an assumption of emergency powers of the executive, following typically a declaration of a situation involving a threat to national security. But in constitutional countries, a variety of different mechanisms have been designed by fiat or evolved through history in order to make legislation possible, comprising both formal legislatures and mechanisms outside of the national assembly such as the referendum, the judiciary and an independent central bank.

Role of parliaments

Although constitutional countries also recognize the possibility of the executive making law by means of administrative decrees, the overwhelming trend in the modern state is to give representative bodies a large role in legislation. These representative bodies are, no doubt, intrinsically important in constitutional countries (Kornberg 1973; Polsby 1975; Lowenberg and Patterson 1979; Norton 1990a, 1990b). But we ask whether they are also of extrinsic importance, meaning that alternative institutions for the making of legislation mean a difference for policies and outcomes?

Parliaments do not operate in a vacuum, as their institutions are nested together particularly with the executive and to a lesser extent with the judiciary. Thus, it is impossible to discuss the characteristics of legislatures without describing the properties of the executive, when one discusses the pros and cons of presidentialism and parliamentarism. In fact, many aspects of the legislature are intimately connected with overall system properties that characterize democracies and the constitutional states. Here, we will restrict our analysis to legislation as a general function. More institutions than legislatures are involved in the making of rules, which is the reason that this function was identified as multi-structural within functionalism (Almond and Coleman 1960).

Today a rationally instituted legislature in a country that adheres to the Montesquieuan separation of powers handles tasks not only in relation to the constitutional state but also with regard to the demands of a democratic regime. Legislatures may satisfy the various requirements of both the constitutional and the democratic state at one and the same time when it handles representation. But it may also face challenges from the constitutional state and the democratic state, respectively. Thus, legislatures may share legislative competencies with the referendum institution providing the people with direct legislative competence in one form or the other. Or legislatures may have to take into account the activities of independent bodies, for instance within the judicial system, where the ordinary courts or a constitutional court would protect civil and political rights, especially so-called immunities.

Parliaments are important in relation to the democratic regime as the mechanism for representative democracy and parliamentarism. In a democracy, the common and minimum basic institutional requirements are two-fold: (1) one man, one vote; (2) majority rule. What varies is the institutional interpretation of these two requirements. In many democratic states, parliaments are the sole or chief expressions of the will of the people. In others, parliaments have to compete with popular elected presidents or be restricted in their operations by the employment of the referendum institution or the allocation of legislative functions to the judiciary.

When parliaments are the only vehicles for the expression of citizen opinions and when they control the executive through the institution of Parliamentarism – investiture and vote of no-confidence – then they dominate the political life of the country. However, in countries with referendum democracy or in countries where the head of state is directly elected by the people, then parliaments face severe competition concerning popular legitimacy.

It should be emphasized that independent bodies are more and more employed in relation to legislative tasks. First, there is the judicial branch which may take on a major role in legislation by means of the special mechanism of legal review. Judicial review, whether practised in the form of a supreme court or in the form of a constitutional court, entails that judges form a kind of supervisory chamber, examining in particular legislation by parliament – see Chapter 8. Second, there is the strong movement towards central bank autonomy on crucial economic matters. If monetary policy is placed outside of the political process and if policy-making concerning the supply of money and interest rates is vested with an independent body, then how much is there left for government, and not least parliament, in relation to policy-making concerning economic growth, unemployment and economic stability?

In the constitutional state, parliaments have formidable power resources. They may legitimately claim to exercise most of the competencies under legislation, given the adherence to the separation of powers. And they receive on regular occasions the mandate of the people to rule, because they constitute the representative assemblies of the people. If uncontested parliaments can claim legislative supremacy and monopolize the people's mandate. Yet, parliaments are often contested by other players.

Parliaments, presidents and judges

The variation in the position of parliaments reflects how the power of other players are recognized institutionally: executive actors such as presidents or premiers, judicial actors such as judges or courts as well as the electorate and independent bodies.

First, parliaments may be challenged by presidents, especially under the institutions of pure presidentialism or strong European presidentialism which gives to the president real executive prerogatives besides those that the premier may exercise. Presidents may restrict parliamentary legislation by either blocking power or the competence to issue decrees or by-laws. Presidents may exercise budgetary powers that infringe upon the general competence of legislatures to decide taxation and spending.

Even in parliamentary systems where the premier is fully in command of the executive – weak presidential systems or monarchies – Parliament has to come to grips with executive interference in its legislative domain. It may be pointed out that there are no pure presidential systems in Europe, but a number of countries practise a combination of parliamentarism and presidentialism resulting in strong presidentialism.

Second, presidents may challenge the claim of parliaments to be the sole representative of the people, especially when they are directly elected. In strong European presidentialism, presidents are involved in the forming and dismissing of cabinets and cabinet members as well as in the dissolution of parliament. Presidents may actually be stronger than premiers in exercising these competencies, especially if they have a people's mandate to rule alongside the representative assembly.

Third, parliaments have to come to grips with the judicialization of politics. Increasingly, the judiciary, either all judges or in the form of a special constitutional court, encroach upon the legislative competence of parliaments. Testing statute law for constitutionality adds to the tasks of the judiciary, making it almost into an additional chamber of parliament, exercising blocking power.

Fourth, the voice of the people could be heard through another channel than the national assembly, namely that of the referendum. When the referendum mechanism involves obligatory and decisive referenda on matters of constitutional law as well as facultative or consultative decisions on major policy issues, then parliament cannot claim to have the sovereignty of the people completely in its own hands.

Thus, we face a most interesting institutional variation with regard to how legislation may be done in the political system of a country. National assemblies may have to share legislative powers with other bodies in the political system. And parliaments can be structured differently. Does this institutional variation matter?

Extrinsic importance

There is an impressive literature on legislative institutions on a case study basis, probing into minute details of how legislation is accomplished and which bodies or actors are involved in what roles. Using social choice theory, these case studies reveal that minor changes in the institutions governing the legislative process, such as the voting rules for the adoption of a bill or an amendment, may change the outcome. However, what is problematic for our study is that these abstract and formal models concerning institutional effects of the variation in legislative structures have little relevance for understanding the macro outputs and outcomes that we wish to explain. How would one go about theorizing institutional effects at the macro level from legislative institutions?

Legislation is about the making of laws and finance bills. Alternative institutions regulating legislation may be assumed to promote certain outputs and outcomes, if one can specify a mechanism through which the institution would impact on first the making of these policies and next the occurrence of relevant outcomes. The main thrust of theories about the impact of alternative legislative institutions deals with how more complex rules for legislation limit legislative activities and thus bring about a lower number of laws and less public expenditure. Suppose that this theory about complex legislative institutions as reducing the tendency of legislatures to expand the scope of state or the size of the public sector is correct, then what would be the testable implications?

First, we would expect to find that two-chamber systems, referendum systems and systems where there is an independent central bank have lower public expenditures and lower state deficits than countries with less complex legislative institutions. Let us test this public finance theory in its various appearances.

Second, we will examine the political stability implication, i.e. whether there is an institutional effect from complex legislative institutions upon democratic stability. One could, it seems, put forward an argument focusing upon the capacity of complex legislative institutions, such as a two-chamber parliament or a referendum system, to stabilize democracy by acting as a bulwark against impetuous decisions – the inertia argument – or against executive invasion of the legislature – the balance argument.

Testing these two kinds of models about extrinsic importance from legislative institutions, one faces a number of choices ranging from a global test strategy covering as many countries as possible to a case study strategy, greatly limiting the countries to be included to the point of there being only one country. All countries of the world tend to have some more or less elaborate institutions for the making of legislative decisions. If these arrangements were all alike, then they could not possibly explain differential macro outputs or outcomes. However, if they are structured differently, then they may be investigated for their possible consequences upon outcomes such as political stability, or policy outputs such as public expenditure.

We will pursue the global strategy below, albeit with restrictions stemming from how differently legislative institutions tend to be implemented. Several countries have constructed legislative institutions, which have nice formal characteristics but tend to be badly institutionalized. Thus, many Latin-American countries have cherished judicial review, for instance Peru, but it has largely been on paper rather than a real commitment, at least for long periods of time since the Second World War. Similarly, countries in Africa and Asia employ the referendum, but then the institution seldom operates as an alternative source of legitimacy to the established institutions. Finally, one can point out that central banks in some countries have formally received increased autonomy, but in reality it is the executive that conducts all forms of economic policy.

The often weak institutionalization of rules guiding legislation in a wide sense makes it very difficult to probe the institutional effects in legislation. We suggest a research strategy with two steps: (a) we examine as many countries as we have data on; (b) we attempt to focus the analysis upon countries where we are certain that the various legislative institutions are fully institutionalized.

Much of the discussion of legislative institutional effects will refer to constitutional states, i.e. to countries where there is an institutionalized division of power between the executive, the legislature and the judiciary, following the classic model formulated by Baron de Montesquieu in 1748, thus securing an important degree of independence between the three powers. Typical of dictatorships is executive dominance, which reduces legislatures to mere rubber stamping of decisions taken elsewhere, when the country is not simply run on the basis of the declaration of martial law or the transfer of emergency powers from the legislature to the executive.

The referendum

The referendum is a classical legislative institution (Butler and Ranney 1994; Luthardt 1994; Gallagher and Uleri 1996; Bjorklund 1997). It is employed by many countries in order to arrive at constitutional legislation, but by only one country when it comes to day-to-day legislation, viz. Switzerland. The established manner of analysing the referendum is to employ the distinction between obligatory and facultative, as well as between decisive and consultative. Thus, we arrive at the following Table:

Table 7.1 Types of referenda

	Decisive	*Consultative*
Obligatory	Ireland, Denmark	Saar 1935
Facultative	Switzerland, Italy	Finland

Source: Suksi 1993: 31.

Perhaps more interesting than the distinctions in Table 7.1 between decisive and consultative referenda is the separation between the positive and the negative uses of the referendum. When referenda are employed, then they tend to be decisive even if they are consultative on paper. In some countries, constitutional decisions are always to be confirmed by an obligatory referendum. Positive referenda are those which change the status quo, whereas negative referenda are those that kill a parliamentary bill that intends to change the status quo. One could mention, in addition, the use of the referendum which allows for the so-called peoples' initiative, which may either suggest the making of a law or test a bill that has been enacted, following a petition involving a certain number of signatures.

When referenda can be demanded by a small number of petitioners, then it is often used negatively as a reaction towards legislation in parliament that minorities wish to undo. It should be pointed out that a peoples' initiative may also concern a positive initiative to introduce new legislation, not merely stopping parliamentary legislation. However, there is tendency for the peoples' initiative to be used as a minority weapon against majorities, especially if the participation rate is low, meaning that a small minority in the whole population can prevail in the referendum. Let us briefly relate some of the Swiss experience with popular initiatives. Up to mid-1988 there had been a total of 451 federal referenda among which 121, or 26.8 per cent, were popular initiatives. While the rate of acceptation for all referenda was 48.8 per cent the corresponding rate for popular initiatives was only 9.9 per cent, that is, only twelve popular initiatives were accepted at the referendum stage.

Yet, for comparative institutional analysis, the basic distinction in relation to the referendum institution is whether it is actually used or not. We may call the countries which use the referendum frequently the referendum democracies. Table 7.2 indicates that referenda are employed frequently in a few of the OECD countries, in some Latin-American countries and in a few post-communist countries.

One observes from Table 7.2 that the referendum institution is employed more and more around the world with the exception of Asia, where it is not very frequent. The increased employment is dramatic in the post-Communist countries where it plays a role in legitimizing the new institutions replacing the old ones. Within the OECD countries, the referendum continues to be widely used, especially in countries such as Switzerland, Denmark, Italy, Ireland, New Zealand and Australia.

Speaking about a country as a referendum democracy, one should note the distinction between the use of the referendum at the national level of government and its use at lower levels of government. An instance is the United States where the referendum is never used at the top level but occurs frequently at the lowest level in the state hierarchy in some states. Let us look at the occurrence of the referendum in so-called constitutional countries (Table 7.3).

We observe from Table 7.3 that there is a considerable variation in the use of the referendum institution between democracies. In a few countries it tends to be employed frequently: Switzerland, Italy, Ireland, New Zealand, Australia and Denmark. In contrast, some countries never use this institution, at least at the national level.

Table 7.2 Number of referenda (Ln)

Countries	1970	1980	1990	n	First factor
OECD	0.75	0.66	0.71	24	87.1
Latin America	0.19	0.30	0.52		
Africa	0.40	0.27	0.41		
Asia	0.23	0.20	0.10		
Post-com	0.09	0.22	1.11		
Total	0.37	0.32	0.53	130	72.6
Eta-squared	0.10	0.07	0.19		

Source: C2D 1998.

Table 7.3 Number of national referenda in the OECD countries 1970–97: ranking-order

Country	Absolute number	Country	Absolute number
Switzerland	221	Sweden	2
Italy	47	Canada	1
Australia	17	Finland	1
Ireland	16	United Kingdom	1
New Zealand	13	Belgium	0
Denmark	6	Germany	0
France	3	Iceland	0
Spain	3	Japan	0
Turkey	3	Luxembourg	0
Austria	2	Netherlands	0
Greece	2	Portugal	0
Norway	2	USA	0

Source: See Table 7.2.

Does it matter if a country is a referendum democracy or not? One model that is often referred to claims that referendum democracy pulls down the total size of the public sector. An active employment of the referendum would prevent public expenditures from increasing due to a tendency or inclination of the normal parliamentary process to be affected by so-called fiscal illusions. The referenda make it less likely that the public sector can be increased for the simple reason that one does not understand what is going on.

Thus, first, it is argued that the referendum enhances transparency and predictability in decisions about taxes and expenditures. And, second, it is claimed that when the employment of the referendum reveals in a more truthful manner the preferences of voters, then it will act as a brake upon the public sector expansion. Here, we have an interesting model about an institutional effect, namely that referenda are conducive to a smaller size of public expenditure, all other things being equal.

The model about many referenda being conducive to a small public sector constitutes one cornerstone in the public choice school. It was developed by scholars with an expertise in the Swiss political system and its employment of the referendum not only at the national level but also at the cantonal and communal levels in the country (Feld and Savioz 1997).

Why is Switzerland the only country in Europe with a public sector of a size that is reminiscent of the welfare societies outside of Europe, such as the United States and Japan? The answer is clearly a strong institutional one, arguing that the frequent use of the referendum reduces the scope for various distributional coalitions to press for increased public expenditure. It may, however, be pointed out that the OECD has revised its numbers for the size of the public sector in Switzerland sharply upwards, using another method of calculation. It remains to be seen whether this recalculation will also result in a reconsideration of the theory about a link between the referendum and public outlays.

Below, we will evaluate the referendum model with regard to public expenditure, i.e. the use of the referendum will disclose the fiscal illusions behind creeping public sector expansion and thus reduce some of the pressures for public sector growth. If the public choice theory about the impact of the referendum is correct, we would also expect to find low fiscal deficits in referendum countries, as voters would continually be conscious about the so-called Ricardo equivalence between present borrowing and future taxation. We will also examine whether there is evidence to the effect that the referendum institution stabilizes democracy.

One must realize that few countries are true referendum democracies, as they rely more upon representative institutions to make laws and budgets. Several democracies hardly use the referendum mechanism at all. And in a few countries it is not even recognized constitutionally.

There are basically two explanations for the infrequent employment of the referendum: (a) transaction costs; (b) a preference for representation over participation. While the first argument is more technical in nature, claiming that referenda are costly or difficult to organize often, the other argument is based upon values, giving precedence to representative institutions before participatory ones. It is difficult to tell which argument explains best how a country employs the referendum. However, technological advances within mass communication seem to reduce the relevance of the transaction cost consideration (Budge 1996).

The definition of the referendum and its various forms refers to whether the people should rule directly or indirectly by means of national assemblies. Although there exist various modes of the referendum, few countries in Europe are real referendum democracies. It is typical that none of the new democracies in Eastern Europe have opted for strong referendum institutions, although some do employ the referendum. Actually, as we have stressed before, only Switzerland is a genuine referendum democracy.

Legislatures

Legislatures play a most prominent role in achieving legislation in all constitutional states, also within the states which recognize and use the referendum. A number of different institutions are employed in legislatures, which regulate competencies (initiative, decision and veto), the conduct of the work (one or two chambers, committees) as well as voting procedures and voting rules (elimination – successive procedure). There is little reason to doubt the importance attributed to legislatures in general in constitutional democracies, i.e. as long as we speak about intrinsic importance.

M.L. Mezey states in his *Comparative Legislatures* (1979):

> I think of a legislature as a predominantly elected body of people that acts collectively and that has at least the formal but not necessarily the exclusive power to enact laws binding on all members of a geopolitical entity.
>
> (p. 6)

Mezey identifies three main different activities that such elected bodies of people engage in: policy-making, representation and system maintenance. This is, though, a functional and not an institutional classification.

Mezey distinguishes between little, modest and strong policy-making power of a legislature, on the one hand, and the extent of support it receives from its neighbourhood environment, for instance by various elites or the mass public, on the other hand. Based upon these concepts, his classification of legislatures includes the following five types: (a) vulnerable legislatures; (b) marginal legislatures; (c) active legislatures; (d) reactive legislatures; (e) minimal legislatures (Mezy 1979: 36). If one wishes to employ a comparative institutional approach to legislatures, then one may focus upon the distinction between unicameralism and bicameralism.

Perhaps the most conspicuous characteristic of a legislature is whether it works by means of one or two chambers. Actually, the first things a casual observer asks about a parliament is whether it has one or two chambers, a lower house and an upper house or a senate. Federal countries have, with no exception, two-chamber parliaments. However, focusing upon the set of unitary states, which is far larger than the set of federal states, one finds that it is far from always the case that unitary states have only one chamber. Why?

Going around the world, one observes that many states with a unitary constitutional framework have double-chamber structures. The hypothesis about a relationship between state format – unitary, federal – and type of legislature – unicameral, bicameral – could be saved, however, when confronted with the numerous occurrences of parliaments with two chambers in unitary countries. The explanation for the anomaly would be that there is, in reality, only one chamber even in these double-chamber structures, because one chamber is the critically important one. This is the asymmetrical bicameralism argument, or the thesis that when there are two chambers in a unitary state, then one must prevail over the other. Now, is this explanation always correct?

The British parliament has of tradition been the model in the argument that unitary states tend towards asymmetrical bicameralism, when they are not simply unicameral systems. Evidently, the House of Lords constitutes such a politically insignificant upper house, although it is not entirely without importance, as one section of it fulfils the juridical function as the supreme court of the United Kingdom.

Yet, bicameralism in a unitary state is not necessarily a redundant institution (Riker 1992). At least two arguments have been identified. First, it has been argued that stability and continuity in a democracy require that decisions taken in a lower, directly elected chamber be tested a second time in a higher chamber, elected somehow in a different manner. Since bicameralism of this kind would restrict the powers of the democratically elected national assembly, it tends to take the form of asymmetrical bicameralism, i.e. the competency of the higher chamber is limited in the sense that its decisions can be overturned by a new decision in the lower chamber. A reminiscent institution resulting in asymmetry between the chambers would be that the higher chamber lacks the power of initiation or can only make recommendations.

Second, a different reason for a second chamber is the mere size of a country. Large countries in terms of territory or population could use a second chamber in order to increase the legitimacy of its representative bodies, by allowing territories or groups to send additional representatives, complementing the lower chamber in the national assembly. Such a complement to the popular chamber could accommodate special regions or minorities. Given this reason for a two-chamber system, it does not, however, follow that bicameralism would have to be asymmetrical.

One could turn the problem around and question whether a second chamber could claim that it is to be equal in competencies to a directly elected first chamber. Evidently, a gerontocratic second chamber could hardly challenge a lower chamber. Its own legitimacy would decline when the whole notion of a group of wise men or women situated above the population loses its grip. Things are different with a regionally composed second chamber, which when representing the people in the regions of the country could claim full democratic accountability. What matters for legitimacy is the method of selection, whether the upper house is merely co-opted, appointed or indirectly elected, or whether it is elected directly.

The second chamber in Canada seems to be a double anomaly, as it is a British-type upper house in a country with a federal system, at the same time as having symmetrical powers with the lower chamber, formally speaking. In reality, though, the Canadian upper house is not as strong as the lower chamber in terms of powers. The Australian senate could be seen as another anomaly, as it is a directly elected body, representing the people in the six provinces of the Australian federation, but it does not exercise equal competences with the lower house.

One may wish to point out that the borderline between symmetrical and asymmetrical bicameralism is far from clear-cut. Constitutional articles do not decide the matter, because the power relations between the chambers in parliament may depend upon shifting circumstances and evolving practices. Thus, a parliament may operate different forms of bicameralism over time. This is the case with the Dutch parliament, which used to display much asymmetrical bicameralism but seems to have moved towards more of symmetrical bicameralism. The same observation holds in relation to the French and the Spanish parliaments. In Italy, we have the clearest case of bicameralism of the symmetrical type in a unitary state, as the higher chamber has regional legitimacy.

Perhaps permanent asymmetrical bicameralism is only possible when the higher or second chamber is an appointed or co-opted body. Starting from asymmetrical chamber arrangements, if the higher chamber has democratic legitimacy, then that chamber will sooner or later move to demand equality with the lower chamber.

Table 7.4 gives an overview of the occurrence of various legislatures, focusing only upon the numerical separation between one-chamber and two-chamber systems, without any attempt to identify countries with strong or weak bicameralism.

It appears from Table 7.4 that the chamber structure is rather stable over time in most countries. There is a clear preference for the one-chamber format, although the number of two-chamber systems is not low. Since the number of federal states is only about twenty but the number of states with a two-chamber system about fifty, one may conclude that many unitary states employ the two-chamber format. The number of one-chamber states is almost double the number of two-chamber states, but it is impossible to tell

Table 7.4 Chamber system

Countries	1970 Chambers		1980 Chambers		1990 Chambers		n	First factor
	1	2	1	2	1	2		
OECD	9	15	10	14	10	14	24	96.3
Latin America	9	13	9	12	9	13		
Africa	33	4	34	5	36	6		
Asia	22	9	27	6	25	8		
Post-com	5	3	5	3	17	10		
Total	78	44	85	40	97	1	127	79.9
Eta-squared	0.19		0.19		0.14			

Sources: Blondel 1972; Encyclopaedia Britannica 1985, 1996.

whether all two-chamber systems in unitary states practise asymmetrical bicameralism – such a proposition would need to checked for each country case. Now, could the distinction between a one-chamber and a two-chamber system matter for macro outputs or outcomes?

First, one must take into account the direct link between federalism and the two-chamber format. It is difficult to conceive of a federal state having only one chamber. The closest approximation to that category is Canada, which has an English-type upper house and no federal senate. But the remaining federal states have the typical federal two-chamber system. Since, however, many more states are two-chamber unitary states, one cannot conclude that the two-chamber format leads to federalism. The connection is the reversed one, i.e. federalism is conducive to the two-chamber format.

Thus, the small number of one-chamber countries is usually increased considerably by the recognition of asymmetrical bicameralism, i.e. a type of bicameralism that is closer to one-cameralism than real two-cameralism. Yet, the separation between symmetrical and asymmetrical two-cameralism is not easily made and it may be done in different ways depending upon when it is made. Thus, in the 1990s several so-called senates have activated themselves, trying to live up to some of the competencies awarded them in the formal constitution.

Chamber symmetry and asymmetry

There can be little doubt that the chamber strucure plays a major role for legislative behaviour. This is the position taken by G. Tsebelis and J. Money in *Bicameralism* (1997), which is based upon a game theoretical argument, supported by empirical evidence. Legislative behaviour will be different when legislative work is divided into two chambers, because such a division necessitates more complex behaviour than when legislation takes place in a one-chamber system. Operating two chambers in legislation involves not the mere duplication of the work by one chamber, but it creates the need for co-ordination in the interaction between the two chambers, especially when they have different opinions on a piece of legislation.

Tsebelis and Money show that legislative deadlocks or intercameral reconciliation can be handled by several institutional techniques: (a) the right of only one of the chambers to introduce a bill – agenda setting (b) the stopping rule which may involve a right for one of the chambers to take a final decision after a limited number of rounds of bidding and counter-bidding, with simple majority or qualified majority – the navette system; (c) the use of joint sessions; and (d) the use of conference or conciliation committees.

Since these institutional techniques may be combined in various ways, we face a complex web of interactions between the two chambers in such a legislature, which is totally absent in a one-chamber legislature. Take the example of Switzerland with its symmetrical bicameralism, typical of a true federal state. Legislative proposals may be introduced in both the lower and the upper house, where legislation requires the consent of both. When the two chambers are not in agreement, then a *navette* system is employed in three rounds, after which a conciliation committee is employed consisting of thirty members from each chamber, should the navette not lead to a compromise decision.

Tsebelis and Money claim: 'Our account demonstrates that bicameral institutions share features that differentiate their outcomes from unicameral ones' (1997: 73). But, aside from the methodological counter-argument that one cannot really demonstrate in a logical or mathematical fashion that empirical generalizations about the link between an institution and outcome are true, we wish to learn more about the outcomes of bicameralism: What are they, more specifically?

Tsebelis and Money identify two very different types of consequences of bicameral institutions. On the one hand, these institutions effect the power relations between the two chambers. On the other hand, these institutions have an impact upon the kinds of decisions taken by the legislature. More specifically, they argue that bicameralism tends to (1) preserve the status quo and (2) to focus political life upon one single dimension, which becomes the conflict cleavage between the two chambers. This is very much in line with game theoretical assumptions about so-called Euclidean preferences and the necessity of a navette system or conciliation committee. What does it mean for legislative outputs?

It has, as a matter of fact, often been argued that complicated methods of legislation give conservative or right-wing results, but this is not quite the same as saying that bicameralism favours the status quo. Since the status quo could be anywhere along the left–right scale depending upon where the country in question happens to be positioned, nothing more specific about which policy outputs symmetrical bicameralism favours can be deduced.

The Tsebelis and Money argument about the importance of bicameral institutions is more orientated towards intrinsic importance than extrinsic importance. They are no doubt right when claiming that these institutions influence the power relations between the two chambers. Thus, the relative power of each house depends upon the initiation rule, the stopping rule and the number of rounds (Tsebelis and Money 1997: 89–105). Yet, the interesting question for empirical research on policy outputs and outcomes is whether such decision rules that favour one of the chambers in terms of agenda power or final decision-making power, also uniquely result in a determinate set of outcomes.

Speculating about the impact of bicameralism on specific outputs or outcomes, one may first focus upon public expenditure. If the Tsebelis and Money formal results are accepted, then bicameralism would result in a restraint upon total public sector size, given that the status quo is a small public sector. Thus, bicameralism would entail a smaller public sector in countries with these institutions, since the major trend in public expenditure in the post-war period has been expansion from a rather low level (Heller 1997).

One may suggest a more specific version of this argument by focusing upon one major type of public expenditure, income redistribution or transfer payments. This category is, generally speaking, much more contested than other items of public outlay, meaning that an institution that gives a bias to the status quo would halt the expansionary pressures in transfer payments programmes.

Following the traditional line of argument about bicameralism in relation to outcomes, emphasizing inertia and wisdom, one could suggest that bicameralism enhances the probability of human rights protection. An upper house would provide better protection of rights, human rights as well as constitutional rights in general, since it could act as a restraint upon hasty decisions by the lower house or the president. In symmetrical bicameral systems the upper house has a vested interest in protecting the constitution, because its power is usually entrenched there. The upper house has the role of guardian of tradition, meaning that it would enhance constitutional longevity. Is there any empirical evidence for the argument that strong bicameralism promotes democratic stability, constitutional longevity and human rights?

To examine the consequences of strong bicameralism one needs to have accurate information about which countries really practise this institution. We will use the classification by Tsebelis and Money of some forty countries, separating two sets, one with asymmetrical bicameralism and the other with symmetrical bicameralism. Table 7.5 presents their classification.

We expect that the countries in Table 7.5 having strong bicameralism enhance democratic stability, on the one hand, and make public sector expansion more difficult, on the other hand, when compared with countries practising asymmetrical bicameralism. Thus, public expenditures should generally be lower in countries with more complicated decision methods in legislation. Correspondingly, public deficits should also be lower and democratic stability should be higher.

Table 7.5 Asymmetrical and symmetrical bicameralism

Asymmetrical bicameralism:

> Australia, Austria, Belgium, Congo, Czech Republic, France,
> India, Ireland, Jamaica, Japan, Madagascar, Malaysia, Mauritania,
> The Netherlands, Pakistan, Paraguay, Poland, South Africa,
> Spain, Thailand, Trinidad, United Kingdom, Russia
> and Croatia.

Symmetrical bicameralism:

> Argentina, Bolivia, Brazil, Canada, Chile, Colombia, Dominican Republic,
> Germany, Haiti, Italy, Jordan, Liberia, Mexico, Niger, the Philippines,
> Romania, Switzerland, USA, Venezuela and Yugoslavia.

Source: Tsebelis and Money 1997: 54–69.

Size of legislatures

A word of caution is necessary. Bicameral parliaments tend to have many parliamentarians. The size of national assemblies must depend somehow upon the size of the country in terms of first and foremost population. Holding the population constant, it seems still evident that one-chamber parliaments must be smaller than two-chamber parliaments. One could argue that the more numerous the parliamentarians, the more likely is it that public expenditure will increase and deficits increase. Bicameralism would thus result in outcomes that tend to cancel each other out.

This is a specific hypothesis about an institutional effect, focusing upon a possible impact of the sheer size of the parliament. The size of the public sector would be affected by the parliament, as public expenditure will be larger when the parliament has many members, because this will give many opportunities for special interests groups to argue their case. If the parliament is compact, then it may better withstand interest group pressure for expenditure increases. A more radical version of this argument would focus upon the occurrence of rent-seeking in the public sector, by means of which interest organizations place burdens upon society, either by directly receiving subsidies or by securing legislation that favours their interests.

This hypothesis about the expenditure-increasing implications of parliament should be contrasted with the alternative hypothesis that two-chamber parliaments with symmetrical bicameralism put a break upon public expenditure, because getting a positive decision in both chambers is more difficult than obtaining a positive decision in a one-chamber system.

How would one test the hypothesis that large parliamentary assemblies are conducive to a huge public sector? One way of testing this hypothesis is through the use of a measure of parliament size as formulated in the so-called inverse cube law. It states that the size of the lower chamber of the national assembly will vary from one country to another as a function of the cube root of the county population. Thus, national assemblies in countries with a huge population will be larger than national assemblies in small countries, i.e. with regard to the lower house (Taagepera and Shugart 1989: 173–83).

If the so-called cube root law of assemblies really holds, then the expenditure hypothesis about sizeable parliaments would have to be modified accordingly. Since lower houses will not differ too much in terms of absolute size, a considerable difference in the number of parliamentarians could only result from populous countries adhering to bicameralism. But perhaps it is not the absolute size of the national assembly that is crucial but the relative size, i.e. the number of parliamentarians per capita? Data is displayed in Table 7.6.

The absolute number of parliamentarians in the lower house varies from a tiny number of sixty to a high number of 3,000 for China, although most national assemblies number between 300 and 500. There is an interesting difference between the relative size of the lower house in the OECD countries, compared with Latin America. Taking the population differences into account, there is about twice as many parliamentarians in the lower houses in the OECD countries as in Latin America. Can one suggest such a simple mechanism as that the more numerous the parliamentarians, the stronger the institutionalization of democracy?

Can we detect the mechanism of the cube root law of assemblies? Figure 7.1 portrays the relationship between the absolute number of parliamentarians and the cube root of the population.

Examining Figure 7.1, we find ample support for the well-known cube root law of national assemblies. However, it does not make a big difference if one predicts the size of the lower house from the square root of the population. As a matter of fact, if one includes the gigantic national assembly in China with its 3,000 members, then the square root predicts somewhat better than the cube root. The correlation coefficient is 0.73 for the square root and 0.68 for the cube root when the outlier is included, and 0.72, 0.73 respectively when China is excluded.

Table 7.6 Absolute and relative size of national assemblies in the 1990s (lower house)

	Absolute size	*Relative size*
OECD	300	34.2
Latin America	166	16.5
Africa	203	23.1
Asia	307	20.3
Post-com	205	29.4
Total	237	24.4
Eta-squared	0.04	0.04

Source: See Table 7.4.

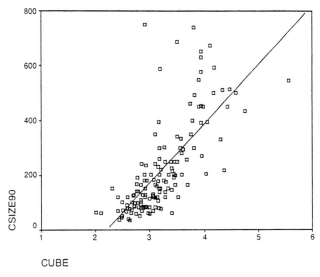

Figure 7.1 The cube root law of national assemblies.

Source: See Table 7.6.

Note: CSIZE90=absolute number of parliamentarians; CUBE=cube root of the population.

Independent central banks

One could also argue that parliamentary legislation should not be all-encompassing in a constitutional democracy. One mechanism to reduce the degrees of freedom of parliaments in the exercise of legislative supremacy is the installation of an independent central bank, responsible for certain key instruments that have an impact upon the conduct of economic policy (Goodman 1990; Alesina and Summers 1993; Busch 1994; Da Haan and Van 'T Hag 1995; Simmons 1996; Elgie and Thompson 1998). A division of the responsibility for economic policy-making is the implication of rules that protect the autonomy of a central bank handling monetary policies. The classical examples of this institution is the American Federal Reserve Board and the German Bundesbank, but, increasingly, other countries have also accepted a divided responsibility for economic policy-making between government, (that is, basically, parliament in the last resort) and a central bank. Does an independent central bank make a difference?

According to monetarist theory (Friedman 1968), central banks have one major task and that is to guarantee the stability of money, meaning keeping inflation in check. Public expenditure should not be decided by central banks. Mainly monetary measures such as interest rates are within the domain of central banks. The basic macro economic argument is that central banks should have discretion to decide these monetary instruments in accordance with strictly economic objectives. A low level of inflation is considered as the means for arriving at sustained and strong economic growth.

The key interpretation of the policy stance of the central bank is that it should avoid short-term fluctuations and focus upon stability, not engaging in discretionary or fine-tuning activities. One could debate whether a monetarist regime could be feasible without an independent central bank, but probably such an institution is needed to arrive at policy credibility. The higher the autonomy of the central bank the lower the average fiscal deficits, one may assume. Without fiscal stringency, any strict monetary policy would lack credibility. Can we detect institutional impacts from the status of the central bank?

The independence of central banks as well as their power has been identified in scales measuring various aspects of their role in governing the economy. Table 7.7 has such a measurement, covering a number of states worldwide with respect to the legal status of the central banks..

One may question whether the measures for most of the countries outside the set of OECD countries make much sense. Are they based upon formal rules or actually operating institutions? How long have these central banks really exercised independence from the executive? The figures for the communist and post-communist countries make little sense, which could also be said about the African and Latin-American countries. Yet, some countries in Asia are known for their monetary toughness, at least so before the Asian debacle in 1997. At the same time we must note the stability over time for this institutional variable.

Let us therefore concentrate upon the OECD countries. Table 7.8 lists the variation in central bank independence as it has been estimated by different scholars like Cukierman, Grilli *et al.* and Alesina *et al.*

If the scale had covered more recent information, then a few countries would most probably have displayed higher scores such as France and the United Kingdom. The trend is at the moment towards increasing central bank autonomy, focusing upon stable money. There is, though, a clear country variation from countries which institutionalize a high degree of central bank autonomy – Germany, Austria, the Netherlands – to countries which provide little autonomy to their central banks: Belgium, Norway, Sweden. Does it matter for the rate of inflation, for instance?

Table 7.7 Status of central banks

Countries	1960	1970	1980	n	First factor
OECD	0.37	0.37	0.37	22	99.9
Latin America	0.33	0.35	0.35		
Africa	0.33	0.34	0.33		
Asia	0.33	0.33	0.34		
Post-com	0.30	0.24	0.24		
Total	0.34	0.34	0.34	61	96.4
Eta-squared	0.03	0.07	0.08		

Source: Coding based upon data in Appendix A of Cukierman 1992.

Table 7.8 Autonomy of the central bank 1970–1990 in OECD countries

Countries	CBANK1	CBANK2	CBANK3	CBANK4
Australia	0.39	0.31	0.60	0.500
Austria	0.57	0.58	0.60	0.625
Belgium	0.16	0.19	0.47	0.500
Canada	0.42	0.46	0.73	0.625
Denmark	0.41	0.47	0.53	0.625
Finland	0.32	–	–	–
France	0.32	0.28	0.47	0.500
Germany	0.67	0.66	0.87	1.000
Greece	0.55	–	–	–
Iceland	0.42	–	–	–
Ireland	0.46	0.39	0.47	0.625
Italy	0.24	0.16	0.33	0.450
Japan	0.21	0.16	0.40	0.625
Luxembourg	0.40	–	–	–
Netherlands	0.45	0.42	0.67	0.625
New Zealand	0.30	0.27	0.20	0.250
Norway	0.22	0.14	0.44	0.500
Portugal	–	–	–	–
Spain	0.06	0.21	0.33	0.375
Sweden	0.29	0.27	0.44	0.500
Switzerland	0.45	0.68	0.80	1.000
Turkey	0.46	–	–	–
United Kingdom	0.36	0.31	0.40	0.500
USA	0.38	0.51	0.80	0.875

Sources: CBANK1=Cukierman 1992; CBANK2=Cukierman revised from Bernhard 1998; CBANK3=Grilli *et al.* from Bernhard 1998; CBANK4=Alesina *et al.* from Bernhard 1998.

The variation between countries and, over time, in the rate of inflation and the rate of economic growth is so substantial that other factors must be at work than merely an economic institution like an independent central bank. Inflation tends to be very sensitive to state deficits, which in turn depend much upon unemployment, i.e. the business cycle. However, average inflation rates may contain an effect from central bank autonomy, especially if the central bank has had time to build up a strong reputation for policy credibility.

The evidence about institutional effects

We have distilled a number of theoretical reasons why legislative institutions, when firmly in place, could be attended by macro policy outputs and outcomes. Strong arguments for the existence of an institutional impact among legislative institutions are to be found in relation to public expenditures, democratic stability and the average rate of inflation.

Thus, the referendum and a two-chamber system or symmetrical bicameralism would reduce public expenditure, in particular transfer payments, as well as promote budgetary balance. A two-chamber system and symmetrical bicameralism would enhance democratic stability. Finally, central bank autonomy would reduce average inflation. Since legislative institutions change very little in the short-run, we will employ average scores on outputs and outcomes in order to test these models.

Table 7.9 presents a few regression models which besides the legislative institutions mentioned also include background factors, e.g. affluence. The aim is to test the hypotheses mentioned above, which predict that legislative rules impact upon democratic stability and public expenditure.

It should be noted that we have excluded the referendum institution from Table 7.9, because we could not establish any specific institutional effect from this institution. We should also point out that the size of the public sector in Switzerland has most probably been grossly underestimated. The implication being that the most important case in the argument for the referendum reducing public outlay simply does not exist.

Now, a two-chamber parliament means a difference for decision-making about public finances. When there is a symmetrically composed two-chamber national assembly, then public expenditures tend to be lower and surpluses higher. A large parliament, absolutely speaking, goes together with a reduced level of democracy, reflecting the fact that many Third World countries are populous, with numerous parliamentarians.

In Table 7.10, we test the theory that the institutionalization of a high level of central bank autonomy means of difference for one real outcome,

Table 7.9. Impact of legislative institutions: regression analysis

		DEM9196	SOC90	CGR95	DEF95
Sym/asy	coeff	—	−4.64	−6.91	2.50
	t-stat		−1.51	−2.46	2.16
Chasize	coeff	−0.00	—	—	—
	t-stat	−2.63			
Afflu	coeff	2.03	11.62	6.60	−.91
	t-stat	10.75	6.67	4.28	−1.49
Gro8594	coeff	—	—	—	0.67
	t-stat				2.96
Inf9095	coeff	—	—	—	−0.01
	t-stat				−2.67
Const	coeff	−9.82	−78.53	−27.53	2.63
	t-stat	−6.44	−5.03	−2.06	0.50
rsq		0.53	0.67	0.41	0.35
n		103	24	32	30

Sources: DEM9196=see Table 3.3; SOC90, CGR95, DEF95: see Table 3.1; Sym/asy=see Table 7.5; chasize=see Table 7.6; afflu=see Table 3.2; gro8594=see Table 3.2; inf9095=see Table 3.2.

Note: DEM9196=democracy score; SOC90=public expenditures for education and health care as well as transfer payments; CGR95=central government revenue; DEF95=general government surpluses/deficits; sym/asy=symmetrical and asymmetrical bicarmeralism (Table 7.5); chasize=absolute size of legislature (Table 7.6); afflu=affluence (Table 3.2); gro8594=economic growth 1985–94 (Table 3.2); inf9095=inflation 1990–95 (Table 3.2).

Table 7.10 Inflation: regression analysis

		Inflation 1990–95				
CBANK1	coeff	−308.25	0.40	—	—	—
	t-stat	−1.83	0.30			
CBANK2	coeff	—	—	1.10	—	—
	t-stat			1.03		
CBANK3	coeff	—	—	—	0.71	—
	t-stat				0.73	
CBANK4	coeff	—	—	—	—	1.16
	t-stat					1.04
Deficit	coeff	−6.91	−.31	−0.33	−0.32	−0.32
	t-stat	−1.75	−3.72	−4.09	−3.95	−4.09
Const	coeff	124.41	1.42	0.91	1.10	1.09
	t-stat	1.98	2.01	1.19	1.44	1.78
rsq		0.08	0.44	0.48	0.46	0.48
n		50	17	17	17	17

Note and sources: See Tables 7.8 and 7.9.

namely the rate of inflation. The finding is negative, as we cannot corroborate this theory whatever measure on central bank autonomy we employ.

Conclusion

Institutional importance – this is the principal idea in the various brands of neo-institutionalism. But does institutional importance refer to *intrinsic* or *extrinsic* importance?

We find in our examination of legislative institutions that they are primarily intrinsically important. It is difficult to verify that the variation in legislative institutions play a major role for public policies or political outcomes. Yet, few would deny that the rules that govern the making of laws in society must be tremendously important.

Admitting that intrinsic importance seems to prevail over extrinsic importance with regard to legislative institutions, we wish still to emphasize that the public finance theory about the impact of bicameralism upon public expenditures or public policies receives ample support.

8   Judicial institutions

Introduction

Does bicameralism or unicameralism matter, we asked in Chapter 7. Can one conceive of tricameralism? Yes. In his argument for legal review or the power of judges to declare laws or actions unconstitutional, Hans Kelsen interpreted a court having such powers as a third higher chamber (Kelsen 1928). It is no doubt true that the existence of legal review creates a special institutional atmosphere rendering political power to judges, which definitely affects both the style and content of political life. Intrinsic importance? Yes, very much so. But we wish to pin down the extrinsic importance of a legal institution such as legal review.

Legal review is not the only legal institution that is relevant for the understanding of policy outputs and outcomes. It is only the tip of an iceberg, involving many layers of judicial institutions, protecting constitutionalism. Stable democracies today all adhere to the basic principles of the Rule of Law, involving procedural accountability, human rights and the access to complaint and remedies against the state. In new democracies and in countries which hover between dictatorship and democracy, the legal institutions of the Rechtsstaat are not fully implemented.

What we wish to enquire into is whether alternative ways of structuring the institutions of the Rechtsstaat play a role for policy outputs and political outcomes. Judicial institutions make up the legal order – a vast set of mechanisms regulating the private and the public sectors. We can only select a few themes here, focusing on whether alternative legal institutions help us understand the macro variation in public expenditures on the one hand and democratic stability, on the other hand. Which legal institutions could be of crucial importance for these outcomes?

Legal systems

A legal system or law is, declares Kelsen 'an order of human behavior.' And he continues: 'An "order" is a system of rules' (Kelsen 1961: 3). The conclusion of this argument would be that law is a system of rules for human behaviour, which is very much in line with one of the two major approaches to institutions, viz. rational choice institutionalism. The closeness between law and institutions becomes even more apparent when Kelsen goes on to qualify further that law 'is a coercive order' (Kelsen 1961: 19). Without a mechanism for punishing behaviour which fails to comply with the relevant rule, an order is not law. Thus, law is a set of rules that is institutionalized in human behaviour. Yet, although law constitutes an institutional phenomenon, not all institutions are legal institutions.

Kelsen claims that legal and political institutions coincide. He writes:

> The state is that order of human behavior that we call the legal order, the order to which certain human actions are oriented, the idea to which the individuals adapt their behavior.
>
> (Kelsen 1961: 188)

Identifying the state with law and vice versa implies, in our view, a much too broad conception of the state and its political institutions. The legal order is a more comprehensive institutional concept than the state, as it also involves the regulation of society.

In order to identify the legal institutions and separate them from political institutions whenever that is feasible, we may employ the traditional distinction between private and public law, although this separation has been much debated as to its relevance and analytical validity. The main elements of public law are made up of constitutional law and administrative law. In relation to these two, we accept the Kelsen position about a very close link between the state and the legal order (Kelsen 1996).

Private law is considered to consist of the various types of law connected with the making of contracts, including family law, the law of purchase and sale, property law and the law of obligations. Moreover, private law also includes tort law, but criminal law is considered to be placed somewhere in-between public and private law. Here, the analogy that Kelsen makes between law and state breaks down, as private law is society, not state.

Legal systems structure public and private law in different ways. Here, we have an institutional variation that is relevant to the search for institutional effects. We will only focus upon the most basic division of legal systems, namely that suggested by the theory of legal families.

In comparative law, one makes a few basic distinctions between the main families of law, practised around the world. Although the identification of a law family is an issue of debate among scholars, the following list of families may be retrieved from this research: Civil Law, Common Law, Civil and Common Law (mixed), Socialist Law, Sharia Law and Conventional or Customary Law (David and Brierley 1985; Schacht 1993).

The theory of legal families comprises, in addition, other more special categories such as the law of India, the law of Africa and the law of Malaysia. It has been suggested that South Africa has a special legal system,

Table 8.1 Legal families in the world

	Civil law	Common law	Socialist	Muslim	Customary
OECD	17	7	0	0	0
Latin Am	17	4	1	0	0
Africa	4	7	0	8	22
Asia	1	7	3	12	9
Post-com	0	0	27	0	0
Total	39	25	31	20	31
Eta-sq			0.56		

Sources: Rhyne 1978 and CIA 1994.

but it seems more adequate to say that it is a combination of laws from the civil law family: Dutch Law and English Common Law. Yet, for comparative purposes, focusing upon the variation in macro political outcomes, the above list is sufficient. Table 8.1 shows the occurrence of the various legal families around the world.

Surprisingly, a plurality of the countries of the world practise Civil Law, i.e. Roman–Germano law. The countries that use this legal order are more numerous than those who adhere to the Common Law tradition. These two Western legal systems are much spread around the world, because they were exported as part of colonial rule. English Law is, however, less widespread than one would have expected, given the immense size of the British Empire. Most countries in Latin America and Africa employ Roman–Germano law.

One might expect Socialist Law to be replaced by either Civil Law or Common Law, at least outside of China and North Korea. One might also expect Sharia Law to spread to more countries in those parts of the world where Muslims are dominant. On the other hand, the spread of Customary Law will be reduced.

Countries, however, do not change the overall nature of their legal systems quickly. Following Kelsen's theory about a very close link between law and state, we suggest that the variation in legal families helps us explain democratic stability. Since the legal family a country adheres to tends to remain stable, it could help us explain the over time variation in democratic stability, meaning the average score of a country on democracy over a period of thirty years.

Legal review

In all constitutional states there exist institutions and organizations that provide citizens with channels for complaint and remedies against the decisions and actions of the officials of the state. We have here an institutional variation that reflects different legal traditions as well as constitutional choices. A thin constitutional state offers a variety of channels for testing and questioning the functioning of the state with an emphasis upon the correct application of administrative law. In a constitutional state of the thick version, on the other hand, legislatures and executives can be challenged by the judicial system. The judges or the courts become major political players when full-scale legal review is accepted. In Europe, all countries accept the relevance of administrative review in some form or other, either by separate administrative courts or by a mixed system of special tribunals and the ordinary courts. What varies in Europe is the acceptance of the legitimacy of judicial review, i.e. the power of judges to test legislation for constitutionality. Legal review is the power of judges to nullify a law or an executive act if it contradicts the rights of citizens in the constitution (Cappelletti and Cohen 1979; Stone 1990; Volcansek 1992; Shapiro and Stone 1994).

Whereas human rights typically refer to individual rights, collective rights deal with groups. It is often argued that the state has to give recognition to special groups, constituted by ethnic, religious or some other criteria such as, for example, sex or gender. Such collective rights often take the form of immunities or special decision rules. When collective rights are combined with judicial review, then the power of legislatures may be severely restricted. However, it is a contested issue whether collective rights are part of human rights, or whether they ought to be constitutionally recognized. According to one position, democracies need to protect various minorities by means of an intricate system of group rights (Kymlicka 1995).

Legal remedies for citizen complaint against the state may be handled either by the Common Law approach or the Civil Law framework. In the Anglo-Saxon legal system, one resorts to either the ordinary courts or *ad hoc* tribunals in order to handle citizen grievances against public officials. In Continental Europe, where the Romano–Germano family of laws prevails, the basic distinction is that between public and private law, the separation of which is institutionally recognized in a clearly dichotomous court system, having two hierarchically structured parts: ordinary courts versus administrative courts. In a Common Law country, legal remedies tend, at the end of the day, to be framed by case law, stated by the ordinary courts, overlooking the work of the various tribunals. In a Civil Law system, only the administrative courts handle public administration cases in terms of a unified system of codified rules.

Whether a country employs the Common Law framework or the Civil Law approach is independent of whether the country in question adheres to legal review or not. There are countries which practice Anglo-Saxon law and which have legal review on a major scale such as the USA, but a country like the United Kingdom does not know legal review. Similarly, many Roman–Germano Law countries do not accept legal review – the Netherlands, Belgium, Sweden, Finland, Denmark – whereas some do, like Germany, Austria, Italy and many East European countries. Whereas all countries who recognize the Rule of Law system have weak legal review in the sense that there are possibilities for remedies checking whether the law has been applied correctly, only a proper subset of constitutional democracies accept strong legal review, or the power of judges to check for constitutionality or whether the law is correct from a constitutional perspective, including human rights.

When it comes to strong legal review one should point out that its modes differ very much. One may distinguish three institutions: the American Supreme Court, the Austrian Constitutional Court and the French Conseil constitutionnel. In the American institution for judicial review, this competence belongs to each and every judge in the federal or the state courts. Since any exercise of this competence by a single judge within the lower levels in the court system will almost certainly be challenged by an appeal, legal review will be mainly exercised by the Supreme Court, which is the highest court of appeal. The federal Supreme Court has a general mandate to test legislation as well as executive acts for constitutionality, besides being the chief court for interpreting the division of competences between the federal and the state governments. Judicial review in the USA is not enshrined in the written constitution, but since 1803 has informed constitutional practice.

The German or, as it is also called, the Austrian model is very different from the American model. Whereas judicial review in the USA takes place in a Common Law system, the Kelsen approach was launched within a Civil Law system, characterized by its sharp separation between public and private law. According to the Kelsen framework, the constitutional court is a special court with one sole preoccupation, viz. to safeguard the written constitution. Thus, its judges are the only ones who can engage in legal review. The constitutional court is separate from the public administrative courts and the ordinary courts. Most European countries where legal review is practised follow the Kelsen type of court. One exception is the French Conseil constitutionnel, which examines laws before they are enacted. Thus, it has no power to squash laws or executive decisions.

Judicial review may be done either by a separate constitutional court – the Continental European model – or by means of the ordinary courts – the American model (Shapiro 1981). The East European countries have all endorsed judicial review but opted for the Continental model, setting up a separate constitutional court. A constitutional court may operate in two different ways, judicial review *ex ante* legislation as in France, or judicial review *ex post* legislation as in Germany. The East European countries have chosen the German model.

As Hans Kelsen argued at the end of World War I, judicial review when put into practice with full force amounts to the addition of a new legislative chamber to the already existing parliament structures. A constitutional court is basically given a final veto on legislation. If the constitution is malleable, then judge-made law may overrule statute law on numerous important issues such as the rights of women or unborn children. How powerful the judiciary will be in relation to the legislature depends on the amount of judicial activism (Holland 1991).

Several countries around the world recognize judicial review in their constitutions, but only in the democracies can one speak of real legal review, meaning that the decisions of courts about constitutionality are respected. However, far from all democracies accept judicial review, or at least the full and unreserved recognition of judges to test laws for constitutionality, as is the case, for instance, in the United States and Germany. In all democracies, we find the institutions of the Rechtsstaat, including numerous avenues for correcting the decisions of public authorities. In some but certainly not all of the constitutional democracies there is, in addition, a mechanism by means of which a judicial institution can squash parliamentary legislation and sometimes executive actions. Separating between the institutionalization of weak and strong judicial review among the constitutional democracies we investigate whether the employment of the one or the other institution has any impact upon outcomes. First, we must specify the outcomes that would be relevant. Second, we must describe the variation in institutions that handle legal review.

Judicial review is the process through which courts test parliamentary legislation against a code of rights, which may be laid down in a constitutional document or which may constitute a bulk of principles of right reason, laid down in case law. These rights typically regulate either human rights or the competencies of public bodies in relation to each other. Is it the case that strong legal review affords a better protection for human rights than weak legal review? One of the key issues in the interpretation of human rights today is the protection for women rights and the rights of minorities. Does strong legal review protect better than weak legal review?

The special mechanism of judicial review allowing judges to test legislation against constitutionality is hardly a widespread phenomenon, although it tends to attract much attention in the political life of a country. It occurs in a stronger version as a real phenomenon in some sixty of the hundred and forty-six countries studied. One must make sure not to confuse the existence of legal review with the practice of constitutionalism. Many OECD countries do not recognize legal review, but they uphold the Rule of Law, albeit with other types of judicial mechanisms than judicial review.

Let us look a little more closely on the countries with some form of legal review. They include: Australia, Austria, Brazil, Germany, Italy, Portugal, Mexico, Spain and the USA, which have strong versions, as well as Canada, France, Greece, India, Ireland, Iceland, Japan, Norway, Portugal, Switzerland and Venezuela. It is debatable whether judicial review really occurs in Latin America, as there may be a gulf between the formal constitution and constitutional realities in these countries.

Although the institution of judicial review has received much attention lately and its relevance in constitutional engineering has increased sharply in the transition from authoritarian regimes to democratic ones, it remains a

Table 8.2 Occurrence of judicial review around the world

	Legal review	No or weak legal review
OECD	12	12
Latin America	14	8
Africa	20	21
Asia	8	24
Post-communist	4	23
Total	58	88
Eta-sq	0.12	

Sources: Based upon reports in Rhyne 1978; CIA 1994; Maddex 1996.

fact that the countries that do not accept this judicialization of politics are more numerous than the countries which practice legal review. This generalization also remains valid for constitutional democracies.

To sum up: institutions for strong legal review come in different forms. One may distinguish between the American model, the German model and the French model. Most countries of the world adhere to the German model, which is close to the one recommended by Kelsen after the First World War. Some of the countries that do not endorse strong legal review have begun to adopt some of its features in combination with weak legal review, which focuses upon public accountability and fairness in procedures, and thus not upon the constitutionality of legislation. Now, is it the case that strong judicial review makes a difference in the sense that countries that harbour it score higher on indices of human rights protection, minority protection as well as gender issues development?

The question of an institutional effect from legal review is difficult to answer by means of empirical research. Countries may formally adhere to the Rule of Law, having either weak or strong judicial review, but in reality they use these institutions as merely Potemkin facades. Increasingly, many countries employ only weak legal review but complement it with the protection of rights by means of the operations of an ombudsman, which is not a court. What then, more specifically, is this institution?

The ombudsman institution

Theorizing the ombudsman institution raises a number of fascinating questions about how the Rule of Law is constructed in modern democracies (Stacey 1978; Rowat 1985, 1997). Understanding the role of the ombudsman for implementing the right of citizens to express grievances against what they consider maltreatment as well as seek redress against government, entails that one must examine the major organs of the Rechtsstaat in present-day democratic countries. This involves relating the ombudsman office to the key bodies in the judicial branch of government, including the plethora of courts, ordinary ones as well as possibly administrative ones. Finally, the rules guiding the work of the ombudsman must be related to how the relationship between the executive and the legislative branches of government works out in practice, as the ombudsman, although constituting an independent body, tends to be a mechanism of the legislature to check the executive.

The Scandinavian countries and Finland are particularly interesting from a comparative perspective on the ombudsman institution. Not only were the first institutions of this kind established in these countries, but there is an interesting systematic difference between what is called the Swedish system and the Danish system. Countries setting up new ombudsman institutions face a choice between the Swedish model and the Danish model when structuring the ombudsman office. The two models are truly distinct as they involve entirely different roles for the ombudsman, which has an impact upon the relationship with the authorities whose activities lie in the domain of the ombudsman. Some countries have adopted the Swedish model, but many more follow the Danish model.

The way the Danish and Norwegian ombudsman offices function in the political system of these two countries is interesting, not only because of the international reputation of the so-called Danish model, but also due to the emergence of a practice in both these two countries that tells us much of the role of this type of body in a Rechtsstaat that is also a democracy. Proceeding from blueprint to actual practice will also allow the statement of a few pertinent differences between the way the ombudsman operates in the respective political systems, which may not be clear to an international audience that wishes to see their own country adopt the so-called Danish model.

The ombudsman may be either a prosecutor or only an investigator. He/she may constitute an addition to a system of administrative courts, without being one itself, or it may operate as a court of appeal in relation to numerous administrative tribunals and boards which are not integrated into a system of administrative courts. The ombudsman may have the entire public sector under its domain or it may be constricted by various omissions such as, for instance, the courts, either ordinary or administrative ones.

The reports of the ombudsman may constitute only recommendations to an agency or board, or they may constitute the basis for taking legal action in the courts against individual officials. He/she may himself decide to turn over the relevant materials to a prosecutor in a criminal law case, or the materials disclosed by the ombudsman may be employed by a litigant seeking compensation in a civil law case. The recommendations of the ombudsman may be considered as merely guidance for the future development of administrative practice or they may be regarded as a quasi-juridical verdict which must be implemented fully, especially when they target a single decision, demanding that it be remade or changed.

The ombudsman may concentrate upon the decisions made by authorities, testing their validity against standard operating procedures in public law. Or they may target individual officials, examining whether their behaviour is in accordance with criminal law. When the ombudsman only looks at authorities as collective bodies, enquiring into their decision procedures, then it does not isolate the single officials who are responsible for the decisions taken. What is important is that the agency or board changes its general administrative practice so that a wrong decision will not be repeated. On the other hand, when the ombudsman targets the behaviour of single office-holders, then it is usually a matter of initiating disciplinary measures.

The actual role of the ombudsman in the political system of a country may not be the one enshrined in the formal documents connected with a historical decision to introduce an ombudsman office. One must look at how the ombudsman operates in reality and how he/she relates to the key organs in the judicial system. The relationship between the ombudsman and parliament is also extremely important in shaping actual operations, as the ombudsman may or may not work in close co-operation with the committee in parliament responsible for overseeing the legality of the actions of the executive branch of government.

These distinctions are critical for the comparative understanding of the ombudsman institution that is emerging in more and more countries. An understanding of the power that an ombudsman can exercise in a political system must be based upon the distinction between power *ex ante* – power by anticipation – and power *ex post*, i.e. power actually exercised in the form of changing what would have occurred had not the ombudsman intervened.

One could argue that parliamentary legislation should not be absolute in a constitutional democracy. There must be limits upon the capacity of a representative body to create law by means of its legislative supremacy, derived from the concept of state sovereignty. The institutions of strong legal review, as well as the ombudsman mechanism, offer such a limitation on the power of states to change or create new law, as legislatures must stay within certain limits established by itself in constitutional documents or by an independent body interpreting such a constitutional legacy. Since strong legal review may restrain the operations of democracy though these limits upon the degrees of freedom of the legislative body, the institutions of legal review are highly contested ones. This is especially the case when the key principles of equity admit of widely different interpretations, opening up the way for the judicialization of politics or, inversely, the politicization of the judicial system (Bennett 1997).

In Table 8.3 an attempt has been made to map the introduction of the ombudsman institution worldwide, making a distinction here between countries where it was introduced quite early, i.e. 1980 or before, those where it was introduced at a later stage, and those where it has not yet been introduced.

As we may note from the table, there are only a limited number of countries that have attempted to introduce this institution at an earlier date. They are mainly to be found among the set of OECD countries.

Table 8.3 Occurrence of the ombudsman institution around the world

	Early institutionalization	*Later institutionalization*	*No institutionalization*
OECD	18	5	1
Latin America	2	13	7
Africa	4	18	21
Asia	5	4	25
Post-communist	0	14	13
Total	29	54	67
Eta-sq		0.33	

Sources: Based upon reports in Caiden 1983, International Ombudsman Institute 1999.

Note: early institutionalization = 1981 or before; not early institutionalized = between 1982 and 1998; no institutionalization = no ombudsman institution in 1999.

Whether a country follows the Swedish or Danish model matters for the operations of the Rechtsstaat as well as impacting upon the authorities whose activities lie in the domain of the ombudsman. Finland practises the Swedish model whereas Norway is closer to the Danish model. The main differences between the two models can be spelt out by making four critical distinctions:

1   The Swedish ombudsman is a prosecutor, not only an investigator. The office constitutes an addition to a system of administrative courts, without being itself an administrative court. The Danish ombudsman operates as a court of appeal in relation to numerous administrative tribunals and boards which are not integrated into a system of administrative courts. The Swedish ombudsman has the entire public sector under its domain and is thus not constricted by various omissions, such as, for instance, the courts, either ordinary or administrative ones.

2   The reports of the Danish ombudsman constitute recommendations to an agency or board, whereas the Swedish ombudsman may also take legal action in courts against individual officials. The Danish ombudsman may decide to turn over the relevant materials to a prosecutor in a criminal law case, or the materials disclosed by the ombudsman may be employed by a litigant seeking compensation in a civil law case. The statements of the ombudsman may be considered as guidance for the future development of administrative practice. In the Danish model, they are regarded as quasi-juridical verdicts which must be implemented fully, especially when they target a single decision, demanding that it be remade or changed.

3   The Danish ombudsman concentrates upon the decisions made by authorities, testing their validity against standard operating procedures in public law. The Swedish ombudsman targets the behaviour of individual officials, examining whether their behaviour is in accordance

with criminal law. When the ombudsman in the Danish or Swedish model only looks at authorities as collective bodies, enquiring into their decision procedures, then it does not isolate the single officials who are responsible for the decisions taken. What is important is that the agency or board changes its general administrative practice so that a wrong decision will not be repeated. On the other hand, when the ombudsman targets the behaviour of single office-holders, then it is usually a matter of initiating disciplinary measures, as in the Dutch model.

4   The ombudsman may be an institution that complements a number of other institutions having the same function of promoting redress in the Rechtsstaat. Or the ombudsman may play a dominant role, being the chief office for handling grievances and seeking redress. In some countries the ombudsman operates alongside a plethora of mechanisms handling grievances in order to give redress, but in other countries the ombudsman is chiefly responsible for this task, which is so vital for the Rule of Law. Thus, the ombudsman may face competition from other channels for handling complaints, including not only a variety of courts, but also numerous possibilities for administrative remedies, including remaking decisions or the intervention of authorities higher up in the administrative system, including the ministries.

It must be emphasized that the actual role of the ombudsman in the political system of a country may not be the one enshrined in the formal documents connected with a historical decision to introduce an ombudsman office. One must look at how the ombudsman operates in reality and how he/she relates to the key organs in the judicial system and the legislature. The Danish ombudsman works in close co-operation with the committee in parliament responsible for overseeing the legality of the actions of the executive branch of government.

The evidence for institutional effects

Do judicial institutions make a difference to the longevity of democracy in a country? This question seems theoretically very relevant, because under a Montesquieu system of institutional partition the legal institutions have the task of guarding against the risk of power abuses by the executive or legislative branches of government. It is true that a system of checks and balances or a system of legal mechanisms for the protection of the Rule of Law need not necessarily protect a democracy. The constitutional state precedes the democratic regime in Europe by some one hundred years. Yet, strong legal institutions may certainly serve the proper institutionalization of civil and political rights.

Table 8.4 shows in a transparent manner that judicial institutions matter for democratic stability, and also, but to a lesser extent, for the occurrence of corruption. Regressing the average score on the index of democracy upon legal mechanisms, holding the level of affluence constant, we find that most of the legal institutions discussed above matter. When it comes to corruption we only find a negative impact from Common Law but a positive impact on the occurrence of corruption in a Civil Law tradition, while legal review does not matter.

Confronted with the positive findings in Table 8.4, one could still take the position that these are merely spurious correlations. It just happens to be the case that countries which cherish human rights also have all the various forms of judicial mechanisms that make up the core of a constitutional state. We believe this interpretation is too pessimistic.

Western-type legal families much more easily accommodate human rights. Countries having either strong legal review or the ombudsman office must be much better equipped to protect human rights than other countries. And human rights are, after all, fundamental in a democratic regime.

Conclusion

Judicial institutions constitute the last part in the Montesquieu system – *trias politica*. Yet, their importance to Montesquieu was as great as that of the executive and legislative institutions, especially with regard to freedom. We find a large variation in present-day legal mechanisms in the countries of the world.

Table 8.4 Impact from judicial institutions on democracy and corruption: regression analysis

		Democracy 1972–96				Corruption 1980–98			
Afflu	coeff	1.69	1.74	1.55	1.40	2.23	2.30	2.01	2.28
	t-stat	8.82	8.78	7.61	6.88	7.63	7.43	5.69	6.12
Civil law	coeff	0.45	—	—	—	−1.20	—	—	—
	t-stat	1.16				−2.73			
Common law	coeff	–	0.16	—	—	—	0.93	—	—
	t-stat		0.45				2.16		
Legmix	coeff	—	—	−0.65	—	—	—	−0.29	—
	t-stat			−2.13				−0.67	
Legfam	coeff	—	—	—	−0.42	—	—	—	0.17
	t-stat				−3.43				0.78
Legrev	coeff	0.73	0.72	0.68	0.54	−0.44	−0.58	−0.55	−0.44
	t-stat	2.17	2.11	2.05	1.65	−1.05	−1.34	−1.22	−0.94
Ombudsm	coeff	1.52	1.45	1.44	1.34	0.19	0.15	0.25	0.20
	t-stat	6.31	5.75	6.11	5.80	0.56	0.45	0.68	0.56
Const	coeff	−9.78	−9.80	−7.25	−5.84	−11.53	−13.23	−10.19	−13.11
	t-stat	−6.95	−6.65	−4.10	−3.38	−5.19	−5.44	−3.34	−4.08
adj rsq		0.67	0.67	0.68	0.70	0.72	0.70	0.67	0.67
n		107	107	107	107	46	46	46	46

Sources: Democracy and corruption: see Table 3.3; affluence (=Ln RGDPCH 1970)=see Table 3.2; legal families=see Table 8.1; legal review=see Table 8.2; ombudsman=see Table 8.3.

First, one should ask which legal family a country belongs to. This concerns all matters of law in the same country. Does a country practise the two major Western systems of law, Civil Law or Common Law, or does it have another type of legal order, such as Sharia? Second, one would like to know if the judicial bodies in general or one special judicial body can exercise legal review in the strong sense of this concept. Finally, there is the ombudsman office, which may complement or substitute for strong legal review.

The evidence scrutinized above clearly indicates that judicial institutions are as important as Montesquieu conceived. They matter intrinsically but particularly extrinsically in relation to the stability of a democratic regime over time. Perhaps one could state that if a country wishes to introduce democracy, then the best institutional devices it could employ in constitutional engineering are legal institutions such as strong legal review, the ombudsman and elements of the Western legal families. If the state and the legal order are as intimately linked as Kelsen suggested (Kelsen 1979), then alternative legal institutions should mean a difference for the state. Thus we find that Rule of Law institutions promote democratic stability and longevity, as well as counteracting favouritism, clientelism and *patronage*.

Part III

The Lijphart system

An alternative to the Montesquieu system with its division of three state competences is to be found in the work of Arend Lijphart, which since the late 1960s has played a major role in directing comparative research on political institutions. Whereas the Montesquieu scheme is applicable to all states in the world, the Lijphart approach is focused only upon countries with a democratic regime. The basic idea in the Lijphart system is that democratic regimes may be structured from an institutional point of view in very different ways and that it means a difference for policy outputs and outcomes. We will examine the theory about two types of democracy below, searching for the occurrence of institutional effects.

Actually, it was Maurice Duverger who first proposed a theory about the importance of alternative institutions in democracies. Duverger suggested in around 1950 that electoral institutions play a key role in shaping the nature of politics in a democracy. The electoral system has a major impact upon the party system which in its turn has a clear effect upon the nature of democratic government. Since to some extent Lijphart's theory of democracy can be seen as a critique of Duverger, we start this section by examining the so-called Duverger's Law, which is very much an hypothesis about an institutional effect. We then examine the logic of Lijphart's argument about two ideal-types of democracy. Finally, we examine the evidence for institutional effects connected with Westminster democracy and Consensus democracy.

9 The Duverger theory

Impact of election rules

Introduction

In the neo-institutionalist literature one finds both a macro theme and a micro theme concerning institutional impacts. According to the *macro theme* a set of institutions has a profound impact upon highly visible outcomes all around the globe, determining human development or democracy. Here we have what may be called grand social theory, such as the claim of the federalists that federalism will be linked up with better outcomes than unitarism (Chapter 4), the theory that presidentialism harms the prospects of stable democracy (Chapter 6) or the idea that property rights are crucial for economic performance (Chapter 12). One may encounter the macro themes in case studies but one meets them most often in statistical analyses.

The *micro theme* is less grandiose but perhaps more distinct, as under the micro theme one may find arguments about specific institutional effects, one institution having a determinate impact upon political life. The micro theme is to be found in case studies stating that one specific institution has had a large effect in one country, although it should be admitted that the micro theme can employ a statistical approach.

The new institutionalism in political science may well use both macro and micro models as well as employ case study or statistical methods. What at the end of the day is decisive is the amount of empirical support for these models.

To illustrate the difference between the macro and the micro themes in comparative politics we focus in this chapter upon one classical institutional model, Duverger's Law (Duverger 1986). It is a micro theme, focusing upon the effects of two electoral institutions, viz. majoritarian versus proportional techniques. Duverger's model was first employed in a case study explaining the difference between British politics and the politics of France during the Fourth Republic. But it was broadened, harbouring a very well-known and much discussed model about the link between the type of electoral institutions and certain specific political outcomes in all advanced countries with democratic political institutions such as party system fractionalization and governmental durability (Duverger 1951, 1964, 1986). It has recently been argued that the so-called Duverger effects hold primarily on the constituency level, which, if true, would make the model even more a micro theme. What is the evidence today for or against Duverger's law?

Elections in democratic countries

In the debate about the validity of the Duverger theory about the political consequences of electoral institutions, one finds basically two positions. On the one hand, there is a set of scholars who affirm the theory, believing that is its correct – the institutionalists. On the other hand, political sociologists reject the Duverger theory, arguing that it is the party system which comes before the electoral institutions, meaning that countries with few political parties select majoritarian techniques in their choice of institutions. To some extent, this is like the discussion about the hen and the egg: which comes first? What we need to assess is whether there really is such a firm connection between electoral institutions and political realities such as the party system, before we start interpreting whether one comes before the other.

Here, we will test Duverger's theory in relation to data about the countries, which have had roughly one and the same election system in place for some period of time. If one is to explore the macro outcomes connected with the use of alternative election systems, then it is absolutely necessary to include only countries with a stable election system in the analysis. The reason is that institutions take time in order to impact upon their environment. What is the comparative evidence in favour of the Duverger theory when one tests his models in relation to a data set covering all countries that allow democratic elections to take place?

The consequences of election systems could be immediate or distant. The immediate consequences would include the impact upon the participants directly involved in the operation of the election rules, i.e. the political parties or political leaders. The distant consequences would cover outcomes that election rules could have an impact upon, through the mediation of other factors. Thus, government instability could be a distant consequence of election systems, if election rules create a party system which counteracts government durability. The distinction between immediate and distant outcomes is hardly an acute one, but it is important. When it is sometimes argued that election institutions can be linked to very distant outcomes such as policy-making or socio-economic performance, then one must seek the links through which these impacts are transmitted.

Basically, one can look upon Duverger's theory as the first major institutional theory in the post-war period. *Political Parties: Their Organization and Activity in the Modern State* was first published in French in 1951 and in English for the first time in 1954, and consists of two sections: 'Party Structure' and 'Party Systems'. Duverger's law, if true, is very attractive from an institutionalist point of view, because it would provide governments with the possibility of straightforward constitutional engineering. It could manipulate one instrument variables – the election formulas – in order to arrive at desired or desirable outcomes. Thus, by moving back and forth between majoritarian and proportional election formulas, political elites could influence the shape of the party system as well as enhance the occurrence of certain forms of cabinets or government coalitions.

The purpose of this chapter is to examine the empirical evidence for the Duverger models in relation to information about the operation of election systems in democratic polities. We have included some forty countries in the data base, covering countries that have been more or less democratically stable for the last thirty years (Table 9.1).

It is certainly true that not all of the countries in Table 9.1 have experienced democratic stability during the entire time period mentioned. However, all of the countries have had at least some free and fair elections, meaning that the election system is not just a facade.

In the literature on election systems one separates between the institutions on the one hand – the ballot structure, the constituency structure and the formula – and, on the other hand, the outcome: the degree of disproportionality (Blais 1988; Blais and Massicotte 1996, 1997). We shall explain these concepts below and introduce measures for them. Here, we survey the election systems employed in the countries in Table 9.1 in order to establish how stable election systems tend to be.

Looking at democratic countries, we first establish the nature of the election formula used around 1970, 1980 and 1995: (1) majoritarian, (2) simple plurality, (3) mixed and (4) proportional. Second, we measure a few salient properties of election systems such as the amount of disproportionality and the district magnitude. Table 9.2 shows the major features of the electoral systems: electoral formula employed, district magnitude and disproportionality. Actually, the electoral formula tends to be very stable as few countries change from majoritarian to proportional representation (PR) methods. PR methods are more frequently employed than majoritarian methods.

The electoral district magnitude, measuring the number of representatives that each electoral district elects, is connected with the election formula. Since there are many countries that use PR methods, the electoral district magnitude will be higher than 1, which is typical of majoritarian techniques. Disproportionality, or the deviation from strict proportionality between votes received and seats allocated, is also related to the formula employed. Table 9.2 also shows that the degree of disproportionality is not high on average, reflecting again the frequent use of the PR methods.

What is crucial in research on election systems is to clarify these links between the formula, the district magnitude and disproportionality in a much more exact manner. We note the occurrence of only a few major changes from one election system to another in these countries: Chile from proportional to majoritarian in 1988, France from majoritarian to proportional in

Table 9.1 Democratically stable countries (n=45)

Country	1990s	1980s	1970s
Argentina	x	x	–
Australia	x	x	x
Austria	x	x	x
Belgium	x	x	x
Bolivia	x	x	–
Botswana	x	x	x
Brazil	x	x	(x)
Canada	x	x	x
Chile	x	–	x
Colombia	x	x	x
Costa Rica	x	x	x
Denmark	x	x	x
Domin Rep.	x	x	x
Ecuador	x	x	x
Finland	x	x	x
France	x	x	x
Germany	x	x	x
Greece	x	x	–
Honduras	x	x	–
Iceland	x	x	x
India	x	x	x
Ireland	x	x	x
Israel	x	x	x
Italy	x	x	x
Jamaica	x	x	–
Japan	x	x	x
Luxembourg	x	x	x
Malaysia	x	x	–
Mauritius	x	x	–
Netherlands	x	x	x
New Zealand	x	x	x
Norway	x	x	x
Papua N. G.	x	x	–
Philippines	x	–	x
Portugal	x	x	–
Spain	x	x	–
Sri Lanka	x	x	x
Sweden	x	x	x
Switzerland	x	x	x
Trinidad	x	x	x
Turkey	x	(x)	x
United King.	x	x	x
USA	x	x	x
Uruguay	x	x	–
Venezuela	x	x	x

Sources: Dahl 1971; Wesson 1987; Freedom House 1997.

Table 9.2 Electoral systems in the 1990s

	Electoral formulas				District magnitude (nat log)	Dispro- portionality
	Majority	*Plurality*	*Mixed*	*Proportion*		
OECD	2	3	4	15	1.6	10.0
Latin America	1	2	1	9	1.6	8.4
Africa	0	2	0	0	0.0	26.0
Asia	0	4	0	2	1.2	9.2
Total	3	11	5	26	1.5	10.2

Sources: Inter-parliamentary union (annually); Mackie and Rose 1991, 1997.

1986 and back to majoritarian in 1988, Honduras from proportional to mixed, Italy from proportional to mixed in 1994, Japan from plurality to mixed in 1996, New Zealand from plurality to mixed in 1995, and Sri Lanka from plurality to proportional in 1978. However, the overall picture of the election systems in democratic countries is one of stability as we can see from Table 9.3.

We will focus upon two outcomes of the operation of electoral institutions: (a) party system fractionalization – an immediate result; (b) government durability – a distant outcome. Two research strategies are available:- either one examines whether one and the same election system tends to result in the same outcomes in a number of countries, or one focuses upon the occurrence of a major change of the election system in order to see if it is accompanied by all together different outcomes. We will pursue the first research strategy, examining correlations between stable electoral institutions and political outcomes in a cross-sectional approach.

Now, assuming that election systems influence politics directly or indirectly, can we then find a strong corroboration of the specific Duverger model(s) in data about elections to the national legislature in these forty-five countries? What are these models, more precisely?

Table 9.3 Electoral systems: stability over time: 1970s to the 1990s

	Total set		OECD set	
	First factor	*n*	*First factor*	*n*
Electoral formulas	95.6	31	97.3	21
District magnitude	95.9	30	94.1	21
Disproportionality	72.3	28	83.7	21

Sources: See Table 9.2.

Note: First factor stands for the amount of explained variation in data accounted for by the first factor in a factor analysis based on data for three time periods.

Duverger's models

From the very beginning it is necessary to identify the Duverger theory clearly. Actually, it may be decomposed into a couple of models. In an article from 1986 'Duverger's Law: forty years later' Duverger commented upon his theory, explaining a few often made misinterpretations of his original statement. What, then, is the original version of what has been referred to as Duverger's law?

As a matter of fact, Duverger had already made the first presentation of his theory in 1945. In 1955 he called it a 'threefold sociological law', a description that he embraced in 1986, quoting again his 1955 formulation, which contains three ideas linking the election system with the party system:

> (1) Proportional representation tends to lead to the formation of many independent parties . . .   (2) the two-ballot majority system tends to lead to the formation of many parties that are allied with each other . . . (3) the plurality rule tends to produce a two-party system.
>
> (Duverger 1986: 70)

One may argue against Duverger himself that in relation to all these three 'laws' it is really a matter of one basic association, namely that between the election system and the party system, i.e. model (1) above. Whether one claims that PR gives rise to multipartism or that plurality rules result in two-partism, it is merely a manner of speaking and does not involve two different laws. The special case made for the two-ballot system – the French majoritarian method – seems to be somewhat of an *ad hoc* hypothesis, because this election system often involves even more disproportionality between votes and seats than the English plurality technique. It should, then, be conducive to strict two-partism.

First, we face here one model linking the election formula with one overall characteristic of the party system, namely the number of parties. Thus, we have:

(D1) Party system=F (Election formula)

where the basic idea would be that proportional election formulas when used tend to increase the number of parties. However, Duverger said in 1986 that he did not imply a mathematical multiplication such that the number of parties would keep increasing over time. What is entailed is simply that countries with PR techniques tend to have fractionalized party systems, but it is not stated how much fractionalization there would be.

Second, we face a corresponding claim about the opposite election system – the plurality technique – namely, that it tends to be conducive to a two-party system. However, this idea is just a reformulation of (D1) and does not need to be stated separately. A reasonable interpretation of Duverger's own caution is that he intends by (D1) a kind of dichotomous statement of a tendency where PR is connected with a multi-party system and plurality with a two-party system.

Third, we face a separate idea about the consequences of the use of the two-ballot technique, namely that it fosters electoral alliances. It may be seen as a hybrid form, where there are more than two parties but they behave in the end as if there were a two-party system. The model (D1) may also be interpreted to cover this idea, as the two-stage French election technique could be interpreted as a version of the plurality formula.

(D1) is a basic model about the consequences of electoral institutions upon the party system. It may be tested empirically. One needs information about a number of countries that have used one and the same election formula for a long period of time in order to test whether there is a clear tendency for PR to go together with a multi-party system and plurality with a two-party system. (D1) could be tested by the use of standard indicators on party system fractionalization such as the number of parties, Rae's fractionalization index or the index on the effective number of parties. (D1) is unproblematic, both theoretically and empirically.

However, from (D1) we do not arrive at the main objective of Duverger, at least not if we follow the theory as it was expounded in 1955. Duverger attempted to explain why at that time of writing the United Kingdom was politically stable whereas France and Italy tended towards instability. The basic difference, states Duverger, was the institutions of the election system. But to reach that conclusion Duverger must also establish a link between the party system and the state. This link is in fact very much discussed in the 1955 version but not mentioned at all in the 1986 comment by Duverger himself. This is why we are concentrating upon *Political Parties*, especially section two, where Duverger suggests a number of links between the party system and the regime.

Duverger distinguishes between three regimes: a presidential regime, a parliamentary regime and an assembly regime, and he confronts this regime classification with his separation between the two types of party systems: two-party system and multi-party system (Duverger 1964: 206–7). Since he actually never speaks about the assembly regime and it is not clear what he refers to, we may focus upon his argument about the links between presidentialism and parliamentarism on the one hand, and two-party system and multi-party system, on the other hand (Figure 9.1).

	Regimes	
	Presidential	Parliamentary
Two-party system	I	III
Multi-party system	II	IV

Figure 9.1 Regimes and party-systems.

All combinations from I to IV are not only feasible but there are real-life counterparts. Let us now quote carefully what Duverger says about each of these combinations:

QI   A presidential regime works best if there is a two-party system: 'In a two-party system the parties are big enough to dwarf the President who appears to be more the leader of one of them than an independent personality.' (Duverger 1964: 412).

QII   In a presidential regime with a multi-party system, the multi-party system increases the power of the president: 'If there is opposition in parliament between the presidential party and the majority party the increase in authority is very marked by comparison with bipartism: instead of finding itself confronted in parliament with a homogeneous and coherent majority the Executive finds only a heterogeneous coalition, and this gives scope for dividing and destroying tactics.' (Duverger 1964: 411).

QIII In a parliamentary regime, a two-party system is conducive to stability in the form of government durability: 'Multi-partism and bi-partism give rise to quite different structures. The two-party system tends to make the opposition into a real institution.' (Duverger 1964: 414).

QIV A multi-party system slips all too easily into government instability: 'Internally weak, multi-party governments are also weak in their relations with parliament' (Duverger 1964: 408).

Although we have already been confronted with QI and QII in Chapter 6 on presidentialism, we will here compress QI to QIV in a general model concerning executive stability, linking it to the party system, whether it is a question of a presidential or a parliamentary regime. Thus, we have:

(D2) Executive stability = F (party system)

The model concerning executive stability in (D2) is absolutely neccessary in order to reach the explanatory purposes that Duverger has set. Now, it follows why the United Kingdom was stable and why France under its Fourth Republic was unstable.

The explanation, using (D1) and (D2) seems plausible when accounting for the politics of the Fourth Republic and the differences between it and the politics of the Fifth Republic. He explains 'the example of France compared with Great Britain' in the following way:

> The absence of a majority party makes it necessary to form heterogeneous French cabinets based upon a coalition, or else minority cabinets relying on the parliamentary support of neighbouring parties.
>
> (Duverger 1964: 407)

The first argument states that PR techniques do not result in 'a majority party' except under very unusual circumstances. This is the first basic model (D1). The second argument claims that neither a 'heterogeneous coalition' nor a 'minority cabinet' works. Let us quote what Duverger predicts about a multi-party coalition government:

> The former are perpetually torn between the contradictory tendencies of their members, for here party solidarity operates against government solidarity instead of strenghthening it. . . . A programme of government action is therefore possible only for a very short period, for limited objectives and very lukewarm measures.
>
> (Duverger 1964: 407–8)

Duverger is equally sceptical towards the viability of minority governments. Although their dynamics is different, especially if it is a one-party minority cabinet, it will still display the same instability:

> Minority cabinets can scarcely function in any other way: they have the advantage of homogeneity but the disadvantage of less-assured parliamentary support; for these reasons they are as a general rule less common.
>
> (Duverger 1964: 408)

Duverger admits the existence of a Scandinavian exceptionalism with durable minority cabinets but 'minority governments are generally transitional cabinets' (Duverger 1964: 408). Here we have the second model, (D2).

The key question is, however, whether the difference between the United Kingdom and France under the Fourth Republic can be used as the basis for a more general induction, linking up the electoral formulas with political outcomes in a manner that would be true of any country. It is evident that Duverger makes this induction, arriving at two basic models, (D1) and (D2).

To sum up: Duverger's theory contain two basic models. There is, first, the link 1 connecting PR with a multi-party system and, second, there is the link 2 connecting a multi-party system with governmental instability. Duverger's theory about the political consequences of the framing of the rules in the electoral system involves two models that are coupled: (D1) and (D2). By putting them together we arrive at:

(D3) Executive stability=F (Election formula)

(D3) is a basic model in what is often referred to as the theme of multipartism or the theory that first links party system fractionalization with PR, and then links up cabinet instability with fractionalization in the party system. No doubt Duverger was more concerned about the first link than the latter. And in his late interpretation of his own position he only mentioned the first link. However, we will examine both (D1) and (D2) below, because they figure prominently in the debate about the outcomes of institutions. Finally, one may wish to point out that there is a strong value premise implicit in the Duverger framework, as the whole argument is based upon the following proposition:

(D4) Two-party systems perform better than multi-party systems

It is hardly difficult to find quotations in Duverger that support his bias against multi-party systems, which operate badly under both parliamentary and presidential regimes. In relation to parliamentary regimes we are told that 'In fact the multi-party system leads to the rule of half-measures and a perpetual preoccupation with current affairs' (Duverger 1964: 408). And as far as presidential regimes are concerned he says that: 'The natural impotence of multi-partism emphasizes with even greater clarity the privileged position of the President, who is alone able to act effectively and with continuity' (Duverger 1964: 412).

When evaluating two-party systems versus multi-party systems along (D3) Duverger restricted himself to political stability considerations. However, one could very well increase the scope of the performance evaluation, looking into other possible consequences of the party system such as, for instance, policy-making or socio-economic outcomes. Below we will follow in Duverger's footsteps and examine the immediate outcomes of the election institutions. Let us first make a short overview of the debate after Duverger and discuss the concepts used to study election institutions and their outcomes.

The debate on Duverger

Much of the research into the political consequences of electoral systems has no doubt been stimulated by Duverger's framework (Eckstein 1963; Rae 1971; Nohlen 1978; Grofman and Lijphart 1984; Taagepera and Shugart 1989; Lijphart 1994b; LeDuc *et al.* 1996; Norris 1997). However, this research has focused much more upon the connections between election techniques and the shape of the party system than upon the relationship between the party system and governmental instability. What has been at stake is the first of Duverger's models (D1). How tight is the connection between electoral formulas and the structure of the party system? Duverger made a simple dichotomy between PR systems and majoritarian techniques, where he separated between plurality and two-ballot methods. The analysis of election systems has been considerably broadened since the publication of Duverger's book, as other factors are also taken into account.

Election systems

The research on how election systems operate has underlined that there are more components that play a role for outcomes than those that Duverger included. Thus, modern election research suggests a more complex model than Duverger's on the basis of comparative research on election systems. The outcome factor is the degree of disparity between votes and seats, which is influenced by several properties of these election systems, not only the formula employed. Disproportionality is a function of not only the election technique – majoritarian versus proportional rules – but is also affected by the nature of the electoral districts and the ballot structure.

Lijphart in *Electoral Systems and Party Systems* (1994) presents a survey of existing electoral research, arguing that the key intervening variable between the electoral institutions and the party system is the amount of disproportionality. He explains this concept in the following way:

> The measures of the deviation of seat shares from vote shares may be alternatively referred to as measures of proportionality or *dis*proportionality – two sides of exactly the same coin.
>
> (Lijphart 1994b: 58)

He then tries to estimate the deviation from such strict proportionality by means of a couple of indices. However, disproportionality is not only effected by the electoral formula itself but also by other properties of the electoral system such as the nature of the constituencies, the existence of legal thresholds and the existence of regional compensation mandates. In addition, the tactics and strategies of the political parties themselves may play a role.

The amount of disparity or disproportionality may be measured with a scale ranging from 0 to 100 per cent. There are a few PR systems which come close to 0 per cent, but not all do so. The amount of disproportionality is affected not only by the formula but also by the constituencies and the ballot. Lijphart focuses upon the effective threshold in a party system, which is the percentage of votes that any party must get in order to be represented, i.e. receive a mandate at all. He takes into consideration the following properties of election systems: formula, district magnitude, number of districts, assembly size and legal threshold. He finds that: 'The strongest relationship is between the two major categories of electoral formula (majoritarian versus PR systems) on the one hand and the effective threshold on the other.' (Lijphart 1994: 50). He finds that the average effective threshold for the twenty-seven countries that he studied is a high 35 per cent for the majoritarian election systems, whereas the corresponding number for the PR countries is only roughly 7 per cent. Clearly, this must mean more parties in the countries with a PR formula than in countries with a majoritarian formula? Is the amount of fractionalization higher in PR countries than in majoritarian countries?

According to Lijphart, the critical mechanism which connects the election system with the party system is the extent of disproportionality. He finds that disproportionality is positively related to the real threshold, but it is far from a strict mathematical relation. Actually, the amount of disproportionality can also be substantial in PR systems, because disproportionality is affected by more factors than the formula used. In our selection of election systems we have a correlation of $r=-0.49$ ($p=0.001$) between the disporportionality scores and the election formula, which indicates that one must be careful when drawing conclusions about the effects of election formula. At the same time, it should be acknowledged that there is a clear link from majoritarian formula to disproportionality over a high effective threshold, but other factors also play a role.

First, constituencies are not always of the same size, meaning that a mandate represents the same number of people in the population. There are considerable divergences between the size of the constituencies not only in the first-past-the-post system but also in countries which use some PR techniques. Only when the whole country is one district will disporportionality be minimized under the use of the PR formulas. Second, some countries try to restrict party system fragmentation by the employment of legal thresholds such as a requirement of a minimum national or regional quota. In a few countries these thresholds are quite harsh, as in Germany and Sweden. Third, one must realize that PR techniques also involve deviation from strict and linear proportionality between votes received and mandates allocated, for example under the d'Hondt procedure, which favours large parties. However, such deviations may be counteracted by the use of regional compensation mandates, and in fact some countries do employ the allocation of equalizing mandates in order to increase proportionality.

The use of legal thresholds increases disproportionality as, after all, proportionality is not the sole concern of election systems. In several countries the districts are not of the same size populationwise, as some types of districts, such as agricultural districts, have a smaller population basis. When the quota between the mandate and the people represented is not the same all over the country, one is bound to have deviations from strict proportionality. The construction of election districts is often changed, reflecting the composition of the population, where so-called gerrymandering considerations can play a role.

Taagepera and Shugart employ in their *Seats and Votes* (1989) the two effects that Duverger used to explain why the majoritarian election technique is conducive to a two-party system by means of the disproportionality index. On the one hand, there is the mechanical effect of electoral rules, i.e. the mere mathematical result that in an election with a high degree of disproportionality each vote will not count equally. On the other hand, there is the psychological impact of this disproportionality upon the voter, who will try to resist wasting his vote, if it does not count as much as any other vote (Taagepera and Shugart 1989).

Moreover, Taagepera and Shugart argue that it is, rather, district magnitude that is the decisive factor for the variation in disproportionality. The larger the electoral districts, i.e. the more representatives each district elects, the smaller the deviation from proportionality. Focusing on the district magnitude allows one to arrive at a quantitative interpretation of Duverger, since with the majoritarian techniques the district magnitude is small whereas with the proportional techniques the district magnitude is high. What matters according to Taagepera and Shugart is the large variation in district magnitude among the proportional systems:

> The degree of proportionality in representation achieved is strongly influenced by the choice of M – more so than by the choice of allocation formula. The allocation formula does make a difference, but varying M matters more than varying the formula.
>
> (Taagepera and Shugart 1989: 124)

Here, 'M' stands for the district magnitude, or the number of seats filled at an election in a district on an average basis.

Thus, recent research on election systems have delivered a refined analysis of how electoral formulas work in real-life, including additional factors which Duverger did not pay attention to. At the same time, orientation of the research has been framed by Duverger's first model, i.e. (D1). In his overview of the debate, Cox in *Making Votes Count* (1997) contrasts a sociological approach to election systems with an institutional one, where the key problem is whether the party system is dependent upon the election formula – institutionalism – or whether the employment of certain election techniques reflects the party system (Cox 1997: 13–33). The sociological position is that party systems are more dependent upon long-run prevailing social cleavages than the construction of election systems – social determinism.

Cox mentions three questions that are relevant in relation to research on Duverger's propositions: (1) how social cleavages are transformed into electoral preferences; (2) how electoral preferences are transformed into votes; and (3) how votes are transformed into seats (Cox 1997: 26). However, he also observes that 'electoral systems tend to be, and to be perceived as, rather long-lived' (Cox 1997: 18). If this is so, then one could ask an additional question about election systems: do they matter for the party system or government formation and durability?

Cox's basic argument is that the so-called Duverger effects (mechanical and psychological) from majoritarian election techniques will show up at the lowest level, i.e. the constituency where the actual voting takes place. He writes:

> Duverger clearly recognized that both the wasted vote argument and the prudent withdrawal argument operated only at the district level. He thus acknowledged that the 'true effect' of plurality elections was to promote local bipartism but argued that local bipartism would 'project' into national bipartism when parties nationalized.
>
> (Cox 1997: 200–1)

The so-called projection argument has been much discussed (Wildavsky 1959; Sartori 1994), as it has a much weaker status from a methodological point of view. Whereas the mechanical and psychological effect at the constituency level are well in agreement with game theoretical predictions from a rational choice model, the conditions for arriving at the same effects at the national level are far less general. It is conceivable that one arrives at a multi-party system result at the national level, even when there is complete local bipartism, as one need only assume that it is not the same parties that are active in every constituency.

The projection argument entails the possibility of slippage in the first Duverger model. If national co-ordination is not forthcoming for some reason, then there could be a multi-party system on the basis of a majoritarian or plurality election technique, as in today's Italy. The occurrence of slippages in the links that Duverger modelled is what we wish to research here: from election system to party system to government formation and durability. This kind of slippage is bound to occur mostly on one side of the equation: majoritarian or plurality technique results in two-partism which results in a stable single party government. However, the reverse situation could also occur: PR resulting in multipartism which leads to unstable minority or multi-party governments. It is conceivable that national co-ordination is also forthcoming in PR systems, meaning that two big parties tend to emerge, as in Germany. It depends upon factors other than Duverger's.

In order to show the relevance of the occurrence of slippage in relation to the first and perhaps the major Duverger model, i.e. '(D1) Party system fractionalization=F(Election formula)', it is interesting to look at how the amount of disproportionality (Lijphart) and the district magnitude (Taagepera and Shugart) varies in real-life election systems. The Duverger implication is that disproportionality will be high when district magnitude is low, i.e. a strong inverse relationship.

Table 9.4 shows how different election systems vary in terms of disproportionality and district magnitude at various points in time.

Table 9.4 Disproportionality and district magnitude (natural logarithm) by election systems: means

	Disproportionality			District magnitude (Ln)		
	1970	*1980*	*1995*	*1970*	*1980*	*1995*
Majoritarian	18.4	17.1	17.8	0.00	0.00	0.23
Plurality	15.4	19.1	16.5	0.14	0.11	0.00
Mixed	1.1	1.6	8.3	0.70	0.70	0.82
Proportional	5.7	6.7	7.5	2.38	2.38	2.35
n	31	42	42	31	42	45
Eta-sq	0.46	0.59	0.30	0.66	0.70	0.70

Sources: See Table 9.2.

Generally speaking, the plurality systems and the majoritarian systems are characterized by the highest levels of disproportionality; at the same time, the differences between these two formula systems are not that large. Both these systems display considerable disporportionality of about 15 to 20 per cent. However, we note the occurrence of a slippage, as the proportional systems can also display disporportionality, although not to the same degree at about 5 to 8 per cent, on average. The decline in the eta-squared score for 1995 is remarkable, warning us against any simple notion that electoral formulas have unambiguous and clear-cut consequences. Looking at the variation in district magnitude it is obvious that what it shows is trivially true: M or district magnitude is really only substantial in PR systems.

We may now enquire into the relationship between the disproportionality measures in and the district magnitude figures in Table 9.4 in order to find out whether the claim of Taagepera and Shugart that disproportionality is a function of district magnitude, is empirically corroborated. Looking at the correlations for the three periods of time, where the scores for district magnitude have been transformed logarithmically, we may establish that they are quite high, from $r = -0.51$ to $r = -0.72$. The direction of the relationship between district magnitude and disproportionality is clearly what Taagepera and Shugart have predicted, viz. a negative relationship, but the strength of the interaction is weaker than what they have in mind. Here, we have another slippage, as the correlation is about -0.50, meaning that there could be substantial disproportionality even when M is high.

According to Duverger's second model, (D2), election formulas tend to have an impact upon executive stability by means of their impact upon the party system. When it comes to researching party systems, the debate after Duverger has also moved towards a recognition of greater complexity. Again, we are interested in the possibility of slippage in the links that Duverger modelled.

Party systems

The section 'Party Systems' introduces the separation between two-party systems and multi-party systems, which is very much focused in terms of his model (D2), meaning that he takes considerations about cabinet formation explicitly into account. On the one hand, two-party systems are analysed in the following manner:

> In one case for practical purposes only two parties share the parliamentary seats: the one assumes the entire responsibility for government, the other limits itself to the free expression of criticism in opposition; a homogeneous and powerful Cabinet has at its disposition a stable and coherent majority.
>
> (Duverger 1964: 207)

On the other hand, the multi-party system is described as a situation where not only two or more parties need to set up a coalition government but also as a situation where such a government would tend to be weak:

> In the other case a coalition between several parties, differing in their programmes and their supporters, is required to set up a ministry, which remains paralysed by its internal divisions as well as by the necessity of maintaining amidst considerable difficulties the precarious alliance on which its parliamentary majority is based.
>
> (Duverger 1964: 207)

Thus, in addition to the link between the election system and the party system, Duverger speaks of the connection between the party system and government stability. Thus, two-partism goes with government efficiency: 'the two-party system too has strengthened the authority of the government but without destroying the apparatus of democracy' (Duverger 1964: 403). But multipartism results in unstable or ineffective governments: '. . . multi-party governments are . . . weak in their relations with parliament' (Duverger 1964: 408).

Duverger's classification of two-party systems versus multi-party systems has been criticized as too simplistic. There is a large party system literature that has offered other and more complex taxonomies. First, the Duverger classification is based on a simple numerical criterion, which does not capture much of the variation in many party systems, which tend to comprise more than two parties. It may actually be more important for the politics of a country if it has a multi-party system with roughly five or six parties or a multi-party system with an excessive number of parties such as, for instance, fifteen parties or more. Second, it has been argued that other properties of party systems must be taken into consideration. Sartori emphasized ideological distance, which in combination with multipartism could create a threat to political stability, especially if so-called anti-system parties receive considerable support.

A number of indices have been devised for the analysis of party system dimensions, including measures of volatility. The Laakso–Taagepera index is one attempt to take into account both the number of parties in the party system and the voting support for the parties, arriving at a measure of the so-called effective number of parties. It is considered more adequate than indicators which merely focus upon the number of parties in a party system (Laakso and Taagepera 1979; see also Gaines 1997). We will use this index in the analysis below of party system effects, resorting to two versions of the index. In addition we will enquire into other indicators of party systems: party system fractionalization and share of largest party as measured by votes and seats (Table 9.5).

Let us first see how much the party systems vary when related to the election systems in terms of the Laakso–Taagepera index, when calculated

Table 9.5 Party system properties by election systems in the 1990s

	Effective number of parties		Party system fractionalization	Share of largest party	
	(votes)	(seats)		(votes)	(seats)
Majoritarian	4.1	2.8	0.699	39.4	50.7
Plurality	3.0	2.6	0.526	50.6	59.7
Mixed	3.7	3.0	0.613	38.2	44.5
Proportional	4.6	4.1	0.715	34.2	37.1
n	42	45	44	42	45
Eta-sq	0.15	0.19	0.30	0.29	0.32

Sources: See Table 9.2; party fractionalization = see Table 3.3.

on data about election results concerning the votes received by a party (Table 9.5). One observes two important findings in the table. On the one hand, it is true that plurality systems tend to have a low number of effective parties. But on the other hand, it is also the case that the difference between PR systems and majoritarian systems is marginal, on average. This is surprising in the light of Duverger's theory, as it loosens the link between the election system and the party system. Looking at the measures of party system fractionalization confirms even more strongly that the differences between the election systems are not as large as Duverger believed.

Perhaps the differences become clearer when we look at another version of the Laakso–Taagepera index, now calculated on the basis of seats allocated in the national assembly. Here we may better observe the two Duverger effects of election formulas. Majoritarian and plurality formulas tend to reduce the fractionalization in the party system by favouring big parties. Although the information pertains to the national scene, the effective number of parties is, on average, below three in majoritarian and plurality election systems, whereas it is above four in PR systems. The mechanical impact is most clear, but perhaps the psychological effect appears better looking at the measures of effective number of parties as the willingness to put up political parties for electoral choice is reduced in plurality and majoritarian systems, people knowing that there is the automatic effect. Yet, the eta-squared scores for effective number of parties (seats) are not that very much higher, meaning that it is more problematic to link up the party system with the election formula than Duverger thought. The difficulty is the projection from the local constituency level to the aggregate national level, as emphasized by Cox. The resulting slippage could actually be rather high in the links from election technique to party system characteristics.

No doubt, Duverger favours a large party receiving a majority share of the votes or the seats. How frequent is that in various election systems? Table 9.5 also contains information about the share of the largest party in terms of votes and seats.

It is actually surprising that the differences are not larger between the four election systems when it comes to favouring the largest party. However, if we add the mechanical effect to the psychological effect in Duverger's terms, then the differences become larger when considering the corresponding information for seats. On average, the share of the largest party in terms of seats in the national assembly reaches about 50 per cent in majoritarian systems and more than that in plurality systems, which should promote executive stability. However, it does not follow that there must be executive instability since the largest party in the other systems never reach the same amount of support. If coalition governments or minority governments can be stable, then Duverger's effect will not show up. Since the share of the largest party in PR systems is, on average, as high as 37 per cent, one could predict that it should not be too difficult to put together a government that could be stable, even if it has to be a coalition government or a minority government. If this prediction holds true, then we have another kind of slippage in the Duverger links.

We wish to underline that one must not miss link two in Duveger's model, more specifically the link between two-partism and government durability, i.e. (D2) above. It is true that Duverger paid much attention to explicating why the electoral formula shaped the party system, but said relatively little about why multi-party systems would tend to produce unstable governments. One of his basic ideas is that PR formulas must result in multi-party systems and that majoritarian election formulas must produce two-party systems. But he also claims, a little less vaguely, that where a large number of parties exists they will find it difficult to form and uphold a stable government.

Perhaps one could argue that Duverger really had in mind two 'laws', one linking the election system with the party system and the other connecting the party system with government durability and efficiency. On the one hand, he has stated: '*the simple majority single ballot system favours the two-party system*. Of all the hypotheses that have been defined in this book, this approaches the most nearly perhaps to a true sociological law' (Duverger 1964: 217). On the other hand, he has also very much insisted that two-partism goes with government durability whereas multipartism would be linked with government instability, and that the critical institution for manifacturing multipartism or two-partism is the choice of the election system. Let us examine the model (D2).

Governmental stability

Duverger starts from the observation that two-party systems are more stable than multi-party systems, at least when the UK is compared with France under the Fourth Republic. And he offers the election formula as the explanation of this fact. Now, stability is a notoriously difficult concept to handle. It is not only a value-loaded concept – is political stability a positive or negative? – but it is also a concept which is difficult to measure unambiguously. Yet, testing Duverger entails that one must focus upon these difficulties.

Bypassing the normative problem as to whether political stability is something positive or negative, as well as restricting the discussion of the concept to governmental stability, we wish to point out a basic difference between parliamentary regimes and presidential ones. Whereas it is meaningful to measure cabinet durability in parliamentary regimes by the number of governments that have served during a normal election period, one can argue that measuring executive stability in presidential regimes is far more difficult. Presidents are elected by a majoritarian election formula of some sort and they tend to stay in power for a full election period, unless something very spectacular occurs. Since presidents are not responsible politically to the national assembly, the whole debate about cabinet stability in parliamentary regimes seems irrelevant to presidential regimes.

One must be aware of an interaction between the election formula and the regime, as presidential regimes must be based upon some majoritarian formula, for practical reasons. Thus, one may wish to restrict the evaluation of the pros and cons of PR techniques to only parliamentary regimes. However, this seems to be much too restrictive, as presidential regimes are so numerous, especially if one also includes the mixed parliamentary and presidential regimes. It is still possible to have a multi-party system in a presidential regime, and presidents may come and go due to conflicts with the national assembly. Aware of the difficulties in measuring executive stability, we offer three alternative measures in Table 9.6.

First, we offer a proxy for measuring executive stability in democratic countries, namely the number of presidents or prime ministers during a specific period of time in terms of averages for each type of election system. One may argue that countries with numerous changes in presidents or prime ministers during a period of time are more unstable than countries where the government remains in power uninterruptedly for a whole normal election period, all other things being equal.

Table 9.6 Government instability properties by election systems in the 1990s: all and parliamentarian countries

	Presidents and prime ministers		Cabinet changes		Effective executive changes	
	All	*Parliam*	*All*	*Parliam*	*All*	*Parliam*
Majoritarian	4.0	4.5	0.61	0.67	0.22	0.17
Plurality	2.8	3.3	0.38	0.44	0.18	0.21
Mixed	4.0	4.3	0.60	0.63	0.43	0.46
Proportional	3.2	3.2	0.39	0.37	0.22	0.22
n	45	29	45	29	45	29
Eta-sq	0.06	0.07	0.10	0.14	0.15	0.18

Sources: Presidents and prime ministers = based upon reports in Keesing's record of world events; cabinet changes = Banks 1996; effective executive changes = see Table 3.3.

Note: The lower the value, the more stability.

The surprising finding in Table 9.6 is that on this measure of executive instability – number of presidents or premiers – the various election systems do not differ much. Very low scores are to be found among the countries that employ the plurality method, especially in presidential systems. Table 9.6 also offers two more measures – number of cabinet changes, and number of effective executive changes – on executive stability, which may complement the earlier measure.

This measure on executive stability is broader than the previous one used. Government changes could involve reshufflings without a change in the leader of the government. However, the eta-squared scores remain relatively low, indicating little difference between the countries who use alternative election systems. Actually, the PR countries score lower than the countries employing mixed or majoritarian techniques and only slightly higher than countries with the plurality method. The table finally states a general measure on executive changes. Although the countries with plurality techniques tend to display fewer executive changes than the PR systems do, the differences between the systems are much too small to serve as evidence for any claim that executive instability is higher in PR systems.

To sum up: we have noted the possibility of slippage in the links that Duverger established in his two models: (1) election technique and the party system; (2) the party system and government formation and durability. Even if his two effects, the mechanical and the psychological impact, hold true, they would do so only at the constituency level. The projection argument to the national level is so uncertain that there could be considerable slippage in the two links. Since election systems involve factors other than those considered by Duverger, the risk of slippages increases even more. Let us now look at estimations of the Duverger links in order to see how much slippage occurs in real life.

Testing the Duverger models

Examining Duverger's theory more closely, we have detected that he has not one model in mind – PR causing party system fractionalization – but also another model linking in the election formula with political instability, or perhaps more correctly executive instability (Druckman 1996; Neto and Cox 1997; Taagepera 1998). Looking at the countries which have had a stable election system for a considerable period of time, what is the evidence for the two Duverger models, (D1) and (D2) (Table 9.1)? One may claim that Duverger's general preference for two-party systems over multi-party systems (D4) results from a combination of (D1) and (D2), which gives us the basic model (D3). However, combining (D1) and (D2) involves a risk, as each link may be too loose due to slippages of various kinds, in order to allow one to arrive at (D3). If the election formula only partly impacts upon the party system, and the party system only partly impacts upon executive stability, then the connection between the election formula and executive stability may not be tight enough to allow the conclusion that majoritarian election institutions are superior to PR techniques in terms of their outcomes. Let us look at the empirical evidence in favour of (D1) and (D2).

Link 1: PR methods and multipartism

The nature of election institutions is rather well-known today, given the extensive research on election formulas, especially in the OECD countries. Thus, one employs not only the all too simple classification of proportional techniques versus majoritarian methods, but one looks carefully at the use of various methods within these two sets, especially in the PR set. There are different majoritarian methods (MT), as for instance the Anglo-Saxon first-past-the-post technique – plurality – and the French double ballot method. Similarly, one must distinguish between different PR techniques, such as d'Hondt, Saint-Lague, Largest Remainder and Single Transferable Vote or Single Non-transferable Vote. What complicates any neat classification is, however, that one may combine the different methods, i.e. Mixed, such as the technique employed in Germany.

Let us look at the evidence for the first Duverger model, i.e.: '(D1) Party system fractionalization=F (Election formula).'

How is one to test (D1) empirically? One needs to look at empirical evidence from many elections in various countries and not only refer to the immense differences between the Fourth and Fifth French Republics or the contrast between the UK and France during its Third or Fourth Republics. And one must look at countries where election institutions have been firmly in place for a long period of time, allowing them to have an impact upon real life, such as electoral rules impacting upon the party system or executive stability.

One may in all earnesty say that Duverger did not pay much attention to other aspects of electoral institutions other than the basic formula distinction: MT versus PR. Yet, as stated above when speaking of the real-life effects of electoral institutions, one needs also to take into account the following properties: (1) the nature and number of the constituency; (2) the use of legal thresholds; (3) the employment of regional compensation mandates: (4) the regulation of list construction and the making of electoral strategies by the parties. When one takes these additional properties of electoral systems into account, then the question becomes whether matters are as transparent as Duverger believed.

Following Lijphart, one may interpret the model (D1) as consisting of two links:

(D1A) Disproportionality=F (Election formula)

and

(D1B) Twopartism=F (Disproportionality)

It is true that if one pays no attention to the other properties of election systems, then one can model situations where it is rational for parties to accept a two-party format, given the use of an election formula that entails the possibility of extreme disproportionality. However, the opposite does not hold. If one takes all the characteristics of election systems into account, then it is far from certain that only majoritarian election systems produce high disproportionality. Only an empirical analysis can tell whether (D1A) is true. In relation to (D1B) one can make the same kind of argument. If there can also be considerable disproportionality in PR systems, then the election system could not make the distinction between a two-party system and a multi-party system.

Following Taagepera and Shugart, we may interpret (D1) somewhat differently, as:

(D1C) District magnitude=F (Election formula)

and

(D1D) Party system fractionalization=F (District magnitude)

We will now argue that the four connections listed above are far from as tight as Duverger thought, which implies that the empirical correlations that are relevant for the evaluation of the models (D1B) and (D1D) are far weaker than needed for the validation of the Duverger argument. Table 9.7 states the correlations between disproportionality, district magnitude and the effective number of parties for votes and seats.

The evidence shows that the connections that Lijphart, and Taagepera and Shugart have suggested in order to account for Duverger's model (D1) are far from tight enough to warrant the conclusion that party system fractionalization is caused by the election institutions. Although it is true

Table 9.7 Party system and election system: correlations

Party system		1970s		1980s		1990s	
		Disp	Magnit	Disp	Magnit	Disp	Magnit
Votes	r	−0.12	0.60	−0.21	0.24	−0.06	0.35
	p	0.266	0.000	0.105	0.072	0.343	0.011
Fractionaliz.	r	−0.48	0.68	−0.43	0.49	−0.32	0.45
	p	0.003	0.000	0.003	0.000	0.019	0.001
Seats	r	−0.40	0.73	−0.40	0.45	−0.33	0.49
	p	0.014	0.000	0.005	0.002	0.016	0.000

Sources: See Table 9.2.

Note: Party system: votes = effective number of parties (votes), fractionalization = party system fractionalization, seats = effective number of parties (seats). Election system: disp = disproportionality, magnit = district magnitude.

that disproportionality reduces the effective number of parties, both in terms of votes and seats, and that the district magnitude increases the effective number of parties, we can establish that the correlations are not strong enough to warrant the Duverger claim (D1). The correlation for 1980 and 1970 are no different from the correlations for 1995 meaning that the negative finding is robust.

Link II: Fractionalization and government durability

We may now turn to the second Duverger model, stating a link between the nature of the party system and performance outcomes, where Duverger focused exclusively upon political stability in the form of government durability, i.e.:

(D2) Government stability = F (party system fractionalization)

Duverger focused upon political stability in the form of government durability, because he thought that rapid turnover of cabinets indicated a profound state of instability. This is not necessarily the case though, as one needs to assess independently how dangerous government instability is. One could argue that the Fourth French Republic was characterized not only by extreme government instability but also by profound state instability, as the long period of rapid cabinet turnover spilled over into a questioning of the institutions. In addition, two major political groupings, the Gaullist Right and the Communists, questioned the Fourth Republic already from its initiation. Such a tight connection between cabinet instability and state instability or constitutional instability may not be necessary. In the 1980s or the 1990s several countries have experienced numerous cabinet crises, but the general acceptance of the state has not been put on the agenda – see e.g. Denmark and The Netherlands.

Yet, it is a widely held belief that multi-party systems are conducive to executive instability. Taagepera and Shugart argue this way, with what they call the 'inverse square law of coalition durability', i.e. that the larger the number of parties, the lower the degree of government durability (Taagepera and Shugart 1989: 99–103). Taagepera and Shugart do not link this law with Duverger, but it is certainly implicit in his theory about the institutional effects of election formulas. What is the evidence in favour of (D2)?

Table 9.8 contains the correlations between the party system – votes and seats – and the indicators on executive stability used here: the number of presidents and prime ministers as well as the number of cabinet changes and effective executive changes.

These findings only very weakly support the Duverger second model. In general, there is hardly any association between party system fractionalization or a high effective number of parties – votes or seats – on the one hand, and executive instability on the other hand. The direction of the connections

Table 9.8 Government instability and party systems: correlations

Gov. instab		1970s			1980s			1990s		
		Vote	Frac	Seat	Vote	Frac	Seat	Vote	Frac	Seat
Prime/presid	r	0.33	0.09	0.33	0.15	0.33	0.18	0.35	0.34	0.29
	p	0.035	0.269	0.35	0.176	0.013	0.128	0.011	0.013	0.025
Cabinet	r	0.29	0.21	0.21	0.21	0.17	0.20	0.14	0.09	0.12
	p	0.059	0.129	0.130	0.097	0.150	0.102	0.181	0.295	0.221
Executive	r	0.26	0.43	0.26	0.10	0.11	0.20	0.03	0.18	0.13
	p	0.082	0.008	0.082	0.265	0.244	0.102	0.437	0.124	0.201

Sources: See Tables 9.2 and 9.6.

Table 9.9 Government instability and election system: correlations

Gov. instab		1970s		1980s		1990s	
		Disp	Magnit	Disp	Magnit	Disp	Magnit
Prime/presid	r	−0.13	0.33	−0.16	0.21	0.15	−0.08
	p	0.241	0.033	0.167	0.090	0.170	0.293
Cabinet	r	0.02	0.19	−0.20	0.21	0.24	−0.15
	p	0.462	0.159	0.117	0.091	0.065	0.155
Executive	r	−0.18	0.34	−0.18	0.28	−0.00	−0.01
	p	0.171	0.033	0.142	0.038	0.492	0.469

Sources: See Table 9.2 and 9.6.

is in accordance with Duverger's argument, but the strength is much too low. Again, we observe slippage, as other factors impact.

Let us look finally at the macro association between election system and government stability, remembering Duverger's starting point: why is the UK stable whereas France is not (under the Fourth Republic). Will majoritarian techniques automatically enhance executive stability? Table 9.9 suggests not, because of the occurrence of slippage in the connections outlined above. The correlations between election system properties and indicators of government instability are simply too low.

Conclusion

We have found that Duverger's law is far more complex and uncertain than recognized in the literature. It harbours not one but several institutional outcome models, which all receive rather scanty support. However, it is clearly one of the most attractive institutional theories, as it has a middle-range scope and can easily be transformed from a micro theory explaining West-European experiences to a macro theory, covering democratic politics in general and the place of institutions in them. Now, can the Duverger set of models be generalized even further into a grand theory of institutions, contrasting British democracy with non-English democracy?

When testing the Duverger models, the strategy has been to select cases which at some period during the post-war period have been classified as democracies (Dahl 1971; Wesson 1987). Among these states we have selected three periods of time, circa 1995, 1980 and 1970, in order to look at the stability over time of these institutional arrangements: are electoral systems stable over time or not?

The outcomes we have looked at represent the following aspects of the political system: disproportionality of the system (i.e. disproportionality between distributions of votes and seats), fragmentation of the party system (effective number of parties based on votes and seats), the incidence of majorities (majority achieved by the largest party in terms of votes and seats), and the stability of government (here measured by three proxies: the number of prime ministers or presidents, number of government changes, and executive changes).

The empirical findings are based upon three conditions that happen to be true: (a) electoral systems tend to be stable over time; this applies to electoral formulas and district magnitudes; (b) party systems properties are also rather stable over time; this also applies to effective number of parties and incidence of majorities; (c) government stability is also stable over time. The findings include the following results:

1 PR systems display less of disproportionality
2 PR systems show more of party system fractionalization
3 PR systems have less incidence of majorities among voters and in terms of seats
4 PR systems have slightly higher number of prime ministers/presidents

All these findings are in accordance with the Duverger theory, but the connections are too weak to warrant the strong Duverger conclusions. Thus, neither (D1) nor (D2) can be empirically corroborated, as the correlations between disproportionality and effective number of parties as well as between effective number of parties and executive stability are too weak.

One may start from the Duverger opposition between the UK and Continental Europe, but interpret the facts in a totally different way. Instead of focusing upon France during its Fourth Republic, one may wish to contrast British democracy with stable West European countries like Switzerland, The Netherlands, Belgium, Austria and Germany after the Second World War. Then, what are the institutional effects? If these countries are even more politically stable than the United Kingdom, then perhaps Duverger was completely wrong to admire British democracy even at the start. Lijphart has published a few books about institutional effects which have played a prominant role in comparative politics ever since the publication of the first study, *The Politics of Accommodation*, in 1968. Lijphart's theme started out as a micro theme, interpreting the Dutch case, but he generalized it into a grand social theory step by step, where the basic idea is that there are better forms of democracy than the Westminster model. The next two chapters examine the Lijphart models, their development as well as the evidence in favour of them.

Evaluating the Lijphart theory, we first face the task of clarifying how democratic institutions may vary. Second, we must enquire as to whether such an institutional variation matters for policies and outcomes. This leads us to an enquiry into institutional performance and causality.

10 Westminster versus Consensus democracy – a tenable distinction?

Introduction

A classical distinction in the social sciences separates between two kinds of theory, grand theory, on the one hand, and middle-range theory, on the other (Merton 1957: 3–17). In the neo-institutionalist literature, one finds examples of both types of theory. Duverger's law amounts to a middle-range theory. Lijphart's model of democracy comes readily to one's mind, when one searches for an example of grand theory in neo-institutionalism.

His *Democracies: Patterns of majoritarian and consensus government in twenty-one countries* from 1984 is perhaps the most influential institutionalist text in political science during the post-war period. A middle-range approach like Duverger's is very different from a macro theme like Lijphart's, as in grand social theory one presents a framework covering many institutions at the same time and their presumed effects. How is one to handle such a macro theme as Lijphart's theory when searching for empirical evidence for the occurrence of institutional effects?

We suggest that one tries to unpack Lijphart's grand theory into several middle-range hypotheses or models that may be tested empirically. Actually, one will then arrive at the negation of the Duverger's argument, Lijphart claiming that PR election techniques are superior to majoritarian methods. In this chapter we first look at the sources of Lijphart's model and then examine its basic claim about institutional convergence toward only two ideal-types of democracy. In the next chapter, we examine one middle-range theory from the Lijphart grand theory, namely that Consensus democracy as a whole works better than Westminster democracy. This is a prediction about the real world that needs to be submitted to the most difficult test possible – falsification.

Dutch consociational practices

Lijphart's grand theory is that there are fundamentally only two kinds of democracy, i.e. Westminster democracy and Consensus democracy. Here we have in a very pronounced manner two ideal-types in the Max Weber sense, as Westminster and Consensus democracy are constructions consisting of a whole sets of institutions. In reality, most if not all countries only come more or less close to these ideal-types, which in pure form do not exist in real life.

Our strategy here is to unpack these two ideal-types into separate institutions and probe the instituional impacts of each institution taken one by one. However, it is interesting to ask how the general Lijphart model developed from the first presentation of this theme in 1968, which was far more restricted both conceptually and empirically, dealing with consociational practices in The Netherlands.

Lijphart's democracy theory is an example of how one may make an induction from one case study to a grand theory, as he has successively generalized his Dutch findings from 1968 into an analysis of all democracies of the world. We wish below to pin down some of the critical steps in this inductive process up until 1999 (Lijphart 1999).

Lijphart's first major study dealt only with one case, the Netherlands, attempting to explain its long record of political stability despite a deep religious cleavage and the occurrence of so-called Zuilen in society and state. He focused upon the chiefly informal institutions structuring elite behaviour in this country, referring to these mechanisms or institutions – broad coalitions, elite cartels, social pacts – by a special technical expression: 'consociationalism', borrowing the latin word 'consociatio', meaning pact or agreement, from a classical text in the history of political theory: Althusius' *Systematic Politics* from 1610.

In the 1950s and 1960s, scholars debated the conditions for political stability and democratic longevity, which attracted widespread interest (Almond 1956; Lipset 1959; Dahl 1971). Three related questions were discussed. On the one hand, one wished to explain why certain advanced industrial countries manifested expressions of political instability, although they adhered to democratic institutions, such as Germany under the Weimar Republic, France during the Third and Fourth Republics, as well as Italy and Finland after the Second World War. On the other hand, one focused upon why some advanced countries during the twentieth century had given up their democratic regimes and moved towards authoritarianism: Italy, Germany, Spain, and Portugal. Why fascism in affluent countries? Finally, one wished to understand why there was political instability in some specific countries resulting in civil war or anarchy such as in Northern Ireland, Spain or later in Lebanon and Sri Lanka. Thus, the concept of political stability in this discourse was a complex one, covering both the distinction between democracy and non-democracy and the separation between political stability and instability.

The Politics of Accommodation (1968) entered the debate about the condition for stable democracy, with the argument that there exist other and different arrangements than those typical of Anglo-Saxon democracy – the Westminster model. Another form of democracy – consociational democracy – emphasizing elite accommodation may be just as stable politically as the British type.

Dutch democracy has a special flavour, argued Lijphart, which has not been captured in the prevailing theories of democracy at that time, especially in the work on stable democracy, which approach dominated the discourse in political science in the late 1950s and early 1960s (Almond 1956; Almond and Coleman 1960; Almond and Powell 1966). What, then, was special about Dutch politics in the eyes of this case study? Elite accommodation or consociationalism, was the answer.

Lijphart started from the so-called cleavage framework when discussing the conditions of democratic stability. This approach tends to look upon politics as a reflection of the social structure, where a high level of fragmentation, i.e. the occurrence of divisive and mutually reinforcing cleavages, would be conducive to political instability in the form of recurrent government crises as well as the occurrence of protest phenomena and political violence. However, Lijphart argued that certain forms of elite behaviour – consociationalism – could compensate for the instability implications of social fragmentation. He employed this new idea when interpreting Dutch politics in the twentieth century, as The Netherlands had experienced both sharp religious cleavages and political stability.

Let us pin down what Lijphart meant by 'elite accommodation', which he used as a general term for several different kinds of mechanisms of elite co-operation, including political institutions. Let us quote from the 1968 book:

> Dutch politics is a politics of accommodation. That is the secret of its success. The term accommodation is here used in the sense of settlement of divisive issues and conflicts where only a minimal consensus exists.
>
> (Lijphart 1975 (2nd edition): 103)

It seems as if Lijphart, in 1968, interpreted consociationalism more behaviourally than institutionally, focusing particularly upon the occurrence of grand coalitions.

The politics of accommodation is the opposite to adversarial politics, as it occurs in English-type democracy. It is the politics of bargaining and agreements among political elites. These agreements or pacts need not be institutionally sanctioned or explicitly translated into institutions, as long as all important players are brought on board. What matters is the actual elite behaviour, consisting of all kinds of behaviour from participation in oversized governments or grand coalitions to the making of formal or informal pacts outside of government, which promote a mutual understanding of politics and policies, accommodating differences. It was not until the 1977 book *Democracy in Plural Societies* that Lijphart gave his theory a distinctly institutional emphasis. Let us now turn to the 1977 book, which involved a major attempt at making the 1968 argument into an institutional format.

The plural societies and their politics

In the 1977 book, Lijphart paid much attention to introducing clear comparative concepts while maintaining the focus upon the relationship between social structure in the form of cleavages and democratic stability. On the one hand, the concept of social fragmentation is made more precise by identifying the so-called deeply divided societies. On the other hand, the notion of elite accommodation was unpacked into a whole set of so-called consociational devices, among which the grand coalition was only one such mechanism. Interestingly, the focus is clearly much more institutional than behavioural.

Broadening the focus from a case study to a comparative analysis, Lijphart examines a set of countries which have employed what he calls 'consociational practices'. These countries are, argues Lijphart, typically countries with strong ethnic or religious cleavages, that would if unmatched by consociational devices result in political instability, such as the occurrence of civil war in the worst case or merely governmental instability in the best case. The set of so-called plural societies included in the 1977 study comprised, for instance, the Benelux countries, Switzerland, Yugoslavia, Lebanon and Sri Lanka.

The notion of a plural society is Lijphart's interpretation of the theory of cleavages as the main cause of conflict in society (Rokkan *et al.* 1970; Flora *et al.* 1999). When there is extensive social fragmentation along ethnic, religious or class cleavages, then democratic institutions based upon majoritarian principles simple do not work. Power-sharing mechanisms are needed in such plural societies – this is the 1977 message.

The concept of a plural society involves not only the Rokkanian cleavages that express in a latent or manifest manner the conflict bases in the social structure (Lipset and Rokkan 1967; Rokkan *et al.* 1970). Lijphart also requires that the cleavages that structure conflict among social groups be 'deep-seated', involving a historical dimension of conflict, and be cumulative, i.e. two or more cleavages coincide, which means in the language of Lipset, that the cleavages are mutually reinforcing (Lipset 1959).

In the publications from the early 1990s, Lijphart, however, takes a much more assertive standpoint, claiming that whatever the social structure may look like, power-sharing institutions perform better than majoritarian institutions (Lijphart 1985, 1991, 1992, 1994a; see also Van Schendelen 1984; Halpern 1986; Lustick 1997). The 1977 position is a cautious conditional one, claiming that power-sharing works in a special set of societies, whereas the later position is a much more general and unconditional preference for any type of power-sharing regime.

In the 1977 book, Lijphart gives consociationalism much more content as well as variety. What we are interested in here is the specification of the so-called 'consociational mechanisms'. It is not a question merely of general elite co-operation at the behavioural level, but a matter of the occurrence of a set of special and distinct mechanisms, identified institutionally or by means of norms and sometimes constitutional rules. Let us quote from a key passage:

> Consociational democracy can be defined in terms of four character-istics. The first and most important element is government by a grand coalition of the political leaders of all significant segments of the plural society.
>
> (Lijphart 1977: 25)

Besides the grand coalition, there are three other consociational mechan-isms: (1) mutual veto, meaning rules about the protection of minority interests; (2) proportionality, or rules about the allocation of political representation and positions in the bureaucracy; (3) autonomy, or rules about decentralization (Lijphart 1977: 25). It is these three additional aspects of consociationalism, besides elite accommodation in a grand coalition, that allow for institutionalization in the form of constitutional recognition of special majorities and federalism, or in alternative ways of constructing election systems.

What is consociationalism?

The key term in Lijphart's early work is 'consociationalism'. What does it mean? Elite accommodation, one may answer, as in the 1968 book. But this is such a vague concept, denoting all forms of elite bargaining and mutual understanding. The 1968 study identified first and foremost the oversized government coalition or the grand coalition as typical for consociationalism, arguing that:

> (L1) Grand coalitions promote democratic stability in fractionalised societies.

The requirement that the government format be not only a real coalition involving more than one player, but also that it should take the form of an oversized coalition having more parliamentary support than strictly neces-sary, is not an innocuous one. It militates against the very simple idea that to rule in a democracy you most often need only 51 per cent – why bring more players on board than necessary? Game theory modelling coalitions predict that the minimum winning sized format is the most likely outcome in deliberations about government and that only such governments will be durable (Riker 1964). Grand coalition will not be stable, as there is more to be gained in reducing the size of the coalition. And minority coalitions will not be stable either, as they will not have sufficient legislative support for their policies.

As a matter of fact, one finds all three types of government coalitions in democracies: oversized, minimum winning and minority coalitions. The making and remaking of coalitions indicate a political culture of bargaining with a strong wish to negotiate differences and respect others by making binding agreements, which is characteristic of a democracy. Why, then, should consociationalism be restricted to one special form of coalition government, the oversized government format. One could focus equally well, it seems, upon all kinds of coalitions, i.e. besides grand coalitions, also those with a simple majority or even minority, claiming that:

> (L2) Coalition governments promote democratic stability in fractionalised societies.

Both (L1) and (L2) may be interpreted as stating a contributing condition for democratic stabilty. What the Lijphart framework definitely rules out is that single-party simple majority governments – the Westminster model – do better than real coalitions with several parties involved in societies with strong cleavages.

The occurrence of coalition governments would, one may theorize, have one clear consequence, namely that it promotes democracy as well as political stability. Accordingly, it is not so much the grand coalition which is conducive to democratic stability as the mere occurrence of a coalition government, whether majoritarian, grand coalition or in the minority coalition format. How crucial is it for the Lijphart argument that the elite co-operation takes the form of a grand coalition, i.e. that the coalition is oversized ? The question is no doubt a higly relevant one, as grand coalitions occur less and less. Perhaps Lijphart would claim that the other three aspects of consociationalism listed above – mutual veto, proportionality and autonomy – have increased their relevance in order to compensate for the decreasing relevance of grand coalitions. In any case, scales measuring consociationalism tend to target the occurrence of grand coalitions.

In his early work, Lijphart definitely favoured the case study method over the so-called comparative methods. In certain special countries, one may observe how a high degree of social fragmentation – mainly ethnic and religious cleavage – works itself out in the form of sharp political instability and also how consociational mechanisms may counteract the momentum towards political instability or fail to do so. One needs to take into account the interaction between social conditions and consociational mechanisms – this remains the core of the Lijphart framework.

Should analysis of consociationalism be restricted to a special set of countries, the so-called plural societies? Are these societies distinct in the sense that the occurrence of cleavages weigh very heavily upon politics, perhaps because social cleavages tend to be mutually reinforcing? Or are these countries distinct in the other sense, meaning through the special use made of consociational practices? The plural societies may constitute a very special set of countries which happen to be both deeply divided and practise heavily consociational practices. Perhaps a country that is very deeply divided needs many of these consociational mechanisms at the same time, in order to handle or counteract the negative consequences of sharp cleavages for political stability. We are talking here about the uniqueness of the cases, whether it be The Netherlands, as in the 1968 statement, or a set of deeply divided societies as in the 1977 statement.

One could approach consociational institutions one at a time or one could single out a special set of countries where they are practised as a whole – the so-called consociational democracies. What could be decisive for political stability or democratic viability is not whether a country scores higher or lower on the employment of each of these devices separately but whether all of them occur more or less simultaneously. Yet, despite the strong concentration upon special countries in the 1968 and 1977 formulations of his theme, Lijphart in 1984 proceeded to elaborate a full comparative statement of his main ideas, covering all democratic countries and dividing democratic institutions into two model sets: Consensus democracy and Westminster democracy.

Two ideal-types of democracy

Democracies (1984) claims that the world of democratic countries, which is certainly not a static one, can best be understood if we start from two extreme models of democracy and then classify existing countries as somewhere in-between these two polar types. These two ideal-types of democracy are based upon the opposition that Lijphart studied in his case studies, namely British or Anglo-Saxon democracy, on the one hand, and Continental European or consociational democracy, on the other hand. What was new in the 1984 book was that this distinction was worked out almost entirely with institutional characteristics as well as in a most comprehensive fashion, covering potentially the entire set of democratic countries (Lijphart 1998a, b).

Lijphart employed nine characteristics to identify the Westminster model of democracy (WM) and the Consensus model of democracy (CM) by means of a correlate and its opposition. Besides institutions, Lijphart also included behavioural characteristics such as the nature of the party system. Below we will examine WM and CD, but only look at their institutional features.

Now, institutions are rules or norms by which men/women live, either abiding by them or violating them. The institutionalization of rules results in organization. Political life is to a large extent institutionalized and the most basic political institution in modern times is the state, comprising a huge variety of public organizations. Thus, institutions are bits and pieces but also patterns of norms.

Lijphart's main argument is that we have two ideal-types of democracy, one adhering to the spirit of power fusion and the other converging upon the opposite spirit of power-sharing. Democratic political institutions may vary along a number of dimensions, but underneath all the country variation in different mechanisms for democratic government there is fundamentally two, and only two, logics of institutional coherence.

The greatest institutionalist of all the founders of the modern theory of constitutional government, Baron de Montesquieu, argued that each country has its own spirit of laws or norms. The institutions of a country have emerged through institutional evolution over the centuries, and institutional legacies reflect the past history of that country. This is a holist position in institutionalism, claiming that each country's institutions make sense when they are understood as single pieces of a larger puzzle.

Weber made no such claim about institutional coherence or convergence, as he looked upon institutions as every single norm that carry sanctions against non observation. Institutionalization is, in Weber, connected with the universal drive towards rationality and his legal–rational type of authority is unthinkable without the concept of an institution as a key element, making this type different from patrimonial, feudal and charismatic domination where personal ties prevail.

We wish to argue for this atomistic position, treating each political institution as a separate entity. The election system is one such institution with a few basic alternatives that appear to be capable of occurring together with a large variety of other political institutions. PR methods occur in unitary as well as federal states, in countries with or without legal review, where government can be of any kind of coalition, and together with any kind of chamber system. PR methods can be constitutional law or mere law. It is, we claim, the same with almost all other key political institutions. Institutional convergence is a myth.

Institutional logic or the spirit of institutions

Political institutions can be conventions or laid down in statute law or in constitutional law. They can be codified constitutional law or constitutional practice. Democracy at the macro level of society is always an institutional phenomenon, as institutions have been designed or have evolved to make the rule of the people possible. Democratic government is one form of constitutional rule, where constitutional law or practices safeguard human rights, on the one hand, and the separation of powers, on the other hand. Thus arises the question: how do the various institutions that bring about democracy in constitutional states hang together? What is their logic or spirit? How do they co-vary empirically?

The institutions of Westminster democracy (WM) are said to converge on executive dominance. But one needs to remember that stable democracies are constitutional states. Thus, they will have institutions promoting the Rule of Law, limiting executive dominance. True executive dominance one finds in unlimited presidential systems, which are not constitutional states. The institutions of Consensus democracy (CM) are claimed to adhere to the opposite spirit, namely power-sharing. Yet, in all constitutional democracies there are many institutions that guarantee power-sharing, also in the British state. Thus, citizens have extensive rights against the Westminster state and the legal system is outside of the system of legislative supremacy of parliament. Correspondingly, limited presidential systems as conceived by Montesquieu or Madison provide for executive dominance, but in such systems they are power-sharing systems with *trias politica* as well as checks and balances.

The institutions of democracy are so numerous that any attempt to cover them all is futile. Lijphart focuses upon a handful of them. We will follow his line of argument but add one more institution that is very much relevant for the macro theme, namely independent central banks. We will omit his behavioural items, because the purpose is to discuss only institutional coherence.

Institutions adhere to an institutional logic, state March and Olsen (1989). Institutions do not exist in a vacuum, but they constitute a pattern with a logic of its own, which rejects institutional inconsistencies or contradictions. Theories of institutional evolution emphasize that the institutions that evolve tend to be adapted towards each other. An even stronger argument in neo-institutionalism claims that institutions that survive tend to be optimal or equilibrium institutions. Following this line of thought, we ask in relation to Lijphart's democracy theory: are WM and the CM internally coherent?

This is not an empirical question. Lijphart's two democracy models are not empirical generalizations, but belong to the special way of constructing social science concepts that Max Weber called 'ideal-types'. An ideal-type captures not merely the given characteristics, though in an exaggerated form, but it attempts to pin down the logic of a pattern of such items. The logic of WM is power-fusion whereas the logic of the CM is power-sharing. Thus, the various institutional items – seven – in the two models combine to express this core logic of the two models.

Let us first ask of each of the seven institutions in each model if they adhere to the logic of power-fusion or logic of power-sharing – the context is all the time a constitutional democracy. One may separate between two different institutional logics. First, does an institution by itself operate in such a manner that it implies power-fusion or power-sharing? Second, does an institution when it is combined with another institution or enters a pattern of institutions entail power-sharing or power-fusion? Or could it be the case that some of the institutions in these two models are, taken separately, neutral in relation to power-fusion or power-sharing?

Westminster logic

Basically, WM is the logic of executive government, emanating from the sovereignty of Parliament. What institutions are involved in power-fusion or executive dominance? If the logic of WM is power-fusion, then we must ask whether all the institutional items in this ideal-type entail executive dominance, or do they form a coherent pattern to that effect? More specifically, the WM harbours the following institutions: (a) minimum winning sized coalitions; (b) unicameral or asymmetrical bicameral parliaments; (c) plurality or majoritarian election techniques; (d) no legal review; (e) a unitary state; and (f) an unwritten constitution. Is Lijphart saying that when there is executive dominance, then we find: a + b + c + d + e + f? Or is he saying that when there is a or b or c or d or e or f, then there is power-fusion? Whereas the first version is about one complex necessary condition, the second version is about many separate sufficient conditions.

An uncodified constitution (f) is hardly necessary for power-fusion. It is true that British parliamentarism is Austinian, i.e. the government is the first executive of parliament and all public powers emanate from the legislative supremacy of parliament. Yet, codified constitutions may enshrine the very same institutions that constitute conventions in British constitutional practice – see, for instance, the Nordic democracies, e.g. Norway. French presidentialism would, we assume, adhere to the same logic of power-fusion, i.e. executive dominance, especially if one bypasses Cohabitation, but it is certainly bolstered by the 1958 constitution. Power-fusion does not entail an unwritten constitution. Central European countries all have written constitutions but vary in terms of executive dominance.

A major disadvantage in the Lijphart approach is that presidentialism, which is a most important executive institution both in terms of power and in terms of frequency of occurrence, does not really fit. What is the logic of presidentialism: power-fusion or power-sharing? Consider the relevance of European presidentialism – strong Head of state and strong premier – which just increases as more and more countries move towards this non-American model. European presidentialism or semi-presidentialism in Western and Central Europe – executive dominance or not?

Lijphart's general 1984 model includes as one element executive institutions, where he makes the distinction between majoritarian executives and consociational ones, which, strictly speaking, only applies to the set of parliamentary regimes. How about presidentialism? One could interpret presidentialism as a majoritarian institution, given the obvious need in such regimes for majoritarian election formulas for the selection of the head of state. However, one could also interpret presidentialism as institutions for power-sharing, especially if the power of the president is limited by various addition institutions.

But power-sharing implies the Consensus model with Lijphart. It would thus seem natural to argue that presidentialism belongs to the Consensus model, because the pure model of presidentialism entails a division of powers between the executive, the legislature and the judiciary. After all, the Consensus model is all about diffusion of political power. But Lijphart has argued very much in favour of parliamentarism when it comes to choosing new constitutions in countries that are searching for new institutions after the fall of communism and fascism (Lijphart 1992).

A unitary state (e) does not imply power-fusion, as lower levels of government may exercise not only considerable financial autonomy but also be responsible for a large number of state competencies involving discretion. A unitary state may allow its local governments complete financial autonomy as in Denmark and Sweden or a unitary state may allow a sizeable area such as the island of Aland almost complete home rule. Unitary states may be centralized as in Central Europe and in the UK and France, Greece and Portugal or decentralized as in Northern Europe and Spain and Italy.

The occurrence of legal review, or the power of judges or a constitutional court, to test statute laws for their constitutionality, implies clearly a major restriction on executive dominance. However, the conclusion that (d) the lack of legal review implies executive dominance does not follow. In any democracy that adheres to the Rule of Law there will be judicial institutions that limit the power of the executive branch of government. Thus, all countries in Europe with no legal review have various judicial or quasi-judicial institutions where citizens may seek redress against public adminis-tration. Parliaments have their own ombudsman for examining the executive branch of government. For example, the Danish ombudsman brought down the Schluter government in 1992. The French Conseil constitutionnel limits executive dominance more than it enhances it. All Central European democracies recognize legal review in the Austrian–Kelsen model of a constitutional court, although they all practise centralized government.

It is also true that one kind of election system implies power-fusion, according to the Duverger principle that the plurality method or major-itarian techniques brings about manufactured majorities, upon which simple majority governments may be formed. However, the opposite conclusion does not hold, namely that (c) PR techniques entail lack of executive dominance. Long periods of executive dominance such as the DC rule in Italy, the DNA government, the SAP government and the Gonzales government, stemmed from PR election systems. A most spectacular reform of the election system took place in Italy in 1994, but this change in favour of WM did not alter much in terms of executive dominance.

A one-chamber parliament or a two-chamber parliament where the lower house prevails over the upper house (b) could not *per se* imply executive dominance, as it depends, of course, on the constellation of forces in each particular parliament. However, a two-chamber symmetrical parliament would limit executive dominance, if the two chambers have a different composition of political forces – that is trivially true. The capacity of a one-chamber parliament or asymmetrical bicameralism to bolster power-fusion is thus entirely dependent upon which other institutions it is combined with. In principle, unicameralism is neutral in relation to executive dominance, although executive dominance is made easier in unicameralism.

The distinction between one-chamber and two-chamber parliaments seems of very limited relevance in relation to Western and Central Europe, especially if one inserts the symmetrical–asymmetrical restriction. Almost all

European democracies would end up in the asymmetrical one-chamber category, as if they were all WM. Only the federal countries would remain outside, but is the amount of executive dominance really the same in Germany, Austria and Switzerland, taking into account that only the Helvetic Republic operates true dualistic federalism?

Finally, executive dominance seems to imply (a) minimum winning and minimum-sized coalitions. But is it also true that executive dominance could not occur under another type of government, for instance an oversized government? The obvious candidate for executive dominance would be a grand coalition of the Austrian type, where the two large parties have managed to monopolize political power for decades, ruling Austria from Vienna. Minority coalitions, on the other hand, would have to be based upon parliamentary committees compromising.

The argument about the WM logic is a theory about the necessary institutions for executive dominance: if there is executive dominance, then a + b + c + d + e + f. This statement is hardly true, as executive government could occur under a different set of combinations of conditions, for instance where there is a dominant party like the DC, the CDU, or the SAP and the DNA. However, the statement about sufficient conditions is definitely not true: If a or b or c or d or e or f, then executive dominance. The fact that each of the Westminster institutions is not sufficient for executive dominance opens up the possibility that each one of them may occur without executive dominance.

Logic of consensus democracy

When one employs Weberian ideal-types, then one employs conceptual opposites in order to arrive at the theoretical effect that Weber emphasized so much: conceptual purity or exaggeration of the key feature(s). In reality, such purity does not exist. Lijphart spoke of New Zealand before the election reform in 1996 as the concrete case that was most close to his pure type – Westminster democracy. This was probably empirically inaccurate, because Lijphart had not realized the impact of Maori ethnic politics upon government in New Zealand, especially the critical implications of the Waitangi Treaty from 1840, one of the founding documents of the country's state, i.e. a document with great constitutional import. In any case, an ideal-type is an imaginative construction, using polar extremes. But are we, then, talking about contradictory or contrary concepts?

The construction of an ideal-type reflects the imagination of the scholar, but he/she also looks at existing real types. Sometimes there are two and only two polar types – contradictory concepts, but at other times it is only a question of contrary concepts, meaning there will be many opposites. Lijphart constructs his CM by proceeding in the same manner as with the WM, stating the opposites. All the institutions of the CM are to be conducive to power-sharing, which again raises the question about necessary or sufficient conditions.

A   Governments would be coalitions between two or more parties. One single party government with simple majority is WM par preference. But what kind of coalition is typical of CM? One bid would be grand coalitions, or oversized coalitions, but they are only contrary types as the minority coalition would also be a contrary type. We are not quite sure which is the polar type to the WM cabinet: grand coalitions as in consociational theory or any kind of coalition government that is not minimum winning and minimum-sized. Power-sharing may occur in the form of a single party minority government who negotiates temporary coalitions in parliament – is that CM? The problem with oversized cabinets is simply that they hardly ever exist! In Central Europe we have none, and in The Netherlands and Belgium they are going out of fashion.

B   There is power-sharing, when the parliament practises symmetrical bicameralism. This is definitely in agreement with the predictions from game theory (Tsebelis and Money 1997), but the caveat is that the two chambers must have different majority wills. If a majority is in command of both houses, then power-sharing must rely upon other institutions. Italian bicameralism which leans towards symmetry, has not been conducive to power-sharing, at least not as long as the DC dominated Italian politics. Whether there will be power-sharing in Belgium after the introduction of the symmetrical bicameral parliament, remains to be seen.

C   PR-election techniques would clearly be the best institutional candidate for being a necessary condition for power-sharing, but it is not a sufficient condition. If there is power-sharing, then there is PR, but the reverse is not true. One can easily imagine a single party receiving a majority of the votes under some PR method, especially one that is not highly proportional in its outcomes, meaning that the party could rule in the form of executive dominance. Take the cases of Spain and Portugal in the 1980s and 1990s as real examples.

D   Does power-sharing really entail legal review, or the capacity of judges to squash legislation by testing laws against criteria of constitutionality and right reason? Lijphart states that Switzerland is the closest country to his CM, but Switzerland does definitely not accept or endorse legal review. How could judges kill what the people wish in a referendum democracy? Does legal review imply power-sharing? The judicial branch of government could have such power in a country ruled by a one-chamber parliament – as is the case in most of Central Europe. All of the Central European countries recognize legal review, but how much of a spirit of power-sharing is there in these new democracies?

E   The federal state format – is it a necessary or sufficient condition for power sharing ? Power-sharing in a federal state could take place either through a strict division of competencies between the central govern-ment and the regional governments – Switzerland. Or power-sharing could occur in the centre through bargaining between the two chambers – Germany. Austrian federalism has never been described as a power-sharing mechanism. And Belgian federalism does not really seem to operate. On the other hand, power-sharing between the centre and the regions seems to take place to some extent in some unitary states like Spain, Italy and France. In Central Europe, only Serbia and Montenegro are a federal state, but no one would describe Milosevic's rule as power-sharing.

F   Does power-sharing really necessitate a written constitution? The distinction between a written and an unwritten constitution is not that clear-cut. All constitutions that have been codified at one stage need practice in order to operate. Power-sharing in Switzerland is based upon *La Formule Magique* from 1959, but it is not codified. The German 1949 Basic Law says little about interlocking federalism and *Politikverflechtung*. If there is a codified constitution, like in Sweden from 1809 to 1974 and another one from 1975 onwards, is there *ipso facto* power-sharing? We think not. All constitutions are a mixture of codified law and practice or case law. All countries have constitutional documents of one kind or another, supplemented by legal interpretation and conventions.

Surprisingly, one may argue that the Consensus model is less coherent than the Westminster model. It is probably not correct to argue that: power-sharing only if A + B + C + D + E + F. But it is certainly not correct to argue: if A or B or C or D or E or F, then power-sharing.

This is all about ideal-types of democracy, dealing with the amount of coherence in the conceptual constructs. Now we must enter the empirically given realities in order to assess how much convergence there really is.

Real institutional convergence?

Thus far we have looked at the logical coherence of the two ideal-types of democracy. We found in relation to Lijphart's two ideal-types that it is sometimes difficult to penetrate the logic of the connection between a huge variety of democratic institutions and the two outcomes that characterize the two ideal-types: power-fusing and power-sharing, respectively. Sometimes it seems logical to argue that an institution entails power-sharing or power-fusion, but at other times this logical relation may simply be missing.

Ideal-types should be internally consistent, but reality need not be so. On the contrary, scholars who employ ideal-types underline that they correspond to nothing in reality. Phenomena in the real world are always more or less in the affinity of the ideal-type, but never 100 per cent close. Closeness is the concept to employ when ideal-types of institutional arrangements are compared with real-life institutions in a country, whereas complete correspondence never occurs. The extent to which there exist copies of WM or CM in the world of phenomena is a different question from that of the internal coherence of these two constructs.

Yet, empirical matters are not unimportant and cannot be neglected. Why construct special or artificial concepts if they denote nothing? An ideal-type is not just a concept that is extremely skilfully constructed and thus may have theoretical beauty or be parsimonious in terms of characteristics. It is first and foremost a tool for the analysis of reality. Our doubt in relation to the empirical validity of the Lijphart models is that the two patterns of institutional configurations exist in simply too few countries. When, as happens most often, countries mix institutions from the two models, then what democracy does the country have? The problem of institutional mixtures is a very relevant one.

There are numerous countries that mix completely. Take the Scandinavian countries: adversarial politics in government formation but a PR-election formula, unitary states and unicameral parliaments but a written constitutions and, at the same time, no legal review. Clearly, this is more Westminster than Consensus, but is it really either? Or let us go to Southern Europe. Italy, for example, has adversarial politics with a mixed election formula, it has a written constitution and legal review, plus it has symmetrical bicameralism, but it is not a federal state. Then, what is it: WM or CM? Finally, take Greece: it has a PR system but governments have been simple majority ones, it has no legal review and a written constitution but it is a unitary state and it has a unicameral Parliament. Is this WM or CM?

Can we use these two models for future explorations or even predictions? How would one describe a United Kingdom where there was a mixed election system combining plurality and proportional methods in addition to devolved competencies (now under way) for Scotland, Wales and Northern Ireland. Has the UK become another type of democracy? We think not.

All of the institutional items in both WM and CM are legal ones, having a clear definition in constitutional law or practice, except one, viz. the rule about the proper form of government. In CM, power-sharing implies bringing all players on board, i.e. the use of oversized coalitions or even grand coalitions. But what is the opposite? In WM, the convention is clearly that governments must be capable of directing the work of parliament, preferably in the form of a single party government that is a minimum winning and minimum-sized coalition. But many countries fall short of fulfilling this WM institution without ever aspiring towards the CM rule about oversized coalitions. How, then, is the minority government to be classified in relation to WM and CM?

Minority coalitions seem neutral in relation to WM and CM, as they fit neither. At the same time, their relevance has increased, as they tend to occur more and more often, whereas the rule about oversized coalitions is only adhered to now by Switzerland, Austria and Finland to some extent. One could argue that minority coalitions are conducive to power-sharing as the governments needs to build temporary coalitions with different parties almost as if there was a grand coalition. One may, however, equally well argue that minority coalitions are only simply majority coalition failures.

Lijphart has made up for this indeterminacy concerning the minority coalition by adding one more institution, which is also conventional and not constitutional law, namely corporatism. The type of corporatism that we are talking about here is macro corporatism, which used to be strongly institutionalized in some European democracies like the Nordic countries and Austria. Despite the fact that corporatism has been reduced in terms of both relevance and legitimacy in the 1990s, Lijphart includes it as a power-sharing device. If this is correct, then a number of countries with minority governments could be classified as adhering to CM. One could, though, argue that corporatism is not really a political institution on par with the other constitutionally sanctioned rules, and that its institutionalization is far less clear-cut.

In support of his claim about institutional configurations, Lijphart presented a factor analysis of the separate institutional items. The finding was that both the WM and CM institutions clustered in two different ways, one relating to the federalism–unitarism division and the other to the executive dominance versus power-sharing separation. Thus, we would have two pure ideal-types, but there would exist four empirical clusters of democratic institutions among twenty-two democracies.

In any case, let us now test whether one gets the same finding when one looks at all the democracies in the 1990s – almost sixty cases. In the factor analysis reported on in Table 10.1 we have deleted the behavioural items that Lijphart used and replaced them with two more institutional items, which seems appropriate when doing neo-institutional research.

If institutional items correlate perfectly according to the two ideal-types WM and CM, then we would receive a one-factor solution in Table 10.1. Such an amount of institutional coherence when examining real-life macro institutions cannot, however, be accomplished in relation to the set of fifty-six electoral, democracies. In relation to the 1990s, and with regard to these countries, we argue that not even a two-factor solution is achievable, because the occurrence of political institutions varies too much in relation to each other. Table 10.1 indicates that a three-factor solution is more proper, resulting in six types of democratic institutions.

Factor 1 could be interpreted as federalism versus unitarism, while Factor 2 would be legislative power-sharing, i.e. the placement of legislative com-

Table 10.1 Factor analysis of institutions in democracies: 1990s

Chamber system	0.90	−0.12	−0.01
Federalism	0.85	0.25	−0.02
Legal review	0.05	0.73	0.32
Central bank auton.	0.05	0.67	−0.12
Presidentialism	−0.02 .	0.34	0.73
Electoral formula	−0.02	−0.37	0.67
Expl. variance:	27.1	20.6	16.8
Number of cases:	56		

Sources: See Tables 7.4, 4.3, 8.2, 7.7, 6.2, 9.2.

Note: These three factors with Eigenvalue >1.0 cover more than 60 per cent of the institutional variation.

petencies outside of the national assembly, with either a central bank or with a constitutional court. Factor 3 would be executive power-sharing: presidential power as an alternative to parliamentarism or the fusion of the executive with the legislature.

This interpretation of a pattern is not evidently empirically true or the only theoretically meaningful one, but it does indicate that a dichotomy between WM and CM fails in relation to the set of democracies today.

Institutional superiority

Democracy is considered at the end of the twentieth century to be the system that basically triumphed over its competitors, communism and fascism. The question, however, that Lijphart raises is whether one type of democracy performs better than another type. He claims that CM is superior to WM – how would one test such a claim? Lijphart examines socio-economic performance, arguing that CM does at least no worse than WM. He also looks at political outcomes, stating that CM does better than WM in respect of representativity, participation and political stability, which is very much at odds with the Duverger argument examined in Chapter 9.

We find the socio-economic argument strange, if not simply misleading. Why would economic growth depend upon WM or CM? Take one decade's data and correlate it with some of the institutions of WM of CM and one may have a slightly positive finding. But take another decade and one has a negative finding. Economic growth hovers and thus the correlations are not stable. There was much talk about the 'ugliness' of the English in the 1970s and 1980s, as growth tended to be low in the Commonwealth area, but in the 1990s things look less gloomy. Yet, the institutions have not changed. Socio-economic outcomes in general and economic growth in particular depend more upon other factors than constitutional characteristics.

Political outputs and outcomes are linked more with institutions – the occurrence of institutional effects – as it were. However, these various institutional items of WM and CM do not operate in the same way with regard to outputs and outcomes. One has to be much more specific about institutional impact. Showing the occurrence of an institutional impact requires elaborate research on each institutional item, as other factors – social conditions, culture, historical legacies – also impact.

WM is orientated towards governmental efficiency and the sovereignty of parliament in representing the people. CM is orientated towards maximum representation and the recognition of so-called veto-players. Lijphart states that CM is superior or better than WM. Why? CM may, as Duverger pointed out long ago, result in governmental immobilism as well as minorities fooling the majority. WM may result in strong governments capable of major reforms that cannot be blocked by small minorities, engaging in cycling or the paradox of voting. Both WM and CM have advantages and disadvantages. British democracy is no worse than Continental democracy. It would appear that British democracy could become increasingly attractive in Europe, where old cleavages are losing their relevance. When the electorate is volatile and the party system highly fractionalized, then perhaps WM does stabilize the situation. Why use CM when there is not a so-called divided society?

In order to test the argument about a better performance record for CM than for WM, we will devote the whole of the next chapter to the performance evaluation of the institutions of Consensus democracy.

Conclusion

One may distinguish between general institutional theories and middle-range institutional hypotheses, although the dividing line between the two is anything but clear. Middle-range theories remain attractive, because the propositions of a middle-range theory contain transparent models that are in principle testable (Merton 1957: 3–16). General theories of institutions tend to attempt to cover everything with the risk that they state nothing that is strictly testable. Since we are focusing here not upon the methodology for analysing institutions but dealing with specific institutional models which link certain institutions with determinate outcomes, we will examine first and foremost middle-range theories.

Lijphart's theory about two ideal-types of democracy is grand social theory. But examining the lack of coherence of the pure types in this theory, we find that it is better to decompose it into a number of middle-range hypotheses about democratic institutions and their consequences. There is more to the variation in democratic institutions than contained merely in the Westminster model and the Consensus model.

The first strong commitment to the existence of institutional effects was launched by Duverger in his theory about the critical importance of the election system. First, Lijphart questioned the validity of Duverger's argument in favour of majoritarian democracy by examining one country employing the PR method – The Netherlands, which combined a plural society with political stability. Second, he launched a grand institutional theory about convergence among the institutions of democracy. Alternative executive, legislative and judicial institutions go together not only with each other but also with the state format (federalism) and the nature of the constitution (codification). Third, Lijphart came down in favour of one of the two ideal-types of democracy, namely Consensus democracy, with which he combined the institutions of Konkordanzdemokratie. Sometimes he claimed that Consensus democracies have a better performance profile than Westminster democracies. Sometimes he argued that the former do at least as well as the latter on various evaluation criteria, including political, social and economic aspects. Let us examine these claims about institutional performance more closely in the next chapter, relating the institutions of Konkordanz to the institutions of corporatism.

11 Konkordanzdemokratie and corporatism

Introduction

Democracies can utilize alternative institutional arrangements. A key question that democratic theory currently addresses is the impact of these alternative institutional set-ups upon policy outputs and outcomes. In a Continental European context, the institutions of Konkordanzdemokratie and corporatism are particularly interesting (Lehmbruch 1996). Can we claim that they have had a critical impact on the political, social and economic outcomes of the post-war period? We will focus on these institutions from the same angle as we regarded institutional effects, because 'for the corporatist analyst, differences in the nature of these institutions tend to be crucial in determining the policies adopted and their eventual outcomes' (Schmitter 1996: 3).

Corporatist theory offers a wide variety of insights into the workings of institutions for interrelating the polity and the economy. It plays a major role in political economy (Czada 1992), which involves discussions concerning the impact of corporatist institutions on public policies as well as on social and economic outcomes. The subject of macro-corporatism is truly interesting from a neo-institutionalist point of view, because it raises a number of issues concerning the connection between institutions, policies and outcomes (Keman and Pennings 1995). The institutionalization of macro-corporatism as distinct from that of meso- or micro-corporatism takes the form of the society-wide creation and implementation of consensus instititutions. Has this process of institutionalization of corporatism been linked to the set of institutions for political democracy that we examined in Chapter 10, viz. those of Consensus democracy constituting – as we will call it here – Konkordanzdemokratie?

What is institutional closeness or interdependency?

If institutions constitute alternatives in the sense that a society may choose one or another, then what are the relationships between these alternatives? First, two institutions may be in some kind of opposition as a society cannot operate both at the same time. They are substitutes, meaning that one replaces the other and vice versa. Second, two institutions may be complementary, meaning that two tend to go together, one requiring the other and vice versa. Finally, two institutions may be orthogonal, occurring completely independently of each other. Let us apply these distinctions in an evaluation of the argument that the institutions of Konkordanz and those of corporatism are closely connected.

One finds this claim about a closeness or interdependency between the institutions of Consensus democracy and corporatism among the so-called consociational scholars (Lijphart and Crepaz 1991). We believe that this belief about corporatist institutions should be examined more closely, both theoretically and empirically. It has been formulated by an expert on corporatism and Konkordanzdemokratie in the following manner:

> The European Consensus Democracies display right through strong neo-corporatist elements, and their historical emergence is closely connected.
> (Lehmbruch 1992: 210–11)

This hypothesis about institutional similarities or institutional combinations can be researched by submitting it to a comparative analysis. It raises important questions about institutional convergence, equivalence and substitutes (Keman 1996).

The thesis which supports the close connection between the regimes of Konkordanz and of corporatism is related to research on issues concerning the sources of political stability and democratic viability, as well as alluding to problems in political economy concerning institutional factors that enhance outcomes, such as affluence, economic growth, inflation and unemployment (Abromeit 1993). The argument which supports the institutional equivalence between corporatism and Konkordanz is impossible to bypass when one constructs scales that measure the existence or importance of these institutions. Looking at these scales, can one find evidence that supports the hypothesis that corporatism and Konkordanzdemokratie are closely connected? Also, what does this expression 'closely connected' mean when used about institutions?

Two institutions can be 'close' in the connotation sense of being similar or basically one and the same thing. One may argue that corporatism and Konkordanzdemokratie are similar institutions, because they both entail power-sharing. Or two institutions may be 'close' in the denotation sense of occurring simultaneously. These two meanings of 'closely connected' should be clearly distinguished, because they are two entirely different concepts of sameness or convergence.

Researching institutional interdependencies between two types of democracy – Konkordanz and corporatism – one may proceed in two different ways. Either one examines the connotation of these two concepts in order to establish if they have a common conceptual core. Or one employs an empirical approach, examining whether the countries that adhere to one set of democratic institutions also adhere to the other set of democratic institutions. This way of framing the question means that one favours the denotation approach.

If indeed the scales on corporatism and Konkordanzdemokratie are not strongly correlated as in the denotation approach, then are there really sufficient theoretical reasons for claiming that these two phenomena are close or identical? Yes, because there is also the connotation version of this argument, distinct institutions expressing the same phenomenon, viz. the power-sharing effort instead of the adversary spirit. If two institutions are close in the connotation sense, then they could still be substitutes, meaning that when one occurs, the other is absent. Thus, merely the lack of constant occurrence of the two institutions together does not answer the question of closeness.

Theories about corporatism or Konkordanzdemokratie focus almost exclusively upon rich democratic countries with a capitalist economy. We restrict our examination of the occurrence of the institutions of Konkordanz and corporatism to twenty-three OECD countries at most, given that this is the area that the argument has been applied to.

Following neo-institutionalist theory, institutions, if accepted as legitimate or considered purposive, tend to be in practice for quite some time. Thus, one can model their operation in time by taking average measures of their longevity. One would correspondingly favour the choice of a cross-sectional approach. As institutions tend to be rather stable over time, their impact would also tend to remain the same over time. When institutions have been in place more or less uninterruptedly, then one may look at long-run average scores measuring the sources and effects of these institutions.

Although the OECD countries constitute a rather homogenous set of rich countries, they tend to vary considerably institutionally. Which institutions, more specifically, do corporatism and Konkordanzdemokratie harbour, respectively? Before one enquires into the effects of institutions, one needs to identify the institutions in question. Quantitative indicators may be employed to describe the occurrence of both corporatism and Konkordanzdemokratie.

Macro-corporatism

Numerous attempts of measuring the occurrence of corporatist institutions within the set of OECD countries have been made. Sometimes only a dichotomy is made between corporatist and liberal societies. At other times countries are ranked on a scale in terms of their level of corporatism. Thus, Crouch places Austria, The Netherlands, Switzerland and Germany as belonging to the neo-corporatist set along with the Nordic countries. And Belgium, France, Ireland, the UK and Italy are classified as belonging to the liberal set along with the US, Canada, Australia and New Zealand (Crouch

1993). Such a dichotomous classification contains a lot less information than the scales that rank each country in terms of their level of corporatism. It does not say anything about whether The Netherlands, Belgium, Switzerland and Germany are closer to the hard core corporatist countries such as Sweden and Austria or whether they actually are nearer to the typical non-corporatist countries such as the US and Japan.

Table 11.1 presents some of the main efforts of scaling corporatism in some seventeen countries in terms of a ranking order tapping the extent of corporatism during the 1980s (see also Wilensky 1975; Marks 1986; Tarantelli 1986; Mitchell 1996).

The six alternative scales differ from each other in several respects, as the correlations between the scales goes from r=0.63 to r=0.97. The Crepaz–Lijphart scale resembles the Bruno–Sachs scale, but these two scales are substantially different from the Cameron and the Alvarez scales. The Schmitter scale could be seen as a compromise solution, which also applies to Calmfors's and Drifill's scale.

Table 11.1 Scales of macro-corporatism

	CORP1	*CORP2*	*CORP3*	*CORP4*	*CORP5*	*CORP6*
AUT	18	17	17	14	14	13
BEL	10	10	9	8	13	10
DEN	14	14	11	11	11	12
FIN	11	13	10	10	12	11
FRA	7	7	5	3	2	2
GER	12	12	16	7	9	6
GRE	—	—	—	—	—	—
ICE	—	—	—	—	—	—
IRE	8	—	—	—	—	—
ITA	6	5	4	1	5	5
LUX	—	—	—	—	—	—
NET	15	11	15	9	10	8
NOR	17	16	14	13	15	14
POR	—	—	—	—	—	—
SPA	—	—	—	—	—	—
SWE	16	15	13	12	16	15
SWI	13	3	12	6	6	—
UK	5	6	6	2	8	9
CAN	2	1	2	4	4	3
US	1	2	1	5	3	4
JAP	9	4	8	—	1	1
AUS	4	8	3	—	7	7
NZ	3	9	7	—	—	—

Sources: Lijphart and Crepaz 1991; Calmfors and Drifill 1988; Bruno and Sachs 1985; Schmitter 1981; Cameron 1984; Alvarez *et al.* 1991.

Note: Corporatism scales: CORP1=Crepaz-Lijphart; CORP2=Calmfors-Drifill; CORP3= Bruno-Sachs; CORP4=Schmitter; CORP5=Cameron; CORP6=Alvarez. The higher the rank order, the more corporatism.

The differences between the scales concern the ranking of the following countries: Switzerland, Japan, the UK, France, Belgium, The Netherlands, Germany, Italy, the US and New Zealand. This amounts to a significant degree of disagreement about how macro-corporatism surfaces. Could it be that the term 'corporatism' does not have a single connotation? If the US, Japan and New Zealand are classified as having a low level of corporatism, then how are Switzerland, Belgium, The Netherlands and the UK to be ranked?

From a connotation point of view, 'corporatism' may mean either a special structure of the interest organizations in civil society, i.e. encompassing hierarchical interest organizations, or the meaning of the term may refer to institutional mechanisms that create reciprocities between government, business and trade unions, or both. How are corporatist patterns of interest intermediation and policy concertation to be identified and measured empirically? Evidently, corporatism is different from lobbyism as it requires so-called tripartism, or Drittelparität, or that organized labour is recognized and plays an important role in tripartite consultation. 'Corporatism' is not just another word for strong pressure groups, given that it involves more than that. Nor is corporatism the same as trade union density, although the existence of a high level of union organization may be conducive to corporatist patterns. Table 11.2 has the trade union density figures as well as indicators on tripartism.

How about corporatism and trade union density? The Cameron and Alvarez scales correlate highly with the measures of trade union density, r = 0.80 and r=0.76, respectively. On the contrary, the Crepaz and Lijphart scale and the Bruno and Sachs scale each have little in common with the scores of trade union density, r=0.31 and r=0.20, respectively. Perhaps one is measuring different things when one talks about 'corporatism'? The Calmfors and Drifill scale and the Schmitter scale agree on how the various countries are to be ranked, r=0.86, and they also correlate to some extent with trade union density, r=0.63 and r=0.54, respectively. They both place three of the difficult cases – Switzerland, The Netherlands and Belgium – in the same way, but differ considerably on the placement of the UK, Germany and France.

It seems hard to arrive at an agreement concerning the extent of macro-corporatism in various countries. From an institutional point of view, this is not satisfactory enough. Actually, one may argue that corporatist institutions appear in two forms which are somewhat different from each other, the first type being linked with trade union density and the second type with the occurrence of Drittelparität, as measured by a country's acceptance of international conventions concerning tripartite consultation.

Trade union density, as measured according to various scales reported in Table 11.2, is only weakly correlated with the institutions of Drittelparität; however, these are identified and measured (r=0.30 between TUD1 and TRIP4).

Table 11.2 Trade union density and Drittelparität

	TUD1	*TUD2*	*TUD3*	*TRIP1*	*TRIP2*	*TRIP3*	*TRIP4*
AUT	58	60.8	58.2	48	9	1	1
BEL	68	—	77.5	85	10	1	1
DEN	83	88.9	86.0	69	9	1	1
FIN	81	86.6	90.0	86	10	1	2
FRA	15	17.7	12.0	115	10	1	2
GER	38	41.5	40.1	75	10	1	2
GRE	—	—	25.0	66	10	1	2
ICE	—	—	—	—	—	—	—
IRE	48	61.2	58.4	60	9	1	1
ITA	51	42.0	62.7	102	10	1	2
LUX	—	—	—	—	—	—	—
NET	28	34.4	30.2	94	10	1	2
NOR	64	67.9	67.7	99	10	1	2
POR	—	—	30.0	68	9	1	1
SPA	—	—	—	124	10	1	2
SWE	91	94.4	96.1	84	10	1	2
SWI	32	34.4	30.0	51	5	0	0
UK	44	49.8	46.1	80	7	1	1
CAN	33	36.2	34.6	28	5	0	0
US	17	17.4	—	11	2	1	0
JAP	29	28.8	26.8	41	5	0	0
AUS	51	56.7	53.4	54	9	1	1
NZ	41	54.9	50.5	56	6	1	1

Sources: Tripartism=World Bank 1995: 150–51; trade union density 1=Western 1995; trade union density 2=Armingeon 1989; trade union density 3=OECD 1994: 97–134 (Visser).

Note: TUD1–TUD3=measures of trade union density; TRIP1: total number of ILO conventions ratified; TRIP2: number of basic ILO conventions ratified; TRIP3: ratification of tripartite consultation, convention no. 144; TRIP4: Summary index of TRIP1–TRIP3.

The fact that the occurrence of corporatism as Drittelparität changes over time, as its legitimacy tends to be questioned more as the market values spread, should be pointed out (Crepaz 1995; see also Prisching 1996). Thus, the acceptance of corporatist patterns of interaction is not stable but may fluctuate, reflecting broad social change. Thus, in the Scandinavian context the relevance and legitimacy of corporatism may differ considerably from one decade to another (Ruin 1972; Lewin 1994). Yet, trade union participation also changes slowly over time. There are also other indications suggesting that the ranking order of the extent of corporatism among various countries seems to be rather stable over time (see Compston 1997; Wallerstein *et al.* 1997).

One must seriously consider the fact that corporatist patterns of interaction may occur at three levels: micro, meso and macro. In some countries emphasis is placed on the macro level but in others most of this type of interaction takes place at the meso level (Knoke *et al.* 1996). Thus, corporatism may be strong in certain industrial sectors although it also remains weak at the macro level. The actual occurrence of corporatist interaction may be researched through the policy network approach (Pappi and König 1995). Below, we focus on corporatism at the macro level, either in society or in the state, for instance as tripartism or the use of Paritätische Kommission.

When corporatism is said to be similar to Konkordanzdemokratie, then it must be explained in terms of the second connotation of corporatism listed above, viz. the occurrence of the institutions of Drittelparität in policy-making and implementation. Both Konkordanzdemokratie and Drittel-parität would handle social problems in the same way, nameley by means of negotiation, bargaining and compromise. The first connotation of cor-poratism, the structure of interest organizations or the amount of centraliz-ation in industrial relations, could lead to the evolution of a culture of Drittelparität, but it would not necessarily have anything to do with Konkordanzdemokratie. The classification of Germany and the UK depends very much on the connotation that 'corporatism' adopts. Trade union density is somewhat higher in the UK than in Germany, but Drittelparität has occurred more often in the latter than in the former. Therefore, which are the institutions of Konkordanzdemokratie?

Konkordanzdemokratie

The concept of Konkordanzdemokratie or Consensus democracy can only be understood in terms of the opposite concept, called 'Konkurrenzdemo-kratie' or the Westminster model. What is crucial here is the rejection of adversarial politics, or the institutions which allow the victor to claim the spoils entirely. Konkordanzdemokratie backs up the inclusion of minorities in the decision-making process as emphasized by Abromeit (1993), and it may involve various mechanisms such as oversized coalitions, qualified majority decision-making rules and minority veto (Schmidt 1995).

One may treat the concept of Konkordanzdemokratie either as offering a dichotomy, separating two different kinds of democracy, or one may try to employ it in order to measure and rank countries according to a scale of Consensus democracy. Taking the denotation approach, one may be certain of the countries that belong to Konkordanz, and then suggest a theory which explains what the properties that form the common core of these countries are, the connotation as it were. Or one may pursue the connotation approach, first by specifying the properties that define 'Konkordanzdemo-kratie' and then move on to observe which countries come close to the connotation.

Both approaches are available in the literature. On the one hand, there is the Lehmbruch classification, which is an overall characterization which explains whether or not a country belongs to the set of Konkordanzdemo-kratie. On the other hand, there are scales by Lijphart measuring aspects of what he calls 'consensus democracy' (Lijphart 1984). Let us compare Lehmbruch's classification with Lijphart's scales in order to try to figure out what the connotation that lies behind the country listings is. Whereas the Lehmbruch classification basically identifies countries as either Konkurrenz- or Konkordanzdemokratie on a scale from 0 to 2, the Lijphart scale involves refined measurements of the occurrence of various institutional features using factor scores as was discussed in the previous Chapter 10.

Lijphart is careful to point out that his Consensus model consists of two dimensions, which are independent of each other at the denotation level, the first being called 'Konsensus-Mehrheits-Dimension' and the other 'Föderalismus-Unitarismus-Dimension' – according to the interpretation by Manfred Schmidt (1995: 233, 244). For the measurement of the occurrence of the institutions of the first kind, the Konsensus dimension, Lijphart offers two indices, one from 1984 and another scale from 1991. Table 11.3 gives the country scores for these indices, the higher the scores the stronger the institutions of Konsensus; Schmidt's own index is also included.

Lehmbruch's classification and the two Lijphart scales do show a correlation of r=0.51 and r=0.69, as we have several countries which are classified in different ways: Denmark, Italy, Norway, Austria, Portugal and Sweden. In fact, Lehmbruch has five clear cases of Konkordanzdemokratie,

Table 11.3 Indices of Konkordanzdemokratie

	Lehmbruch	Schmidt	Lijphart84	Lijphart91
AUT	2	−0.84	−1.50	−0.37
BEL	2	0.74	0.55	0.64
DEN	1	0.89	0.78	0.77
FIN	1	1.65	1.49	1.47
FRA	0	0.11	0.18	0.16
GER	1	−0.11	−0.68	−0.07
GRE	0	−0.90	—	—
ICE	0	0.30	0.06	—
IRE	0	−0.73	−0.61	−0.73
ITA	1	1.18	0.10	1.04
LUX	2	−0.30	−0.08	—
NET	2	1.58	1.69	1.40
NOR	0	0.30	−0.42	0.24
POR	0	0.50	—	—
SPA	0	−0.11	—	—
SWE	0	0.14	−0.48	0.08
SWI	2	1.88	1.65	1.67
UK	0	−1.30	−1.16	−1.25
CAN	0	−1.55	−0.81	−1.48
US	0	−0.97	−1.11	−0.96
JAP	0	0.01	−0.12	−0.04
AUS	0	−0.95	−0.67	−0.92
NZ	0	−1.36	−1.42	−1.32

Sources: Schmidt 1995; Lijphart 1984; Lijphart and Crepaz 1991.

Note: The Lehmbruch scale is taken from Schmidt 1995, who constructs it himself following various texts by Lehmbruch. Schmidt's own index is an adaptation of Lijphart's scales. Lijphart refers to scales created by Lipjhart himself.

whereas Lijphart counts no less than seven or eight countries as more or less consensus democracies. What is actually the core connotation for Lehmbruch and Lijphart?

Examing these classifications, we argue that the core connotation of Konkordanzdemokratie is the occurrence of one institution, viz. the grand coalition or the employment of oversized cabinets with two or more parties. As stated above, in Lijphart's general institutional model, there are two basic and independent dimensions: Konsensus-Mehrheit versus Föderalismus-Unitarismus. Lehmbruch's identification is related to the first dimension, and not to the second one.

Both Lehmbruch and Lijphart agree on the fact that the US is a competitive democracy meaning that it scores low on Konsensus-Mehrheit. In all other respects, the US must be classified outside of the Westminster model. In the other and different Lijphart scale, which taps the occurrence of federalism, the US emerges as having the political system that differs most with regard to that of the Westminster model. Of course, in a presidential system one can only have Konkordanz if the presidency has many heads as in Switzerland. Otherwise, presidents, if powerful, tend to be elected by a majoritarian procedure.

If the core connotation of 'Konkordanzdemokratie' or 'Konsensus-Mehrheit' focuses upon government formation, then the US is a competitive democracy. If it is a matter of federalism, then the US is far from the Westminster camp. Lehmbruch's five cases of Konkordanzdemokratie do not rank high on Lijphart's second dimension of consensus democracy, given that only Switzerland comes close to the US on that scale. The Lehmbruch Konkordanz countries of Belgium, The Netherlands, Luxembourg and Austria are classified as either unitary cases or mixed according to Lijphart.

Thus, we conclude that the countries which Lehmbruch or Lijphart call 'Konkordanzdemokratie' are first and foremost a set of countries where there is broad-based elite co-operation in government, i.e. the participation of two or more political parties in a cabinet that has more support than is strictly necessary. It is true that Lijphart includes more institutions in his first dimension of Consensus democracy such as e.g. party system characteristics. Yet, it is clear that Konkordanzdemokratie is not the same as the federal state, because at its core it rejects the relevance of the one government model, the minimum winning coalition that is also of minimum size.

Thus, Konkordanzdemokatie occurs in those countries which tend to have grand coalitions. A grand coalition involves all major players being brought on board, thus negating the adversarial government – opposition interaction that is a characteristic feature of the Westminster model. Which countries practise oversized coalitions? One may distinguish between a minority government, a simple majority government and oversized coalitions, where the line separating the last two is somewhat arbitrary. Let us use the criterion of more than 60 per cent support in Parliament. Table 11.4 records the occurrence of various kinds of governments between 1945 and 1994.

Table 11.4 Types of governments after World War II: 1945–1994

	Number	Months in power	Party support	Number of parties	Average duration (%)
AUT	19	32.6	75.8	1.8	68.0
BEL	32	17.7	61.8	3.1	36.5
DEN	30	20.0	40.9	2.0	41.0
FIN	42	13.5	58.2	2.9	28.0
FRA	47	12.3	59.0	4.1	20.5
GER	18	31.8	58.3	2.2	66.1
GRE	41	11.6	62.7	1.1	24.1
ICE	22	25.5	55.5	2.3	53.1
IRE	21	30.2	51.2	1.6	60.9
ITA	48	12.1	52.5	2.8	19.8
LUX	13	43.2	68.2	2.0	70.8
NET	20	30.1	61.0	3.3	60.2
NOR	24	25.0	46.9	1.7	52.2
POR	15	14.2	60.0	1.6	29.2
SPA	7	31.5	49.9	1.0	65.8
SWE	24	25.7	47.3	1.5	64.3
SWI	13	44.0	79.3	3.8	91.7
UK	19	30.6	54.5	1.0	60.9
CAN	20	29.6	55.1	1.0	49.9
US	15	40.6	49.6	1.0	84.6
JAP	38	15.9	51.9	1.3	35.6
AUS	27	22.4	58.5	1.6	62.0
NZ	22	28.5	57.4	1.0	78.5

Source: Lane, McKay and Newton 1996.

The countries where the average support in parliament was over 60 per cent between 1945 and 1994 and where, in addition, two or more parties were involved in a coalition are the following: Austria, Belgium, Greece, The Netherlands, Luxembourg and Switzerland. The only other countries that come close to this criterion are Finland, France, Portugal and Germany.

Comparing Table 11.4 with Table 11.3, it is clear that Lijphart's ranking of Denmark, Italy and Austria is based on facts other than the occurrence of a grand coalition. To us, the former two would be competitive democracies whereas the latter should definitely be classified as belonging to Konkordanzdemokratie. It would be hard to place Denmark and Italy in a mixed position. Denmark does not employ oversized cabinets at all and in Italy the major party on the left-wing was excluded from government during the entire post-war period. Lehmbruch's scale could be expanded, at least by classifying Finland and maybe Germany as Konkordanzdemokratie. The employment of the grand coalition tends, however, to vary over time, which means that a few countries could shift back and forth from simple majority governments to oversized coalitions, like, for instance, Belgium.

Thus, we have arrived at a set of institutions that apply to what is referred to as 'Konkordanzdemokratie', and which only apply to those countries.

Whereas Konkordanzdemokratie, or Consensus democracy, is a neat institutional concept, corporatism is a messy concept for referring to a distinct set of institutions. What is the relationship between these two sets of institutions?

Institutional convergence?

We now know much more about the denotation of 'corporatism' and 'Konkordanzdemokratie'. There are certain difficulties concerning the classification of some countries, especially on the scales of corporatism. Yet, the classification of the hard core corporatist countries, as well as the tendency of the typically non-corporatist countries, is clear. The argument which states that the institutions of corporatism and Konkordanzdemokratie are related, may refer to these institutions as being equivalent, substitutable or complementary to each other. Basically, there is one argument about institutional convergence at the denotation level and another at the connotation level.

First, the institutions of corporatism and Konkordanzdemokratie may co-exist in space and across time. Wherever there is corporatism, Konkordanzdemokratie is also present, speaking extensionally or referentially. Thus, we have the first interpretation:

(I1) Corporatism and Konkordanzdemokratie tend to co-vary.

(I1) is hardly empirically correct. Table 11.5 has the correlations between the six scales measuring corporatism, on the one hand, and the three scales tapping the existence of Konkordanzdemokratie or Consensus democracy (Lehmbruch, Schmidt and Lijphart), on the other.

There are countries which rank very high on the scales of corporatism but which are classified as competitive democracies, like the Scandinavian ones. And there are countries which are truly Konkordanzdemokratie but which

Table 11.5 Correlations between corporatism and Konkordanzdemokratie

	Lehmbruch		Schmidt		Lijphart91	
	r	p	r	p	r	p
Corporatism 1 (L-C)	0.53	(0.01)	0.61	(0.00)	0.64	(0.00)
Corporatism 2 (C-D)	0.29	(0.13)	0.28	(0.14)	0.30	(0.12)
Corporatism 3 (B-S)	0.57	(0.01)	0.46	(0.03)	0.50	(0.02)
Corporatism 4 (Sch)	0.26	(0.18)	0.26	(0.18)	0.30	(0.15)
Corporatism 5 (Cam)	0.35	(0.10)	0.30	(0.13)	0.32	(0.11)
Corporatism 6 (Alv)	0.31	(0.13)	0.32	(0.12)	0.37	(0.10)

Sources: See Tables 11.1 and 11.3.

Note: Spearman's rank-order correlation. The significance values are given in parentheses.

do not rank very high on the scale of corporatism, like Switzerland (Blaas 1992, Lehmbruch 1993), The Netherlands and Belgium. The uncertainty concerning how these three countries are to be classified with regard to corporatism, affects the possibility that a relationship between the two phenomena exist. When Switzerland and The Netherlands are considered corporatist as in Corporatism Index 1 and Corporatism Index 3, then there is modest interaction. But when Switzerland and The Netherlands are ranked lower on the scales of corporatism, then there is little or no interaction. In any case, on the denotational level the set of Konkordanz countries is one set and the set of corporatist countries is another set, where only Austria and perhaps Finland are placed in the intersection of both sets. Corporatism is neither a sufficient nor a necessary condition for Konkordanzdemokratie.

Second, another interpretation of the argument which states that corporatism and Konkordanzdemokratie refer to the same entity may rely on the connotations of these concepts, not their denotation. The non-existence of a correlation between empirically-given phenomena cannot be presented as evidence against the connotation interpretation. On the contrary, the lack of an empirical association strengthens the argument, because a country does not need to have both kinds of institutions since these institutions could very well be substitutable or complementary.

The second interpretation is perhaps the most interesting one, at least from a theoretical point of view. The connotation interpretation may be stated as follows:

(I2) Corporatism and Konkondanzdemokratie are two alternative expressions of power-sharing.

If corporatism and Konkordanzdemokratie are closer to being substitutable than complementary, then the fact that there is no correlation between the two is not surprising.

(I2) raises an entirely different question concerning the possible modes of power-sharing: are there institutions other than those of corporatism and Konkordanzdemokratie that also express power-sharing? Perhaps countries which have numerous institutions for power-sharing are the same countries as those that have corporatist institutions or the institutions of Konkordanzdemokratie?

The concept of power-sharing is a very general one, given that the institutions of power-sharing include all the mechanisms in a constitutional state that provide for so-called concurrent majorities (Calhoun [1850] 1953, 1992). A number of indices have been suggested for tapping the existence of such institutions (Schmidt 1995) and they do not correlate with either Lehmbruch's classification of Konkordanzdemokratie or with the scales concerning Konsensus-Mehrheit (Table 11.6).

Thus, Konkordansdemokratie is generally a specific set of institutions and not just constitutionalism. One could, perhaps, reach different conclusions

Table 11.6 Power-sharing institutions and Konkordanzdemokratie

	Lehmbruch		Schmidt		Lijphart84		Lijphart91	
	r	*p*	*r*	*p*	*r*	*p*	*r*	*p*
CONST1	0.28	(0.095)	0.01	(0.476)	−0.03	(0.455)	0.03	(0.461)
CONST2	−0.08	(0.386)	−0.38	(0.069)	−0.23	(0.184)	−0.35	(0.087)
CONST3	0.61	(0.005)	0.40	(0.057)	0.26	(0.182)	0.38	(0.102)

Sources: Schmidt 1995: 252; Huber *et al.* 1993: 728; and Colomer 1996: 13.

Note: Spearman's rank order correlation. The indices on constitutional devices stands for the following: CONST1=Schmidt's index; CONST2=Huber's index; and CONST3=Colomer's index.

concerning the degree of similarity between the institutions of corporatism and Konkordanzdemokratie, if one looks at their sources as well as their effects.

On the one hand, can we prove that there is a common foundation for the emergence of these two sets of institutions? What supports the institutions of corporatism and of Konkordanzdemokratie? If key groups or chief actors tend to support the institutions that are compatible with their power resources, then, which actors support corporatism and Konkordanzdemokratie, respectively? On the other hand, what are the policy outputs and socio-economic consequences, or outcomes, of corporatism and Konkordanzdemokratie? Is the configutaion the same for both sets of countries?

Sources of corporatism and Konkordanzdemokratie

Both corporatism and Konkordanzdemokratie are institutional set-ups. They regulate the flow of power through the political system. The key actors support them only if they support their interests, both on a short- and long-term basis. Which are the key groups behind these alternative sets of institutions?

Institutions may be regarded as rational and permanent responses to the search for rules of human interaction (Shepsle 1989). In addition, the danger of institutional inertia exists, meaning that, once created by fiat, the institutions begin developing their own vested interests. Both the institutions of corporatism and those of Konkordanz have been in practice for quite some time in the post-war period, which means that they have adopted the characteristics of the so-called equilibrium institutions. Measuring the power of the political forces in democracies according to the support for parties, governments and trade unions, one may draw a picture that explains which group has had a dominating position; the right, the centre or the left, in lending their support to certain institutional arrangements.

Table 11.7 presents data pertaining to the issue of the sources of support for corporatism and Konkordanzdemokratie among these groups of countries.

Table 11.7 Sources of corporatism and Konkordanzdemokratie

		Corp 1 Lijphart/ Crepaz*	Corp 2 Calmfors/ Drifill*	Corp 6 Alvarez*	Konkordanzdemokratie Lehmbruch*	Schmidt**	Lijphart91**
Left governments	r	0.63	0.87	0.90	0.05	0.08	0.18
1950–94	p	0.002	0.000	0.000	0.418	0.361	0.234
Centre governments	r	0.07	−0.12	−0.13	0.51	0.21	0.33
1950–94	P	0.391	0.318	0.316	0.007	0.172	0.089
Liberal governments	r	0.58	0.33	0.22	0.53	0.54	0.76
1950–94	p	0.005	0.094	0.127	0.005	0.004	0.000
Conservative gov.	r	−0.60	−0.52	−0.55	−0.48	−0.49	−0.62
1950–94	P	0.004	0.017	0.018	0.011	0.009	0.003
Left dominance	r	0.74	0.70	0.74	0.39	0.33	0.46
1950–94	P	0.000	0.001	0.001	0.033	0.060	0.026
Major right party	r	−0.65	−0.57	−0.67	−0.28	−0.38	−0.46
1950–94	p	0.002	0.008	0.003	0.097	0.035	0.027
Size of Parl Supp	r	0.13	−0.05	−0.11	0.54	0.12	0.22
1945–94	p	0.306	0.432	0.350	0.004	0.299	0.187
TUD1 1990s	r	0.44	0.68	0.83	0.17	0.27	0.29
	p	0.033	0.001	0.000	0.244	0.135	0.120
TUD2 1980s	r	0.45	0.76	0.87	0.02	0.17	0.180
	p	0.034	0.000	0.000	0.470	0.259	0.241
TUD3 1990s	r	0.31	0.63	0.80	0.22	0.22	0.21
	p	0.112	0.004	0.000	0.180	0.179	0.204

Sources: Schmidt 1996; see Tables 11.4, 11.2.

Note: *Spearman's rank order correlation; **Pearson's correlation.
The first five indicators measure the party composition of governments between 1950 and 1994; the average size of parliamentary support for cabinets; the last three indicators are measures of trade union membership.

A similar thing may be expressed differently. Corporatism and Konkordanzdemokratie could be similar in the sense that they have a common source, although they do not appear together. However, in Table 11.7 there is little support in favour of this interpretation. Corporatist institutions stand strong where the left is powerful, either in the state (government) or in society (trade union density). Konkordanzdemokratie has much more to do with the inclusiveness of governments than with the power of the left, as these institutions are strongly endorsed where the Centre is powerful and they are not related to trade union density. The only thing that corporatism and Konkordanzdemokratie have in common is that these institutions cannot thrive where there are strong conservative parties such as neo-liberal parties. Neither corporatism nor Konkordanz occur in the Anglo-Saxon world, that is in, the US, the UK, Canada, Australia and New Zealand.

It is perhaps not surprising that the bases of support for the institutions of corporatism and of Konkordanzdemokratie are different, because the processes of formation of these institutions have little in common. The first arose during the 1930s as an institutionalized response to the regulation of class conflict during the Great Depression (Karvonen 1993), whereas, the second grew out of ethnic or religious fragmentation in so-called deeply divided societies, where cultural conflicts had been strongly present for centuries (Lehmbruch 1967, 1991; Lijphart 1975; Lorwin 1974; Steiner 1974). Institutionalized responses to conflict regulation may acquire a life of their own, persisting despite the fact that the conflicts that gave rise to these institutions have subsided. But, if both corporatism and Konkordanz-demokratie are mechanisms for bridging groups that are in conflict with each other, then one must remember that the patterns of conflicts were entirely different in the corporatist countries compared with those of the countries which practise Konkordanzdemokratie.

If the sources of support for corporatist institutions are different from those of the institutions of Konkordanzdemokratie, then perhaps these institutions are similar in a different sense. One could argue that these two sets of institutions result in the same configuration of outputs and outcomes within a policy perspective.

Policy outputs of corporatism and Konkordanzdemokratie

Since both corporatism and Konkordanz are made up of institutions of considerable longevity throughout the course of the second half of the twentieth century, one may wish to examine the average policy outputs and socio-economic outcomes that accompany these two institutional set-ups. Since policy outputs and outcomes are caused by conditions other than the institutional ones, such as social factors or actor-related ones, one may wish to speak of institutional 'configurations' and not 'consequences'. In any case, since it would be a question of average scores on various outputs and outcomes, any person living under these two institutional set-ups, or in the two sets of countries that adhere to them, would experience these outputs and outcomes.

Are the institutions of Konkordanzdemokratie and corporatism accompanied by the same public policies? Table 11.8 contains a few clues that point towards the output configurations of these institutional set-ups covering the variation within the set of OECD countries.

Table 11.8 reports cross-sectional correlations between policy outputs and measures of corporatism and Konkordanz for the set of OECD-countries during the post-Second World War period. Policy outputs appear either in the form of allocative or redistributive programmes. Government consumption (GGC) is the allocative part of the state where government provides goods and services. Corporatism tends to favour big spending on allocative programmes whereas in Konkordanz countries the allocative size of the state tends to be smaller, relatively speaking. Also, when considering the level of taxation we find more significant correlations among the corporatist countries. This is a different institutional effect which holds for both the 1980s and the 1990s.

Table 11.8 Corporatism, Konkordanz and policy outputs

		Corp1*	Corp2*	Corp6*	Lehmbruch*	Schmidt**	Lijphart91**
GGC80	r	0.01	0.38	0.46	−0.01	−0.15	−0.16
	p	0.480	0.066	0.041	0.476	0.245	0.257
GGC95	r	0.25	0.52	0.55	−0.18	−0.05	−0.03
	p	0.157	0.017	0.017	0.222	0.413	0.458
SOCB85	r	0.70	0.74	0.61	0.40	0.20	0.34
	p	0.001	0.000	0.008	0.030	0.175	0.082
SOCB94	r	0.54	0.60	0.56	0.54	0.35	0.50
	p	0.013	0.007	0.018	0.006	0.060	0.019
CGE80	r	0.24	0.44	0.37	0.26	0.20	0.22
	p	0.165	0.040	0.085	0.130	0.192	0.189
CGE95	r	0.29	0.36	0.29	0.30	0.31	0.35
	p	0.133	0.085	0.154	0.098	0.090	0.084
TAX85	r	0.67	0.78	0.73	0.44	0.25	0.37
	p	0.001	0.000	0.001	0.018	0.125	0.063
TAX94	r	0.60	0.70	0.60	0.52	0.37	0.51
	p	0.004	0.001	0.009	0.006	0.039	0.015

Sources: See Tables 11.1, 11.3 , 3.1 (GGC, SOCB), 4.5 (CGE), 4.4 (TAX).

Note: *Spearman's rank order correlation; **Pearson's correlation.

The other section of the state is engaged in redistribution, measured, for example, by the proportion of social security payments as a percentage of GDP (SOCB). Both corporatist and Konkordanz countries have huge redistributive public expenditures, significantly more in countries with corporatist institutions than in countries which have grand coalitions. In terms of policy outputs, measured by public expenditures as a percentage of GNP (CGE), corporatist institutions are accompanied by huge government allocative expenditures, whereas Konkordanz is attended by a higher market allocation, at the same time as there is redistribution but not to the same extent as in corporatist countries. Thus, the policy output configurations are not the same.

Policy outcomes of corporatism and Konkordanzdemokratie

In the corporatist literature, the claims advanced in favour of the corporatist institutions, suggesting that corporatism supports both quality of life and economic stability (Streeck 1992; Crouch 1993; Kenworthy 1996), undoubtedly loom large. The hypothesis which states that corporatist institutions perform well, along with the claim argued by Lijphart, which states that the institutions of Konkordanzdemokratie have beneficial effects on society, should be analysed in a comparative test (Lijphart 1994a).

The human development index (HDI), the rate of inflation (INFL) as well as the unemployment rate (UN) reflect whether the outcome configuration is influenced by the institutions of corporatism and Konkordanzdemokratie within the OECD world. Examining policy outcomes, one may also wish to include a whole range of other socio-economic development indicators. The level of affluence, measured by GNP per capita (RGDPCH), would be determined by a number of factors, among which we would find these political institutions. The same applies to economic growth (GRO), measured by the average growth rates. We also consider the impact of institutions on female representation in parliament (FEMR) as well as income distribution (GINI).

There are minor differences between the corporatist and Konkordanz countries concerning the indicators of economic outcome. In the OECD set of countries it rather seems to be the case that the market regimes that have Westminster regimes, like the US and Japan, outperform most of the corporatist and Konkordanz countries (Table 11.9).

Table 11.9 Konkordanz, corporatism and policy outcomes: correlations

		Corp1*	Corp2*	Corp6*	Lehmbruch*	Schmidt**	Lijphart91**
RGDPCH80	r	−0.02	−0.16	−0.00	0.14	0.06	0.02
	p	0.468	0.264	0.496	0.258	0.399	0.475
RGDPCH92	r	−0.03	−0.37	−0.33	0.11	−0.04	−0.04
	p	0.458	0.073	0.114	0.320	0.436	0.445
GRO7385	r	0.18	0.22	−0.11	0.18	0.05	0.12
	p	0.239	0.200	0.344	0.203	0.402	0.319
GRO8594	r	0.16	0.06	−0.26	0.07	−0.09	−0.13
	p	0.266	0.407	0.173	0.377	0.347	0.302
INF8090	r	−0.28	0.14	0.30	−0.55	−0.05	-0.29
	p	0.132	0.290	0.141	0.003	0.407	0.122
INF9095	r	0.26	0.12	0.26	0.01	−0.08	0.21
	p	0.152	0.318	0.178	0.486	0.367	0.203
UN8089	r	−0.38	−0.23	−0.30	0.06	−0.16	−0.20
	p	0.060	0.183	0.140	0.399	0.239	0.21
UN95	r	−0.18	0.10	0.02	−0.05	0.12	0.20
	p	0.233	0.348	0.478	0.418	0.295	0.208
GINI80	r	−0.38	−0.42	−0.43	−0.38	−0.13	−0.23
	p	0.067	0.051	0.062	0.043	0.282	0.190
GINI90	r	−0.30	−0.12	−0.18	−0.66	−0.50	−0.54
	p	0.157	0.352	0.293	0.005	0.034	0.029
HDI80	r	−0.08	−0.36	−0.26	−0.22	−0.10	−0.22
	p	0.379	0.078	0.173	0.157	0.324	0.185
HDI90	r	0.08	−0.30	−0.24	−0.04	−0.03	−0.08
	p	0.374	0.122	0.194	0.436	0.453	0.377
FEMR80	r	0.68	0.65	0.73	0.41	0.48	0.48
	p	0.001	0.003	0.001	0.027	0.010	0.022
FEMR90	r	0.66	0.71	0.75	0.35	0.41	0.42
	p	0.001	0.001	0.001	0.053	0.040	0.026

Sources: See Tables 11.1, 11.3, 3.2 (RGDPCH, GRO, INF, GINI, HDI), 3.3 (FEMR); UN=unemployment=see OECD 1998.

Note: * Spearman's rank order correlation; ** Pearson's correlation.

The profile of the performance of the institutions of corporatism and those of Konkordanz is not as impressive as the adherents to these institutions have claimed, at least if one looks at the economic and social outcomes of the rich democratic countries.

Table 11.9 indicates that there are differences between corporatism and Konkordanz when we look at social outcomes. In relation to female parliamentary representation (FEMR), corporatist countries are as advanced as Konkordanz countries, promoting equality between men and woman. The same applies to another aspect of equality, the income distribution, which, however, seems to be less uneven in Konkordanz countries (GINI) (see also Birchfield and Crepaz 1998). In relation to economic growth, inflation and unemployment, there are no noticeable differences, as neither corporatist nor Konkordanz countries have a specifically advantageous profile on these outcomes.

Both the institutions of macro-corporatism and Konkordanzdemoktatie pose interesting questions for institutional research. Can we connect specific configurations of policy outputs and policy outcomes with the operation of these institutions over a long period of time? In order to discuss this matter seriously, we need to think about how one can identify and possibly measure the operation of these institutions across time and space.

We do not wish to consider corporatism and Konkordanzdemokratie in the same category, because neither the evidence derived from the denotation nor connotation theory would support a category which would include them both. Corporatism is the set of institutions that particularly characterize a few countries: the Nordic countries, Austria and possibly Germany. Konkordanzdemokratie occurs in the central European democracies: Switzerland, Austria and the Benelux countries. Only Austria is included in both categories, denotationally speaking.

Connotationally speaking, corporatism and Konkordanzdemokratie share a common core with respect to the notion of power-sharing. But the mechanisms of power-sharing are much more diverse and also take place extensively outside of countries with corporatist institutions and the key institution of Konkordanzdemokratie, which is basically the employment of oversized coalitions which have excessive parliamentary support. Most indicators tapping the existence of power-sharing institutions rank the US at the top, but the US falls outside of Lehmbruch's classification of Konkordanz and of Lijphart's scale of consensus. By briefly examining the sources and consequences of these two different institutional set-ups, once again we find that the differences are more striking than the similarities.

By exploring the configurations of policy outputs and outcomes we find that the claims made concerning the superiority of either corporatism or Konkordanz in promoting socio-economic development are not corroborated by data concerning the variation in the outcomes of the OECD set of countries. Corporatism means big government, especially huge allocative expenditures, and equality, but does not mean an increase in affluence nor economic stability, relatively speaking, when compared with other regimes within the set of rich countries. The institutions of Konkordanz occur in a set of highly affluent countries characterized by a considerable redistributional ambition, but there is little evidence supporting the fact that they promote socio-economic outcomes.

We are strongly inclined to answer 'No' to the main question raised in this chapter. One should make a clear distinction between the institutions of Konkordanzdemokratie and of corporatism, both in terms of the denotation and connotation aspects. Perhaps Austria is the only country where we find that these institutions are closely connected, but one swallow does not make a summer. The Scandinavian countries score high on what Lehner calls 'liberale Korporatismus' but they do not accept the legitimacy of the typical institutions of Konkordanz. Whether Switzerland, the jewel among the Konkordanz countries, practises 'liberale Korporatismus' is contested:

> Opposed to it Swiss Konkordanzdemokratie works under conditions of a pluralistic and decentralized mediation of interests and incorporates organized interest on a broad basis into the decision making processes.
>
> (Lehner 1986: 154)

If the classical cases harbouring *either* the institutions of Konkordanz *or* corporatism, respectively, do not practise *both* sets of institutions, then how can they be 'closely connected'?

Conclusion

We have, in this chapter, focused upon the relevance of the Lijphart institutional theory in relation to the occurrence of institutional effects. The findings indicate that one should keep the institutional items that enter into Consensus democracy separate and enquire into the impact of each one of them on socio-economic outcomes and political results. In particular, we have raised objections towards the identification of the institutions of Konkordanz and the institutions of macro-corporatism, especially on the denotation level.

Searching for institutional effects, we find that the operation of the institutions of Konkordanz and the institutions of macro-corporatism do not have the same effects. There are clear institutional effects from these two types of institutions, but they are not the same ones, corporatism resulting in much more equality than Konkordanz, partly as a result of the huge welfare state expenditures that the corporatist countries tend to have.

We have not been able to confirm any notion about a better performance profile for the Consensus institutions than for the Westminster institutions. On the contrary, the evaluation data for the 1990s indicate that the countries that stay away from macro-corporatism, favouring a market economy instead of a huge welfare state, tend to do better than the corporatist countries. A neo-institutionalist perspective may be employed to illustrate how the institutions of Konkordanzdemokratie and macro-corporatism are related, both in terms of their origins as well as their policy outputs and outcomes. Both the conditions and the configuration of outputs and outcomes of Konkordanzdemokratie and corporatism are different. Therefore, one should clearly distinguish between these two sets of institutions. In a cross-sectional approach, the configuration of socio-economic outcomes connected with these institutions are not as impressive as often claimed by the adherents of Konkordanz and macro-corporatism.

Macro-corporatism is an institution that regulates economic policy-making and the interaction between the major interest organizations. In the next part we will take a broader look at state institutions with a basic economic import, i.e. so-called politico-economic regimes.

Part IV

The Friedman system

One often encounters arguments to the effect that major economic outcomes such as affluence or economic growth over time are conditioned by institutions. Chapter 11 examined such an argument in relation to macro-corporatism. The new theories within neo-institutionalism or the new institutionalism emphasize the link between institutions and economic development to such an extent that we need to raise the entire question about how much institutions matter for economic outcomes.

In politico-economic regimes, institutions regulate the role of the public and the private sectors as well as clarify the borderline between state and market. Alternative institutions for the state and the market result in different politico-economic regimes. Does the evidence about outcomes in the late twentieth century support the claim advanced that the overall structuring of politico-economic institutions matters? We will focus upon two outcomes: average economic growth and political freedom.

It may be pointed out that in the traditional economic growth literature, for instance in the neo-classical growth model, institutions are not given such a prominent causal position as neo-institutionalism entails, because other factors are emphasized. In the three chapters below, we try to pin down the contribution of politico-economic regimes against the background of the theoretical debate (Chapter 12) in order first, to average economic growth (Chapter 13) and second, to evaluate political freedom, or democracy (Chapter 14).

12 The economic outcomes of market institutions
Theory

Introduction

This chapter examines the logic of the argument that institutions enhance economic affluence, focusing upon the amount of economic freedom that the prevailing politico-economic regime in a country allows for. As Table 12.1 shows, the connection between economic institutions and economic development has been researched with somewhat varying findings in the last decade. In this research on the outcomes of economic institutions one is confronted with a number of critical methodological questions, to be discussed below, about how to identify institutions, how to measure economic development (level of affluence or growth rates) as well as which countries to focus upon.

From Table 12.1 it appears that the empirical tests of economic neo-institutionalism tend to support the hypothesis that institutions matter for economic growth, but they are not conclusive. Why? Before we examine this empirical

Table 12.1 Research on the connection between economic freedom and economic growth

Studies	Countries	Economic data	Scales on economic freedom	Findings
Spindler (1991)	rich and poor	level	Wright (1982)	mixed
Vanssay/Spindler (1994)	rich and poor	level	Scully/Slottje (1991)	positive
Torstensson (1994)	rich and poor	change 1976–85	Scully/Slottje (1991)	positive
Abrams/Lewis (1995)	rich and poor	change 1968–87	Pourgerami	positive
	poor	change 1968–87	Pourgerami	positive
Goldsmith (1995)	poor	change 1988–93	Johnson and Sheehy (1995)	positive
Leblang (1996)	rich and poor	change 1960–90	proxies för Wright (1982)	positive
Islam (1996)	rich and poor	change 1980–92	Easton (1992)	positive
	rich	change 1980–92	Easton (1992)	positive
	poor	change 1980–92	Easton (1992)	none
Easton/Walker (1997)	rich and poor	level	Gwartney (1996)	positive

question in the next chapter, we look into the theoretical debate about economic institutions in order to identify certain macro institutions that would be relevant to the understanding of socio-economic development. Which are the economic institutions that promote affluence or economic growth? Answer, those that enhance economic efficiency, either micro or macro. But which ones are they?

Role of the state in institutional design of the economy

We are particularly interested in the role of government in designing and implementing institutions that enhance economic development. Thus, we ask some of the classical questions in political economy: What is the role of private property as against public ownership? How does extensive government intervention in markets affect affluence and economic growth? The institutions that structure economic life tend to be legal ones, meaning that they receive much of their backing from government. The state and the legal order are inseparable entities. When government designs and implements legal institutions for economic life, then it can provide itself with a major role, or it can trust the private sector to handle economic interactions.

Basically, there are two key questions involved here. First, there is the problem of identifying the possible variation in economic institutions, especially from the perspective of modelling their impact upon economic life. At the macro level, this cannot be done without taking into account the role of the state in economic life. Major economic institutions constitute part of the politico-economic regime, which is sometimes laid down in the constitution but always clarified in the legal order. Second, there is the question of describing accurately the economic institutions of each and every country. That this is far from a simple and straightforward issue is readily seen in relation to the debate about economic development in South East Asia (Krugman 1994). Which institutions have been utilized among the Baby Tigers? Changing the institutional description of the countries in South East Asia affects the analysis of the causes of economic prosperity.

What difference does it make for economic outcomes, especially long-term growth, if (a) there is little or heavy government intervention, or (b) there is extensive or little public ownership? Starting from the ideal-type of a laissez-faire regime, where government intervention or regulation is minimal and public ownership tiny, we ask if countries coming close to the model of the physiocrats and Manchester liberalism do well on economic growth. Increasing the role of government either along the interventionist or regulative dimension or in terms of public ownership, we arrive at institutional alternatives to laissez-faire, from the Wagner–Keynesian ideal of a mixed economy to economic statism, as well as, finally and at the other extreme, the command economy, where the role of markets and private ownership is minimal. How do countries which have rejected the laissez-faire framework and adopted one or another alternative institutional set-up, perform on economic growth?

This is not the place to start an extensive evaluation of various theories about economic growth. What we wish to look at is only the contribution of one factor in these arguments, namely the nature of the institutions that would promote economic development conceived of as economic growth. What are the institutional conditions for economic prosperity? We argue that the link between institutions structuring economic life and economic output involves efficiency. The key question is then: which institutions promote micro or macro efficiency? We suggest that the answer to that question focuses either upon information or upon incentives.

Information

In the Austrian School one encounters a theory about the social prerequisites of affluence. Economic development is impossible without a proper institutional basis for the economy. Affluence results from the productive employment of inputs. Affluence is the money value of the goods and services produced during a period of time, say one year. The chief question for the Austrians was not to analyse how inputs were being transformed into outputs, or how the monetary value of inputs and outputs was forthcoming. These things had been taken care by the Lausanne School. Instead, the argument focused upon the necessity of a laissez-faire regime for economic development. Why this essential link between laissez-faire and economic growth?

Austrian institutionalism may be seen as a response to two influential schools of thought in the early twentieth century: the Lausanne School and the Socialist School. The Lausanne School focused upon mathematical solutions to equilibrium questions in market resource allocation. Not much was said about the institutional setting in which markets operate. Thus, it was possible to launch a socialist interpretation of the findings of the Lausanne School, claiming that a quite different institutional set-up could find and implement the equilibrium, namely government. Barone in 1908 launched his model of the Ministry of Production, calculating the Pareto efficient solutions in allocation. Given that the Ministry of Production knows the preferences of consumers and the production functions in industry, then a socialist economy could also be efficient, claimed Barone. To the Austrians, the Barone theorem was faulty, opening up a much too great a role for government in the economy, in both allocation and ownership: the command economy model.

Calculation: von Mises

Mises' rejection of the planned economy is a practical one, focusing upon the role of calculations implicit in the Barone equations. How is the Ministry of Production to behave in order to be able to calculate the equilibrium in all markets? To Mises, only market prices can carry all the information necessary for arriving at the decisions which equilibrate demand and supply in various markets. Thus, decentralized decision-making is necessary for economic efficiency, which competitive prices bring about through the invisible hand.

The Austrians rejected not only a pure command economy but also the attempt to mix market and state in the form of market socialism. Markets and private property go together for the Austrians. There can be no decentralized markets and, at the same time, state ownership of the means of production. Mises' position was very clear on this point:

> the market and its functions in regard to the formation of prices cannot be divorced from private property and the freedom of capitalists, landlords and entrepreneurs to dispose of their property as they see fit.
>
> (Mises 1936: 138)

The Mises argument makes private property only medially relevant for a high level of economic output. What is critically important in the economy is the capacity to calculate, and only market prices can arrive at the correct economic calculations, resulting in economic efficiency fostering growth.

Mises' classical position targets micro efficiency, but is vulnerable to all kinds of arguments focusing upon the scope of market failures and the possible contribution of government towards macro efficiency in the form of Keynesian demand management. Why is government so weak on economic calculation when markets seem, to Mises, so cognitively advanced?

Knowledge and discovery: Hayek

The Hayek argument in favour of laissez-faire is distinctly evolutionary but at the same time focused upon knowledge. Hayek starts from the assumption that rational behaviour is impossible due to the cognitive limitations of man/woman. Thus, not only is socialist calculation not feasible, but markets will also never identify or attain the Walras' equilibrium. Knowledge being dispersed throughout society, rationality can only be enhanced though the exchange of information in decentralized forms, which improves upon collective wisdom but never attains the perfect knowledge conceived in the rational choice model.

To Hayek, the capacity to calculate correctly belongs to no one except those taking part in the development of a spontaneous order such as the market. Collective wisdom is forthcoming when the foolishness of individuals confronts each other. In this evolutionary process, discovery becomes a mechanism that advances mankind towards more truthful knowledge without ever attaining the goal of perfect rationality. The implications for economic organization are straightforward as economic efficiency can only be enhanced by institutions that allow for decentralized exchange of information, i.e. a decentralized market economy. There will at any point of time be market inefficiencies, but they can only be overcome if the invisible hand is allowed to do its job in a longer time perspective. Hayek rejects any attempt to correct for market imperfections, because of the bounded rationality assumption. If there is laissez-faire, then in the long run markets function adequately enough to advance rationality, whereas government, as every actor, has a limited cognitive perspective and cannot replace the private entrepreneur when it comes to discovery, which plays a major role in increasing economic efficiency (Hayek 1978).

Private property rights enter the Hayek preference for laissez-faire in the same way as they do with von Mises, ignoring the fact that Hayek, like Friedman, also believes that private property is an essential feature of any free society, or a necessary condition for political freedom. A regime of private property rights is the institutional bedrock for the proper functioning of markets, because without private property competition, risk-taking and entrepreneurship will not work, i.e. be conducive to economic efficiency.

Thus, institutions safeguard rationality, man and woman do not. And one of the great spontaneous orders is the market, whose proper functioning is intimately connected with private property rights. To the Austrians, the Lausanne School was wrong in two respects. On the one hand, it neglected the institutional embeddedness of markets. On the other hand, it assumed erroneously that single men or women can calculate rational solutions to economic problems.

To the Austrians, the link between economic institutions and affluence or economic growth, is not a direct one. It is mediated by the nature of human knowledge, its acquisition and diffusion. If one accepts the Austrian theory of bounded rationality, then the conclusions in favour of laissez-faire seem to follow. However, starting from a rational choice perspective, admitting the possibility of rational expectations, then another argument must be found in order to link up private property and the invisible hand with economic development.

Hayek looked upon the modern economy as the co-ordination of millions of individual decisions, resulting in a succession of co-ordination failures and co-ordination successes, i.e. the business cycle. What makes economic activity efficient is the evolution over time of rules which regulate what single individuals do – a so-called spontaneous order as the 'results of human action but not of human design'. But, if one rejects the assumption about bounded rationality, then what is really inherited from past wisdom? Could not governments by design improve economic institutions? Knowing about the ups and downs of the business cycle, could not government smooth out the curve?

Yet, more fundamental objections may be raised against the Austrian institutional analysis. One may question both legs of the argument: Is the main advantage of the market economy really its capacity of finding, communicating and evaluating information? The market economy may be important for other reasons than the transmission of information, for instance for handling incentives. Cannot government play a role in advancing the cognitive capacity in a society? The heavy commitment of many governments towards research and education indicates that information and the search for new knowledge may be a public good, in relation to which market myopia and opportunism entail market failure. Perhaps there are other goods or services with which markets face similar difficulties – economies of scale, externalities, information asymmetries on the part of consumers?

The early Chicago position

If the Austrians were one of the intellectual sources in the twentieth century theorizing the connection between economic institutions and economic output, then the developments in the so-called Chicago School of Economics can be considered as the second major source for research into the role of economic institutions. The interesting point to be made is that the strong preference for laissez-faire that is typically associated with the Chicago scholars after the Second World War is not discernible among the early champions.

The quite negative analysis of laissez-faire economics by T. Veblen around 1900 was only barely counter-balanced by other scholars, such as Commons and Knight, who, like Veblen, clearly saw the connection between the operations of markets and economic institutions. Knight took a positive view of laissez-faire as a beneficial mechanism combining interest seeking with knowledge search, expressing the typical Chicago School preference for economic freedom and the competitive market model as the most suitable mechanism for solving economic problems. However, he was fundamentally ambiguous about the overall virtues of laissez-faire, taking a negative long-term view of the development of a laissez-faire society, tending towards monopolies and sharp income inequalities. A Manchester liberal society, or laissez-faire, resulted in micro economic efficiency, especially because of the uncertainty links between risk-taking and profits that laissez-faire harboured. But its macro outcomes were not ethical, argued Knight.

Commons presented government with a major role in reforming the institutions of capitalism. Government could facilitate collective action resulting in negotiations between trade unions and business, which would improve upon the social consequences of laissez-faire. Property rights play a major role in the functioning of the capitalism system, but it is an evolutionary system which can be affected by government, for instance in the form of judicial intervention. Capitalism generates distributional conflicts all the time, whose resolution requires institutional responses facilitating bargaining, resulting in compromise between organized interests. Actually, Commons equated institutions and collective action, regarding the 'working rules' (Veblen's customs) of the economy as the outcome of various forms of collective action, changing capitalism in an evolutionary manner. In the last resort, these working rules would be sanctioned by legal action, especially by the Supreme Court – 'the supreme faculty of political economy'.

If Veblen, Commons and Knight to some extent anticipated the arrival of the New Deal institutions, a sort of miniature welfare state or mixed economy, then it was not until the arrival of Friedman and Coase that the Chicago position turned definitively in favour of laissez-faire. One must, though, not believe that all kinds of institutional economics have favoured laissez-faire (Knight 1982).

Incentives

The emphasis with the Austrians as well as with the early institutionalists in America was upon the cognitive functions in an economy, i.e. the storing and transmission of correct knowledge as well as the search for new knowledge. Yet, institutions should be related not only to cognition but also to volition, meaning that economic institutions may enhance or hinder the flow of incentives in the economy, promoting or stopping the working out of man's/woman's natural tendencies towards the furthering of their self-interests. Which politico-economic regime is most suitable for the incentives given in an economy? Or, which set of economic institutions is most incentive compatible?

Transferability: Alchian

Whereas the Austrian focused primarily upon the market, neo-institutionalists tend to deal directly with property rights and their impact upon economic life, as for instance Alchian. Alchian looks upon property rights as natural rights that people claim in ordinary life, even when the state is feeble in backing these rights. In most societies, the state protects rights including property rights. However, property rights are not, in Alchian's view, of a fixed nature. Typical of private property rights is the large variety of forms of property rights corresponding to different methods for partitioning property by means of mutually agreeable forms of sharing of objects, or more correctly rights to objects: 'private, public, bailments, easements, leases, licenses, franchises, inheritances, etc' (Alchian 1977: 135), to which one may add various forms of joint action involving property rights: corporations, partnerships, non-voting common stock, trusts, agencies, employee–employer relationships as well as marriages.

All these types of property rights testify to man's ingenuity in inventing rules about costs and rewards in human interaction and co-operation, but the basic difference is that between public and private ownership. The contribution of private ownership to economic efficiency is its transferability, meaning that private property rights can be bought and sold quite easily. Alchian focuses upon the restrictive nature of public ownership:

Public ownership must be borne by all members of the public, and no member can divest himself of that ownership. Ownership of public property is not voluntary; it is compulsory as long as one is a member of the public.

(Alchian 1977: 139)

And he derives two basic properties of public ownership: (a) the risk of dilution; (b) the lack of transferability. When something is placed in the public domain, then it is easily subject to invasion, meaning that people may enjoin the property without sharing in the payment of its cost. This tendency to dilute public ownership is actually only the other side of the coin, the lack of transferability. When a property right cannot be bought or sold, then it is more likely that it will be diluted somehow.

The Alchian analysis does not target so much the mechanism of transferability as the incentive consequences of transferability of ownership. If public ownership was transferable, then there follow a number of important consequences for economic efficiency: (1) concentration of rewards and costs more directly on each person responsible for them; and (2) comparable advantage effects of specialized applications of (a) knowledge in control and (b) of risk-bearing. (Alchian 1977: 140).

There can be little doubt that these three implications – the connection between rewards and costs at the personal level, specialization and risk analysis – enhance economic efficiency. When private ownership works well, then one can observe the three Alchian effects: cost-reward internalization, specialization and risk analysis. But when is transferability possible to implement?

Transferability enhances appropriability, and with appropriability comes efficiency-enhancing consequences: marginal productivity rewarding schemes, specialization in knowledge and rational risk management. But we are moving in circles: transferability promotes appropriability in both the short-term and the long-term, but appropriability presupposes transferability. If, indeed, 'public ownership could be sold', then why not reduce public ownership? But can public property always be sold in an efficient manner? Perhaps it is efficiency-enhancing to protect some types of assets (common property) by placing them under protection in the public domain so that they cannot be dissipated – counteracting the so-called tragedy of the commons.

What Alchian is focusing upon is appropriability. He must show that appropriability works for public ownership, meaning that it can satisfy transferability. But suppose it does not. Then we are moved back to enquire into the conditions for transferability of property, i.e. to transaction cost analysis. There is a variety of forms of contracting that may serve various types of property rights differently. Instead of simply equating private property with transferability and transferability with economic efficiency, one must look at alternative contractual regimes, where one regime may be appropriate for one kind of property but inappropriate for another.

Transaction costs: Williamson

Institutions that minimize transaction costs will prevail, the new institutionalism claim. What is crucially important in a flourishing economy is not only that production costs are low but also that transaction costs are manageable. What does this imply institutionally speaking? Which institutions minimize transaction costs? Williamson starts from the transaction costs approach in his *The Economic Institutions of Capitalism* (1985) in order to show what understanding it can bring about concerning a capitalist organization of economic life. It is obvious that Williamson denotes by 'capitalism' the market economy. He writes:

> Contrary to earlier conceptions – where the economic institutions of capitalism are explained by reference to class interests, technology, and/or monopoly power – the transaction cost approach maintains that these institutions have the main purpose and effect of economizing on transaction costs.
>
> (Williamson 1985: 1)

Williamson's general idea is that institutions have an impact upon transaction costs, but such a general hypothesis needs to be specified more concretely. On the one hand, there is the question of the pool of institutions from which one draws when one argues that economic institutions are important for outcomes. One can identify lots of economic institutions, but which ones are the relevant ones? Answer: those institutions which economize on transaction costs. But what costs are truly transaction costs? How about the dissipation of rents, which play a major role in the law and economics approach? As we noted above, governments are given a role in handling dissipation costs, resulting from the practices of laissez-faire, i.e. the Prisoner's Dilemma situation where individual rationality prevails over collective rationality.

The basic Williamson argument is that governance structures that deviate from the institutions of laissez-faire may be transaction cost saving, and thus they – hierarchy, regulation – enhance efficiency in the economy. However, the market economy itself is also transaction cost saving, because economic institutions that remain in place over a longer period of time are – *ipso facto* – transaction cost saving, thus increasing efficiency. And the market economy is, at the end of the twentieth century, the institutional alternative which not only seems to perform the best but, of all feasible alternatives, has stayed in place for the longest time period.

In relation to transaction cost theory, one must separate between assumption and empirical finding. If one assumes that economic institutions survive because they economize on transaction costs, then one must assemble some kind of evidence that supports the hypothesis. It is possible to explain the existence of economic institutions by means of other theories, for example a theory which makes no assumption about institutional teleology, i.e. that institutions exist because they fulfil a beneficial purpose. The Williamson argument is open-ended in one very important aspect: it does not specify the length of time that an institution must have existed in order to qualify as useful. It has happened several times that an institutional arrangement works well at first and then starts to malfunction after some years. Was it first useful and then useless? How much time must elapse before one can test its usefulness?

There is a set of alternative feasible institutional arrangements about which one may enquire into their usefulness. The test is an empirical one. Basically, one would want to know if the impact upon economic outcomes differs when the institutional set-up changes. Thus, one must ask: if labour can be organized very differently in corporatist and non-corporatist regimes, then does it matter? Similarly, market regulation can be more or less extensive or detailed: does it matter? 'Matter' here means causality, which entails a question that can only be answered by empirical evidence at the end of the day. Yet, Williamson provides little empirical evidence about the functioning of alternative institutional arrangements.

Williamson is right that in an affluent economy exchanges occur in several markets. As a matter of fact, the complexity of the modern economy is immense due to the interlinkages between various markets. Thus, economic efficiency is very much promoted if exchanges are facilitated in numerous markets. Transaction costs arise when exchanges are made. These are the costs of negotiating an agreement as well as implementing the agreement. Transaction cost is the effort and time devoted to writing contracts, including also the time and effort devoted to solving disputes about the content of the contract. Yet, there are more factors to be taken into account: the level of education, the entrepreneurial spirit, infrastructure, trade as well as peace, the tax system, work ethic, the level of corruption, etc.

Economic institutions: property and contracting

To the basic insight into the multiplicity of property rights one must add that the neo-institutionalists add the variety of contractual forms, not only in the transfer of such rights, but also in their employment. Some contracts tend to be more efficient than others, especially if one holds the nature of the property rights constant (Barzel 1997). The connection between property rights and market transacting is crystal clear, as property rights involve either the consumption of a good or its exchange.

In the law and economics literature, inspired by the Coase theorem, it is considered to be a state task to define the basic framework for generating property rights. It is the government which lays down the basic rules about what is to be placed inside the so-called public domain and what is to be placed outside it. This distinction is not a dichotomy, but resources or goods may fall in-between, reflecting that property rights are imperfectly defined. The economic approach to social cost and collective action tends to view imperfectly specified property rights as a source of inefficiency, calling for state action to clarify them if transaction costs start to run high.

If the distinction between common property, the public domain and private property is not crystal clear, then it is also true that this separation evolves in the legal system. Property rights will be created when there is an opportunity to do so (Libecap 1993). Economic forces that increase the value of a resource will tend to elicit a legal recognition of the owner of that resource. Thus, what is left inside the public domain is what people decide not to claim rights on. When the costs of metering and policing a resource is higher than its value in use, then it will be left as a common property, subject to open access. Thus, property rights are continuously revised reflecting economic development, and the possibilities for rents in the use of resources. What, then, is the role of the state?

First, the state provides for the courts which handle disputes about property rights. Ideally, such disputes should be settled by means of the principles of justice. However, according to law and also economics the outcomes of disputes about property rights will be driven by efficiency considerations, the courts favouring solutions which involve that the difference between overall gains and losses is maximized. Or if such disputes are settled out of court, then the persons with the most to gain will prevail.

Second, government plays a major role in regulating access to the public domain, where the costs of policing, metering and pricing are too prohibitive for any person to invest in the creation of property rights. Can government itself be considered a player which maximises its gain from holding resources in the domain? In the law and economics approach, governments can contract with other governments about common pool resources in order to clarify property rights, which can then either be kept by government or be sold off to the private sector. Yet, in the law and economic perspective upon property rights, it is up to government first and foremost to handle transaction problems in relation to the use of resources, involving the dissipation of rents as well as costly pricing, metering and policing. What, then, more specifically does transaction cost analysis imply for wealth or economic growth?

It seems possible to argue either way. On the one hand, property rights enhance wealth by finding the most efficient rules for the use and exchange of resources. On the other hand, property rights cannot solve problems involved in the use of common property, which requires government. The larger the public domain, the less the impact of property rights schemes upon wealth. Finally, it may be added that one must not commit the sin of teleology, i.e. assuming that efficient institutions are always forthcoming. It is far from obvious that the parties reach optimal contracts, which maximize output and minimize the dissipation of rents (Cheung 1969).

Testing economic regime hypotheses

If one stays outside of the camp of socialist theories about economic institutions, then one meets the hypotheses that private property rights and market allocation enhance affluence or economic growth. The explanation of this connection may focus upon the diffusion of knowledge, the capacity to appropriate or the saving in transaction costs. We argue that these explanations are theoretically plausible, but their empirical validation is absolutely necessary.

It seems theoretically valid to argue that institutions that improve the spread of knowledge, allow for appropriability or promote transferability by reducing transaction costs, improve economic efficiency. However, this is basically a micro argument. In order to arrive at a macro argument about the impact of economic institutions upon economic growth and overall affluence one needs to take into account that the operation of economic regimes may involve a variety of consequences that may have contradictory effects upon economic growth. Why take only factors like knowledge, appropriability or transferability into account?

Perhaps one should focus upon the protection of infant industries or the promotion of infrastructureas in the doctrine of economic nationalism? Perhaps the distribution of income is also important, as the adherents of the mixed economy argue? One needs to arrive at an overall assessment, based upon empirical evidence. Examining different institutional arrangements for the economy, referring to the scope for market allocation in relation to government intervention or regulation as well as the size of private property in relation to public ownership, would only laissez-faire score high on the capacity of the institutions to advance knowledge and safeguard incentive compatibility? With the exception of the command economy, we believe it is an open question which mix of the private and the public promotes the highest degree of economic growth.

Conclusion

Economic growth varies considerably not only between countries but also over time. Countries displaying high economic growth at one period of time may come out otherwise at another period, and this holds true both for the narrow OECD set of countries and the total set (Figure 12.1; see also Table 3.2). The period 1960–73 was indeed a period of economic growth in most parts of the world, whereas there is more variation in the other two periods considered. Latin-American countries had, on average, negative figures for the 1973–85 period while the same was true for the African countries during the 1985–94 period. What is also obvious from Figure 12.1 is that countries experiencing high growth rates during one period of time need not do so during another period of time.

Can we detect any institutional effect in these growth data? There is sufficient variation in the long-term growth rates to warrant an analysis of

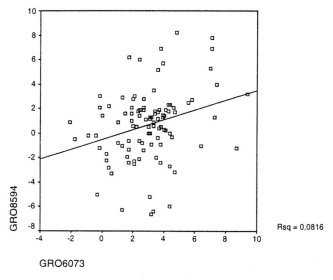

GRO6073

Figure 12.1 Economic growth 1960–73 and 1985–94.

Sources: World Bank Atlas 1975 (1960–73); World Bank Atlas 1996 (1985–94).

determinants. What is the role of economic institutions? The next chapter presents an attempt to test empirically whether economic regimes matter for economic growth.

13   The economic outcomes of market institutions

Empirical tests

Introduction

The theories about the effects of economic regimes examined in Chapter 12 favour laissez-faire, i.e. market allocation based upon clear and transparent property rights. The regime of laissez-faire implies, first, market institutions, and, second, property rights. The connection between economic efficiency, market allocation and property rights has received its most precise formulation in the so-called Coase theorem, stating that markets will allocate resources effectively when transactions costs are zero, independently of the structure of ownership of resources. In real life, transaction costs are most often not negligible, presenting governments with two alternatives: either state intervention or more transparent property rights. How to identify and classify real politico-economic regimes?

Types of real economic regimes

Existing economic regimes are in reality a combination of laissez-faire institutions with state intervention. We identify four such real-life economic regimes following a more refined classification made in the early 1980s (Gastil 1987):

1   Decentralized capitalism or the market economy
2   The mixed economy
3   State-capitalism
4   The planned economy

The two underlying dimensions in this classification are the amount of public ownership and the degree of governmental intervention. The mixed economy has less public ownership than state-capitalism and the planned economy, thus respecting markets more. What is typical of the mixed economy is the heavy commitment towards income maintenance and redistribution. State-capitalism, on the other hand, involves public ownership of key industries as well as government regulation in order to promote infant industries. This type of economic regime is not committed to income redistribution, as trade union activity tends to be controlled by government. Finally, the planned economy involves an economic system that rejects the employment of markets, except for simple nutrition goods. The dream of market socialism has not been realized in any existing country, although attempts were made in former Yugoslavia and Hungary. A basic problem in relation to the four categories above – (1–4) – is that countries may move in and out of them during a short time span. Thus, there are hardly any planned economies in the 1990s and several state-capitalist economies and mixed economies have been reformed towards the ideal of the market economy.

If one were to conduct macro research looking at the country variation in overall economic institutions following the theories discussed above, then the one obvious distinction would be the separation between capitalism and socialism. After all, the capitalist countries recognize the institutions of capitalism whereas the socialist countries did not. However, the dichotomy of capitalism versus socialism is much too simple in relation to the realities after the Second World War, to which the categories from the Great Debate have become more and more inadequate or inapplicable.

The concept of socialism is far from clear, as it may cover not only the planned economy but also the welfare state regimes which accept the institutions of capitalism, although in the form of a mixed economy (Kornai 1992). The same observation may actually be made in relation to capitalism, which occur in two forms: the decentralized market economy and economic nationalism or state-capitalism. A few attempts have been made to introduce scales with which to measure the amount of economic freedom in a country, taking into account both the role of markets and the extent of state ownership and intervention. We will use these scales below, but we wish to state one reservation in relation to their employment: the classification of the Baby Tigers in South East Asia as well as the NICs (newly industrialized countries) in the same area. The classification of the countries in South East Asia is not only a matter of description as it also affects the model estimations used for the evaluation of theories about the consequences of economic regimes. In our empirical tests we will leave the question of the description of the South East Asian economies open, using alternative and contrary descriptions.

In this chapter we will examine a few questions. First, we look at the classification of countries according to economic regime categories. Is the identification of a single country a straightforward, rather uncomplicated matter? Second, we will take a look into the pattern of variation in innovations, i.e. inventions developed into patents. Finally, we also wish to probe causality: does the type of economic regime play a role in the economic growth that the new institutional economics presents it with? Has innovation any impact on economic growth?

Classification and scales: economic regimes

It is unavoidable not to pay attention to the problem of classifying the countries according to economic regime, as it is not a straightforward task. There are both validity and reliability problems connected with the description of economic regimes. Not only is it problematic identifying the scales to be employed in the classification of countries, there is also the question of descriptive accuracy, especially in relation to certain key countries such as the so-called Baby Tigers in South East Asia. We have to deal with these two matters before we examine the evidence concerning interaction between institutions and economic growth.

In the literature, we find two types of scales. On the one hand, there is the nine-category classification used by Gastil in order to cover the 1980s (1980, 1982, 1983–4, 1986–7, 1987–8). It covers more than one hundred countries, classified on the basis of categories that recognize much more than merely capitalism versus socialism. Not only are various kinds of capitalism and socialism identified, but also economic nationalism is recognized.

The Gastil framework is not simply a nominal scale with nine categories or types of economic regimes, identified *ad hoc*. The idea behind these nine categories is a sort of ordinal scale, where low scores involve less state involvement in the economy and high scores refer to greater state involvement. Yet one may discuss whether all categories are strictly placed according to less–more state involvement, as well as whether all the relevant categories have been identified. Gastil's approach is much focused upon a classification of actually existing regimes at one point in time, the 1980s. If economic regimes change over a decade in the sense that some of the categories have no countries that practise them, then the framework runs the risk of becoming rapidly irrelevant. Let us look at the Gastil classification of countries (Table 13.1).

It is fair to say that Gastil starts out from three categories, capitalist, capitalism-statist and socialist regimes, and then goes on to introduce more subtypes within the three overall groups, which is what makes the framework very dependent upon how countries look at a specific point in time. In the empirical classification, Gastil finds that out of 128 cases no less than 33 are capitalist-statist while 34 are placed in the socialist camp. Many countries are classified as mixed-capitalist – all in all 21, but should the mixed economies really be placed after the capitalist-statist ones if the scale is less–more state involvement? This is why we have reclassified the Gastil framework somewhat, placing his state-capitalist countries after the mixed capitalist countries but ahead of the socialist countries (Table 13.1).

Perhaps the employment of the word 'capitalism' is unfortunate, whether in itself or in all these combinations (scores 1–5). 'Capitalism' is a value-laden concept, where the emotive part is larger than the cognitive one. What is disturbing is, however, that both the emotive and cognitive content of the concept is ambiguous. Thus, 'capitalism' raises positive emotions with marketers but is vehemently rejected among egalitarians (Wildavsky 1991).

Table 13.1 Economic systems around 1985 (Gastil)

	Scores Old	Scores New	OECD	Latin America	Africa	Asia	Post-commun	Total
Capitalism inclusive	1	1	12	5	1	3	—	21
Capitalism non-inclusive	2	2	—	4	11	4	—	19
Mixed capitalism	5	3	10	2	7	2	—	21
Capitalist-statist inclusive	3	4	2	7	3	6	—	18
Capitalist-statist non-inclusive	4	5	—	3	5	7	—	15
Mixed socialist inclusive	6	6	—	—	1	2	2	5
Mixed socialist non-inclusive	7	7	—	—	8	1	—	9
Socialist inclusive	8	8	—	1	1	3	6	11
Socialist non-inclusive	9	9	—	—	5	4	—	9

Source: Gastil 1987.
Note: Old score=the classification of Gastil; new score=our reclassification.

There is a whole literature on what 'capitalism' stands for, discussing when and where capitalism emerged, how it has developed, as well as what its future could be predicted to be. This is not the place to enter into the debate about the spiritual or motivational sources of capitalism nor to evaluate the many predictions about its viability in the future. Suffice it to say that two major predictions in the early twentieth century about the evolution of capitalism – Sombart's (1927) and Schumpeters's (1944, 1989) – seem to have been erroneous, as one looks at the evidence about the performance of the market economy after the Second World War. Such an assessment depends, of course, on what one means by 'the market economy' and whether one takes into account not merely economic growth rates but also the social consequences of capitalism, whatever they may be – for instance child labour and drug trafficking.

It seems better to use the word 'market economy' than 'capitalism' and then make distinctions between different types of market economies, especially whether there is a small or large welfare state. Instead of 'capitalist-state' or 'state-capitalism' one could speak of 'economic nationalism' or, finally, of 'the mixed economy' as a proper term for what is sometimes called 'welfare state capitalism'. What we are talking about here are not merely words, but the criteria of evaluation of economic regimes. Assessing capitalism only on the basis of data about economic output may be taking a too restrictive point of view. At the same time, speaking of 'capitalism' in a neutral manner, examining a broad set of evaluation criteria, may be an impossible enterprise.

On the other hand, as an alternative to the Gastil framework one can find various attempts to measure the degree of economic freedom on a ratio scale basis (Gwartney *et al.* 1996; Messick 1996; Holmes *et al.* 1997). The basic idea is that the pure market economy is characterized by a high degree of economic freedom, whereas the pure command economy displays a low degree of economic freedom. But how does one rank countries in-between these two polar opposites? What is to count as economic freedom? Is economic freedom larger or much larger in a market economy with a small welfare state than in a country which adheres to economic nationalism or the mixed economy? One may wish to answer the first question with a clear 'Yes', but it is not given that countries that vary in their type of welfare state also vary – *ipso facto* – in economic freedom.

One may consult these attempts at measuring the amount of economic freedom in various countries around the world, covering almost one hundred cases, allowing for an 'over time' development analysis. Table 13.2 contains the scores for three different time periods constructed by the Fraser Institute (Gwartney *et al.* 1996, 1997).

The scores for the 1990s are, on average, higher than the scores for the 1970s and 1980s. The 1989 initiated regime transitions had profound implications all around the world, affecting not only the command economies but also countries adhering to economic nationalism, as well as to a lesser extent the mixed economies. The profound process of globalization has involved not only a dramatic increase in trade, foreign direct investments and financial transactions, but also a spread of regime changes, modelled first and foremost upon the basis of laissez-faire notions.

What we must discuss here is, however, the reliability in the coding of various countries according to these scales. Can one really be sure that these scales have identified the economic regime of each and every country correctly? There are two ways that one can test for reliability. First, one may consider generally whether these scales tend to co-vary, allowing for the fact that they do not measure economic regimes at the very same point in time. Second, one may focus upon a few countries to check whether there are large differences in the scaling in a few critical cases.

When one is faced with a number of indicators and derived scales, then one may enquire into whether they all tap the same dimension or latent

Table 13.2 Economic freedom index 1975–95

| | 1975 | 1985 | 1995 | Factor analysis | |
				First factor	n
OECD	4.66	5.21	6.36	82.1	23
Latin America	4.60	4.28	5.77		
Africa	3.33	3.56	4.21		
Asia	4.48	4.84	5.65		
Post-com	2.73	2.69	4.25		
Total	4.17	4.28	5.23	77.4	89

Sources: Gwartney *et al.* 1996, 1997.

variable. Here, we have one classification of nine types of economic regime (Gastil), on the one hand, and a number of measurements on economic freedom, on the other. Taking into account that these scales do not pertain to the very same point in time, we would still expect a fairly high degree of co-variation between the measures, because an economic regime does not change rapidly over time, except in a revolutionary situation like the one in Eastern Europe in the 1990s.

It is obvious that the various measures of economic systems and economic freedom tend to co-vary. Comparing the indices for the 1990s, we find that there is a high degree of agreement between them as to the rankings of most countries. This is positive and adds credibility to the attempts to identify economic regimes correctly around the world. Yet, classifying South East Asia is problematic.

Regimes in South East Asia

Looking at individual country scores on the different scales as another method of testing for reliability, it is pertinent to examine the countries in the chief economic growth zone in the world, i.e. South East Asia. How have the NICs been classified, including also Hong Kong although it is neither a country nor a state? Table 13.3 shows the different economic system measures for the South East Asian countries.

The interesting thing with Gastil's classification is that only three of the countries in the South East Asia growth region receive an unambiguous laissez-faire scoring: Hong Kong, Japan and Malaysia. Indonesia, South Korea, the Philippines, Taiwan and Thailand are placed as capitalist-states whereas Singapore is considered to be a mixed economy. How are these

Table 13.3 Economic systems in South East Asia

	Economic system (1) 1982	(1) 1987	Economic freedom (2) 1995	(3) 1975	(3) 1990	(4) 1995	(5) 1995	(5) 1998	(6) 1980
Hong Kong	1	1	—	9.1	9.2	9.3	1.25	1.25	—
Indonesia	5	5	6	4.9	6.4	6.3	3.35	2.85	3
Japan	1	1	13	5.3	7.4	6.7	1.95	2.05	1
Korea South	1	4	7	3.8	4.9	6.7	2.15	2.30	3
Malaysia	1	1	12	5.5	7.3	7.0	2.15	2.40	3
Philippines	5	5	10	4.2	5.2	7.0	3.30	2.65	3
Singapore	3	3	12	6.4	8.5	8.2	1.25	1.30	3
Taiwan	4	4	11	4.9	6.1	6.8	1.95	1.95	—
Thailand	2	2	12	4.4	6.0	7.2	2.30	2.40	2

Note: (1): Economic systems: 1=capitalism inclusive , 2=capitalism non-inclusive, 3=mixed capitalism, 4=capitalist-statist inclusive, 5=capitalist-statist non-inclusive. Source: Gastil 1987; (2)-(4): the higher the value, the more economic freedom. Sources: Messick 1996, Gwartney *et al.* 1996, 1997; (5)-(6): the lower the value, the more economic freedom. Sources: Holmes *et al.* 1998; Wright 1982.

countries placed on the other scales tapping the extent of economic freedom? Let us consult a couple of these ratings and look at the scores as they pertain to different points in time.

Looking at the country scores in Tables 13.3 for columns (2 to 4), one observes two things. First, the scores increase over time, reflecting the general impression that the degree of economic freedom has changed for the better in the 1990s. Second, it is still the case that the countries are classified differently and that some have less economic freedom than others. Actually, Hong Kong stands alone as having a laissez-faire regime, with Singapore, Taiwan and Thailand closing in on Hong Kong's ranking, where the difference in scores reflects much government interference or regulation in the past. Indonesia, Malaysia and the Philippines are never classified as laissez-faire, whereas the identification of Japan and South Korea is more ambiguous.

One may point out that there is agreement that around 1980 most of the NICs in South East Asia were not regarded as laissez-faire systems. On the contrary, they were all, with the exception of Japan and Thailand, looked upon as economies with only a medium degree of economic freedom, reflecting no doubt their state-capitalist features according to the Gastil framework. The doctrine of economic nationalism presents the state with a major role in the economy that deviates from all the conceptions of laissez-aller (Wade 1990). First, the government should own the key industries, setting an example of good management in the national interest. Second, the government should promote the development of industry by the use of tariffs and quotas as well as subsidies – the infant industry argument. Finally, the government should regulate the different sectors of the economy in order to capture economies of scale and see that the infrastructure is supplied. Thus, economic growth is to be fostered by means of state guidance of the economy, not by means of market forces.

All the classifications seem to agree that the economies in this region of the world have been transformed towards much greater laissez-faire. Import substitutions have been massively replaced by export substitution and state involvement has been reduced. However, this impression was seriously questioned in a much discussed article by Paul Krugman, published in 1994. Krugman argues that the amount of state intervention has been totally underestimated, the economies in South East Asia being much closer to the command economies than realized in all attempts to identify the economic regimes in these countries. The miracle of the Baby Tigers is based upon forced labour, providing companies with cheap labour and marginalizing trade unions (Krugman 1994).

This is not the place to enter into the extensive debate about the causes of highly sustained economic growth in South East Asia. Suffice it to say that Krugman adds to a long list of factors that range from purely economic ones like investment and trade patterns to social and political ones including religion, the strength of the state and the ethics of work. Since we only wish to estimate the contribution of economic institutions to economic growth, we will recognize the Krugman rejection of the identification of the regimes in South East Asia by providing below two alternative sets of estimates, one including the NICs in South East Asia and another excluding them.

Correlation with economic growth

If the structure of economic institutions matter for economic growth, then one would expect to find some evidence to that effect, first in correlations and second in regressions. Economic growth varies considerably from one year to another, whereas economic regimes tend to be stable over time. Using a cross-sectional approach one would then have to examine the interaction between stable economic regimes, on the one hand, and long-term economic growth, on the other, averaging out the impact of temporary ups and downs. Is there any surface evidence of the claims of the neo-institutionalists that economic institutions are crucial for promoting long-term economic development?

Let us first look at the evidence from a set of countries covering the entire world, where three alternative sets are employed, one including South East Asia (total set), another excluding these countries due to the difficulty in identifying the type of economic regime, and a third referring only to the OECD set of countries. Three period of time are covered.

Looking at Table 13.4 one observes two findings. First, the correlations appear to substantiate the predictions of the neo-institutionalist theory concerning institutional impact, but the strength of the association is somewhat disappointing, especially when one takes into account the second finding. When the countries in South East Asia are excluded due to the difficulties in identifying, unambiguously, the nature of the regimes with regard to their economies, then we see that the strength of the association is lowered considerably. This is a most disturbing finding as the evidence for

Table 13.4 Correlations: economic systems and economic growth

		Total set economic growth			South East Asia excluded economic growth			OECD set economic growth		
		1960 –73	1973 –85	1985 –94	1960 –73	1973 –85	1985 –94	1960 –73	1973 –85	1985 –94
Economic	r	−0.20	−0.06	−0.28	−0.19	−0.04	−0.28	—	—	—
system 87	p	0.018	0.282	0.001	0.027	0.345	0.002			
Economic	r	0.28	0.17	0.11	0.18	0.02	−0.04	−0.29	0.01	−0.14
freedom 75	p	0.005	0.056	0.163	0.066	0.439	0.365	0.086	0.480	0.261
Economic	r	—	0.43	0.36	—	0.30	0.22	—	0.05	−0.07
freedom 85	p		0.000	0.000		0.003	0.017		0.405	0.374
Economic	r	—	—	0.53	—	—	0.45	—	—	−0.16
freedom 95	p			0.000			0.000			0.236

Sources: See Tables 3.2, 13.1 and 13.2.

the neo-institutionalist theory about regime impact depends upon how a few key countries are classified. During the post-war period, the NICs have been the growth area of the world *par preference* – they constitute so-called outliers and they are numerous enough to have a large effect upon the association between economic growth and economic regime. Thus, there is a risk that the estimates of the interaction are not robust.

Despite these uncertainties, one may establish that we have a corroboration of the theory that economic institutions matter for economic growth. When one examines the entire world, then the institutional effect is not that pronounced. How about a subset of countries like the OECD?

Here, however, the findings are disappointing from the point of view of theoretical expectations. Very few correlations are statistically significant, i.e. $p < 0.05$. Most of the empirical associations are negative, which implies a refutation of the theory about the impact of economic regimes, at least in this set of countries.

Take, for instance, the correlation between economic freedom 1975 and overall economic growth between 1960 and 1973, which is: -0.29. Positive corroboration of the neo-institutionalist theory is neither to be found for the most recent decade, i.e. the correlation between economic freedom 1995 and real economic growth 1985–94.

Most of the countries that have experienced high economic growth during the post-war period come from an economic regime with much governmental intervention. When one looks at the association in the most recent decade, when the extent of economic freedom has increased considerably in most of the countries that used to practise economic nationalism, then it is true that the association is positive, but it is weak.

Although the extent of economic freedom increases in the entire OECD area over the time period covered, pushing down the country differences, it is still the case that all countries are not the same. Economic freedom is high in the Anglo-Saxon countries as well as in Switzerland, Germany, The Netherlands and Japan. A lower degree of economic freedom is to be found in the countries around the Mediterranean Sea as well as in the Nordic countries.

Patterns of innovations

Let us finally take a look at the pattern of innovations worldwide. As an indicator of innovations we have chosen the number of patents per capita registered in the USA by inventor country. The idea is that for most inventions there are strong incentives to have it registered in the largest market in the world, i.e. the US market. However, this creates a problem when comparing the US score with the scores for other countries. One can solve it in at least two ways; either we drop the USA from the analysis or we assign it the highest score; we have chosen the second option. The number of patents has been collected from the US Patent Database. Data for the period 1981 to 1995 is presented in Table 13.5.

Table 13.5 Number of patents (per capita ×1000) registered in the USA by inventor country

	1981–85	1986–90	1991–95	Factor analysis First factor	n
OECD	259.1	314.3	330.3	98.0%	24
Latin Am	2.9	1.9	2.5		
Africa	0.5	0.4	0.5		
Asia	10.2	18.8	34.3		
Post-com	13.7	14.4	3.1		
Total	51.9	64.2	61.7	98.2%	130

Source: US Patent Database; data collected in June 1998.

The lead for the OECD countries in terms of inventiveness is simply immense. Among the top countries in terms of innovation we find: the USA, Japan, Switzerland, Luxembourg, Israel, Sweden, Canada and Germany, but it is also evident that we find the highest growth rates in inventions among South East Asian countries like Taiwan, Hong Kong, South Korea and Singapore. The scores for Latin America and Africa are very low. It is also obvious that for these three periods of time there is a high degree of stability over time.

We may also note that the correlation between patent/capita for 1997–98 and economic freedom is clearly substantive, with the Fraser institute index for 1995 ($r=0.41$), the Freedom House index for 1995 ($r=0.46$) and the Heritage foundation index for 1998 ($r=-0.48$). Table 13.6 displays the correlations between innovations and economic growth.

Yet, the clear positive association between number of patents registered and economic growth is not an institutional finding. To corroborate the entire Hayek argument we must show that innovation can only be high in a laissez-faire regime and that economic growth is chiefly determined by the innovative capacity. The findings above do not allow such an interpretation.

Table 13.6 Correlations: innovations (Ln of patents per capita) and economic growth

		Growth 1973–85	Growth 1985–94	Growth 1960–94
Patents 1981	r	0.17	0.20	0.36
	p	0.043	0.014	0.000
Patents 1986	r	0.19	0.21	0.40
	p	0.023	0.011	0.000
Patents 1991	r	0.21	0.30	0.45
	p	0.013	0.000	0.000
Patents 1997	r	0.24	0.28	0.45
	p	0.007	0.001	0.000

Sources: See Tables 3.2 and 13.5.
Note: *n* varies from 91 to 130.

Regression findings

In order to test the impact of economic institutions and innovations on economic growth, it is necessary to control for the effect of other factors which may be conducive to economic growth. In the models tested below we include variables measuring, on the one hand, changes in gross domestic investments (GDI) over time, as well as the wealth of a country measured at a time when it may have impact on the economic growth, here transformed into the natural logarithm of real GDP per capita (LN RGDP/CAP). We also include innovations into the regression analysis. In addition we will use dummy variables which will pick up the effect of whether a country belongs to the OECD set of nations or whether it is part of South East Asia.

The design of the regression analysis is the following: first, we estimate models explaining economic growth for four various time periods (1960–73 1973–85 1985–94 and 1960–94) using the dummy variables in various combinations (Equations 1–4); second, we introduce the impact of innovations as measured by a variable, averaging patents per capita for the entire period 1981 to 1998 (Equation 5).

The estimations of these five equations are displayed in Table 13.7. The dependent variable is economic growth for 1960–73 (Eq 1) 1973–85 (Eq 2) 1985–94 (Eq 3) and also averaged for the period 1960–94 (Eq 4 and 5). Our focus here is upon the impact of the economic institutions, i.e. the indices measuring economic freedom at various periods of time. The following findings are worth emphasizing.

The institutional effect

For the first period (1960–73) it is obvious that economic freedom has no impact on economic growth when controlling for a number of relevant factors. It may be partly due to the fact that we have to rely on a measure of economic freedom covering the mid-1970s, but it is also important to remember that economic freedom tends to be rather stable over time, at least up to the late 1980s. Thus it seems to be reasonable to conclude that for this period prior to the oil crisis there is no causal relation between economic freedom and economic growth. Next, Equation 2 presents the results of the analysis for the period after the oil crisis, i.e. economic growth from 1973 to 1985. Controlling for other factors we find no impact from economic institutions on economic growth.

However, looking at the findings in Equation 3, which covers the last period of economic growth, i.e. 1985–94, we find an impact from economic freedom. Here it is obvious that we have found the institutional impact upon economic growth which holds true even when controlling for the impact of other factors. The picture changes again when we look at the impact on economic growth for the whole period 1960–94. When controlling for other factors there is no further impact from the economic freedom index. To summarize, we may establish that an economic institution like economic

Table 13.7 Regression analysis: economic growth 1960–94 and economic institutions

		Eq 1	Eq 2	Eq 3	Eq 4	Eq 5
Econ freedom 1975	coeff	−0.01	—	—	—	—
	t-stat	−0.07				
Econ freedom 1985	coeff	—	0.21	—	—	—
	t-stat		1.35			
Econ freedom 1993	coeff	—	—	0.55	—	—
	t-stat			2.98		
Econ freedom 1975–93	coeff	—	—	—	0.09	0.05
	t-stat				0.80	0.34
GDI growth 1960–70	coeff	0.27	—	—	—	—
	t-stat	6.66				
GDI growth 1970–80	coeff	—	0.15	—	—	—
	t-stat		4.35			
GDI growth 1980–93	coeff	—	—	0.37	—	—
	t-stat			8.33		
GDI growth 1960–93	coeff	—	—	—	0.34	0.34
	t-stat				6.38	6.28
LN RGDP/CAP 1960	coeff	0.33	—	—	0.31	0.22
	t-stat	1.08			1.29	0.81
LN RGDP/CAP 1970	coeff	—	0.11	—	—	—
	t-stat		0.36			
LN RGDP/CAP 1980	coeff	—	—	0.37	—	—
	-stat			1.18		
Ln patent/capita 1981–98	coeff	—	—	—	—	0.10
	t-stat					0.70
OECD dummy	coeff	1.73	1.11	−0.73	1.21	1.00
	t-stat	3.35	1.65	−1.22	3.24	2.05
SEASIA dummy	coeff	1.01	2.70	2.04	1.91	1.88
	t-stat	1.58	3.42	2.64	3.57	3.51
Constant	coeff	−1.95	−2.06	−5.44	−3.17	−2.38
	t-stat	−0.94	−0.91	−2.69	−1.94	−1.19
R2adj		0.56	0.41	0.70	0.73	0.73
n		77	80	86	67	67

Sources: See Tables 3.3, 13.2, 13.5, 13.3; GDI growth data is based upon World Bank 1983, 1997.

Note: Eq 1: dependent variable=economic growth 1960–73; Eq 2: dependent variable= economic growth 1973–85; Eq 3: dependent variable=economic growth 1985–94; Eq 4: dependent variable=economic growth 1960–94; Eq 5: dependent variable=economic growth 1960–94.

freedom only has an impact on economic growth during certain time periods and in certain contexts. Thus there seems to be no general positive impact from this variable on economic growth.

Impact of economic factors

Two economic factors which according to economic theory have an impact on economic growth are included in the regression analyses: gross domestic investment growth (GDI growth) and level of economic output (Ln RGDP/CAP). GDI growth has a consistent and strong impact on economic growth in all five equations. The strong impact of investments reduces any positive effect from a previous level of economic output.

In Equation 5 we are testing the impact of innovations on economic growth, adding here a variable measuring the average number of patents per capita for the period 1981–98, transformed into natural logarithms. We may note that the amount of explained variance only increases slightly when adding the innovation variable.

Thus, among the economic factors tested, it is only investment growth which shows an impact on economic growth. Controlling for GDI growth, other factors only have a limited impact.

Impact of South East Asian institutions and OECD

The institutional impact as expressed by South East Asian or OECD institutions is also tested in Table 13.7. Dummy variables for OECD and South East Asia have been entered in all the equations. The impact of these institutions on economic growth is highly changeable. The South East Asia variable displays a significant impact on economic growth except for the period 1960–73. In all the other equations, economic growth is strongly associated with the South East Asian set of countries. The pattern is almost the reverse for the OECD variable. It is only for the early period that we may identify a positive relation between being a member of OECD and economic growth.

Thus, these institutions have an impact on economic growth, but this impact varies over time: prior to the oil crisis, economic growth was high in the OECD countries, while during the 1980s and the 1990s economic growth has been strong in South East Asia.

Summary

All in all from the equations reported upon in Table 13.7, we may establish that economic freedom has a significant impact on economic growth in one of these equations. There is a variation in the impact over time, and it is strongest during the most recent period, i.e. economic growth between 1985 and 1994. Other factors have a stronger impact on economic growth, and among them we may identify investment growth but also what we may call the South East Asian factor, at least up to the mid-1990s.

Conclusion

Economic neo-institutionalism adds to the neo-classical growth model one factor that is of interest to the student of government, namely economic regimes. The basic characteristics of economic regimes tend to be laid down in constitutional documents and they are always protected by the state. How much is an economic outcome, such as long-term growth, dependent upon the institutional set-up for the economy, when the traditional behaviour factors such as, for instance, investments have been taken into account?

In the literature, economic institutions have been given more and more attention. Here we find several theories about the link between economic institutions and economic output: correct information, appropriability and transferability. Although very few doubt that economic output increases when these very conditions are present, it is not the whole story, as economic growth depends upon other factors too, such as the availability of infrastructure, the level of education of the workforce and the political stability of the country.

Empirically, we have partly been able to corroborate the hypothesis that economic institutions matter, although not all problems concerning the identification of economic regimes have been resolved. Yet, we must conclude that economic institutions cannot match behaviour factors, e.g. investments.

If economic institutions matter for affluence, then which kind of institutions would enhance long-run economic growth? Possible answers include institutions that enhance calculation, knowledge and discovery, or rules that favour appropriability and transferability, as well as institutions that are transaction cost saving. It is true that the market economy accomplishes these conditions for economic efficiency, but economic growth depends upon other conditions as well, which other kinds of economic regimes may fulfil. We have examined the variation in economic regimes around the world and related it to the variation in average economic growth during the postwar period. The main finding is that economic institutions matter during certain periods of time and in certain contexts. There is, at times, an institutional effect, an impact from institutions that provides for economic freedom to a sustained high level of economic growth. Do economic institutions also have an impact on political outcomes? This is an issue to be addressed in the next chapter.

14 Economic institutions and political freedom
Friedman

Introduction

In the last chapter we examined the link between the economic regime and affluence, in particular economic growth or the development over time of affluence. We turn now to a classical question in political economy: is there an institutional impact from the legal framework of the economy onto a major outcome in the set of political systems, namely political freedom (Schumpeter 1944; Lindblom 1977). Interestingly, we find among two well-known economists an argument concerning such an impact.

It should be pointed out that the thesis that economic regimes impact upon political liberty is different from another much discussed theory about the sources of human rights, including among them political freedom. Sociologists and political scientists have debated the link between affluence and democracy for some time, following the argument by S.M. Lipset that these two entities are intimately connected. Since several of the rich countries have one type of economic system – the decentralized market economy – and one standard indicator on the spread of democracy is the implementation of civil and political rights, it is almost impossible not to mix the two questions:

(Q1) Do economic institutions matter for political freedom?

(Q2) Does affluence enhance the probability of democracy?

Both these two questions are examined in *Capitalist Development and Democracy* (1992) in the form of profound historical analyses of the evolution over time of capitalist institutions and economic development in the form of output, on the one hand, and the varying fortunes of democratic institutions in the same period, on the other. The authors state:

> That capitalism and democracy go hand in hand is a widely held belief. Indeed it is a commonplace of western political discourse. Editorials and political pronouncements insist regularly that capitalist develop-ment – economic development driven by capital interests in competition with each other, will also bring about political freedom and democratic participation in government. In fact, democracy and capitalism are often seen as virtually identical.
>
> (Rueschemeyer, Stephens and Stephens 1992: 1)

The definition of 'capitalism' in this quotation is not a very precise one, as in different kinds of economic regimes economic development could be 'driven by capital interests in competition with each other'. This is true of at least decentralized capitalism, the mixed economy and state-capitalism. Only the pure command economy is excluded by this characteristic. Why would democracy occur in the same manner in these three types of capitalist regimes? Moreover, it is not clear whether the text is arguing that it is economic development that promotes democracy or whether it is a special type of economic regime which promotes democracy. One must separate analytically between economic institutions and economic output. When the authors claim that democracy and capitalism are 'virtually identical', then are we moving on the connotation or the denotation level, i.e. is the presumed identity a conceptual or an empirical one?

The Friedman argument

The classical statement of M. Friedman's position is *Capitalism and Freedom* first published in 1962. Suppose one asks why Friedman is so much in favour of laissez-faire? Because it brings about wealth, resulting from a long-term sustained process of economic growth? Surprisingly, Friedman says nothing, literally nothing about the connection between capitalism and economic output, or whether laissez-faire is conducive to efficiency or the maximization of total output. His basic argument is totally different, as it states that capitalism is a necessary and sufficient condition for political liberty. Let us quote a few key passages:

> Fundamentally, there are two ways of co-ordinating the economic activities of millions. One is central direction involving the use of coercion – the technique of the army and of the modern totalitarian state. The other is voluntary co-operation of indivuduals – the technique of the market place.
>
> (Friedman 1964: 13)

As will be seen below, this is hardly a very accurate description of the variety of economic regimes in the real world, focusing only upon the dichotomy between pure capitalism and pure socialism. Laissez-faire is an economy based upon voluntary exchange:

> As in that simple model, so in the complex enterprise and money-exchange economy, co-operation is strictly private and voluntary provided: (a) that enterprises are private, so that the ultimate contracting parties are individuals and (b) that individuals are effectively free to enter or not to enter into any particular exchange, so that every transaction is strictly voluntary.
>
> (Friedman 1964: 14)

Thus, 'competitive capitalism' is based upon institutions that safeguard the operation of private firms and that make economic transactions 'strictly voluntary'. Not quite, though, as Friedman acknowledges a role for government, but it is a residual one, deriving from what needs to be done but which the market cannot do itself. He states:

> The existence of a free market does not of course eliminate the need for government. On the contrary, government is essential both as a forum for determining the 'rules of the game' and as an umpire to interpret and enforce the rules decided on.
>
> (Friedman 1964: 15)

In reality, Friedman identifies a few things government can do to supplement the workings of the free market economy, such as public education and poverty relief programmes. However, what we wish to stress here is not internal coherence or lack of coherence in the Friedman analysis but the basic idea of the message, namely that the market first reduces the need for government and, second, enhances political freedom by means of its contribution to economic freedom:

> By removing the organization of economic activity from the control of political authority, the market eliminates this source of coercive power. It enables economic strength to be a check to political power rather than a reinforcement.
>
> (Friedman 1964: 15)

This argument is nothing less than a logical fallacy. A market economy limiting the role of government can only in itself bring about economic freedom, not political freedom. Analytically speaking, economic freedom and democracy are logically independent. It is an empirical question – a matter of probabilities – whether institutions that promote economic freedom co-vary with institutions that provide political freedom. Estimating these probabilities for the post-war period, what is the evidence?

One may point out that the economic argument for the acceptance of the institutions of competitive capitalism is, strangely enough, lacking in Friedman. Chapter 12 contained an examination of the main economic arguments in favour of laissez-faire, but we can see that Friedman launches none of them. His whole case in favour of laissez-faire is not based upon economic efficiency or economic growth but political freedom. This is actually not entirely surprising, as we find a similar kind of argument with another prominent economist, namely Hayek. However, Hayek also suggested a purely economic argument in favour of laissez-faire. Before we look at Hayek's position concerning the link between laissez-faire and political freedom, we should point out that Friedman quite naturally assumes that a laissez-faire regime will bring about development (Friedman 1988). As we saw in Chapter 13, there is ample evidence for this implicit belief when it is a matter of economic growth, but how are things in relation to broader aspects of socio-economic development?

Hayek

Whereas Friedman conceives of the relation between laissez-faire and political freedom as a link between two distinct entities, Hayek looks at the composite elements of a free society, one of which is the market economy. Thus, Friedman's position lends itself easily to a causal interpretation, while Hayek's standpoint in *The Constitution of Liberty* (1960) is holistic. Hayek begins his examination of the place of laissez-faire in a free society by saying:

> The classical argument for freedom in economic affairs rests on the tacit postulate that the rule of law should govern policy in this as in all other spheres.
>
> (Hayek 1960: 220)

Hayek's argument about the link between the market economy and freedom outside of economic life is seemingly not of a causal nature. It is not the case that the market economy increases the amount of freedom in other spheres of social life. Rather, without a market economy a free society is not completely free. It is not a relation of concomitant co-variation that Hayek has in mind but rather adding one free sector to another in order to make liberty complete.

Liberty in Hayek's interpretation is a concept whose contradiction is coercion. It follows from such an approach to the conception of freedom that government interference in the economy is a threat to freedom only when it involves coercion. When government simply implements the rules of the market economy – 'regular enforcement of the general law' (Hayek 1960: 221) – then it is not a matter of an encroachement upon liberty. If the market economy itself is in accordance with the requirements of liberty, then what kinds of state interference in the economy constitute coercion? Hayek separates this kind of illegitimate state intervention from legitimate state intervention, but he also considers lots of state intervention that is perfectly legitimate as foolish or without expediency.

First, government should have the monopoly of coercion. Second, this is the only monopoly of government: 'in all other respects it operates on the same terms as everybody else' (Hayek 1960: 223). Third, there is a set of desirable activities for government, i.e. services 'which are clearly desirable but which will not be provided by competitive enterprise' (Hayek 1960: 223). Here Hayek includes sanitary and health services, construction and maintenance of roads, municipal amenities, etc. What is outside of proper government activities and thus involves the use of coercion, is any kind of government action which involves 'arbitrary discrimination between persons' or any kind of public purpose which 'cannot be achieved by merely enforcing general rules' (Hayek 1960: 227). Here, we have the gist of the Hayek message, which allows him to restrict state intervention to the laissez-faire ideal.

What the concept of freedom rules out is, according to Hayek, a whole set of government decisions, namely:

> The most important among them are decisions as to who is to be allowed to provide different services or commodities, at what prices or in what quantities – in other words, measures designed to control the access to different trades and occupations, the terms of trade, and the amounts to be produced or sold.
>
> (Hayek 1960: 227)

What does this principle against government coercion entail? First, it excludes government regulation of markets in terms of price controls or restrictions on output or trade. Second, and more importantly, Hayek cannot accept the redistribution of income that is typical of a welfare state, or 'it precludes the pursuit of distributive, as opposed to commutative, justice' (Hayek 1960: 232). Thus, a mixed economy with its considerable income redistribution programmes is not in congruence with liberty.

Hayek emphatically states that he can accept more government than what the Manchester liberal theory of the state implies. Thus, he would accept government decisions for: (a) security or the protection against risks common to all, including security against severe physical privation, the assurance of a given minimum of sustenance for all; and (b) public amenities such as parks, museums, theatres and facilities for sports. What he cannot accept is 'the desire to use the powers of government to insure that particular people get particular things', because it involves 'a kind of discrimination between, and an unequal treatment of, different people which is irreconcilable with a free society' (Hayek 1960: 259–60).

Although flexible enough to accept government intervention to help poor people and to undo certain private monopolies, Hayek cannot approve of the welfare state. As in his analysis of socialism, stated in his *The Road to Serfdom* from 1944, Hayek regards the welfare state as the unintended result of a creeping process of state expansion at the expense of the market economy:

> Though some of the aims of the welfare state can be achieved only by methods inimical to liberty, all its aims may be pursued by such methods. The chief danger today is that, once an aim of government is accepted as legitimate, it is then assumed that even means contrary to the principles of freedom may be legitimately employed.
>
> (Hayek 1960: 260)

Starting out with benevolent objectives, government is pushed slowly in the direction of more and more intervention until 'the welfare state becomes a household state in which a paternalistic power controls most of the income of the community and allocates it to individuals in the forms and quantities which it thinks they need or deserve' (Hayek 1960: 260–61).

This is not the place to examine the key concept in Hayek's analysis, viz. freedom. To Hayek, 'liberty' seems to mean either 'according to common law' or 'what is in the common interest'. In any case, the analysis implies the prediction that a large public sector not only limits the market economy but also endangers the overall position of freedom in society. Is it true?

The political consequences of economic institutions

In relation to the Friedman and Hayek arguments, one must make sure that one measures economic freedom independently of political freedom. A proper index of the position of overall freedom is the indicator of human rights, which comes in different forms. They take into account economic freedom, especially property rights, but only to a small degree, as they tend to focus upon other types of freedom such as civil and political rights. Thus, the relationship between economic regime and the measures of liberty would be an open one, conceptually speaking.

An argument to the effect that the market economy brings about political freedom would be a closed one, if any deviation from laissez-faire would *ipso facto* be considered as a violation of freedom. Then there would be no need for an empirical test. However, such an argument is methodologically unsound, making the entire problem only a matter of definitions. It would also prejudge the entire issue, since we know that one type of economic regime that is very frequent in Western Europe, the mixed economy or the welfare state, operates with a high degree of implementation of human rights. Is there any evidence at all that the greater the public expenditure, the weaker the protection of human rights?

Let us start examining the empirical evidence. Table 14.1 has the correlations between two indices on economic regime, on the one hand, and an index on human rights, or democracy, on the other. With regard to the Gastil classification of economic regimes, we note that the protection of human rights declines as the amount of state intervention increases. But it is far from a perfect association. Actually, the correlation declines as we move

Table 14.1 Economic regime and democracy: correlations

		DEMO 1972–83	DEMO 1982–93	DEMO 1991–96
Econ system 1987	r	−0.63	−0.58	−0.41
	p	0.000	0.000	0.000
Econ freedom 1975	r	0.33	0.26	0.28
	p	0.001	0.007	0.003
Econ freedom 1985	r	—	0.35	0.63
	p		0.000	0.000
Econ freedom 1995	r	—	—	0.55
	p			0.000

Sources: See Tables 3.3, 13.1, 13.2.

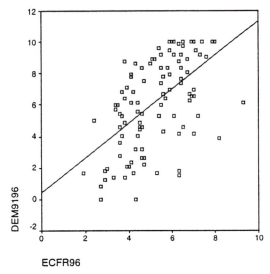

Figure 14.1 Economic freedom and democracy: 1990s.

into the 1990s, reflecting not only the change of several countries towards another kind of regime but also a general increase in respect for human rights.

The other indicator on institutions is the degree of economic freedom. It correlates positively with the implementation of human rights, but the strength of the association is not so high (although it still shows significance), that one may question the Friedman-Hayek argument. Let us examine Figure 14.1, where we are plotting human rights, i.e. democracy (DEM9196), onto the degree of economic freedom for the 1990s (ECFR96).

We can see that several countries score only medium on economic freedom but high on human rights, the mixed economies or the welfare states. Only very few countries score high on economic freedom and low on human rights. And similarly a few countries only score low on economic freedom but high on human rights, i.e. democracy. For the 1990s it is, though, quite obvious that we have a fairly strong positive relation between these two entities.

One may question the Friedman–Hayek argument more profoundly by looking at the association between economic freedom and the size of the public sector. Is it really true that big government only occurs in economic regimes characterized by a low degree of economic freedom? If this is so, then one can be quite sure that high public expenditure must mean less economic freedom in general. Table 14.2 has the correlations for economic freedom (ECFR) and central government revenue (CGR) for three different periods of time.

The finding is an almost perfect confirmation of the null hypothesis. Economic freedom and the size of the public sector are two phenomena that

Table 14.2 Economic freedom and public sector size: correlations

		CGR 1972	CGR 1980	CGR 1995
ECFR75	r	0.18	0.07	0.10
	p	0.068	0.259	0.219
ECFR85	r	—	0.04	0.03
	p		0.361	0.411
ECFR95	r	—	—	0.06
	p			0.298

Sources: See Tables 3.1 and 13.2.

are not related to each other. A country can have economic freedom and a large public sector. One can go into more detail about the relationship between public expenditures and economic freedom by examining the Hayek position that huge redistributive expenditures involve a threat against freedom. Is this argument true in relation to economic freedom? Table 14.3 has the information about social expenditures which includes income transfers (SOCB) and economic regime (ECFR).

The finding in Table 14.3 is clearly counter-evidence against the Friedman–Hayek position. It is not the case that the more an economic regime involves economic freedom the less its social expenditures, as Hayek claims. The connection between economic freedom (ECFR96) and social expenditures (SOCB94) is also positive, although only weakly so. Let us look at Figure 14.2, where this relation is displayed for the 1990s.

One can see from Figure 14.2 that several countries have very high social expenditures but at the same time they score high or medium on the economic freedom index. Even countries which adhere to laissez-faire (decentralized capitalism) may have social expenditures that are not marginal, whereas countries which practise much more of state intervention may have very low social expenditures. The error in the Friedman–Hayek argument is that it neglects affluence as the basic background condition, not only for social expenditures but also for economic freedom itself.

Table 14.3 Economic freedom and social expenditures: correlations

		SOCB 1975	SOCB 1985	SOCB 1995
ECFR75	r	0.30	0.29	0.34
	p	0.013	0.006	0.002
ECFR85	r	—	0.26	0.30
	p		0.010	0.006
ECFR95	r	—	—	0.32
	p			0.002

Sources: See Tables 3.1 and 13.2.

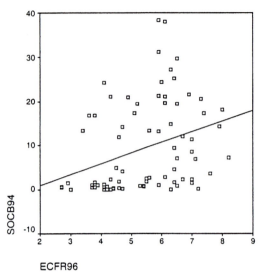

Figure 14.2 Economic freedom and social expenditures: 1990s.

Affluence matters

Theorizing the relation between economic institutions and political freedom without taking into account affluence could involve a sinful omission. Most rich countries have a certain degree of economic freedom meaning that they are either welfare societies or welfare states. Human rights tend to be strongly protected among rich countries. What, then, is the interaction between these three entities: human rights, economic freedom and wealth?

Hayek argues that state expansion involves a threat to liberty. But political freedom tends to increase with affluence and affluence is created by institutions that allow for economic freedom. Thus, perhaps economic and political freedom are both associated with affluence in the same manner: as affluence increases, so does economic freedom and political freedom, meaning that affluence is the crucial factor, and not the size of government. Perhaps Hayek's view of government as coercion is too simplistic?

Friedman claims that a high degree of economic freedom is a guarantee for political freedom. And only the economic institutions of laissez-faire can achieve a high degree of economic freedom, according to Friedman. But what if the size of government obeys the Wagner principle, meaning that it tends to increase along with more affluence, which goes together with economic freedom? The difficulty with the Friedman argument is the existence of the mixed economy, which scores high on political freedom and affluence while, at the same time, economic freedom is much higher than in state-capitalism and the command economy. Is economic freedom truly substantially lower in a welfare state than in a welfare society?

Table 14.4 regresses the implementation of human rights upon affluence and economic freedom. What matters most, we ask, in relation to data about the 1980s and 1990s? In addition to the previously used democracy index, we also employ here a more straightforward human rights index as it has been developed in somewhat different versions by Humana (1983, 1992).

The major empirical finding is that affluence is more important for democracy, i.e. civil and political liberties, than the type of economic institution, as is obvious from the low t-statistics for the economic freedom variables. This holds true especially if we examine the macro variation in political freedom in the 1990s, when so many countries have given up the command economy and reformed their state-capitalist institutions. Since public expenditures tend to increase with affluence, we arrive at the un-avoidable conclusion that the Friedman–Hayek argument about an intimate link between economic freedom and political freedom is wrong. It is falsified by the existence of many mixed economies, where government expenditures are large at the same time as human rights are observed and economic freedom remains only marginally lower than in the laissez-faire countries.

To sum up: we are sceptical to the institutional argument that economic freedom is a necessary and sufficient condition for political freedom. It is not the case that the size of government varies inversely with the protection of human rights. But if laissez-faire is not the only regime that can harbour political freedom, then laissez-faire may result in other outcomes, for instance social development. What is the evidence?

Social outcomes of laissez-faire

There can be little doubt that the overall performance record of laissez-faire is impressive, when economic outcomes are evaluated. We have already

Table 14.4 Regression equations: the effect of economic freedom and wealth on democracy and human rights

		Eq 1 DEMO 1982–93	Eq 2 HUMA 1983	Eq 3 DEMO 1991–96	Eq 4 HUMA 1992
ECFR	coeff	0.22	2.88	0.06	−0.51
	t-stat	1.64	1.84	0.40	−0.48
LNRGDP	coeff	2.49	10.50	2.11	15.57
	t-stat	11.45	3.98	8.54	8.12
Const	coeff	−14.53	−29.07	−10.91	−52.08
	t-stat	−9.30	−1.52	−6.44	−3.91
adj rsq		0.64	0.39	0.53	0.52
n		96	60	98	85

Note and sources: DEMO=democracy index based upon Freedom House ratings, see Table 3.3; HUMA=human rights scores based upon ratings by Humana 1983, 1992; ECFR=economic freedom index, see Table 13.2; LnRGDP=nat log of real GDP per capita, see Table 3.2.

established a link between economic freedom and economic growth (see Table 13.4). Table 14.5 further corroborates such a finding when enquiring into the relations between economic freedom and human development as this is measured by the human development index (HDI).

There is a strong tendency for higher levels of human development to be found among laissez-faire countries, although the relationship is not perfect, because the mixed economies also do well on the human development index.

Interestingly, on other social evaluation criteria the laissez-faire countries perform in a less impressive manner. Table 14.6 displays the connections between laissez-faire (ECFR) and female parliamentary representation (FEMR) as well as with income inequalities (GINI).

We learn from Table 14.6 that laissez-faire is neutral in relation to social equality, as it has no impact whatsoever upon female parliamentary representation or income distributions.

Conclusion

In this chapter we have continued the analysis of economic institutional effects. However, this time the finding involves a falsification of a well-known

Table 14.5   Economic freedom and human development: correlations

		HDI 1970	HDI 1980	HDI 1992
ECFR75	r	0.42	0.45	0.68
	p	0.000	0.000	0.000
ECFR85	r	—	0.45	0.46
	p		0.000	0.000
ECFR95	r	—	—	0.68
	p			0.000

Sources: See Tables 3.3 and 13.2.

Table 14.6 Economic freedom and female parliamentary representation and income inequalities: correlations

		FEMR 1970	FEMR 1980	FEMR 1990	GINI 1970	GINI 1980	GINI 1990
ECFR75	r	−0.07	−0.00	0.11	−0.22	0.10	−0.06
	p	0.260	0.482	0.148	0.056	0.218	0.355
ECFR85	r	—	−0.10	0.06	—	0.11	−0.05
	p		0.165	0.297		0.182 .	0.363
ECFR95	r	—	—	0.29	—	—	−0.04
	p			0.001			0.387

Sources: See Tables 3.3 and 13.2.

institutional argument, viz. the Friedman–Hayek thesis that laissez-faire is a necessary and sufficient condition for political freedom.

Whereas the previous chapter established a confirmation of the argument that economic freedom is conducive to economic wealth, this chapter has not been able to arrive at a similar conclusion concerning economic freedom and political freedom. The implementation of human rights today varies more with affluence than with the type of economic regime. And there is a whole set of countries where the public sector, i.e. the welfare state, is much larger than what Friedman and Hayek would accept as being able to perform well on political freedom. This is also obvious when we look at other kinds of socio-economic outcomes. There are also factors other than economic institutions at work, which have a stronger impact on political and socio-economic outcomes.

15 Conclusion
Constitutionalism matters

Introduction

What does it all add up to one may ask, after having examined a number of key political institutions and a set of outputs and outcomes in order to clarify and answer the often raised question: Do institutions matter? In this final chapter we do not wish to make a survey of the findings in each of the chapters of the book, but to state a new interpretation of the theory that political institutions are important. We now suggest that among the conceivable institutional effects that are relevant when examining the successful operation of a written constitution one should include *constitutionalism*, or the outcome that the constitution is a basic document that constrains state power or power-holders in government. If institutions can produce constitutionalism in a country, then this is a very worthwhile effort.

Federalism, or the theory that federal states perform differently, was examined in Chapter 4, where the institutional effects were sought among public expenditures, deficits, democracy, economic growth and executive durability. Chapter 5 asked whether human rights institutions in general make any difference. The Linz theory about presidentialism was researched in Chapter 6 which enquired into the links between various types of executives and democracy as well as a host of other outcomes. Chapter 7 dealt with the institutions of the legislative branch of government, attempting to trace institutional effects from central bank autonomy, two-chamber systems and the referendum, while Chapter 8 enquired into the impact of legal systems, judicial review, and the ombudsman institution on the size of public expenditure, fiscal deficits, democracy, economic growth and inflation rates. In Chapter 9 we examined the Duverger theory about the electoral system and its outcomes, viz. the party system and government durability, whereas Chapter 10 discussed the Lijphart theory about two basic types of democracy. In Chapter 11 this analysis was continued when the institutions of corporatism and Consensus democracy (Konkordanz) where compared with reference to a variety of different outputs and outcomes including the level of human development, income equality and gender equality, public sector size, fiscal deficits, executive stability and economic growth as well as inflation. Chapter 12 enquired into theories about economic regimes and the institutions guaranteeing economic freedom, with the focus in Chapter 13 being upon one special outcome, namely economic growth. It seemed natural to go somewhat further into the theory of economic institutions, by also testing, in Chapter 14, the Friedman theory about a close link between economic freedom and democracy.

Political institutions are the rules that states uphold by means of their monopoly on the use of legitimate physical violence. Once these rules have been institutionalized properly, they constitute mechanisms which determine how a country is governed. Some of these rules are so critically important that they are codified in legal documents, called constitutions. Here, we wish to argue that what is crucial when assessing constitutional importance is what constitutionalist institutions have in common, not what differentiates them.

Constitutionalism

Constitutionalism is the theory that seeks to devise institutions which will implement the Rule of Law in the public sector. One may identify two versions of constitutionalism, one thin and one thick depending on the number and strength of the institutional set-up devised. No doubt, the thick version of constitutionalism has received more and more attention on the European scene. Constitutionalism, whether in its thin or thick versions, starts from the distinction between state organs and state powers or competencies. According to the classical Montesquieu model the state organs are the head of state, parliament and the judiciary. And the state competencies are the following: executive, legislative and judicial powers. From a constitutional perspective parliaments are basically legislatures, delivering statute law and tax bills.

The thin version of the Rule of Law requires procedural accountability, representation and division of powers. Besides these mechanisms, the thick version also requires the following: a rigid constitution, a bill of rights and minority protection as well as judicial review. The thin version of constitutionalism is institutionalized by the Westminster state whereas the German constitution may be regarded as an example of thick constitutionalism. Actually, one may place the remaning European countries somewhere in between these two polar types. Legislatures play an important role in both thin and thick constitutionalism.

Thin constitutionalism

In a constitutional state, legislatures are relied upon to supply some of the basic materials of constitutionalism itself, i.e. rules. One critical question is how many rules it is the task of the legislature to supply, the main competitors being the executive and the judicial branch of government.

Furthermore, legislatures play a key role in representing the people legitimating government. Legislatures meet in Europe in the form of national assemblies with one or two chambers, representing always the people of the country and sometimes the regions of the country. Both the legislative power and the representative capacity of legislatures vary to some extent in Europe. Finally, and in accordance with the tasks of legislatures outlined above, they constitute one of the three key branches of government, the other two being the executive and the judiciary. The constitutional state requires that legislatures define themselves in relation to the executive and the judiciary and maintain the basic pattern of the balance of power typical of the Rule of Law.

The thin constitutional state can easily harbour a strong legislature. One may even argue that the principles of the Rule of Law requires an active and assertive legislature, making rules, representing the people and checking the executive while giving guidance to the judiciary. At the same time, it should be pointed out that the division of powers principle entails that legislatures have to compete with the other two main state organs, the executive and the judiciary, for power. If a country practises parliamentarism, then the relations between the executive and the legislature will be complex, involving many reciprocities. Under the Montesquieu separation of powers doctrine the legislature should be in command of the competence to deliver legislation. However, legislation is not a clear-cut phenomenon that may be identified in a straightforward manner at one time. As law involves more than statute law, the activities of legislatures are orientated towards maintaining an area that may be encroached upon by other state organs.

First, legislatures have to protect their domain against the executive, which is interested in promulgating rules directly to the administration without taking the route via parliament. All the evidence points to a rise in the number of by-laws or ministerial or agency regulations. Legislatures have grown more suspicious of framework legislation, as it reduces the legislative competence of parliaments to the advantage of the executive. Legislatures cannot be too broad in their statement of legislative ends and means, as it allows for the ministries and the agencies to step in and fill empty buckets.

Some European countries provide the president with special prerogatives in the field of legislation. Here we include such things as package or partial veto with or without override, the competence to issue decrees, budgetary powers, introduction of legislation and proposals of referenda. It is characteristic of European presidentialism, this hybrid form of pure presidentialism, with numerous prerogatives, and parliamentarism, where the head of state is a ceremonial person, that few European presidents have any rights in legislation with the exception of the Russian president, if Russia now belongs to Europe. Yet, the Polish, Portuguese, Lithuanian and Macedonian presidents have certain veto possibilities and the French president may issue decrees.

Second, legislatures must take care to be specific enough not to allow too much room for judges to manoeuvre when interpreting statutes. If there is ample room for judicial interpretation, then legislative competence is transferred to judges, legal precedents becoming more important than statute law.

To sum up, in order to guard their legislative competencies, parliament must be specific when making laws. But in a complex society this demand runs into conflict with another demand, namely that of flexibility. If legislatures were to pass a law on each specific issue, then they would rapidly be overburdened. Thus, transaction costs pull in the other direction in making legislation more open-ended and broadly defined. This, however, opens up opportunities for other players to enter into the legislative competencies.

Thick constitutionalism

Yet, in relation to the thick version of constitutionalism, things are less clear. Ambiguity arises when the requirements of thick constitutionalism are to be combined with the identity of legislatures as perhaps the leading state organ. After all, a constitutional state can only be ruled by legislation, which is the main task of the legislature and the area where it may claim a certain exclusiveness.

Thick constitutionalism requires much more than thin constitutionalism. Thin constitutionalism may be accomodated within the framework of a doctrine of legislative supremacy as in the British theory of the sovereignty of parliament. Thick constitutionalism is a Continental European framework which demands a written and preferably rigid constitution, a fundamental bill of rights to be implemented by judicial review in a special constitutional court, as well as institutions that offer special protection for minorities, for example in the form of decision rules which involve more than simple majorities, and also immunities, or collective rights, which the legislature may not infringe upon.

To see how such a thick interpretation of the Rule of Law idea comes into conflict with the role and tasks of parliaments, we examine each element one by one, giving examples from the European scene.

A rigid constitution   This restricts the power of legislatures, as it hold up a body of rules which a parliament can change, if at all, only by a slower process of decision-making than ordinary legislation. A set of written constitutional documents set up standards against which the executive and the legislature may be evaluated by the judiciary, if the rigid constitution is combined with extensive judicial review. There is no necessary link between the two, as in several countries there are more or less rigid constitutions but no judicial review, such as in the Nordic countries, the Benelux countries and Greece. One must remember the distinction between administrative review and judicial review, the latter standing for the capacity of a court to squash legislation.

When there is a rigid constitution, then legislative supremacy is limited. The constitution takes over parts of the sovereignty of parliament, especially if it contains numerous immunities such as rights which the legislature may never change. If the rigid constitution comprises special rules requiring separate forms of legislation on, for example, urgent matters of constitutional relevance or demands that parliament legislation on certain matters be validated by outside bodies such as referendum, then again legislative supremacy is limited. Thus, many countries in Europe involve the referendum, i.e. the people in the process of making constitutional law.

Special decision rules in parliaments need not restrict the power of legislatures, but they may limit their freedom of action. When special majorities need to be manifactured, then parliaments may fail to take action, because consensus may be difficult to come by. Special decision rules may also strengthen the executive in relation to the legislature, as the government may step in and take over when legislatures fail to deliver. A very intersting example of qualified majority rules enhancing executive power and weakening legislative power was the Finnish constitutional requirement for a possible 67 per cent majority in the Edeskunta for legislative decisions, including taxation. Let us quote from a country expert:

> According to the Finnish Parliament Act, one third of all MPs can postpone an adopted bill to be considered anew by parliament. This second consideration does not take place in the next annual parliamentary session, but in the session that follows thereafter.
>
> (Anckar 1992: 161)

Since tax bills cannot be postponed for such a long time, the government needed to make sure it had the 2/3rds majority in Parliament to get its budget accepted as law. This fact called for oversized coalitions governments in Finland, strengthening no doubt the executive at the expense of the legislature (Anckar 1992). However, in 1992 this rule was changed giving Finland a simple majority rule as is the case in most parliamentarian systems (Mattila 1997).

A bill of rights   Due to the increasing relevance of public international law European parliaments have given constitutional or legal recognition to a bill of rights. This amounts to nothing but a concurrence to the fact that all European countries are now members of the Council of Europe, which implements the European Convention on Human Rights. Yet, when a constitutional bill of rights is combined with judicial review, then such a regulation of the relationships between the citizen and the state really bites. Immunities are the rights in constitutions which, once established, cannot be changed or at least require some very special procedure for change.

In the constitution-making process in Eastern Europe, all countries opted for a bill of rights. In Western Europe, countries like Sweden have moved to a strengthening of the position for human rights either by constitutional amendments or by the transfer of the European Convention into their municipal law. European parliaments face similar restrictions when they engage in legislation in the form of a bulk of civil and political rights which constitute immunities to a higher or lesser degree. If a country fails to implement these human rights, then it may be tried in the European Court in Strasbourg and have to pay fines if found guilty of neglect.

To sum up, constitutions are important due to their capacity to identify, uphold and maintain competences as well as divide them among the state organs, the executive, the legislature and the judiciary. Whether a country adheres to thin or thick constitutionalism, it in any case institutionalizes a body of rules that restricts the power of the state, internally within the state and externally in relation to society.

Institutions and constitutional engineering

In the 1990s, there has been much debate concerning the possibilities of constitutional engineering. Constitutions tend to be looked upon as man-made mechanisms that can be introduced, changed and eliminated at will within the so-called neo-institutionalist movement in the social sciences. Constitutional design is regarded as a real choice option where the choice of one constitutional set-up over another has consequences for real life, at least so the argument has it. If one pursues this line of argument, then one rapidly arrives at the position 'Constitutions matter'. Yet, we need to reflect upon what this means.

Turning to constitutional institutions, we would like to point out three elements of importance for making institutions: norms, behaviour and sanctions. Things become somewhat more complicated when we deal with the subset of institutions that make up constitutions, as the concept of a constitution is ambiguous.

It is no exaggeration to say that the basic argument by neo-institutionalists in political science and economics is that institutions matter in the sense that they have an impact upon real life. Constitutional institutions comprise, people agree, important institutions. Some then argue that constitutions offer the most important institutions of a country. One would expect not only legal scholars to be highly receptive to such an argument, as, after all, jurisprudence is the study of if not all institutions then those that are enforced by the use of state apparatus (and one subset of institutions is the constitutional rules). One would also expect that neo-institutionalism, as a new approach in the social sciences, would emphasize constitutional rules.

Institutions are rules guiding or restraining behaviour. Whenever one conceptualizes institutions one needs to distinguish between the norm, the behaviour and the sanction. By clearly distinguishing between these three elements one may interpret the argument that constitutions matter in two radically different ways, as outlined below.

Following this conceptualization of an institution, it is always an open question whether rules are obeyed in the sense of behaviour intentionally complying with the norm or whether the norm is disobeyed, meaning that behaviour intentionally deviates from the norm. Rules guide behaviour by commanding what is to be done in various situations. Commands may be obeyed or disobeyed and commands may be backed by the employment of sanctions. Institutions are rules backed by sanctions, which help enforce the observation of the rules or punish persons who disobey the rules. Rules are not behaviour or behaviour regularities, but guide or restrain behaviour. Rules may be written or unwritten. Now, stating that 'institutions matter' might stand for two different states of affairs.

The reference of the word 'institution' is extremely broad, as it stands for both the simple rules of elementary behaviour and the complex rules of organizations. When one refers to constitutional institutions, then we face a set of phenomena that ranges from a single particular rule, such as the right to freedom of expression or the right of association, to the set of complex rules of organizations, such as the parliament or the supreme court of a country.

Sometimes 'institutions' refer to the rules of interaction but not to the actors. Sometimes 'institutions' stand for complex behaviour, which when it takes on the form of institutionalization appears as formal organizations that are capable of actors. This ambiguity in the basic concept of an institution surfaces again when one looks at a subset of institutions, the constitutional ones.

Institutions matter when behaviour is oriented in terms of certain institutions, i.e. the institutions are obeyed. Institutions also matter when behaviour takes the rules into account but intentionally neglects or breaks the rules. This is *the compliance interpretation*. Although it is far from self-evident that institutions are important in the sense of complying with rules, it is frequently observed that institutions matter in this sense. Much behaviour is orientated towards rules, either towards complying with them or towards rejecting them. Thus, traffic rules would be an almost perfect case of the importance of institutions.

However, when institutions are claimed to be of importance for social life, then one most often has something more ambitious in mind, namely an assertion that when institutions operate well, then they cause outcomes beyond the mere observation of the rules. This is the *outcome interpretation*. Thus, it is asserted that private property rights promote economic growth, that majoritarian election formulas enhance government durability, that parliamentarism are more in agreement with democratic stability than presidentialism.

It is vital to separate between these two interpretations of importance, which are both covered by the phrase: 'institutions matter'. Let us develop this distinction between (1) institutions are observed, and (2) institutions cause results, by focusing upon a true subset of institutions, namely constitutional institutions.

To sum up: institutions may be deemed important, because (a) they are interesting; (b) they structure behaviour; (c) they determine outcomes. The two senses b and c, in particular, will be discussed below in relation to a subset of institutions, i.e. constitutions. However, (a) is not irrelevant, as some institutions may receive attention simply because of their specific nature.

Constitutional longevity

There is a strong belief in what one might call the constitutional fix (Sartori 1994). By resorting to constitutional engineering or the making and implementation of constitutional policies things may be changed. It is not necessary to refer to major constitutional changes in Eastern Europe, or constitutional revolutions when the entire framework of constitutional rule has been supplanted, in order to find a case of constitutional engineering. Constitutional change may also encompass minor changes in a constitution, which are believed to enhance specific outcomes, such as for instance in Italy. At the same time, the theme emphasizing constitutional inertia entails a clear qualification of the idea of constitutional fix, as it argues that constitutions tend to change slowly and that it takes time before they are imbedded enough to have an impact upon real life.

But how does one identify constitutional institutions? As one readily recognizes, the entire set of institutions contains a non-empty subset of constitutional institutions. Can one specify which institutions are in that subset and which institutions are not? We will show that raising this innocent question poses some problems concerning the identification criteria of constitutional institutions, which are very relevant for the main problem of whether constitutions matter.

In constitutional theory two traditions may be separated, one linking 'constitution' with the formal or written constitution – the Kelsen approach, and another framework underlining the real constitution, or working, constitutional practice – the Weber definition of 'constitution'. How this distinction between the formal and the real constitution is made plays a major role in assessing the claim that constitutions matter. Are constitutional paragraphs important? What impacts does the real constitution have? In the Kelsen approach, a constitution is based upon a formally laid down basic norm, from which constitutional paragraphs may be deduced. In the Weberian framework, the constitution is the set of rules actually followed in the way a country is governed. In many countries either there is no written constitution or the written constitution has been cast aside by means of a declaration of martial law.

Since the written constitution is never the same as the real constitution one may not only enquire into how great the distance is between them, but also discuss the fascinating question of interaction: Does the formal constitution impact upon the real, or is it the real constitution that impacts upon the formal? In the literature one finds two hypotheses. When the real constitution takes precedence over the written documents, then we have the theory of the obsolete elements of a constitution. In intended institutional change processes we have the opposing theory, claiming that changes in the written documents bring about changes in constitutional practice.

One arrives at a constitutional dialectics where the real institutions are most important in some situations and the written constitution is primary in other situations. The dialectics of paragraphs versus institutions includes all the phenomena that one associates with constitutional plagiarism, constitutional veneration and constitutional inertia. They boil down to the problem of constitutional validity – what is it? Constitutional theory has to reconcile both the impact of written rules and the role of case law. In American constitutional practice one leans towards giving priority to the latter as with Dworkin (1986). The classical examples would be the variation in the interpretation of key constitutional terms such as 'due process' and 'equal protection'. Dworkin's position may be contrasted with the importance of codification in civil law systems, which give priority to the formally laid down wishes of the legislator, or the sovereign.

We suggest one road out of the dialectics of the written and the real constitution. Clarity is enhanced if one speaks of the constitution as the written documents, but that one examines continually whether the constitution is applied or not, i.e. is valid or effective. Consequently, we suggest a qualification, namely: constitutions that are valid matter.

It seems reasonable to assume that constitutions play a role in real social life, when they are applied. Of course, they can figure prominently in discourse, even when they are only constitutional blueprints and have not been enforced. However, in neo-institutionalism the basic argument is that institutions matter for behaviour, not only as ideas. If constitutions are to be important, then clearly they must be valid either in the short-term or in the long-term.

There are two different interpretations of institutional importance: the compliance interpretation and the outcome interpretation. In relation to the subset of institutions – the constitutional institutions – the same distinction applies. Thus, constitutional paragraphs are important, because they are observed. Or constitutional realities are important, because they are conducive to outcomes beyond the mere observation of constitutional paragraphs. Under both interpretations, constitutions are deemed important.

If constitutions matter, then they must exist for some time. This is entailed in both the compliance and the outcome interpretations. But do constitutions really last? One may arrive at an understanding of how fragile written constitutions are by examining how long they tend to be in place. Constitutions are formally enacted as valid at a specific point in time, which means that one may measure the length of time that they have been considered as valid. It is, again, an open question as to whether the constitution is also applied, as it could be considered valid but without being respected. Table 15.1 maps the length of time a constitution has been in place in various countries around the world for three different periods of time.

Table 15.1 Constitutional longevity in years by major world regions: means

	Longevity in 1978	Longevity in 1985	Longevity in 1996
OECD	69.0	68.2	64.9
Latin America	24.9	27.1	20.2
Africa	13.1	21.2	10.4
Asia	16.3	19.2	22.0
Post-comm	12.5	19.5	6.6
All	26.2	30.3	22.2
n	125	125	144

Source: See Table 3.3

Note: UK is not included in the OECD set above.

There is in reality only one set of countries where constitutional longevity is a real phenomenon, namely the industrial democracies. The constitution, written or unwritten, now in place (1978–1996) has been operating for a long time without major interruptions. Constitutions do not survive long in Third World countries. One may actually observe a tendency towards even less constitutional longevity when one compares the data for 1996 with the data for 1978. It remains to be seen whether the new constitutions in the many post-communist societies will last longer.

Thus, constitutions are fragile phenomena. However, the finding in Table 15.1 must be interpreted with caution. Sometimes a new constitution is only the confirmation of long existing practice. At other times, the constitution is given an overhaul, although only certains parts of it are changed. Recognizing that it is far from clear-cut what is to be counted as a 'new' constitution, we may observe that constitutional validity is not a dominant feature in the states of the world. This speaks in favour of the compliance interpretation of constitutional importance. Constitutions matter simply when they can be put into operation, which tends to be a real phenomenon in the short-term. Table 15.2 presents data about constitutional longevity in the 1990s in more detail when broken down for a number of various regions of the globe.

Constitutional longevity is very high in North America and Oceania, although we should point out that constitutional matters have been very much an issue of contention in Canada. There, it is just that an agreement about a new constitution between the English-speaking provinces and Quebec is never arrived at. In Western Europe, the present constitutions have been in operation for several decades, on average. However, we also find here countries where the basic rules of the game have been a source of conflict and change, e.g. France and Italy, and also the former authoritarian regimes of the countries of Southern Europe.

Constitutional stability is a formidable problem in Sub-Saharan Africa, where the problem is not so much the frequent change from one framework

Table 15.2 Constitutional longevity in various regions in 1996

	Longevity in 1996
West Europe	56.9
East Europe	6.8
North America	110.5
Cent America	24.8
South America	14.7
North Africa/Mid East	22.6
Subs Africa	9.4
East Asia	21.3
South Asia	27.8
Oceania	67.5

Source: See Table 3.3

to another, such as in Latin America, but the complete lack of constitutional implementation at all. South Asia appears to be more stable than, for instance, North Africa and the Middle East, where Islam creates constitutional turbulence.

Thus, in relation to the so-called Second World and the Third World countries there is much to say in favour of the compliance interpretation of constitutional importance. Just getting constitutions into place has often been an extremely difficult task. Constitutional violation is a most frequent occurring phenomena around the world. It is true that liberal constitutions are often put out of operation in Third World countries, but not even authoritarian constitutions last long. At the same time, one must remember that liberal democracies may also engage in vast constitutional overhaul, as for example in France in 1958. And Europe has seen many authoritarian constitutions in the twentieth century.

Yet, the compliance interpretation of constitutional importance is hardly as ambitious as the outcome interpretation. When constitutions are claimed to be of critical importance, then the argument is often that they enhance major social, economic or political outcomes. In order to do so, they must possess validity, i.e. they must have been in operation for some time.

Real constitutionalism

Constitutions are formal documents that may be implemented by the actual behaviour of state officials becoming valid law. In order to be valid, constitutional paragraphs must be backed by sanctions against deviating behaviour. Only in so far as there is a high probability that sanctions are forthcoming and that correct behaviour is in accordance with constitutional norms, can constitutions be said to be valid. Thus, formal constitutions need real constitutions in order to achieve validity. Constitutions that are valid can be considered as important simply due to this fact. However, constitutions can also be effective in bringing about outcomes, i.e. social, economic or political conditions that go beyond the mere implementation of the constitution.

Among neo-institutionalists it is a widely held belief that the variety of constitutional institutions is important. It is, however, not easily shown by means of empirical evidence that one type of constitution brings about different outcomes than another type. Conditions other than institutional ones also play a role. The problem of attributing outcomes to institutions is much more difficult than many neo-institutionalists are aware of. Economic, social and political outcomes depend upon many factors. How can one know what difference the constitution of a country makes to its performance record?

Suppose that a country L has a constitution C in place for a long period of time. Suppose that the country L flourishes and achieves a very nice performance evaluation, scoring high on economic growth, social stability and democracy. Can one then conclude that the constitution C is the cause of the performance of L, merely from observing that L and C go together during this period of time? According to a Humean theory of causality, the answer is clearly No, as the connection may be spurious. Only by conducting comparative research can one make the induction that constitutions of the type C promote outcomes of the kind that L enjoys.

One may interpret the key clause in the theory that 'Constitutionalism Matters' in the following manner: a constitution C matters in a country L, if (a) C is in force in L, (b) C separates between public and private in L, (c) C makes public power responsible to independent bodies in L, and (d) C secures procedural accountability in L. If conditions a–d apply, then the result is the constitutional state.

One can measure the degree of constitutionalism in the states of the world by enquiring into how they have institutionalized civil and political rights in a wide sense. A few standard indices on human rights may be employed to measure the occurrence of constitutionalism around the world. Let us begin with the extent of constitutionalism, which here stands for the implementation of human rights, or democracy as we may also call it, in the world at both the beginning and middle of the twentieth century (Table 15.3).

Constitutionalism is different from constitutional longevity in that the constitution now really binds the state to respect limitations on its exercise of power. These limitations concern both the rights of civil society – the implementation of civil and political rights – but also the internal decentralization of power within the state. Around 1900, constitutionalism was very much an Occidental phenomenon, occurring basically in Western Europe or countries with a so-called white settler tradition originating in Europe. Yet, the data indicate that constitutionalism has become more widespread, especially when one takes into account the situation around 1950, when many more countries are included.

Table 15.3 Constitutionalism in 1900 and 1950 by world regions: means

	Constitutionalism	
	1900	*1950*
West Europe	6.6	8.8
East Europe	1.4	2.7
North America	9.8	10.0
Cent America	4.3	4.2
South America	5.0	4.5
North Africa / Mid East	2.9	4.6
Subs Africa	5.0	4.5
East Asia	3.3	3.3
South Asia	2.0	5.5
Oceania	10.0	9.2
All	4.8	5.4
n	55	82

Source: Based upon scores reported on in Gurr *et al.* (1990).

Note: These scores are arrived at through combining two variables (DEMOC minus AUTOC) and normalizing the new variable so that a score of 10 stands for democracy while the score of 0 represents non-democracy.

After the Second World War, in about half of the countries of the world there was a certain amount of constitutionalism in the state. Constitutionalism in general has increased all over the world in the 1990s, although many countries in Africa and Asia score very low.

The occurrence of constitutionalism in a state involves the operation of a number of institutions that guarantee the observation of rights and competences: human rights. In a full-scale constitutional state not only all kinds of rights are guaranteed, from civil and political rights to property rights, but also public competences are specified and separated. One must be aware of the possibility that states are only semi-constitutinal states, i.e. they protect certain rights such as property but disrespect other rights such as political rights.

What are the narrow or broad outcomes of the constitutional state? Let us look at this question by focusing upon both the full-scale constitutional states and states that respect only some of the principles of constitutionalism, i.e. semi-constitutional states. We argue basically that it is not the variety of constitutions that matter, i.e. whether they are of the Westminster type or the Consensus type. It is not the details of a constitution that make a constitution socially or political important. What matters is whether there is constitutionalism or not.

Outcomes of constitutionalism

What do fully constitutional states enhance most immediately? We answer: state stability. It has been argued that the concept of state stability is fundamentally flawed, expressing a conservative principle favouring the status quo. We believe this is wrong, as state stability is of fundamental importance to mankind. When the state is unstable, then the probability is high that one may witness the occurrence of massive deaths from domestic violence. For ordinary people the occurrence of state instability in the form of anarchy implies meaningless killings of innocent people. Civil war is a horrendous experience wherever it takes place.

Fully constitutional states offer a predictable pattern of behaviour for changing state and society. Radical movements operating in a constitutional state know that their time will come, as long as the established institutions are respected. A fully constitutional state is, in principle, neutral in relation to conservatism or radicalism. Although it has a conservative bias in so far as it protects institutions that restrict state power and provide for the separation of powers, it also has a radical potential in that it offers avenues for groups seeking to transform society.

State instability is much more typical of states that are deficient in terms of constitutionalism. It is true that authoritarian states may be stable for some time, but it is much more likely that such states will suffer from the various expressions of state instability. Table 15.4 has the correlations between constitutionalism and constitutional longevity indicating state stability.

The empirical finding is clearly that constitutional states have a substantial probability of remaining stable. The correlation is not perfect, meaning that there are some non-constitutional states that are also stable over time. But constitutional states tend to be stable more often than non-constitutional states. This is an important outcome, as the consequences of state instability tend to be devastating for the population. Thus, having a constitution that restricts state power is a significant contribution to state integrity and state longevity. This finding has been neglected in the literature on institutional effects, which tends to focus upon whether the impacts of one or another constitutionalist framework are particularly appealing. It is not the different constitutionalist formats that matter. It is what they have in common that impacts upon real life.

Constitutionalism, or the predicament where a constitution of whatever kind it may be restrains the exercise of state power, has a strong impact upon

Table 15.4 Constitutionalism and constitutional longevity: correlations

		Longevity in 1978	*Longevity in 1985*	*Longevity in 1996*
CONST 1900	r	0.47	0.43	0.52
	p	0.000	0.001	0.000
CONST 1950	r	0.38	0.34	0.51
	p	0.000	0.001	0.000

Sources: See Tables 3.3 and 15.3.

the longevity of the state. A constitutionalist framework restricts the use of the immense power resources of the state both in relation to civil society and internally in the state. It safeguards the rights of citizens – political, social and economic – thus protecting civil society, and it offers internal decentraliz-ation within the state, separating executive, legislative and judicial compe-tences from each other, balancing them against each other. Such states last longer than states that operate a non-constitutionalist framework of institutions.

How about socio-economic performance? Do constitutionalist states do better on economic development than non-constitutionalist states?

Socio-economic performance

One may distinguish between full constitutionalist states and semi-constitutionalist states. The first type of constitutionalist state implements the entire set of civil and political rights, whereas the second kind of constitutionalist state only recognizes economic rights, protecting private property, respecting markets and bourses and acknowledging the joint stock company. What are the developmental outcomes of full constitutionalism versus semi-constitutionalism? The rights and duties that define economic freedom tend to be enshrined in constitutional documents regarding the inviolability of private property and the freedom of economic exchange.

We know that there is a firm connection between full constitutionalism and the level of human development. The level of human development (HDI) takes into account not only the size of the GDP per capita but also other indicators on social development such as literacy. Another similar indicator is the physical quality of life index (PQL). Constitutionalist states tend to do much better on measures of the level of human development than non-constitutionalist states. Thus, the rich countries in the world are very often fully constitutional countries, and vice versa. Can we draw the conclusion that constitutionalism enhances economic development?

The strong association between fully constitutionalist states and human development has been much debated, some claiming that it is a mere his-torical accident that capitalism has emerged in countries orientated towards democracy. Others claim that causality goes from affluence to constitutional-ism, the higher the level of GDP the more human rights will be asked for.

Constitutionalism is about rights and economic development is about output. Could rights enhance a huge output connected with a large GDP? In the short run, 'No', but in the long-run, 'Yes'. Poor countries cannot raise their standards of living simply by introducing a new constitution. Yet, in the long run constitutionalist protection of economic freedom may be crucial for sustained economic development. There is virtually no interaction between full constitutionalism and economic growth in the short-term perspective. Countries which reject full constitutionalism may have a high growth rate – consider some of the South East Asian countries! In the short-term, rights cannot produce output. However, there are different kinds of rights connected with constitutionalism.

Whereas countries that harbour full constitutionalism always safeguard economic freedom, it is also the case that countries with semi-constitutionalism protect property rights. What they do not institutionalize is the set of political rights that constitute the core of human rights. This is the so-called South East Asian model of socio-economic development, anchored in so-called Asian values, which combines considerable political authority with economic freedom. Table 15.5 has the correlations between the implementation of constitutionalism, i.e. democracy, at two points in time and the level of human development after the Second World War.

From Table 15.5 we may conclude there are indeed quite strong correlations between an early implementation of democracy and the level of human development. In Table 15.6 we find similar relations between early democracy, or constitutionalism, and perceptions of corruption in the 1980s and the 1990s: countries where democracy was implemented at an early stage tend to score high on the corruption index which means that the level of perceived corruption is low.

Constitutionalism, or the early implementation of democracy, seems to be positively correlated with perceptions of corruption. What is obvious from Table 15.6 is thus that countries with an early democratization also seem to have lower level of perceived corruption.

Table 15.5 Constitutionalism and human development: correlations

		HDI 1970	HDI 1980	HDI 1992	HDI 1995
CONST 1900	r	0.54	0.52	0.44	0.32
	p	0.000	0.000	0.001	0.009
CONST 1950	r	0.56	0.49	0.45	0.45
	p	0.000	0.000	0.000	0.000

Sources: See Table 3.2 and 15.3.

Table 15.6 Constitutionalism and perceptions of corruption: correlations

		CORR 1980	CORR 1983	CORR 1990	CORR 1998
CONST 1900	r	0.51	0.62	0.51	0.52
	p	0.001	0.000	0.001	0.000
CONST 1950	r	0.56	0.51	0.56	0.67
	p	0.000	0.000	0.000	0.000

Sources: See Tables 3.3 and 15.3.

Constitutional equivalents

Constitutions are written documents that institutionalize the state. When they really take hold, then they restrict state power – this is the doctrine of constitutionalism, both externally and internally. Talking about whether constitutions matter, then, involves two things. First, one must look into whether the constitution really restricts the exercise of state power or whether it is merely a fascade. Second, one may investigate whether a constitution that is institutionalized brings about political or socio-economic outcomes.

A constitution that is implemented will always be important in the trivial sense that it orientates behaviour. Thus, one can claim that the 1949 German constitution has had a crucial impact upon the development of German affairs in the post-war period. Since, for instance, the rulings of the Constitutional Court in Karlsruhe has been respected in state and society, one can argue that it is a most important constitutional institution. This is the compliance interpretation.

Turning to the causal interpretation, however, it is far from self-evident that constitutional things have played such a prominent role in bringing about political, social and economic outcomes. Suppose we make the counter-factual (CF) assertion:

> (CF) If Germany had chosen another kind of liberal constitution, then the country developments would have been the same: stability, economic growth, democratic legitimacy.

Is (CF) false? There is no other way to decide the truth or falseness of (CF) except by carrying out comparative research, where alternative constitutional arrangements are correlated with outcomes. The findings in this chapter suggest that (CF) is indeed true, because of the existence of *constitutional equivalents*.

Many countries of the world do not pass threshold one, i.e. manage to operate a constitutionalist state over a long period of time. A full-scale constitutionalist state of whatever kind it may be – Westminster, Consociational, Presidential – enhances state stability, as the more constitutionalist the constitution the longer it has been in place in an uninterrupted fashion.

What is crucial when assessing constitutional importance is what constitutionalist institutions have in common, not what differentiates them. The political outcome of constitutionalism is state longevity or the intactness of the state, which has profound consequences for the general condition of life of the population. When the state begins to shake, then one frequently encounters the misery of social disorder, meaning deaths from domestic violence or outright anarchy.

In terms of the second outcome – socio-economic development – the findings here indicate a qualification as well as a distinction between full constitutional states and semi-constitutional states. A full-scale constitutionalist state does not accomplish socio-economic development. Although there is a clear positive connection between constitutionalism and the level of human development, one could argue that causality works the other way around, output enhancing rights and not vice versa. Speaking of socioeconomic development in the form of economic growth, what is most important is the institutionalization of economic freedom, which does not necessarily entail a full-scale constitutional state. Thus, full-scale constitutional states will not do better than semi-constitutional states on socio-economic development in the short-term perspective.

Bibliography

Abromeit, H. (1992) *Der verkappte Einheitsstaat*. Opladen: Leske und Budrich.
—— (1993) *Interessenvermittlung zwischen Konkurrenz und Konkordanz*, Opladen: Leske and Budrich.
Akerlof, G. (1970) 'The market for lemons: qualitative uncertainty and the market mechanism', *Quarterly Journal of Economics* 84: 488–500.
Alchian, A.A. (1977) *Economic Forces at Work*, Indianapolis: Liberty Press.
Alesina, A. and Summers, L.H. (1993) 'Central bank independence and macroeconomic performance: some comparative evidence', *Journal of Money, Credit and Banking* 25: 151–62.
Alford, R.R. and Friedland, R. (1985) *Powers of Theory: Capitalism, the State, and Democracy*, Cambridge: Cambridge University Press.
Almond, G.A. (1956) Comparative political systems, *Journal of Politics* 18: 391–409.
Almond, G. *et al.* (1993) *Comparative Politics: A Theoretical Framework*, New York: HarperCollins.
Almond, G.A. and Coleman, J.S. (eds) (1960) *The Politics of Developing Areas*, Princeton, NJ: Princeton U.P.
Almond, G.A. and Powell, G.B. (1966) *Comparative Politics: A Developmental Approach*, Boston: Little, Brown and Company.
Althusius, J. ([1610]1964) *The Politics of Johan Althusius*, London: Eyre and Spottiswoode.
Alvarez, M. *et al.* (1991) 'Government partisanship, labor organization, and macroeconomic performance', *American Political Science Review* 85: 539–56.
Alvarez, M. *et al.* (1996) 'Classifying politial regimes', *Studies in Comparative International Development* 31(2): 3–36.
Anckar, D. (1992) 'Finland: Dualism and consensual rule', in Damgaard, E. (ed.) *Parliamentary Change in the Nordic Countries*. Oslo: Scandinavian U.P., pp. 151–90.
Anckar, C. (1998) *Storlek och Partisystem: En studie av 77 stater*, Abo: Abo Akademis forlag.
Anderson, E.N and Anderson, P.R. (1967) *Political Institutions and Social Change in Continental Europe in the Nineteenth Century*, Berkeley, CA: University of California Press.
Apter, D.E. (1991) 'Institutionalism reconsidered', *International Social Science Journal* 129: 463–82.
Armingeon, K. (1989) Arbeitsbeziehungen und Gewerkschaftsentwicklung in den achtziger Jahren: Ein Vergleich den OECD-Ländern. *Politische Viertalsjahresschrift* 30: 603–28.

Armstrong, D.M. (1973) *Belief, Truth and Knowledge*, Cambridge: Cambridge University Press.

—— (1978) *Nominalism and Religion*, Cambridge: Cambridge University Press.

—— (1980) *A Theory of Universals*, Cambridge: Cambridge University Press.

Arrow, K.J. (1963) *Social Choice and Individual Values*, New Haven: Yale University Press

Bagehot, W. ([1867]1993) *The English Constitution*, London: Fontana.

Bahro, H. *et al.* (1998) 'Duverger's concept: Semi-presidential government revisited', *European Journal of Politial Research* 34: 201–24.

Bakvis, H. and Chandler, W.M. (eds)(1987) *Federalism and the Role of the State*, Toronto: University of Toronto Press.

Banks, A.S. (ed.) (1978) *Political Handbook of the World, 1978,* New York: McGraw-Hill.

Banks, A.S. (1996) *Cross-National Time-Series Data Archive.* Binghampton, NY: Center for Social Analysis, State University of New York at Binghampton.

Barrett, D.B. (ed.) (1982) *World Christian Encyclopaedia: A Comparative Study of Churches and Religions in the Modern World, AD 1900–2000*, Nairobi: Oxford University Press.

Barro, R.J. (1997) *Determinants of Economic Growth: A Cross-country Empirical Study*, Cambridge, MA: MIT Press.

Barry, B. and Rae, D.W. (1975) 'Political evaluation'. in: Greenstein, F.I and Polsby, N.W. (eds) *Handbook of Political Science*, volume 3: *Macropolitical Theory*, Reading, MA: Addison-Wesley, pp. 123–76.

Barzel, Y. (1997) *Economic Analysis of Property Rights,* Cambridge: Cambridge University Press.

Baylis, T.A. (1996) 'Presidents versus prime ministers: shaping executive authority in Eastern Europe', *World Politics* 48: 297–323.

Beetham, D. (ed.) (1994) *Defining and Measuring Democracy*, London: Sage.

Bell, D. (1988) *The End of Ideology: On the Exhaustion of Political Ideas in the Fifties* (with a new afterword), Cambridge, MA: Harvard University Press.

Bernhard, W. (1998) 'A political explanation of variations in central banks independence', *American Political Science Review* 92: 311–27.

Bennett, C.J. (1997) 'Understanding ripple effects: the cross-national adoption of policy instruments for bureaucratic accountability', *Governance* 10: 213–33.

Birchfield, V. and Crepaz, M.M.L. (1998) 'The impact of constitutional structures and collective and competitive veto on income inequality in industrialized democracies', *European Journal of Political Research* 34: 175–200.

Bjorklund, T. (1997) *Om Folkeavstemninger: Norge og Norden 1905–1994*, Oslo: Universitetsforlaget.

Blaas, W. (1992) 'The Swiss model: corporatism or liberal capitalism?' in: Pekkarinen, J. *et al.* (eds) *Social corporatism: A Superior Economic System?*, Oxford: Clarendon Press, pp. 363–76.

Black, C. (1966) *The Dynamics of Modernization*, New York: Harper and Row.

Blais, A. (1988) 'The classification of election systems', *European Journal of Political Research* 16: 99–100.

Blais, A. *et al.* (1997) 'Direct presidential elections: a world summary', *Electoral Studies* 16: 441–55.

Blais, A. and Dobrzynska, A. (1998) 'Turnout in electoral democracies', *European Journal of Political Research* 33: 239–61

Blais, A. and Massicotte, L. (1996) 'Electoral systems', in LeDuc, L. *et al.* (eds) *Comparing Democracies: Elections and Voting in Global Perspective*, Thousand Oaks, CA: Sage, pp. 49–81.

—— (1997) 'Electoral formulas: a macroscopic perspective', *European Journal of Political Research* 32: 107–29.

Blaustein, A.P. and Flanz, G. (eds) (1972–) *Constitutions of the Countries of the World*, New York: Oceana Publishers.

Blondel, J. (1969) *An Introduction to Comparative Government*, London: Weidenfeld and Nicolson.

—— (1972) *Comparative Legislatures*. Englewood Cliffs, NJ: Prentice-Hall.

Bollen, K.A. (1980) Issues in the comparative measurement of political democracy, *American Sociological Review* 45: 370–90.

—— (1986) Political rights and political liberties in nations: an evaluation of human right measures, 1950 to 1984, *Human Rights Quarterly* 8: 567–91.

—— (1990) Political democracy: conceptual and measurement traps, *Studies in Comparative International Development* 25: 7–24.

—— (1993) Liberal democracy: validity and method factors in cross-national measures, *American Journal of Political Science* 37: 1207–30.

Borcherding, T.E. (1985) 'The causes of government expenditure: a survey of the U.S. evidence', *Journal of Public Economics* 28: 359–82.

Brennan, G. (1996) 'Selection and the currency of reward', in Goodin, R.E. (ed.) *The Theory of Institutional Design*, Cambridge: Cambridge University Press.

Brinton, M.C. and Nee, V. (eds) (1998) *The New Institutionalism in Sociology*, New York: Russell Sage.

Bromley, D.W. (1989) *Economic Interests and Institutions*, Oxford: Blackwell.

Bruno, M. and Sachs, J. (1985) *Economics of Worldwide Stagflation*, Cambridge, MA: Harvard University Press.

Buchanan, J.M. (1995) 'Federalism as an ideal political order and an objective for constitutional reform', *Publius* 25(2): 19–27.

Budge, I. (1996) *The New Challenge of Direct Democracy*, Cambridge: Polity Press.

Budge, I. and Keman, H. (1990) *Parties and Democracy: Coalition Formation and Government Functioning in Twenty States*, Oxford: Oxford University Press.

Burgess, M. and Gagnon, A.-G. (eds) (1993) *Comparative Federalism and Federation: Competing Trends and Future Directions*, Hemel Hempstead: Harvester Wheatsheaf.

Busch, A. (1994) 'Central bank independence and the Westminster model', *West European Politics* 17(1): 53–72.

Butler, D. and Ranney, A. (eds)(1994) *Referendums Around the World: The Growing Use of Direct Democracy*, Basingstoke: Macmillan.

Caiden, G.E. (ed.) (1983) *International Handbook of the Ombudsman: Evolution and Present Function*, Westport, CT: Greenwood Press.

Calhoun, J.C. ([1850] 1953) *A Disquisition on Government*, Indianapolis: Bobbs-Merrill.

—— (1992) *Union and Liberty. The Political Philosophy of John C. Calhoun*, Indianapolis: Liberty Fund.

Calmfors, L. and Drifill, J. (1988) 'Centralization of wage bargaining', *Economic Policy* 6: 13–61.

Cameron, D.R. (1984) 'Social democracy, corporatism, labour quiescence, and the representation of economic interests in advanced capitalist society', in Goldthorpe, J.H. (ed.) *Order and Conflict in Contemporary Capitalism: Studies in the Political Economy of Western European Nations*, Oxford: Clarendon Press, pp. 143–78.

Campbell, N.N. (1995) *Incentives*, Cambridge: Cambridge University Press.

Cappelletti, M. and Cohen, W. (eds) (1979) *The Modern Systems of Judicial Review: Comparative Constitutional Law*, New York: Bobbs-Merrill.

Cartwright, N. (1994) *Nature's Capacities and Their Measurement*, Oxford: Clarendon Press.

Castles, F.G. (ed.) (1982) *The Impact of Parties: Politics and Policies in Democratic Capitalist States*, London: Sage.

—— (1998) *Comparative Public Policy: Pattern of Post-war Transformation*, Cheltenham: Edward Elgar.

Central Intelligence Agency (CIA) (1994) *The World Factbook 1994–95*, Washington, DC: Brassey's.

Centre d'études et de documentation sur la démocratie directe (C2D) (1998) *La Démocratie Directe dans le Monde*, Geneva: Department of constitutional law. <http/c2d.unige.ch/>

Cheung, S.N.S. (1969) *A Theory of Share Tenancy*, Chicago : University of Chicago Press.

Chubb, F.J.E. (1985) 'The political economy of federalism', *American Political Science Review* 79: 994–1015.

Coase, R.H. (1988) *The Firm, the Market and the Law*, Chicago, IL: University of Chicago Press.

Colomer, J.M. (ed.) (1996) *Political Institutions in Europe*, London: Routledge.

Compston, H. (1997) 'Union power, policy making, and unemployment in Western Europe, 1972–1993', *Comparative Political Studies* 30: 732–51.

Cox, G.W. (1997) *Making Votes Count: Strategic Coordination in the World's Electoral Systems*, Cambridge: Cambridge University Press.

Crepaz, M.M.L. (1992) 'Corporatism in decline? An empirical analysis of the impact of corporatism on macroeconomic performance and industrial disputes in 18 industrialized democracies', *Comparative Political Studies* 25: 139–68.

—— (1995) 'Austrian Corporatism in the Post-Industrial Age', *West European Politics* 18: 64–88.

—— (1996) 'Constitutional structure and regime performance in 18 industrialized democracies: A test of Olson's hypothesis', *European Journal of Political Research* 29: 87–104.

Crouch, C. (1993) *Industrial Relations and European State Traditions*, Oxford: Clarendon Press.

Cukierman, A. (1992) *Central Bank Strategy, Credibility, and Independence: Theory and Evidence*, Cambridge, MA: The MIT Press.

Czada, R. (1992) 'Korporatismus', in: Schmidt, M.G. (ed.) *Lexikon der Politik*, Munich: Beck, pp. 218–24.

Dahl, R.A. (1967) 'The evaluation of political systems', in: Pool, I.S. (ed.) *Contemporary Political Science: Toward Empirical Theory*, New York: McGraw-Hill, pp. 167–81.

—— (1971) *Polyarchy*, New Haven, CT: Yale University Press.

Danto, A.C. (1968). *Analytical Philosophy of Knowledge*, Cambridge: Cambridge University Press.

Danziger, J.N. (1978) *Making Budgets: Public Resorce Allocation*, London: Sage.

David, R. and Brierley, J.E. (1985) *Major Legal Systems in the World Today*, London: Stevens and Sons.

De Haan, J. and Van 'T Hag, G. (1995) 'Variations in central bank independence across countries: some provisional empirical evidence', *Public Choice* 85: 335–51.

Deininger, K. and Squire, L. (1997) *The Deininger-Squire Data Set*; available at: <http://www.worldbank.org/html/prdmg/grthweb/dddeisqu.htm>

Derbyshire, J.D. and Derbyshire, I. (1989) *Political Systems of the World*, Edinburgh: Chambers.

—— (1991) *World Political Systems: An Introduction to Comparative Government*, Edinburgh: Chambers.

—— (1996) *Political Systems of the World*, Oxford: Helicon.

Der Fischer Weltalmanach (1959–) Frankfurt am Main: Fischer Taschenbuchverlag.

De Winter, L. (1995) 'The role of parliament in government formation and resignation', in: Döring, H. (ed.) *Parliaments and Majority Rule in Western Europe*. Frankfurt: Campus, pp. 115–51.

DiMaggio, P. and Powell, W.W. (eds) (1991) *The New Institutionalism in Organizational Analysis*, Chicago, IL: University of Chicago Press.

Döring, H. (ed.) (1995) *Parliaments and Majority Rule in Western Europe*, Frankfurt: Campus Verlag.

—— (1997) 'Parlamentarismus, Präsidentialismus und Staatstätigkeit', *WeltTrends* 17: 143–70.

Druckman, J.N. (1996) 'Party factionalism and cabinet durability', *Party Politics* 2: 397–407.

Duchacek, I.D. (1970) *Comparative Federalism: The Territorial Dimension of Politics*, New York: Holt, Rinehart and Winston.

Dunleavy, P. and O'Leary, B. (1987) *Theories of the State: The Politics of Liberal Democracy*, Basingstoke: Macmillan.

Duverger, M. ([1951] 1964) *Political Parties: Their Organization and Activity in the Modern State*, London: Methuen.

—— (1980) 'A new political system model: semi-presidential government', *European Journal of Political Research* 8: 165–87.

—— (1986) 'Duverger's law: forty years later', in: Grofman, B. and Lijphart, A. (eds) *Electoral Laws and Their Political Consequences*, New York: Agathon Press, pp. 69–84.

Dworkin, R. (1986) *Law's Empire*, Cambridge: Harvard University Press.

Dye, T.R. and Gray, V. (1980) *The Determinants of Public Policy*, Lexington, MA: Lexington Books.

Easton, D. (1965) *A Systems Analysis of Political Life*, New York: Wiley.

Easton, S.T. (ed.) (1992) *Rating Global Economic Freedom*, Vancouver: The Fraser Institute.

Easton, S. and Walker, M.A. (1997) 'Income, growth, and economic freedom', *American Economic Review* 87: 328–32.

Eatwell, J. *et al.* (eds) (1989) *Allocation, Information and Markets*, London: Macmillan.

Eckstein, H. (1963) 'The impact of electoral systems on representative government', in Eckstein, H. and Apter, D.E (eds) *Comparative Politics: A Reader*, New York: Free Press, pp. 247–54.

—— (1966) *Division and Cohesion in Democracy: A study of Norway*, Princeton: Princeton University Press.

Eggertson, T. (1990) *Economic Behaviour and Institutions*, Cambridge: Cambridge University Press.

Eisenstadt, S.H. (1968) 'Social institutions', in: Sills, D.A (ed.) *International Encyclopaedia of the Social Sciences*: volume 14, New York: Macmillan, pp. 409–21.

Elaigwu, J.L. (1994) 'Nigeria: from unitarism to federalism', in Villiers, B. de (ed.) *Evaluating Federal Systems*, Dordrecht: Nijhoff, pp. 225–42.

Elazar, D.J. (1968) 'Federalism', in Sills, D. (ed.) *International Encyclopaedia of the Social Sciences*, vol. 5, New York: Macmillan, pp. 353–67.

—— (1985) 'Federalism and consociational regimes', *Publius* 15(2): 17–34.

—— (1987) *Exploring Federalism*, Tuscaloosa, AL: University of Alabama Press.

—— (ed.) (1991) *Federal Systems of the World*, Harlow, Essex: Longman.

—— (1995) 'Federalism', in Lipset, S.M. (ed.) *The Encyclopedia of Democracy*, London: Routledge, 2: 472–82.

—— (1997) 'Contrasting unitary and federal systems', *International Political Science Review* 18: 237–51.

Elgie, R. (1997) 'Models of executive politics: a framework for the study of executive power relations in parliamentary and semi-presidential regimes', *Political Studies* 45: 217–31.

—— (1998) 'The classification of democratic regime types: conceptual ambiguity and contestable assumptions', *European Journal of Political Research* 33: 219–38.

Elgie, R. and Thompson, H. (1998) *The Politics of Central Banks*, London: Routledge

Elster, J. (1989) *The Cement of Society*, Cambridge: Cambridge University Press.

Encyclopaedia Britannica (annually) *Britannica World Data*, Chicago: Encyclopaedia Britannica.

L'état du monde (1982–) Paris: La Découverte.

Etzioni, A. (1988) *The Moral Dimension*, New York: Free Press.

Eulau, H. (1963) *The Behavioral Persuasion in Politics*, New York: Random House.

Europa Yearbook (1985), London: Europa Publications.

Evans, P.D. *et al.* (eds) (1985) *Bringing the State Back In*, Cambridge: Cambridge University Press.

Fagerberg, J. (1994) 'Technology and international differences in growth rates', *Journal of Economic Literature* 32: 1147–75.

Feld, L.P. and Savioz, M.R. (1997) 'Direct democracy for economic performance: An empirical investigation', *Kyklos* 50: 507–38.

Finer, H. (1962) *The Theory and Practice of Modern Government*, London: Methuen.

Flora, P., Kuhale, S. and Unwin, D. (eds) *State Formation, Nation-building and Mass Politics in Europe*, Oxford: Oxford U.P.

Franck, T. M. *et al.* (1968) *Why Federations Fail: An Inquiry into the Requisites for Successful Federalism*, New York, NY: New York University Press.

Freedom House (ed.) (annually) *Freedom in the World: The Annual Survey of Political Rights and Civil Liberties*, New York: Freedom House.

Friedman, M. (1962) *Capitalism and Freedom*, Chicago, IL: University of Chicago Press.

—— (1968) *Dollars and Deficits*, Englewood Cliffs: Prentice-Hall.

—— (1988) 'A statistical note of the Gastil survey of freedom'. in: Gastil, R.D., *Freedom in the World: Political Rights and Civil Liberties 1987–1988*, New York: Freedom House, pp. 183–7.

Frye, T. (1997) 'A politics of institutional choice: post-communist presidents', *Comparative Political Studies* 30, 523–52.

Gaines, G.J. (1997) 'Where to count parties', *Electoral Studies* 16: 49–58.

Gallagher, M. and Uleri, P.V. (eds) (1996) *The Referendum Experience in Europe*, Basingstoke: Macmillan.

Gastil, R.D. (1987) *Freedom in the World: Political Rights and Civil Liberties, 1987–1988*, New York, NY: Greenwood Press.

Glymour, C. (1980) *Theory and Evidence*, Princeton: Princeton University Press.

Golden, M. (1993) 'The dynamics of trade unionism and national economic performance', *American Political Science Review* 87: 439–54.

Goldsmith, A.A. (1995) 'Democracy, property rights and economic growth', *Journal of Development Studies* 32, 2: 157–74.

Goldstone, J.A. *et al.* (eds) (1991) *Revolutions of the Late Twentieth Century*, Boulder, CO: Westview Press.

Goodin, R.E. (1996) *The Theory of Institutional Design*, Cambridge: Cambridge University Press.

Goodman, J.B. (1990) 'The politics of central bank independence', *Comparative Politics* 23: 329–49.

Goodman N. (1965) *Fact, Fiction and Forecast*, Indianapolis: Bobbs-Merrill.

—— (1972) *Problems and Projects*, Indianapolis: Bobbs-Morrill.

Gress, F. (1994) 'Interstate co-operation in the USA and the FRG', in Villiers, B. de (ed.) *Evaluating Federal Systems*, Dordrecht: Nijhoff, pp. 409–29.

Griliches, Z. (1990) 'Patent statistics as economic indicators: a survey', *Journal of Economic Literature* 28: 1661–707.

Grofman, B. and Lijphart, A. (eds) (1986) *Electoral Laws and their Political Consequences*, New York: Agathon Press.

Gurr, T.R. (1990) *Polity* II: *Political Structures and Regime Change, 1800–1986*, Boulder, CO: Center for Comparative Politics (computer file).

Gwartney, J. *et al.* (1996) *Economic Freedom of the World 1975–1995*, Vancouver: Fraser Institute.

—— (1997) *Economic Freedom of the World: 1997 Annual Report*, Vancouver: Fraser Institute.

Hall, P.A. and Taylor, R.C.R. (1996) 'Political science and the three new institutionalisms', *Political Studies* 44: 936–57.

Halpern, S.M. (1986) 'The disorderly universe of consociational democracy', *West European Politics* 9: 181–97.

Hamilton, A., Jay, J. and Madison, J. ([1787–8] 1961) *The Federalist Papers*.

Hamilton, W.H. (1932) 'Institution', in Seligman, E.R.A. (ed.) *Encyclopaedia of the Social Sciences*, vol. 8, London: Macmillan, pp. 84–89.

Hardin, R. (1996) 'Institutional morality', in Goodin, R.E. (ed.) *The Theory of Institutional Design*, Cambridge: Cambridge University Press, pp. 126–53.

Hayek, F.A. (1944) *The Road to Serfdom*, London: Routledge.

—— (1960) *The Constitution of Liberty*, London: Routledge.

—— (1978) *New Studies in Philosophy, Politics, Economics and the History of Ideas*, Chicago: University of Chicago Press.

Heap, S. Hargreaves (1989) *Rationality in Economics*, Oxford: Blackwell.

Heller, W.B. (1997) 'Bicameralism and budget deficits: the effect of parliamentary structure on government spending', *Legislative Studies Quarterly* 22: 485–516.

Hempel, C.G. (1965). *Aspects of Scientific Explanation and Other Essays in the Philosophy of Science*. New York: Free Press.

Hesse, J.J. (ed.) (1978) *Politikverflechtung im Föderativen Staat*, Baden-Baden: Nomos.

Hesse, J.J. and Goetz, K.H. (1992) *Federalising Europe? The Costs, Benefits and Conditions of Federal Political Systems*, London: Anglo-German Foundation for the Study of Industrial Society.

Hesse, J.J. and Wright, V. (eds) (1996) *Federalizing Europe?: The Costs, Benefits, and Preconditions of Federal Political Systems*, Oxford: Oxford University Press.

Hicks, A.M. and Swank, D.H. (1992) 'Politics, institutions, and welfare spending in industrialized democracies, 1960–82', *American Political Science Review* 86: 658–74.

Hicks, U.K. (1978) *Federalism: Failure and Success: A Comparative Study*, London: Macmillan.

Hiller, B. (1997) *The Economics of Asymmetric Information*, London: Macmillan.

Hogwood, B.W. and Gunn, L.A. (1992) *Policy Analysis in the Real World*, Oxford: Oxford University Press.

Holland, K.M. (ed.) (1991) *Judicial Activism in Comparative Perspective*, Basingstoke: Macmillan.

Holmes, K. *et al.* (1997) *1997 Index of Economic Freedom*, Washington, DC: Heritage Foundation.

—— (1998), *1998 Index of Economic Freedom*, Washington D.C.: Heritage Foundation.

—— (1992) 'Comparing democratic systems', in Lijphart, A. (ed.) *Parliamentary and Presidential Government*, Oxford: Oxford University Press, pp. 203–6.

Horowitz, D.L. (1990) 'Comparing democratic systems', *Journal of Democracy* 1(1): 73–79.

Huber, E. *et al.* (1993) 'Social democracy, christian democracy, constitutional structure and the welfare state', *American Journal of Sociology*, 99: 711–49.

Humana, C. (1983) *World Human Rights Guide*, London: Hutchinson.

—— (1987) *World Human Rights Guide*, London: Pan Books.

—— (1992) *World Human Rights Guide*, 3rd ed., New York: Oxford University Press.

Hume, D. ([1741]1966) *A Treatise of Human Nature II*, London: Everyman's Library.

Huntington, S.P. (1968) *Political Order in Changing Societies*, New Haven, CT: Yale University Press.

ILO (1992) *The Cost of Social Security: Thirteenth International Inquiry, 1984–1986*, Geneva: ILO.

—— (1997) *World Labour Report, 1997–98: Industrial Relations, Democracy and Social Stability*, Geneva: ILO.

—— (1998) *Cost of Social Security – Basic Tables, 1990–1993*, <http://www.ilo.org/public/english/110secso/css/cssindex.htm>

IMF (1994) *Government Finance Statistics Yearbook*, Washington, DC: IMF.

Immergut, E.M. (1998) 'The theoretical core of the new institutionalism', *Politics & Society* 26: 5–34.

International Ombudsman Institute (1999) *International Ombudsman Institute Directory of World-wide Ombudsman Offices*, Edmonton: International Ombudsman Institute.

Inter-Parliamentary Union (IPU) (annually) *Chronicle of Parliamentary Elections and Developments*, Geneva: IPU; also available at:<http://www.ipu.org/english/parlweb.htm>

—— (1995) *Women in Parliaments 1945–1995: A World Statistical Survey*, Geneva: IPU.

Islam, S. (1996) 'Economic freedom, per capita income and economic growth', *Applied Economic Letters* 3: 595–97.

Jabine, T.B. and Claude, R.P. (eds) (1992) *Human Rights and Statistics: Getting the Record Straight*, Philadelphia, PA: University of Pennsylvania Press.

Jackman, R.W. (1993) *Power Without Force: The Political Capacity of Nation-states*, Ann Arbor, MI: The University of Michigan Press.

Jaggers, K. and Gurr, T.R. (1995) Tracking democracy's third wave with the Polity III data, *Journal of Peace Research* 12: 469–82.

Jeffery, C. (1994) 'German unification and the future of the federal system', in: Villiers, B. de (ed.) *Evaluating federal systems*, Dordrecht: Nijhoff, pp. 409–29.

Johnson, B.T. and Sheehy, T.P. (1995) *The Index of Economic Freedom*, Washington DC: Heritage Foundation.

Jones, M.P. (1994) 'Presidential election laws and multipartism in Latin America', *Political Research Quarterly* 47: 41–57.

—— (1995) *Electoral Laws and the Survival of Presidential Democracies*, Notre Dame, IN: University of Notre Dame Press.

Kaplan, A. (1964) *The Conduct of Inquiry*, San Francisco: Chandler.

Karvonen, L. (1993) *Fragmentation and Consensus: Political Organization and the Interwar Crisis in Europe*, Boulder, CO: Social Science Monographs.

Keating, M. (1988) *State and Regional Nationalism*, Hemel Hempstead: Harvester Wheatsheaf.

Kelly, J.S. (1986) *Social Choice Theory*, Berlin: Springer-Verlag.

Kelsen, H. (1928) 'La Garantie jurisdictionelle de la Constitution (la justice constitutionelle)', *Revue de droit public et de la science politique en France et à l'étranger*, pp. 197–257.

—— (1961) *General Theory of Law and State*, New York: Russell and Russell.

—— (1996) *Théorie générale des normes*, Paris: Press Universitaire de France.

Keman, H. (1996) 'Konkordanzdemokratie und Korporatismus aus der Perspektive eines rationale Institutionalismus', *Politische Vierteljahrschrift* 37: 494–516.

—— (1997) 'Approaches to the analysis of institutions', in: Steunenberg, B. and Vught, F. (eds) *Political Institutions and Public Policy: Perspectives on European Decision Making*, Dordrecht: Kluwer, pp. 1–27.

Keman, H. and Pennings, P. (1995) 'Managing political and social conflict in democracies: do consensus or corporatism matter?', *British Journal of Political Science* 25: 271–81.

Kenworthy, L. (1996) 'Unions, wages and the common interest', *Comparative Political Studies* 28: 491–524.

King, P. (1982) *Federalism and Federation*, London: Croom Helm.

Knight, F.H. (1982) *Freedom and Reform*, Indianapolis: Liberty Press.

Knoke, D., Pappi, F.U., Broadbent, J. and Tsujinaka, Y. (1996) *Comparing Policy Networks: Labor Politics in the U.S., Germany and Japan*, Cambridge: Cambridge University Press.

Koelble, T.A. (1995) 'The new institutionalism in political science and sociology', *Comparative Politics* 27: 231–43.

Kornberg, A. (ed.) (1973) *Legislatures in Comparative Perspective*, New York: McKay.

Kriek, D.J. (ed.) (1992) *Federalism: The Solution?*, Pretoria: HSRC Publishers.

Krugman, P. (1994) 'The myth of Asia's miracle', *Foreign Affairs*, 73(6): 62–78.

Kuhn, T. (1962) *The Structure of Scientific Revolutions*, Chicago: University of Chicago Press.

Kymlicka, W. (1995) *Multicultural Citizenship: A Liberal Theory of Minority Rights*, Oxford: Oxford University Press.

Laakso, M. and Taagepera, R. (1979) Effective number of parties: a measure with application to West Europe, *Comparative Political Studies* 12: 3–27.

Lakatos, I. and Musgrave, A (eds) (1970) *Criticism and the Growth of Knowledge*, Cambridge: Cambridge University Press.

Lane, J.-E. *et al.* (1996) *Political Data Handbook: The OECD Countries*, Oxford: Oxford University Press.

Laver, M. and Schofield, N. (1990) *Multiparty Government: The Politics of Coalition in Europe*, Oxford: Oxford University Press.

Leblang, D.A. (1996) 'Property rights, democracy and economy growth', *Political Research Quarterly* 49, 1: 5–26.

—— (1997) 'Political democracy and economic growth: pooled cross-sectional and time-series evidence', *British Journal of Political Science* 27: 453–72.

LeDuc, L. *et al.* (eds) (1996) *Comparing Democracies: Elections and Voting in Global Perspective*, Thousand Oaks, CA: Sage.

Leftwich, A. (1995) *Democracy and Development*, Cambridge: Polity Press.

Lehmbruch, G. (1967) *Proporzdemokratie: Politisches System und Politische Kultur in der Schweiz und in Österreich*, Tübingen: Mohr.

—— (1991) 'The organization of society, administrative strategies, and policy networks', in Czarda, R.M. and Windhoff-Hereitier, A. (eds) *Political Choice*, Frankfurt am Main: Campus Verlag, pp. 121–57.

—— (1992) 'Konkordanzdemokratie', in Schmidt, M. (ed.) *Lexikon der Politik*. München: Piper, Bd 3: 206–11.

—— (1993) 'Consociational democracy and corporatism in Switzerland', *Publius* 23, 2: 43–60.

—— (1996) 'Die korporative Verhandlungsdemokratie in Westmitteleuropa', *Schweizerische Zeitschrift für Politische Wissenschaft* 2(4): 19–41.

Lehner, F. (1986) 'Konkurrenz, Koroporatismus und Konkordanz', in: Kaase, M. (ed.) *Politische Wissenschaft und Politische Ordnung*, Opladen: Westdeutscher Verlag, pp. 146–71.

Leonardy, W. (1994) 'Regionalism within federalism: the German constitution prepared for the European Union', in: Villiers, B. de (ed.) *Evaluating Federal Systems*, Dordrecht: Nijhoff, pp. 299–315.

Levy, F.S., Meltsner, A.J. and Wildavsky, A. (1974) *Urban Outcomes*, Berkeley: University of California Press.

Levy, M.J. (1952) *The Structure of Society*, Princeton: Princeton University Press.

Lewin, L. (1994) 'The decline of corporatism in Sweden', *European Journal of Political Research* 26: 57–79.

—— (1998) 'Majoritarian and consensus democracy: the Swedish experience', *Scandinavian Political Studies* 21: 195–206.

Libecap, G.D. (1993) *Contracting for Property Rights*, Cambridge: Cambridge University Press.

Lijphart, A. ([1968]1975) *The Politics of Accomodation: Pluralism and Democracy in the Netherlands*, Berkeley, CA: University of California Press.

—— (1977) *Democracy in Plural Societies: A Comparative Exploration*, New Haven, CT: Yale University Press.

—— (1984) *Democracies: Patterns of Majoritarian and Consensus Government in Twenty-one Countries*, New Haven, CT: Yale University Press.

—— (1985) *Power-Sharing in South Africa*, Berkeley, CA: Institute of International Studies, University of California.

—— (1991) 'Constitutional choices for new democracies', *Journal of Democracy* 2(1): 72–84.

—— (ed.) (1992) *Parliamentary Versus Presidential Government*, Oxford: Oxford University Press.

—— (1994a) 'Democracies: forms, performance, and constitutional engenieering', *European Journal of Political Research* 25: 1–17.

—— (1994b) *Electoral Systems and Party Systems: A Study of Twenty-seven Democracies, 1945–1990*, Oxford: Oxford University Press.

—— (1998a) 'Consensus and consensus democracy: cultural, structural, functional, and rational-choice explanations', *Scandinavian Political Studies* 21: 99–108.

—— (1998b) 'South African democracy: majoritarian or consociational?' *Democratization* 5(4): 144–50.

—— (1999) *Patterns of Democracy*, New Haven: Yale University Press.

Lijphart, A. *et al.* (1988) 'A mediterranean model of democracy?: the southern European democracies in comparative perspective', *West European Politics* 11(1): 7–25.

Lijphart, A. and Crepaz, M.M.L. (1991) 'Corporatism and consensus democracy in 18 countries', *British Journal of Political Science*, 21: 235–56.

Lindblom, C.E. (1977) *Politics and Markets: The World's Political-economic Systems*, New York: Basic Books.

Linz, J.J. (1990a) 'The perils of presidentialism', *Journal of Democracy* 1(1): 51–69.

—— (1994) 'Presidential or parliamentary democracy: does it make a difference', in: Linz, J.J. and Valenzuela, A. (eds) *The Failure of Presidential Democracy*, volume 1: *Comparative Perspectives*, Baltimore, MD: The Johns Hopkins U.P., pp. 3–87.

—— (1990b) 'The virtues of parliamentarism', *Journal of Democracy* 1(4): 84–91.

Linz, J.J. and Valenzuela, A. (eds)(1994) *The Failure of Presidential Democracy*, volume 1: *Comparative Perspectives*, Baltimore, MD: The Johns Hopkins U.P.

Lipset, S.M. (1959) *Political Man*, Garden City, NY: Doubleday.

Lipset, S.M. and Rokkan, S. (eds) (1967) *Party Systems and Voter Alignments: Cross-national Perspectives*, New York: Free Press.

Locke, J. ([1690]1962) *Two Treatises of Civil Government*, London: Everyman's Library.

Lorwin, V. (1974) 'Belgium: conflict and compromise', in McRae, K. (ed.) *Consociational Democracy: Political Accommodation in Segmented Societies*, Toronto: McClelland and Stewart, pp. 179–206.

Lowenberg, G. and Patterson, S.C. (1979) *Comparing Legislatures*, Boston, MA: Little, Brown and Company.

Lubin, D. (1996) 'The publicity principle', in Goodin, R.E. (ed.) *The Theory of Institutional Design*, Cambridge: Cambridge University Press, pp. 154–98.

Lustick. I.S. (1997) 'Lijphart, Lakatos, and consociationalism', *World Politics* 50: 88–117.

Luthardt, W. (1994) *Direkte Demokratie: Ein Vergleich in Westeuropa*, Baden-Baden: Nomos.

MacIver, R.I. (1965) *The Web of Government*, New York: The Free Press.

Mackie, T.T. and Rose, R. (1991) *The International Almanack of Electoral History*, 3rd ed., Basingstoke: Macmillan.

—— (1997) *A Decade of Election Results: Updating the International Almanack*, University of Strathclyde: Centre for the Study of Public Policy.

McRae, K.D. (1997) 'Contrasting styles of democratic decision-making: adversial versus consensual politics', *International Political Science Review* 18, 279–95.

Maddex, R.L. (1996) *Constitutions of the World*, London: Routledge.

Mainwaring, S (1993) 'Presidentialism, multipartism, and democracy: the difficult combination', *Comparative Political Studies*, 26: 198–228.

Mainwaring, S. and Shugart, M.S. (1997) 'Juan Linz, presidentialism and democracy: A critical appraisal', *Comparative Politics* 29: 449–70.

March, J.G. and Olsen, J.P. (1984) 'The new institutionalism: organizational factors in political life, *American Political Science Review* 78: 734–49.

—— (1989) *Rediscovering Institutions: the Organizational Basis of Politics*, New York: Free Press.

—— (1995) *Democractic Governance*, New York: Free Press.

Marks, G. (1986) 'Neocorporatism and incomes policy in Western Europe and North America', *Comparative Politics* 18: 253–77.

Matthews, R.C.O. (1986) 'The economics of institutions and the sources of economic growth', *Economic Journal* 96: 903–18.

Mattila, M. (1997) 'From qualified majority to simple majority: the effects of the 1992 change in the Finnish constitution', *Scandinavian Political Studies* 20: 331– 45.

Mauro, P. (1995) 'Corruption and growth', *Quarterly Journal of Economics* 110: 681–712.

Merriam, C.E. (1966) *Systematic Politics*, Chicago: Phoenix Books.

Merton, R.K. (1957) *Social Theory and Social Structure*, New York: Free Press.

Messick, R.E. (1996) 'The world survey of economic freedom', *Freedom Review* 27(2): 7–17.

Mezey, M.L. (1979) *Comparative Legislatures*, Durham, NC: Duke U.P.

von Mises, L. (1936) *Socialism: An Economic and Sociological Analysis*, London: Cape.

Mitchell, N.J. (1996) 'Theoretical and empirical issues in the comparative measurement of union power and corporatism', *British Journal of Political Science* 26: 419–28.

Moe, T.M. (1988) *The Organization of Interests*, Chicago: University of Chicago Press.

Moe, T.M. and Caldwell, M. (1994) 'The institutional foundations of democratic government: a comparison of presidential and parliamentary systems', *Journal of Institutional and Theoretical Economics* 150: 171–95.

Molho, J. (1997) *The Economics of Information*, Oxford: Blackwell.

Montesquieu, C.S. ([1748] 1989) *The Spirit of the Laws*, Cambridge: Cambridge University Press.

Moulin, H. (1983) *The Strategy of Social Choice*, Amsterdam: Elsevier.

Mueller, D. (1989) *Public Choice* II, Cambridge; Cambridge University Press.

Mulhall, S. and Swift, A. (1996) *Libertarians and Communitarians*, Oxford: Blackwell.

Myrdal, G. (1968) *The Asian drama: I–III*, New York: Pantheon Books.

Nagel, E. (1961) *The Structure of Science: Problems in the Logic of Scientific Explanation*, London: Routledge.

Neto, O.A. and Cox, G.W. (1997) 'Electoral institutions, cleavage structures, and the number of parties', *American Journal of Political Science* 41: 149–74.

Niskanen, W.E. (1971) *Bureaucracy and Representative Government*, Chicago: Aldine Publishing Company.

Nohlen, D. (1978) *Wahlsysteme der Welt: Daten und Analysen: ein Handbuch*, Munich: Piper.

Norris, P. (1997) 'Choosing electoral systems: proportional, majoritarian and mixed systems', *International Political Science Review* 18: 297–312.

North, D.C. (1989) *Institutions and Economic Performance*, Washington University: The Center in Political Economy (mimeo).

—— (1990) *Institutions, Institutional Change, and Economic Performance*, Cambrige: Cambridge University Press.

Norton, P. (ed.) (1990a) *Legislatures*, Oxford: Oxford University Press.

—— (1990b) 'Parliaments: A framework for analysis', *West European Politics* 13(3): 1–9.

Nummi, H. (1987) *Comparing Voting Systems*, Dordrecht: D. Reidel.

OECD (1998) *OECD in Figures: Statistics on the Member Countries*, Paris: OECD.

—— (1995a) *OECD Employment Outlook*, Paris: OECD.

—— (1995b) *Historical Statistics, 1960–1993*, Paris: OECD.

—— (1996) *Revenue Statistics of Member Countries 1965–1995*, Paris: OECD.

Offe, C. (1996) 'Designing institutions in East European transitions', in Goodin R.E. (ed.) *The Theory of Institutional Design*, Cambridge: Cambridge University Press, pp. 199–226.

Olson, J.P. (1988) Statsstyre og institusjonsutforming, Oslo: Universitetsforlaget.

Ostrom, E. (1990) *Governing the Commons: The Evolution of Institutions for Collective Action.* Cambridge: Cambridge University Press.

Ostrom, V. (1974) 'Can federalism make a difference?', *Publius* 3(3):, 197–238.

—— (1987) *The Meaning of American Federalism: Constituting a Self-governing Society*, San Francisco, CA: ICS Press.

The Oxford English Dictionary (1993), Oxford: Clarendon Press.

Page, E.C. (1992) *Political Authority and Bureaucratic Power*, New York: Harvester Wheatsheaf.

Pap, A. (1958) *Semantics and Necessary Truth*, New Haven: Yale University Press.

Pappi, F.U. and König, T. (1995) 'Les organizations centrales dans les réseaux du domaine politique: une comparaison Allemagne – Etats-Unis dans le champ de la politique du travail', *Reveue française de sociologie* 36: 725–42.

Polsby, N.W. (1975) 'Legislatures', in: Greenstein, F.I. and Polsby, N.W. (eds) *Handbook of Political Science*, volume 5: *Governmental institutions and Processes*, Reading, MA: Addison-Wesley, pp. 275–319.

Pontusson, J. (1995) 'From comparative public-policy to political-economy: putting political-institutions in their place and taking interests seriously', *Comparative Political Studies* 28: 117–47.

Popper, K.R. (1959) *The Logic of Scientific Discovery*, London: Hutchinson.

—— (1963) *Conjectures and Refutations*, London: Routledge and Kegan Paul.

—— (1972) *Objective Knowledge*, Oxford: Clarendon Press.

Posner, R.A. (1992) *The Economic Analysis of Law*, Boston: Little, Brown.

Pourgerami, A. (1988) 'The political economy of development: a cross-national causality test of development-democracy-growth hypothesis', *Public Choice* 58: 123–41.

Powell, W.W. and DiMaggio, P.J. (1991) *The New Institutionalism in Organizational Research*, Chicago: University of Chicago Press.

Pressman, J. and Wildavsky, A. (1984) *Implementation*, Berkeley, CA: University of California Press.

Prisching, M. (1996) *Die Sozialpartnerschaft: Modell der Vergangenheit oder Modell für Europa?*, Wien: Manz.

Quine, W.W. and Ullian, J.S. (1970) *The Web of Belief*, New York: Randon House.

Rae, D.W. (1971) *The Political Consequences of Electoral Laws*, New Haven: Yale U.P.

Rapaport, A., Guyer, M. and Gordon, D.G. (1976) T*he 2×2 Game*, Ann Arbor: University of Michigan Press.

Rhyne, C.S. (ed) (1978) *Law and Judicial Systems of Nations*, Washington, DC: The World Peace Through Law Center.

Ricketts, M. (1987) *The Economics of Business Enterprise*. Hemel Hempstead: Harvester Wheatsheaf.

Riggs, F.W. (1997) 'Presidentialism versus parliamentarism: implications for representativeness and legitimacy', *International Political Science Review* 18: 253–78.

Riker, W.H. (1964) *Federalism: Origin, operation, significance*, Boston: Little, Brown and Company.

—— (1975) 'Federalism', in: Greenstein, F.I. and Polsby, N.W. (eds) *Handbook of political science*, volume 5: *Governmental Institutions and Processes*, Reading, MA: Addison-Wesley, pp. 93–172.

—— (1992) 'The justification of bicameralism', *International Political Science Review* 13: 101–16.

—— (1996) 'European Federalism: the lessons of past experience', in Hesse, J.J. and Wright, V. (eds) *Federalizing Europe*? Oxford: Oxford University Press, pp. 9–24.

Rokkan, S. (1970) *Citizens, Elections, Parties: Approaches to the Comparative Study of the Processes of Development*. Oslo: Universitetsforlaget.

Ross, S.A. (1973) 'The economic theory of agency: the principal's problem', *American Economic Review* 63: 134–9.

Rothstein, B. (1996) 'Political institutions: an overview', in: Goodin, R.E. and Klingemann, H.-D. (eds) *A New Handbook of Political Science*, Oxford: Oxford University Press., pp. 133–66.

Rousseau, J.-J. ([1782] 1972) *Les rêveries du promeneur solitaire*, Paris: Gallimard.

Rowat, D.C. (1985) *The Ombudsman Plan: The Worldwide Spread of an Idea*, 2nd ed., Lanham, MD: University Press of America.

—— (1997) 'A worldwide survey of ombudsmen', Edmonton, Alberta: International Ombudsman Institute: Occasional paper, no. 60.

Rueschemeyer, D. *et al.* (1992) *Capitalist Development and Democracy*, Cambridge: Polity Press.

Ruin, O. (1972) 'Participatory democracy and corporativism: the case of Sweden', *Scandinavian Political Studies* 9: 171–86.

Salmon, W.C. (1984) *Scientific Explanation and the Causal Structure of the World*, Princeton: Princeton University Press.

—— (1998) *Causality and Explanation*, Oxford: Oxford University Press.

Sartori, G. (ed.) (1984) *Social Science Concepts: A Systematic Analysis*, Beverly Hills, CA: Sage.

—— (1994) *Comparative Constitutional Engineering: An Inquiry into Structures, Incentives and Outcomes*, London: Macmillan.

Saunders, C. (1995) 'Constitutional arrangements of federal systems', *Publius* 25, 2: 61–79.

Schacht, J. (1993) *An Introduction to Islamic Law*, Oxford; Clarendon.

Scharpf, F.W. *et al.* (1976) *Politikverflechtung: Theorie und Empirie des kooperativen Föderalismus in der Bundesrepublik*, Kronberg: Hain.

Schmidt, M.G. (1982) *Wohlfartsstaatliche Politik unter bürgerlichen und sozialde-mokratischen Regieriungen: ein internationaler Vergleich*, Frankfurt: Campus.
—— (1995) *Demokratitheorien: eine Einführing*, Opladen: Leske und Budrich.
—— (1996) 'When parties matter', *European Journal of Political Research* 30: 155–83.
—— (1997) 'Determinants of social expenditure in liberal democracies: the post world war II experience, *Acta Politica* 32: 153–73.
Schmitt, N. (1994) 'The foreign policy of Spanish autonomous communities compared to that of Swiss cantons', in Villiers, B. de (ed.) *Evaluating Federal Systems*, Dordrecht: Nijhoff, pp. 362–92.
Schmitter, P.C. (1981) 'Interest intermediation and regime governability in con-temporary Western Europe and North America', in Berger, S. (ed.) *Organizing Interests in Western Europe*, Cambridge: Cambridge University Press., pp. 285–311.
—— (1983) 'Democratic theory and neo-corporatist practice', *Social Research* 50: 885–928.
—— (1996) Corporatist intermediation meets the globalized economy: is there going to be a predictable winner or loser? (mimeo).
Schumpeter, J.A. (1989) *Essays on Entrepreneurs, Innovations, Business Cycles and the Evolution of Capitalism*, New Brunswick: Transaction.
—— (1944) *Capitalism, Socialism and Democracy*, London: Allen and Unwin.
Scully, G.W and Slottje, D.J. (1991) 'Ranking economic liberty across countries', *Public Choice* 69: 121–52.
Selznick, P. (1996) 'Institutionalism "old" and "new"' *Adminsitrative Science Quarterly* 41: 270–77.
Shane, S.A. (1992) 'Why do some societies invent more than others?' *Journal of Business Venturing* 7:29–46.
Shapiro, M. (1981) *Courts: A Comparative and Political Analysis*, Chicago: University of Chicago Press.
Shapiro, M. and Stone, A. (1994) 'The new constitutional politics of Europe', *Comparative Political Studies* 26: 397–420.
Sharpe, L.J. and Newton, K. (1984) *Does Politics Matter?*, Oxford: Clarendon Press
Shepsle, K.A. (1989) 'Studying institutions: Some lessons from the rational choice approach', *Journal of Theoretical Politics* 1: 131–47.
Shugart, M.S. and Carey, J.M. (1992) *Presidents and Assemblies: Constitutional Design and Electoral Dynamics*, Cambridge: Cambridge University Press.
Simmons, D.A. (1996) 'Rulers of the game: central bank independence during the interwar years', *International Organization* 50: 407–43.
Simon, H.A. (1957) *Models of Man*, New York: John Wiley
SIPRI (1980) *World Armaments and Disarmaments*, Oxford: Oxford University Press.
—— (1988) *World Armaments and disarmaments*, Oxford: Oxford University Press.
—— (1997) *World Armaments and disarmaments*, Oxford: Oxford University Press.
Skocpol, T. (1979) *States and Social Revolutions*, Cambridge: Cambridge University Press.
Smith, G. (ed.) (1995) *Federalism: The Multiethnic Challenge*, London: Longman.
Sombart, W. (1916–27) *Der moderne Kapitalismus*, 3 vols, Munich: Duncker & Humboldt.
Sorokin, P.M. (1966) *Sociological Theories of Today*, New York: Harper and Row.
Spindler, Z.A. (1991) 'Liberty and development: a further perspective', *Public Choice* 69: 197–210.
Stacey, F. (1978) *Ombudsmen Compared*, Oxford: Clarendon Press.

The Statesman's Yearbook (annually) Basingstoke: Macmillan.

Steiner, J. (1974) *Amicable Agreement versus Majority Rule: Conflict Resolution in Switzerland*, Chapel Hill: University of North Carolina Press.

Steinmo, S. and Tolbert, C.J. (1998) 'Do institutions really matter?: Taxation in industrialized democracies', *Comparative Political Studies* 31: 165–87.

Steinmo, S. *et al.* (eds) (1992) *Structuring Politics: Historical Institutionalism in Comparative Analysis*, Cambridge: Cambridge University Press.

Stepan, A. and Skatch, C. (1993) 'Constitutional frameworks and democratic consolidation: parliamentarism versus presidentialism', *World Politics* 46: 1–22.

Stigler, G.J. (1975) *The Citizen and the State: Essays on Regulation*, Chicago, IL: University of Chicago Press.

—— (ed.) (1988) *Chicago Studies in Political Economy*, Chicago: University of Chicago Press.

Stinchcombe, A.L. (1997) 'On the virtues of the old institutionalism', *Annual Review of Sociology* 23: 1–18.

Stokey, E. and Stockhauser, R. (1978) *A Primer for Policy Analysis*, New York: Norton.

Stone, A. (1990) 'The birth and development of abstract review: constitutional courts and policymaking in Western Europe', *Policy Studies Journal* 19(1): 81–95.

Streeck, W. (1992) *Social Institutions and Economic Performance*, London: Sage.

Sturm, R. (1994) 'Economic regionalism in a federal state: Germany and the challenge of the single market', in: Villiers, B. de (ed.) *Evaluating Federal Systems*. Dordrecht: Nijhoff, pp. 316–32.

Suksi, M. (1993) *Bringing in the People: A Comparison of Constitutional Forms and Practices of the Referendum*, Dordrecht: Nijhoff.

Suleiman, E.N. (1995) *Les réussites cachées de la republique française*, Paris: Seuil.

Sullivan, M.J. (1991) *Measuring Global Values: The Ranking of 162 Countries*, New York: Greenwood Press.

Summers, R. and Heston, A. (1994) *Penn World Tables, mark 5.6*; available at: <http://www.nber.org/pwt56.html>

Suppes, P.A. (1970) *A Probabilistic Theory of Causality*, Amsterdam: North-Holland.

Taagepera, R. (1998) 'How electoral systems matter for democratization'. *Democratization* 5(3): 68–91.

Taagepera, R. and Shugart, M.S. (1989) *Seats and Votes: The Effects and Determinants of Electoral Systems*, New Haven: Yale University Press.

—— (1993) 'Predicting the number of parties: a quantitative model of Duverger's mechanical effect', *American Political Science Review* 87, 455–64.

Tabatabai, H. (1996) *Statistics on Poverty and Income Distribution: An ILO Compendium of Data*, Geneva: ILO.

Tarantelli, E. (1986) 'The regulation of inflation and unemployment', *Industrial Relations* 25: 1–15.

Taras, R. (ed.) (1997) *Postcommunist Presidents*, Cambridge: Cambridge U.P.

Taylor, C.L. (ed.) (1983) *Why Governments Grow: Measuring Public Sector Size*, Beverly Hills: Sage.

Tocqueville, A. de ([1840] 1990) *Democracy in America: I-II*, New York: Vintage Books.

—— ([1856] 1988) *L'ancien régime et la révolution*, Paris: Flammarion.

Todd, E. (1983) *La Troisième Planète: Structures Familiales et Sytemes Idéologiques*, Paris: Seuil.

Tollison, R.D. (1982) 'Rent-seeking: a survey', *Kyklos* 35: 575–92.

Torstensson, J. (1994) 'Property rights and economic growth: an empirical study'. *Kyklos* 47: 231–47.

Transparency International (1995) *Historical Comparisons*, <http://www.GWDG.DE/~uwvw/histor.htm>

—— (1998), *1998 Corruption Perceptions Index*. <http://www.GWDG.DE/~uwvw/CPI1998.htm>

Tsebelis, G. (1990) *Nested Games: Rational Choice in Comparative Politics*, Berkeley, CA: University of California Press.

Tsebelis, G. and Money, J. (1997) *Bicameralism*, Cambridge: Cambridge University Press.

United Nations Development Programme (UNDP) (annually from 1990) *Human Development Report*, New York: Oxford University Press.

USPTO (1998) *U.S. Patent Database,* <http://patents.uspto.gov/access/search-dvs.html>

Van Schendelen, M.P.C.M. (ed.)(1984) *Consociationalism, Pillarisation and Conflict-Management in the Low Countries*, Rotterdam: Erasmus Universiteit.

Vanhanen, T. (1990) *The Process of Democratization: A Comparative Study of 147 States, 1980–88*, New York: Crane Russak.

Vanssay, X. de and Spindler, Z.A. (1994) 'Freedom and growth: do constitutions matter?', *Public Choice* 78: 359–72.

Vaubel, R. (1995) 'Constitutional safeguards against centralization in federal states: an international cross-section analysis', Mannheim: Universität Mannheim (unpublished).

Villiers, B. de (ed.) (1994) *Evaluating Federal Systems*, Dordrecht: Nijhoff.

Volcansek, M.L. (ed.) (1992) 'Judicial politics and policy-making in Western Europe', *West European Politics* 15, 3.

Wade, R. (1990) *Governing the Market: Economic Theory and the Role of Government in East Asian Industrialization*, Princeton, NJ: Princeton University Press.

Wallerstein, M. *et al.* (1997) 'Unions, employers' associations, and wage-setting institutions in Northern and Central Europe, 1950–1992', *Industrial and Labour Relations Review* 50: 379–401.

Wallerstein, M. and Golden, M. (1997) 'The fragmentation of the bargaining society: wage setting in the Nordic countries, 1950 to 1992', *Comparative Political Studies* 30: 699–731.

Wamala, A. (1994) 'Federalism in Africa: lessons from South Africa', in: Villiers, B. de (ed.) *Evaluating Federal Systems*, Dordrecht: Nijhoff, pp. 251–67.

Watts, R. (1994) 'Contemporary views on federalism', in: Villiers, B. de (ed.) *Evaluating Federal Systems*, Dordrecht: Nijhoff, pp. 1–29.

Watts, R.L. (1996) *Comparing Federal Systems in the 1990s*, Kingston, Ontario: Institute of Intergovernmental Relations.

—— (1998) 'Federalism, federal political systems, and federations', *Annual Review of Political Science* 1: 117–37.

Weaver, K.M. and Rockman, B.A. (eds)(1993) *Do Institutions Matter?: Government Capabilities in the United States and Abroad*, Washington, DC: Brookings.

Weber, M. (1964) *Wirtschaft und Gesellschaft*, Köln: Kiepenheur und Witsch.

Weber, M. ([1922]1978) *Economy and Society: An Outline of Interpretive Sociology*, 2 vols, Berkeley, CA: University of California Press.

Weingast, B.R. (1996) 'Political institutions: rational choice perspectives', in: Goodin, R.E. and Klingemann, H.-D. (eds) *A New Handbook of Political Science*, Oxford: Oxford University Press, pp. 167–90.

Welsh, D. (1994) 'Federalism and the divided society: a South African perspective', in: Villiers, B. de (ed.) *Evaluating federal systems*, Dordrecht: Nijhoff, pp. 267–85.

Wesson, R. (ed.)(1987) *Democracy: A Worldwide Survey*, New York: Praeger.

Western, B. (1995) 'A comparative study of working-class disorganization: union decline in 18 advanced capitalist countries', *American Sociological Review* 60: 179–201.

Whitley, R. (ed.) (1994) *European Business Systems: Firms and Markets in Their National Contexts*, London: Sage.

Wildavsky, A. (1959) 'A methodological critique of Duverger's *Political Parties*', *Journal of Politics* 21: 303–18.

—— (1979) *Speaking Truth to Power: The Art and Craft of Policy Analysis*, Boston, MA: Little, Brown and Company.

—— (1987) 'Choosing preferences by constructing institutions: a cultural theory of preference formation', *American Political Science Review* 81: 3–21.

—— (1991) *The Rise of Radical Egalitarianism*, Washington, DC: The American University Press.

Wilensky, H. (1975) *The Welfare State and Equality*, Berkeley: University of California Press.

—— (1976) *The 'New Corporatism', Centralization and the Welfare State*, London: Sage.

Williamson, O. E. (1975) *Markets and Hierarchies*, New York: Free Press.

—— (1985) *The Economic Institutions of Capitalism*, New York: Free Press.

—— (1986) *Economic Organization*, Hemel Hempstead: Harvester Wheatsheaf.

World Bank (1975) *World Bank Atlas, 1975*, Washington DC: The World Bank.

—— (1983) *World Tables*, 3rd ed., Baltimore: Johns Hopkins U.P.

—— (1987) *World Bank Atlas, 1987*, Washington DC: The World Bank.

—— (1992) *World Development Report, 1992*. New York: Oxford University Press..

—— (1993) *World Development Report, 1993*, New York: Oxford University Press..

—— (1995) *World Bank Atlas, 1995*, Washington, DC: World Bank.

—— (1995) *World Development Report, 1995*, New York: Oxford University Press.

—— (1996) *World Bank Atlas, 1996*, Washington, DC: World Bank.

—— (1997) *World Development Indicators, 1997*, Washington, DC: The World Bank.

Wright, L.M. (1982) 'A comparative survey of economic freedoms', in: Gastil, R.D. (ed.) *Freedom in the World: Political Rights and Civil Liberties, 1982*,Westport, CT: Greenwood Press, pp. 123–45.

Yeung, O.M. and Methieson, J.A. (1998) *Global Benchmarks: Comprehensive Measures of Development*, Washington, DC: Brookings Institution Press.

Young, R.A. (1994) 'How do peaceful secessions happen'? *Canadian Journal of Political Science* 27: 773–92.

Index

affluence 249; effect of market institutions 248; and fascism 208; federalism vs. unitarism 92–4, 97–100; link with democracy 274, 283; and political freedom 282–3
Alchian, A.A. 253–4
Alford, R.R. 25
Almond, G.A. *et al.*: functionalism 61
Althusius, J. 3; federalism 75, 77–101
altruism 40, 41–6
American Supreme Court 170
Anckar, D. 290
Anderson, E.N. and P.R. 25
aristocracy: democracy contrasted 107, 108
asymmetrical bicameralism 144, 154–9
Austrian Constitutional Court 170
Austrian School: social prerequisites of affluence 249

Bagehot, W. 78
Barone model 249
Bell, D. 25
bicameralism 17, 144, 154; *see also* asymmetrical bicameralism, symmetrical bicameralism
bipolar system 124
Black, C. 99
boundary problem 3–4
bounded rationality 50–1
Brazil: constitution 119
Britain: parliamentarism 126–7

capitalism 18, 261; decentralized 53; distributional conflicts 252; evaluation 263; link with democracy 274–6; role of government in reforming institutions 252
Carey, J.M. 17, 123

causality: Humean methodology 59; institutional performance 14–15; problem of induction 72
central banks 144; autonomy 1970–90 in OECD countries 163; independence 144, 161–3; OECD countries 162–3; status 162
chamber system 144, 154–6; executive dominance 217; impact on democratic stability 148; impact on public finance 148
charismatic leadership 39–40
Chicago School 252–3
civil law 167–8, 169
civil society 52, 53; corporatism 52; free market economy 52; trade union activity 53
civil society institutions 53–4
coalition 219; grand coalition 211–12, 233, 234; types 211–212
Coase, R.H. 7
collective rights 169
common law 167–8, 169
Commons, J.R. 252

communitarianism 45
composition problem 3, 4, 5–6
confederal states 79–80
Consensus model of democracy (CM) 16, 114, 207–24; characteristics 213; institutions 218–20; marked by power-sharing 214–15
consociationalism 208; coalition 211; elite accommodation 208, 210–11; meaning 211–13; mechanisms 211
constitution 52; codification 52; doctrine of constitutionalism 54; fragility 295;*see also* constitutionalism
constitutional articles 121

constitutional court in Karlsruhe 11
constitutional democracies 2
constitutional engineering 291–3
constitutional equivalents 302–3
constitutional institutions 291–4
constitutional longevity 293–6, 297; by
    region 295, 296; and
    constitutionalism 299; federalism vs.
    constitutionalism 96, 98, 99, 100
constitutional monarchy 120–1
constitutional practice 121
constitutional theory 121
constitutional validity 294, 296
constitutionalism 54, 57, 286; by region
    298; and constitutional longevity
    299; and human development 301;
    outcomes 298; and perceptions of
    corruption 301; polar versions 287;
    political outcomes 302–3; socio-
    economic performance 300–1; state
    stability 298–300; thick 289–91; thin
    287–9
corporatism 53, 225–44; distinguished
    from lobbyism 229; and
    Drittelparität 229, 230; and
    Konkordanz 226–7, 235, 240, 241;
    policy outcomes 240–3; policy
    outputs 239–40; power-sharing 236;
    social outcomes 242; sources of
    support 237–9
corruption: human relations 111, 114;
    perceptions of, and constitutionalism
    301
Cox, G.W. 193
cube root law of national assemblies 161
customary (conventional) law 167–8

Dahl, R.A. 104–6
decentralization: federal vs. unitary
    states 91–3, 100
democracy 52: alternative institutional
    arrangements 225; aristocracy
    contrasted 107, 108; belief systems
    105; characteristics 106–9; Consensus
    see Consensus model of democracy;
    and economic freedom 280, 283; and
    economic regime 279–80; electoral
    institutions 181–206; favourable
    conditions 105; human rights
    102–14; ideal-types 207–8, 213–14;
    insitutions, 1990s 220; link with
    affluence 274; link with capitalism
    274–6; link with freedom 106;
    outcomes and outputs 110; political

stability 208; relative superiority of
    systems 223–4; socio-economic
    conditions 105; thin and thick
    definitions 103; threats to 106;
    Westminster see Westminster model
    of democracy
democracy index 109
democracy scores: federalism vs.
    unitarism 95–7
democratic effects model 114
democratic institutionalism 16–19
democratic longevity 208
democratic stability: impact of chamber
    system 148; negative impact of
    presidentialism 130–2, 134–5, 136–40
democratically stable countries 184
Derbyshire, I. and J.D. 123
dictatorships 40
disproportionality 191: and district
    magnitude 183, 194–5
district magnitude: and
    disproportionality 183, 194–5
Drittelparität (tripartism) 229; and
    corporatism 229, 230; trade union
    density 230
Duchacek, I.D. 81, 82, 84–6
Duverger, M. 3, 13, 16, 179, 181–207
Duverger's model 181–2, 186; testing
    200–4

Easton, D. 61; systems analysis of
    political life 61
Eckstein, H. 105–6
economic freedom 263–4; and
    democracy 280; and economic
    growth 247; female parliamentary
    representation 284; and human
    development 284; and human rights
    280; and public sector size 281; social
    expenditures 281, 282; variation
    within Europe 268
economic freedom index 264
economic growth: and economic
    freedom 247; and economic
    institutions 271; and economic
    systems 267; federalism vs. unitarism
    92–4, 95; impact of market
    institutions 247–59; in periods
    1960–73 and 1985–94 259; variability
    258
economic institutions 18–19; and
    economic growth 271; link with
    political freedom 274–85; political
    consequences 279–81; see also market

institutions
economic outcomes: effect of
institutions 245, *see also* market
institutions
economic reforms 13
economic regimes 262–5; and
democracy 279–80; problems in
classifying 262
economic systems: distribution around
1985 263; and economic growth 267;
South East Asia 265
economy: role of state in institutional
design 248–9; *see also* market
institutions
egoism 40–6; limited by rules of conduct
40–2
Elazar, D.J. 18, 78, 81–2, 83–4, 101
election formula: and executive stability
189–90; types 183; *see also*
majoritarian and proportional (PR)
election formulas
election rules 181–206
electoral institutions in democracies
181–206; consequences 182;
outcomes 185
electoral system 52; and government
instability 199, 204; in the 1990s 185;
local vs. national level 193–4; and
party system 186–90, 196–7, 202;
proportional 52; stability over time
185
elite accommodation 208, 210–11
Encyclopaedia Britannica: classification
of federal states 81–2
Epicureanism 40–1
epistemological issues 27
equality: formal vs. real 108–9; human
rights 111, 113
Estonia: constitution 120
European presidentialism 117, 118, 122
executive 52; parliamentary 52, 54,
117–40; *see also* parliamentarism;
presidential 52, 54, 117–40; *see also*
presidentialism
executive dominance/power-fusion:
Westminster democracy 214; *see also*
Westminster model of democracy
executive institutions 119–23
executive stability: and election formula
189–90; and party system 188–9,
199–200
extrinsic importance of institutions 10,
143, 145, 148–9, 165

federal states 86; budgetary structure 89;
characteristics 84–8; classification 82;
constitutional competencies 81;
criteria of federalism 84–7;
identification 79–84; not inherently
democratic 78; performance
contrasted with unitary states 77–8,
88–90, 101; sets of 88; symmetrical
bicameralism 144, 154, 156
federalism 18, 75, 77–101; affluence 93,
100; as check on political
opportunism 55; constitutional
longevity 96, 98, 99, 100; criteria
84–7; decentralization 92, 100;
definition 78; democracy scores 97;
economic growth 95; evaluation
78–9; Human Development Index 94;
income distribution 96; potential
outcomes 88–9; public sector size 91;
types 87; unitarism contrasted 77–8,
88–90; whether important 88–90
federative arrangements: states with 83
female parliamentary representation 69;
corporatist vs. Konkordanz countries
242; and economic freedom 284
Finer, H. 25
Finland: 1919 constitution 124
fiscal decentralization: federalism 101
fractionalization of party system 196–7
French Conseil Constitutionnel 170
French presidency 12
Friedland, R. 25
Friedman M. 3, 19, 275–6
Friedman system 245–85

Gastil, R.D. 262–4, 265–6
gender equality 139
Goetz, K.H. 87, 88
Goodin, R.E. 28
government: reform of capitalist
institutions 252
government durability: party system
198–200, 203, 204
government instability: resulting from
election and party systems 204
grand coalition 211–12, 233, 234;
democratic stability 211
gross domestic product (GDP): human
rights 300

Hamilton, W.H. 24
Hardin, R. 28
Hayek, F.A. 3, 53, 250–1, 276–9
Hesse, J.J. 87, 88

holistic institutionalism 29–31
human development: and economic
    freedom 284
Human Development Index 68; and
    constitutionalism 301; federalism vs.
    unitarism 94; GDP 300; social
    indicators 300
human rights 52, 102–14; and
    constitutionalism 301; corruption
    111, 114; country performance
    profile 109–10, 114; democracy
    102–14; effect of economic freedom
    283; equality 111, 113;
    implementation 52; judicial
    institutions 177; link with affluence
    283; link with economic freedom
    280; socio-economic development
    111–12; welfare state 111–13
human rights indices 103–4
Hume, D. 42–5
Humean methodology as to causality
    59; problem of induction 72
Huntington, S.P. 39

ideal-type of democracy 207–8, 213–14;
    institutional consequences 220–3
income distribution (GINI Index) 68;
    corporatist vs. Konkordanz countries
    242; federalism vs. unitarism 96
income equality/inequality 139; and
    economic freedom 284
individualism 108
induction 72
inflation 165
innovations 268–9; impact on economic
    growth 270
institution: ambiguity, 24–27; atomistic
    view 6; as code 29; concept 3, 23–37;
    conflict 39; constitutional
    engineering 291–3; constitutionalism
    286; definition 23–37; economic
    outcomes 245, *see also* market
    institutions; effects 1, 12, 59;
    enforcement 40–2; as governance
    mechanism 38, 51; holistic view 6,
    35; importance 9–12; interpretations
    6; logical patterns 215; as norm 24,
    28; operation 1; as organization 24,
    29; outcomes 1; parameters 23–37;
    rationale 39–40; relationship to
    outcomes 72; structures 3; as system
    of action 28; thin and thick
    interpretations 4, 6
institutional causality 14–15

institutional counter-factuals 10–12
institutional degeneration 56
institutional effects of presidentialism
    138–41
institutional models 2, 20; evaluation 15
institutional performance; causality
    14–15
institutional publicness 28–9
institutional sclerosis 139
institutionalization of human rights
    102–14
intrinsic importance of institutions 10,
    143, 145, 165
Israel: political system 119

Jordan: constitution 122
judicial control on opportunism 55
judicial institutions 166–78; impact on
    democracy and corruption 177;
    impact on democratic longevity
    176–7; *see also* judicial review; legal
    review; legal system; ombudsman
judicial review 169, 170–2; distribution
    172; legal review contrasted 169
judiciary: legal review 52
juridical responsibility 120–1

Kelsen, H. 166–7, 171
key political institutions 52
kingdoms 118, 120–2
Knight, F.H. 252
Konkordanz: and corporatism 226–7,
    235, 240, 241
Konkordanzdemokratie 16, 225–44; and
    corporatism 235; grand coalition
    233; indices 232; institutions 231;
    policy outcomes 240–3; policy
    outputs 239–40; power-sharing
    236–7; social outcomes 242; sources
    of support 237–9

Laakso, M. 196–7
laissez-faire economy 250, 251, 275;
    contrasting views 252; social
    outcomes 283–4; South East Asian
    economies 265–6
Latin America: presidentialism 117
Lausanne School 249
law: imperfect analogy with state 167
legal authority 38
legal review 166, 168, 172; constitutional
    court 55; implication for type of
    democracy 217, 219; judicial review
    contrasted 169; limited to

democracies 171
remedies for citizens against state
168–72; strong 170, 172, 174; weak
169–70
legal systems 52, 166–8; civil and
common law 52; control of political
opportunism 55; families of 167–8
legislation: mechanisms 144, 145; tested
by judicial review 168–9, 170–1
legislative institutions: impact on
politics 143–65
legislature 52, 153, 156; bicameral 52,
54; characteristics 154; framework
legislation 288; self-protection 288–9;
size 159–60;
symmetrical/asymmetrical
competencies 54; unicameral 52, 54
legislatures in Europe: variation in
power 288
Lehmbruch, G. 226, 231
Lehner, F. 243
Levy, F.S. *et al.* 62: policy analysis 62
liberty: market economy 277; negative
vs. positive 108–9; *see also* political
freedom
Lijphart, A. 3, 16, 57, 232–3; democracy
model 207–24; Netherlands study
208–9
Lijphart system 179–244
Lindblom, C.E. 53
Linz, J.J. 17, 117, 123, 124, 129–33
Lipset, S.M. 274
lobbyism 53
Locke, J. 3, 102

macro corporatism 225; scales 228
macro institutions 3; federalism 75,
77–101; institutionalized human
rights 75, 102–14; unitarism 75,
77–101
macro outcomes 1, 2, 58–73; alternative
electoral systems 182; variation 58,
67–71, 73; *see also* outcomes
macro outputs: variation 58, 66, 70–1,
73; *see also* outputs
macro policy outputs 58–73
macro political institutions: impact on
outputs and outcomes 58–73
macro political outcomes: importance of
institutions 1
macro social outcomes: importance of
institutions 1
Madison, J. 56
majoritarian election formulas 181,

191–3, 194, 197–201, 205
March, J.G. 9, 30, 36
market economy 18, 260, 261;
decentralized 53
market institutions: contracting 256–7;
economic growth 258, 267; effect on
outcomes 248, 256, 260–73;
incentives 253; property rights 25–67;
regulation 256; transaction costs
255–6
markets: relationship to private property
250–1
Matthews, R.C.O. 36
Mezey, M.L. 153
Mises, L. von 249–50
mixed economy 260, 261
monarchy 4, 118, 120–2
Money, J. 17, 156–8
Montesquieu, C.S. 3, 115; constitutional
institutions 115; influence 115; *trias
politica* 56–7, 115
Montesquieu system 115–78
motivations and rules 42
motives of individuals in society 40–6
Muslim law 167–8
myopia as human motivation 43

national assemblies: absolute and
relative size in 1990s (lower house)
160; cube root law 161
national legislatures 26
Netherlands: constitution 120–1;
Lijphart study 208–9
new institutional economics 35
new institutionalism 1, 23, 27, 28
non-presidential countries, stable 142
norms 23, 28, 29, 38
North, D.C. 3, 9, 36

OECD countries: institutional variation
227–8; levels of corporatism 229
old institutionalism 31–5; *see also* Weber
Olsen, J.P. 9, 30, 36
ombudsman 55, 172–6; distribution
174–5; role 173–4, 176; Swedish vs.
Danish system 173, 175–6
ontological issues 27
opportunism 38, 50–1; political
institutions 51–2, 53; *see also*
political opportunism
organization: concept 23; definition of
institution 23, 24
organizational interpretation of
institution 24, 26

Ostrom, V. 18
outcomes 1, 2, 14, 19; distinguished
from outputs 61; economic 68;
federal vs. unitary state 90–7;
indicators 65–6; long-term stability in
variation 58–9, 66, 70–1, 73; macro
19; meanings 60–4; measures 64–5;
political 69–70; presidentialism
134–8; relationship to institutions 72
outputs 2, 14, 19; indicators 65–6; long-
term stability of variation 58–9, 66,
70–1, 73; meanings 60–4; measures
64–5

parliament: challenges to power 147–8;
role 145–7
parliamentarism 5, 117–40; continental
Europe 127, 128–9; mapping 126–8;
monarchs 120–2; performance 137–8;
political outcomes 130–40; socio-
economic outcomes 136–8; virtues
128–9
parliamentary constitutions 120–1
parliamentary regimes 1990 and 1995
including mixed executives 127
party systems 54; classification 196;
effect on regime type 187–8; electoral
system 186–90, 196–7; executive
stability 188–9, 199–200;
fractionalization, 70, 196–7, 203;
government durability 198–200;
interaction with presidentialism 133;
two-party vs. multi-party 190, 195–8,
202, 204
patents: economic growth 269;
registered in USA, by inventor
country 269
planned economy 260, 261
plural societies 210–11; need for power-
sharing 210, 213
policies *see* outputs
policy analysis 62
policy outcomes: corporatism 240–3;
Konkordanzdemokratie 240–3;
stability over time 1970s to 1990s 71
policy outputs 66–7; corporatism
239–40; federal vs. unitary states
90–7; Konkordanzdemokratie
239–40; stability over time 1970s to
1990s 71; variation in 1990s 67; *see
also* outputs
political elites: rules for competition
between 54
political freedom: and affluence 282–3;

link with economic institutions
274–85
political institutions: distinct features
vis-à-vis institutions generally 31; *see
also* institutions
political opportunism: checked by
federalism 55; judicial controls 55
political outcomes: of presidentialism
vs. parliamentarism 130–40;
variations in 1990s 69
political stability: federal vs. unitary
states 95–6
political systems: Dahl's typology 104–5
political transitions 12
polyarchy 104–6
Portugal: constitution 121
positive liberties: and real equality 109
power-sharing 219–20, 236–9;
Consensus democracy 214–15; *see
also* Consensus model of democracy
power-sharing institutions and
Konkordanzdemokratie 237
premier 118–119
president: executive powers 119;
extensive powers in Brazil 119
presidential constitutions 119
presidential countries, stable 142
presidentialism 117–40; collective 118;
European 117, 118, 122; institutional
effects 138–41; in Latin America 12,
117; limited vs. unlimited 125–6;
mapping 123–6; negative
consequences 129–34; outcomes for
state 117–18, 134–8; outside Europe
118; performance 134–8; South
Africa 118; strong 118, 119, 122, 129;
successful in USA 117; types 118;
weak 118, 119, 120; whether based on
power-fusion or power-sharing 216
principal-agent 38, 39, 45, 46–8; adverse
selection 48; asymmetric information
47; in authoritarian regimes 49;
conflict of interest 47; contractual
relationship 48; democracy 48–52;
moral hazard 47; political
institutions 51–2; role in institutions
49–50; rules for competition between
elites 54
Prisoner's Dilemma game 43–5
private property: relationship to markets
250–1
private sector contracting 46
'projection' argument (electoral systems)
193–4

property rights 253; and legal system 257
proportional election formulas (PR)
    181, 191–4, 197–201, 205
public contracting: double governance
    52
public finance: impact of chamber
    system 148
public institutions 36
public ownership: restrictive nature
    253–4
public policy 46, 62
public sector: fiscal decentralization in
    federal states 91–2, 97
public sector behaviour 36
public sector size: and economic
    freedom 281

Quine, W.W. 60

rational choice orientation to
    institutions 4, 6, 7–8, 19, 23, 35–36
real economic regimes: types 260–1
real equality and positive liberties 109
Rechtsstaat 55, 166
referendum 144, 149–53; effect on public
    sector 152; number 151; OECD
    countries 151; prevalence 151;
    Switzerland 152; types 150
regime types: classification 124; effect of
    party system 187–8
results *see* outcomes
Riker, W.H. 80–2, 85–6
Rousseau, J.-J. 1
rule: concept 23
Rule of Law 55, 166
rules 23, 26, 27–9, 38, 40–2; choice 45;
    importance for outcomes 1; lack of
    self-enforceability 41; and
    motivations 42

Salmon, W.C. 73
Schmitter, P.C. 7
scientific hypotheses 60
semi-presidentialism 118, 123
Sharia law 167–8
Shugart, M.S. 17, 123, 192–3
Simon, H.A. 50
social equality: federal vs. unitarian
    states 94–5
social expenditures: and economic
    freedom 281, 282
social maxims 40–2; importance 41
social order: and human motivation 43;
    and the state 43–5

socialism 261
socialist law 167–8
Socialist School 249
socio-economic development: human
    rights 111
socio-economic outcomes: of
    presidentialism vs. parliamentarism
    136–8; variations in 1990s 68
socio-economic performance: impact of
    constitutionalism 300–1
sociological approach to institutions 4,
    6, 7–8, 19, 23, 35–36
Sombart, W. 18
Sorokin, P.M. 26
South Africa: presidential system
    118–19
South East Asian economies 261, 265–7;
    classification 265–6; innovation level
    269
stable countries 1970–95 142
state, the 43–5; elites 45; social order
    43–5; necessity for 45
state capitalism 260–1
state format 52; unitary or federal 52
state stability: constitutionalism
    298–300
states: OECD/total set 72
Stoicism 41
Stortinget 11
Switzerland: referendum 152
symmetrical bicameralism 144, 154–9
systems analysis of political life 61

Taagepera, R. 17, 192–3
thick constitutionalism 289–91; bill of
    rights 289, 290–1; need for rigid
    constitution 289–90
thin constitutionalism 287–9
Tocqueville, A. de 53, 106–10
trade union density: and corporatism
    229; Drittelparität 230; measures 229
trade unions: strength 53
traditional authority 39–40
transaction cost theory 255–6
transferability of property 253–4
tripartism 229; *see also* Drittelparität
Tsebelis, G. 17

Ullian, J.S. 60
unicameralism 144, 154, 156
unitarism 18: federalism contrasted
    77–8, 88–90; *see also* federalism
unitary states: budgetary structure 89;
    chamber system 144; local autonomy

217; outcomes 90–7; policy outputs 90–7; *see also* federal states
universal contracts: impossibility 51
US Congress 11
US Patent Database 268–9
USA: presidentialism in 117, 119, 120

Vaubel, R. 89
Veblen, T. 252
violent events 70

Watts, R.L. 78, 81–2
wealth *see* affluence
Weber, M. 7, 24, 31–35, 36–37; authority relations 38; conflict relations 33; corporation 34; legitimacy 33; maxims 32, 34; norms 32; order 32, 36; power as social relation 33; social actions 32
welfare state: human rights 111–3
Westminster model of democracy (WM) 16, 114, 207–24; characteristics 213; institutional logic 215–18; institutions 216; marked by executive dominance/power-fusion 214
Williamson, O.E. 3, 18, 36, 50, 56, 255–6
written constitution 220; institutional effects 286